CONTEMPORARY CHALLENGES TO THE LAWS OF WAR

The laws of war are facing new challenges from emerging technologies and changing methods of warfare, as well as the growth of human rights and international criminal law. International mechanisms of accountability have increased and international criminal law has greater relevance in the calculations of political and military leaders, yet perpetrators often remain at large and the laws of war raise numerous normative, structural and systemic issues and problems. This edited collection brings together leading academic, military and professional experts to examine the key issues for the continuing role and relevance of the laws of war in the twenty-first century. Marking Professor Peter Rowe's contribution to the subject, this book re-examines the purposes of the laws of war and asks whether existing laws found in treaties and customs work to achieve these purposes and, if not, whether they can be fixed by specific reforms or wholesale revision.

CAROLINE HARVEY is a solicitor specialising in international law and obtained her PhD under Professor Peter Rowe's supervision.

JAMES SUMMERS is Lecturer in Law at the University of Lancaster, where he teaches international law, peoples' rights and the law of international institutions.

NIGEL D. WHITE is Professor of Public International Law at the University of Nottingham.

CONTEMPORARY CHALLENGES TO THE LAWS OF WAR

Essays in Honour of Professor Peter Rowe

Edited by

CAROLINE HARVEY

JAMES SUMMERS

and

NIGEL D. WHITE

CAMBRIDGE
UNIVERSITY PRESS

CAMBRIDGE
UNIVERSITY PRESS

University Printing House, Cambridge CB2 8BS, United Kingdom

Cambridge University Press is part of the University of Cambridge.

It furthers the University's mission by disseminating knowledge in the pursuit of education, learning and research at the highest international levels of excellence.

www.cambridge.org
Information on this title: www.cambridge.org/9781107063556

First published 2014

Printed in the United Kingdom by Clays, St Ives plc

A catalogue record for this publication is available from the British Library

Library of Congress Cataloguing in Publication data
Contemporary challenges to the laws of war : essays in honour of Professor Peter Rowe / edited by Caroline Harvey, James Summers, Nigel D. White.
pages cm
ISBN 978-1-107-06355-6 (hardback)
1. War (International law) I. Rowe, P. J. (Peter J.) honouree.
II. Harvey, Caroline, 1977 – editor. III. Summers, James, 1974 – editor.
IV. White, N. D., 1961– editor.
KZ6385.C67 2014
341.6–dc23
2014018500

ISBN 978-1-107-06355-6 Hardback

CONTENTS

CONTRIBUTORS

ALEX BATESMITH is a visiting fellow of the British Institute of International and Comparative Law. Alex spent ten years as a criminal barrister in Leeds and five years as an international prosecutor for the United Nations in Kosovo and Cambodia. He now works as an independent consultant advising governments, companies and other organisations in international criminal law, human rights and transitional justice. He has a particular interest in business and human rights and conflict resolution, and is a qualified mediator. He is married with one daughter and lives in Manchester.

WILLIAM (BILL) BOOTHBY retired in July 2011 as the Deputy Director of Legal Services for the Royal Air Force after thirty years as a member of its Legal Branch. He took his doctorate at the University of Frankfurt (Oder) in Germany in 2009 and in the same year published his first book, *Weapons and the Law of Armed Conflict*. In 2012, he published *The Law of Targeting* and in 2014, he published *Conflict Law*. He was a member of the UK delegation to the Oslo negotiations in 1997 that produced the Ottawa Convention on anti-personnel landmines, was from 2000 to 2006 a member of the UK delegation to the Conventional Weapons Convention negotiations at the UN, Geneva and has been a member of the Groups of Experts that prepared the Harvard Manual on the Law of Air and Missile Warfare and the Tallinn Manual on the Law of Cyber Warfare. He speaks and publishes regularly on a variety of international law issues and teaches at Royal Holloway, University of London and the Australian National University, Canberra.

MAYA BREHM is researcher on weapons law at the Geneva Academy of International Humanitarian Law and Human Rights and works as an independent consultant on disarmament issues. She holds an MA in international relations and an LLM in international humanitarian law. Prior to joining the Geneva Academy, she conducted research on explosive weapons, including cluster munitions, for the United Nations Institute for Disarmament Research (UNIDIR) and authored the study *Protecting Civilians from the Effects of Explosive Weapons: An Analysis of International Legal and Policy Standards* (2012). Previously, she was a protection delegate with the International Committee of the Red Cross, and worked with civil society organisations and think tanks in the field of arms control and disarmament.

ROBERT CRYER is Professor of International and Criminal Law at the University of Birmingham. His major teaching and research interests are in international law and criminal law. In addition to a number of articles and book chapters he is the author of *Prosecuting International Crimes: Selectivity and the International Criminal Law Regime* (Cambridge University Press, 2005) and co-author (with Håkan Friman, Darryl Robinson and Elizabeth Wilmshurst) of *An Introduction to International Criminal Law and Procedure*, 2nd edn (Cambridge University Press, 2010) and (with Neil Boister) *The Tokyo International Military Tribunal: A Reappraisal* (2008). He also co-edited (with Neil Boister) *Documents on the Tokyo International Military Tribunal* (2008). He is co-editor of the *Journal of Conflict and Security Law*.

DIETER FLECK is former Director, International Agreements and Policy, Federal Ministry of Defence, Germany; Honorary President, International Society for Military Law and the Law of War; member of the advisory board of the Amsterdam Centre for International Law; and member of the editorial board of the *Journal of International Peacekeeping*.

CHARLES GARRAWAY served for thirty years as a legal officer in the UK Army Legal Services, initially as a criminal prosecutor but latterly as an adviser in the law of armed conflict and operational law. He represented the Ministry of Defence at numerous international conferences and was part of the UK delegations to the First Review Conference for the 1981 Conventional Weapons Convention, the negotiations on the establishment of an International Criminal Court and the Diplomatic Conference that led to the 1999 Second Protocol to the 1954 Hague Convention on Cultural Property. He was also the senior army lawyer deployed to the Gulf during the 1990–1 Gulf conflict. Whilst still serving, he taught international humanitarian law at King's College London as well as acting as Course Director on the military courses run by the International Institute of Humanitarian Law, San Remo. On retirement, he spent three months in Baghdad working for the Foreign Office on transitional justice issues and six months as a senior research fellow at the British Institute of International and Comparative Law before taking up the Stockton Chair in International Law at the United States Naval War College, Newport, Rhode Island in August 2004 for the year 2004/5. He was a visiting professor at King's College London from 2002 to 2008, teaching the law of armed conflict, and an associate fellow at Chatham House from 2005 to 2012. He is currently a fellow at the Human Rights Centre, University of Essex and was awarded an honorary doctorate by the university in 2012. In December 2006, he was elected to the International Humanitarian Fact-Finding Commission under Article 90 of Additional Protocol I to the Geneva Conventions of 1949, of which he is now a Vice-President. He worked for the British Red Cross from 2007 to 2011 and now works as an independent consultant. He was appointed CBE in 2002. He has worked on a number of expert groups including the ICRC projects on 'direct participation in hostilities' and 'occupation' as well as the Harvard program on humanitarian policy and conflict research project on air and missile warfare. He is currently General Editor of the *United Kingdom Manual on the Law of Armed Conflict* and carries out a number of consultancies for government and international organisations, including the Commonwealth Secretariat. In 2011, he chaired the Commonwealth Working Group that updated the Commonwealth Model Law on the International Criminal Court.

CAROLINE HARVEY studied law at the universities of Keele and Lancaster. She completed both her LLM and PhD under the inspiration and supervision of Peter Rowe, and was his last doctoral candidate. Caroline qualified as a solicitor in 2008 after interning with the ICTY and the Gulf Region Advocacy Center in Houston, Texas and is in private practice. She has published on a variety of issues, including the decisions of German-speaking courts on war crimes, procedural fairness in arbitration proceedings and is the UK correspondent to the *Yearbook of International Humanitarian Law*. Caroline recently completed a post-doctoral fellowship at the Institute of European and Comparative Law at the University of Oxford, in the course of which she published an article in the *European Review of Contract Law* and a book chapter, both on the subject of comparative contract law.

NICHOLAS MERCER was educated at St Andrews University and Oxford University. Admitted as a solicitor in 1990 and commissioned into the Army Legal Service in 1991, he served in Northern Ireland, Bosnia Herzegovina, Cyprus and Germany and was the Command Legal Adviser for the Iraq War 2003 with the HQ 1st (UK) Armoured Division. He has been a member of the teaching staff of the International Institute of Humanitarian Law, San Remo since 2001. He left the Army in 2011 as a Lieutenant Colonel and was ordained in Salisbury Diocese a week after leaving the Army. He has extensive experience in the law of armed conflict and human rights both on the battlefield and in the classroom and has lectured extensively on the subject at defence academies and other forums. He was named the Liberty Human Rights Lawyer of the Year 2011–12 for 'integrity and courage in the face of the dissembling and denial of human rights abuses in Iraq 2003'.

MICHAEL MEYER OBE is head of international law at the British Red Cross. He has worked for the British National Society for over thirty years and is a specialist in international humanitarian law as well as in the protective emblems and in principles and laws relevant to the International Red Cross and Red Crescent Movement. Michael has served on government and Red Cross/Crescent delegations to international meetings, and represents the British Red Cross on the United Kingdom Inter-departmental Committee on International Humanitarian Law. He has also been a member of the governing bodies of the International Institute of Humanitarian Law and of the UK Group of the International Society for Military Law and the Law of War.

LINDSAY MOIR is Professor of International Law and Deputy Director of the McCoubrey Centre for International Law at the University of Hull. He holds degrees from the University of Edinburgh (LLB) and the University of Cambridge (LLM, PhD) and joined the University of Hull Law School as a lecturer in 1997, becoming Professor of International Law in 2005, and serving as Head of the Law School from 2009 to 2012. He has written widely on various aspects of the international laws of armed conflict, with publications including *The Law of Internal Armed Conflict* (Cambridge University Press, 2002) and *Reappraising the Resort to Force: International Law, Jus ad Bellum and the War on Terror* (2010).

GORDON RISIUS was Tony Rogers' successor as Director of Army Legal Services from 1997 to 2003. Following the court martial reforms introduced by the Armed Forces Act 1996, he also became in 1997 the first Prosecuting Authority for the Army, and was appointed CB in 2000. Having been authorised in 1992 to sit in the Crown Court as a Recorder, he became a Circuit Judge in 2003 on his retirement from the Army, when he was seconded temporarily to the Immigration Appeal Tribunal in London as a Vice-President, before moving in 2005 to Reading Crown Court to sit in crime. He is currently the Resident Judge at Oxford Crown Court following his appointment there in 2010. The following year he was elected the Honorary Recorder of Oxford. He is also a senior judge of the Sovereign Base Areas Court in Cyprus. He was active from 1988 in the UK Group of the International Society for Military Law and the Law of War and latterly in its parent Society, of which he is now an Honorary President, and additionally as an instructor at the International Institute of Humanitarian Law in San Remo. He was also Deputy Colonel Commandant of the Adjutant General's Corps from 2004 to 2009.

A. P. V. ROGERS was Director of Army Legal Services from 1994 to 1997 and was awarded the OBE in 1985. He is an honorary president of the International Society for Military Law and the Law of War. Following retirement from the Army, he became a fellow, later a senior fellow, of the Lauterpacht Centre for International Law at the University of Cambridge until he retired from the Centre in 2011. He lectured on the law of armed conflict in the LLM course at the Cambridge Law Faculty from 2000 to 2009 as an affiliated lecturer, and held the title Yorke Distinguished Visiting Fellow from 2003 to 2009. He was also a fellow, later visiting fellow, of the Human Rights Centre at the University of Essex from 1999 to 2007. He was a member of the International Humanitarian Fact-Finding Commission from 2001 to 2006, becoming a vice-president. Having drafted many of its chapters and been involved in much of its revision over the years, he was eventually appointed the general editor of the UK Ministry of Defence *Manual of the Law of Armed Conflict* (2004). He has published many articles on the law of armed conflict, but his principal publication is the prize-winning *Law on the Battlefield*, currently in its 3rd edition (2012).

PETER ROWE is Professor Emeritus at the University of Lancaster. He has also taught at the University of Liverpool where he was professor and head of the Department of Law from 1988 to 1993. He has been chairman of the UK Group of the International Society for Military Law and the Laws of War. He was the Inaugural Sir Ninian Stephen Visiting Scholar at the Asia Pacific Centre for Military law, Faculty of Laws, University of Melbourne (June–July 2003). His main research interests lie in the fields of military law and the international laws of war, and the relationship between them on which he has published a number of articles and book chapters. His latest book is *The Impact of Human Rights Law on Armed Forces* (Cambridge University Press, 2006). He has given lectures to military legal officers over many years, both in the UK and abroad.

JAMES SUMMERS is a graduate of Helsinki University and is a lecturer in international law at the University of Lancaster. A second edition of his book *Peoples and International Law* was published in 2013. He is also the editor of *Kosovo: A Precedent?* (2011). He is currently working on a text, cases and materials book to be published in 2015.

DAVID TURNS is Senior Lecturer in International Laws of Armed Conflict at the Defence Academy of the United Kingdom (Cranfield University). He was previously a lecturer in law at the University of Liverpool (1994–2007) and also taught at the London School of Economics (1990–4). He has been on the visiting faculty of the International Institute of Humanitarian Law, San Remo since 1997. In 2002, he was a visiting professor at the Institute for International Law and International Relations, University of Vienna. Since 2008, he has been the Chairman of the UK National Group of the International Society for Military Law and the Law of War. He has extensive experience of teaching international law to military officers in different parts of the world. He has given many conference papers and published widely on a variety of topics in public international law.

NIGEL D. WHITE is Professor of Public International Law at the University of Nottingham and formerly Professor of International Law at the University of Sheffield. He has held a chair since 2000 and an academic post since 1987. In addition to publishing over sixty articles and essays, many in leading journals and collections, he is co-author and author of eight books. He is sole author of *Keeping the Peace* (1997), *The UN System: Toward International Justice* (2002), *The Law of International Organisations* (2005) and *Democracy Goes to War: British*

Military Deployments under International Law (2009). He recently co-authored *Collective Security: Law, Theory and Practice* (2013) with Nicholas Tsagourias. He is also editor and co-editor of eight collections, including *The UN, Human Rights and Post-Conflict Situations* (2005), *European Security Law* (2007), *International Law and Dispute Settlement* (2010), *International Organizations and the Idea of Autonomy* (2011) and *Counter-Terrorism: International Law and Practice* (2012). He is co-editor of the *Journal of Conflict and Security Law*, which is in its eighteenth year.

FOREWORD BY JUDGE SIR CHRISTOPHER GREENWOOD

It is a great pleasure to contribute this brief foreword to the present collection of essays. There are at least three reasons why that is so. First, the collection honours Peter Rowe, a friend and colleague for many years. Peter Rowe's contribution to the laws of war has been of enormous value. His book *Defence: The Legal Implications* broke new ground in the academic writing on the subject by bringing together in one volume a consideration of the international law of war and UK military law, thereby anchoring the consideration of international law in the legal framework within which the practitioners of that law – the servicemen and women called upon to apply it in combat – are required to operate. That essentially practical approach is also evident in Peter Rowe's own contribution to the present volume, which considers the relationship between the legal framework for the trial by a state of its own service personnel and the way in which such a state complies with its international law obligations regarding the trial of prisoners of war for war crimes and offences committed after capture. His later book, *The Impact of Human Rights Law on Armed Forces*, again went to the heart of important practical issues, including the relationship between international human rights law and the laws of war (a subject which the International Court of Justice has had to face three times in the last twenty years). At the time that book appeared, I was counsel for the Secretary of State for Defence in two cases arising out of the conflict in Iraq (*Al-Skeini* and *Al-Jedda*) then pending before the House of Lords. The book was much used by all the legal teams.

Secondly, a glance at the list of contributors to the present volume shows that the editors have succeeded in bringing together authors from academic, military and Red Cross backgrounds, as well as other walks of life. The different perspectives thus brought to bear enhance the value of this volume. It is also particularly fitting in a tribute to Peter Rowe, who was one of those who were instrumental in creating a series of seminars

Peter Rowe, Emeritus Professor in the Law School, University of Lancaster

in which academics and practitioners with a shared interest in the laws of war took part. One product of that series was the book *The Gulf War 1990–91 in International and English Law*, which Peter Rowe edited and which contained contributions from a range of authors similar to that found in the present volume. It is in part due to that continuing dialogue between the military and academic lawyers that discussion of the laws of war in the United Kingdom has never been detached from reality in the way that it has sometimes been in other communities.

Lastly, the present volume contains a wonderfully rich discussion of the most important issues confronting all of those involved with the laws of war today: whether those laws are capable of coping with the conditions of modern warfare, what relationship they have with international human rights law and other branches of international law, how can their application be strengthened and what role they play in the various operations undertaken with Security Council authorisation. Sixty years ago Sir Hersch Lauterpacht famously remarked that 'if international law is at the vanishing point of law, the laws of war are at the vanishing point of international law'. This collection of essays is a timely reminder that those laws have not vanished yet and it holds the promise that they are unlikely to do so in the immediate future, however great the challenge they face. Lauterpacht would have been delighted.

PREFACE

The increase in violence and conflict in the twenty-first century has emphasised the importance of the laws of war, but has also raised the issue of their impotence as we witness increased unaddressed violations of the laws, many of them shocking and horrific. First fashioned in an age of chivalry, can the laws of war continue to apply in an age of extremes?

Although international mechanisms of accountability have increased and international criminal law has greater relevance in the calculations of political and military leaders when conducting warfare, perpetrators often remain at large; an ever-present reminder of a cycle of violence that, without some form of reckoning, will not be broken.

Nevertheless, the laws of war are not coterminous with international criminal law, nor are they subsumed by human rights law. As *lex specialis* applicable in armed conflicts the laws of war raise numerous normative, structural and systemic issues and problems, the most significant of which are discussed in this book by a range of military, academic and professional experts, brought together to mark Professor Peter Rowe's contribution to the subject. Initial discussions and debates were held during a workshop at Lancaster University in September 2012.

The aim of this book is to consider the continuing role and relevance of the laws of war in the twenty-first century. To understand this we need to re-examine the purposes of the laws of war and ask questions as to whether the existing laws found in treaties and customs work to achieve these purposes; if not, can they be fixed by specific reforms or do we need a wholesale revision? These questions are addressed by the contributors, some by focusing on specific issues of the protections provided by the laws of war, others on broader structural and systemic issues. The contributors are drawn from both academia and practice, bringing their different perspectives to bear on the subject matter, and it is fitting that the book starts with an account of the interface between these two branches.

Following from an Introduction, which contains an overview of the laws of war and places the contributions within that framework, the book contains a number of chapters examining the role of the *jus in bello* and its place within the wider international legal order. These are followed by an examination of aspects of the relationship between the laws of war on the one hand, and international criminal law and human rights law on the other. There then follow some specific chapters considering issues of the protections provided by the laws of war by looking at targeting, weapons, the use of drones, combatant status and the protection of civilians. The aim is not to cover all areas, but to take a sample of contentious areas where the protections provided by the laws of war are under pressure, in order to test the law's workability. The book then closes by looking at the issues of responsibility and accountability for violations of the laws. By these means we will endeavour to find answers to one of the most pressing issues of international law: whether the laws of war are fit for purpose?

The editors would like to thank Lydia Davies-Bright for her editorial work on the chapters.

ABBREVIATIONS

AC	Appeals Cases
ACHPR	African Charter on Human and Peoples' Rights
ACHR	American Convention on Human Rights
ACLU	American Civil Liberties Union
AJIL	*American Journal of International Law*
ALS	Army Legal Services
AMISOM	African Union Mission in Somalia
AO	area of operations
AOAV	Action on Armed Violence
AP I	Additional Protocol I to the Geneva Conventions
AP II	Additional Protocol II to the Geneva Conventions
ATS	Alien Tort Statute
AU	African Union
BOI	board of inquiry
BWC	Biological Weapons Convention
BYBIL	*British Yearbook of International Law*
CCR	Center for Constitutional Rights
CCW	Convention on Certain Conventional Weapons
CERD	Convention on the Elimination of All Forms of Racial Discrimination
COMCAPREPS	Common Capture Reports
CoW	coalition of the willing
CWC	Chemical Weapon Convention
DALS	Director of Army Legal Services
DIME	dense inert metal explosive
DPH	direct participation in hostilities
DPKO	Department of Peacekeeping Operations
DRC	Democratic Republic of the Congo
DU	depleted uranium
DUF	directive on the use of force
ECCC	Extraordinary Chambers in the Courts of Cambodia
ECHR	European Convention on Human Rights
ECtHR	European Court of Human Rights
EHRR	European Human Rights Reports

EJIL	*European Journal of International Law*
ENMOD	Convention on the Prohibition of Military or Any Other Hostile Use of Environmental Modification Techniques
ERW	explosive remnant of war
EWCA	England and Wales (reports) Court of Appeal
EWHC	England and Wales (reports) High Court
FOIA	Freedom of Information Act
GAOR	General Assembly Official Records
GC	Geneva Conventions
GC III	Third Geneva Convention Relative to the Treatment of Prisoners of War
GC IV	Fourth Geneva Convention Relative to the Protection of Civilian Persons in Time of War
HMSO	Her Majesty's Stationery Office
HPCR	Humanitarian Policy and Conflict Research
HRC	Human Rights Council
ICC	International Criminal Court
ICCPR	International Covenant on Civil and Political Rights
ICJ	International Court of Justice
ICL	international criminal law
ICLQ	*International and Comparative Law Quarterly*
ICRC	International Committee of the Red Cross
ICTR	International Criminal Tribunal for Rwanda
ICTY	International Criminal Tribunal for the former Yugoslavia
ICTY RPE	Rules of Procedure and Evidence of the International Criminal Tribunal for the former Yugoslavia
IED	improvised explosive device
IFOR	Implementation Force
IHL	international humanitarian law
IHRL	international human rights law
ILC	International Law Commission
ILM	*International Legal Materials*
ILR	*International Law Reports*
IMT	International Military Tribunal
IMTFE	International Military Tribunal for the Far East
INEW	International Network on Explosive Weapons
INTERFET	International Force for East Timor
IRRC	*International Review of the Red Cross*
ISAF	International Security Assistance Force
ISO	International Organisation for Standardisation
JCE	joint criminal enterprise
JCSL	*Journal of Conflict and Security Law*

JDN	Joint Doctrine Note
JICJ	*Journal of International Criminal Justice*
KFOR	Kosovo Force
LAR	lethal autonomous robot
LJIL	*Leiden Journal of International Law*
MLRS	multiple launch rocket system
MNC	multinational corporation
MOAB	massive ordnance air blast
MOD	Ministry of Defence
MONUSCO	United Nations Organisation Stabilisation Mission in the Democratic Republic of the Congo
MRL	multiple rocket launcher
NATO	North Atlantic Treaty Organization
NGO	non-governmental organisation
NPT	non-proliferation treaty
OECD	Organisation for Economic Cooperation and Development
OIOS	Office of Internal Oversight Services
ONUC	United Nations Operation in the Congo
OTP	Office of the Prosecutor
PDT	pre-deployment training
PJHQ	Permanent Joint Headquarters
PKO	peacekeeping operation
PMSC	private military and security company
POW	prisoner of war
RoE	Rules of Engagement
RPE	Rules of Procedure and Evidence
SALW	small arms and light weapons
SCSL	Special Court for Sierra Leone
SNCO	senior non-commissioned officer
SOFA	Status of Forces Agreement
STL	Special Tribunal for Lebanon
TCN	troop-contributing nation
TNC	transnational corporation
UAV	unmanned aerial vehicle
UCAV	unmanned combat aerial vehicle
UKSC	United Kingdom Supreme Court
UNAMA	United Nations Assistance Mission in Afghanistan
UNAMSIL	United Nations Assistance Mission in Sierra Leone
UNDP	United Nations Development Programme
UNDPKO	United Nations Department of Peacekeeping Operations
UNEF	United Nations Emergency Force
UNGA	United National General Assembly

UNIDIR	United Nations Institute for Disarmament Research
UNOCI	United Nations Operation in the Ivory Coast
UNPROFOR	United Nations Protection Force
UNSC	United Nations Security Council
UNTS	United Nations Treaty Series
VJIL	*Virginia Journal of International Law*
YIHL	*Yearbook of International Humanitarian Law*
WLR	Weekly Law Reports

1

Introduction

JAMES SUMMERS

This edited collection in honour of Peter Rowe explores contemporary challenges to the laws of war. The title of the book is fitting as Peter has not only contributed extensively to the study of the law of armed conflict and related areas in his academic career but has also highlighted new frontiers in its development – especially in relation to human rights. With chapters from experts in the field, this book investigates many of the problems experienced by the law as it copes with new technologies and methods of warfare, as well as its interaction with other legal disciplines, including human rights. This introduction will briefly outline the laws of war and place the chapters in their context.

The structure of the laws of war

Most states, most of the time, exist in a peaceful condition. The very concept of a state encapsulates the idea of a government in control of a territory and a population. That government, in turn, is subject to human rights obligations that derive from custom and various treaty regimes. One of the most fundamental of these standards is the right to life, which cannot be taken by agents of a state arbitrarily and extrajudicially. The outbreak of war changes this. Human life in a conflict becomes subject to a special legal regime, variously known as the laws of war, international humanitarian law (IHL) or the law of armed conflict.[1] As described in *Tadić*, this 'applies from the initiation of such armed conflicts and extends beyond the cessation of hostilities until a general conclusion of peace is reached; or, in the case of internal conflicts, a peaceful settlement is achieved'.[2] This *lex specialis*, the International

[1] See *Jurisdictional Immunities of the State (Germany* v. *Italy; Greece Intervening)*, ICJ Reports 2012, para. 81.

[2] *Prosecutor* v. *Dusko Tadić* (Interlocutory Appeal on Jurisdiction) IT-94-1-AR, 2 October 1995, para. 70.

Court of Justice recognised, exists alongside human rights[3] and changes the interpretation of the arbitrary deprivation in the right to life.[4]

The object of war, American General George S. Patton once noted, is not to die for your country, but to make someone else die for his. The laws of war do not fundamentally challenge this proposition, although they do seek to mitigate and contain it by ensuring that the conduct of warfare is not unlimited.[5] Protections are provided for civilians, the sick and wounded, prisoners of war, the nationals of states not involved in the conflict, civilian property (especially that of cultural significance) and the environment. Indiscriminate killing and unnecessary suffering are expressly prohibited, though killing and suffering, as such, are an accepted part of war and can include protected individuals. The laws of war work within the messy reality of conflict in which even carefully targeted action can result in the deaths of civilians and the destruction of property. This reflects a very different idea of law from that of human rights, which prevails in peacetime, but now coexists with the laws of war in a sometimes difficult relationship.[6] Lastly, IHL does not, by itself, restrict the ability of states to go to war. The decision to initiate a conflict is a separate legal matter (*jus ad bellum*) orientated around the UN Charter. Instead, the laws of war focus on the conduct of hostilities (*jus in bello*) – a legal war could be fought illegally and vice versa.[7]

The laws of war are contained in a series of treaties, as well as customary international law. The most prominent of these are the Hague and Geneva conventions, which have, respectively, given rise to 'Hague Law' and

[3] See *Wall in Occupied Palestinian Territory* (Advisory Opinion), ICJ Reports 2004, para. 106; *Democratic Republic of Congo* v. *Uganda*, ICJ Reports 2005, para. 216.

[4] *Legality of the Threat or Use of Nuclear* Weapons (Advisory Opinion), ICJ Reports 1996, para. 25. See also, *Juan Carlos Abella* v. *Argentina*, Report No. 55/97, Case 11.137, 1997, para. 16.

[5] See Article 22 Hague Regulations 1907: 'The right of belligerents to adopt means of injuring the enemy is not unlimited.' Article 35(1) AP I: 'In any armed conflict, the right of the Parties to the conflict to choose methods and means of warfare is not unlimited.' See also, *Nuclear Weapons* (n. 4, above), para. 77.

[6] See K. Watkin, 'Controlling the Use of Force: A Role for Human Rights Norms in Contemporary Armed Conflict', 98 *AJIL* (2004) 1.

[7] A. Orakhelashvili, 'Overlap and Convergence: The Interaction between *Jus ad Bellum* and *Jus in Bello*', 12 *JCSL* (2007) 158. See Preamble AP I: 'the provisions of the Geneva Conventions of 12 August 1949 and of this Protocol must be fully applied in all circumstances to all persons who are protected by those instruments, without any adverse distinction based on the nature or origin of the armed conflict or on the causes espoused by or attributed to the Parties to the conflict'.

'Geneva Law'.[8] In addition to these two treaty regimes, there are individual instruments that regulate specific weapons, including chemical and biological weapons and landmines.

Hague Law concerns the conduct of hostilities and the means and methods used to pursue them. It can be seen to originate with the St Petersburg Declaration 1868, which prohibited small projectiles under the principle that weapons which uselessly aggravated the sufferings of disabled men, or rendered their death inevitable, exceeded the object of warfare.[9] However, the main instruments behind this law were concluded in two peace conferences in The Hague in 1899 and 1907, which, between them, produced twenty conventions and declarations.[10] The legal status of these instruments differs, but the Hague Regulations attached to the Hague Convention IV 1907, in particular, have been recognised as custom.[11]

Geneva Law is based on the protection of specific classes of individuals who are not engaged in hostilities. Its origins lie with the first Geneva Convention in 1864. This was on the initiative of Swiss businessman Henry Dunant, who, on witnessing the suffering of the wounded left untreated in the Battle of Solferino in 1859, founded the organisation that became the International Committee of the Red Cross (ICRC). The original Convention was updated in 1906 and again in 1929, when it was joined by a second instrument on prisoners of war. These two treaties, in turn, were replaced by the present four Geneva Conventions of 1949, which have 195 states parties.[12] The First Geneva Convention concerns the wounded and sick in armed forces in the field. The Second addresses them at sea, as well as the shipwrecked. The Third covers prisoners of war. The Fourth protects civilians in time of war. These are supplemented by three protocols. Additional Protocol I 1977 (173 parties) encompasses the conduct of hostilities, meaning that much of 'Hague Law' is now found in a Geneva instrument. In keeping with its contemporary setting (the tail-end of post-war decolonisation), the Protocol

[8] See *Nuclear Weapons* (n. 4, above), para. 75.

[9] Declaration Renouncing the Use, in Time of War, of Certain Explosive Projectiles Under 400 Grammes Weight, 29 November/11 December 1868.

[10] Y. Dinstein, *The Conduct of Hostilities under the Law of International Armed Conflict*, 2nd edn (Cambridge: Cambridge University Press, 2010), 14–15.

[11] *Wall in Occupied Palestinian Territory* (Advisory Opinion), ICJ Reports 2004, para. 89; *Democratic Republic of Congo* v. *Uganda*, ICJ Reports 2005, para. 217.

[12] On the status of the instruments, see the ICRC Geneva Conventions website: www.icrc.org/eng/war-and-law/treaties-customary-law/geneva-conventions/index.jsp.

also extended international armed conflicts to include peoples fighting colonial domination, alien occupation and racist regimes. Additional Protocol II 1977 (167 parties) expands Geneva Law into non-international armed conflicts, beyond the minimum provisions of Common Article 3, and is the most comprehensive instrument to address this type of conflict. Finally, Additional Protocol III 2005 (63 parties) added an extra non-religious emblem for the Red Cross and medical services to use, the 'Red Crystal'.

There is a significant overlap between Hague and Geneva Law and not just from Additional Protocol I. This is most evident with civilians. Under Hague Law they are protected by limits on the selection of targets and the types of weapons used. Under Geneva Law there are specific protections attached to them as people. The goals are the same, preserving non-combatants from the devastation of conflict, though the approaches are quite different.

Behind the laws of war is a balance between the pursuit of military objectives and humanitarian protection, informed by the reciprocal interests of states. Belligerent states have an incentive to respect sick, wounded and captured soldiers and the civilians of an enemy state in the expectation that the same treatment will apply to their nationals. This has had an important effect on the structure of the law, creating a distinction between international and non-international armed conflicts. In the first, between two or more states, there is a clear reciprocal relationship between governments. However, in the second, where governments are fighting rebel movements, they have tended to deny such a relationship with groups that they may prefer to dismiss as terrorists or criminals. The result is that the laws of war are more developed for an international armed conflict, creating a notable dichotomy in legal protection.

The foundations of the law, though, clearly go beyond mere reciprocal interests and derive from a wider project to humanise the conduct of war. The independent non-governmental organisation (NGO), the ICRC, has been central to this. As Michael Meyer explains in Chapter 12, it has been integral in developing the laws of war, in particular, by preparing texts that have later been adopted by states. The development of the law is also influenced by the interaction between academics and military lawyers, recounted by Anthony Rogers and Gordon Risius in Chapter 2. But, the humanisation of war is not merely an external imposition. Military forces have, throughout history, sought to define themselves with basic standards by which war could be fought in a disciplined and honourable way.[13] Carl von Clausewitz, writing in 1832, while belittling the international laws of war as they were then, nevertheless distinguished constraints on the devastation of cities and the execution of prisoners as a sign of intelligence and civilisation, as opposed to the impulsive acts of savages.[14] However, what is acceptable in hostilities is open to different views and has evolved over time as methods of warfare and weaponry have changed. In an early work on international law in 1796, Prussian academic Johann G. Fichte condemned the use of snipers as cold-blooded murder and downright illegal.[15] Similarly, as Bill Boothby notes in Chapter 10, aerial bombardment (from balloons) was banned by Hague declarations in both 1899 and 1907.[16] Today, though, both would be seen as regular and lawful methods of combat. Maya Brehm reflects in Chapter 11 that horrific injuries can be accepted if they are seen as a 'normal' part of an armed conflict.

The need for international humanitarian law to be able continuously to adapt to new methods of warfare was specifically recognised in the Hague conventions of 1899 and 1907. With the Marten's Clause, proposed by the international lawyer F. De Martens, 'belligerents remain under the protection and rule of the principles of the law of nations, as they result from the usages established among civilized peoples, from the laws of humanity, and the dictates of the public conscience'.[17] This refers to development by custom (usage), but also specifically incorporates moral humanitarian considerations.[18] These inform the application of basic principles in the laws of war, such as distinction and the prohibition of unnecessary suffering in relation to legitimate military objectives.[19]

[13] An excellent comparison between modern and ancient and medieval codes on warfare is L. C. Green, 'What is – Why is There – the Law of War?' (1994) 5 *Finnish Yearbook of International Law* 99.

[14] C. von Clausewitz, *On War*, ed. and trans. M. Howard and P. Paret (Princeton, NJ: Princeton University Press, 1976), bk. 1, ch. 1, paras 2–3.

[15] J. G. Fichte, *The Science of Rights*, trans. A. E. Kroeger (London: Routledge, 1970), 482.

[16] Hague Declaration IV, 1 1899; Hague Declaration XIV 1907.

[17] Preamble Hague Convention IV 1907. See also Preamble Hague Convention II 1899; Article 1(2) Geneva Conventions; AP I 1977.

[18] On the interpretations of the clause, see T. Meron, 'The Martens Clause, Principles of Humanity, and Dictates of Public Conscience', 94 *AJIL* (2000) 78.

[19] See *Nuclear Weapons* (n. 4, above), para. 78. See also the ICTY in *Prosecutor* v. *Furundžija* (Trial) IT-95-17/1, 10 December 1998, paras 137 and 168; *Prosecutor* v. *Kupreškić* (Trial) IT-95-16-T, 14 January 2000, paras 525–7; *Prosecutor* v. *Martić* (Trial) IT-95-11-T, 12 June 2007, para. 467.

Nonetheless, due to the considerations underpinning them, the laws of was do not form a smooth continuum of protection, but are fragmented into categories, both of conflicts and of individuals, which are, in turn, linked to particular instruments. Some of these distinctions have been mitigated by customary international law, but IHL must be approached through categories. The first is whether an armed conflict is international or non-international. The second is the people and property involved or caught up in the conflict.

The implementation of the laws of war

Another key aspect of the context of the laws of war is implementation. Despite the grave nature of the acts it covers, enforcement has been an area of weakness. As Michael Meyer explains in Chapter 12, the ICRC is currently engaged in consultations to strengthen monitoring states' compliance with IHL obligations. Nonetheless, IHL lacks its own distinct institutions and has been enforced, in particular, by international criminal tribunals in the prosecution of war crimes and also by human rights bodies. Those institutions, however, address the law from the perspective of their own particular legal cultures.

The implementation of the laws of war traditionally grew from the reciprocal relationship between belligerents. From ancient times it was acceptable to take (and kill) hostages and to engage in reprisals to induce enemy forces to comply with their obligations.[20] Hostage-taking was still recognised in the Second World War, but subsequently became a Grave Breach of the Fourth Geneva Convention.[21] Reprisals were also prohibited against protected persons under the Geneva Conventions.[22] In Additional Protocol I there were further protections for civilians, the environment, cultural artefacts, indispensable objects for civilian survival and installations containing dangerous forces.[23] In combination, the effect was to hollow reprisals out to the point of irrelevance as the only legal targets left were combatants, who could be targeted in any

[20] G. I. A. D. Draper, 'The Implementation of the Modern Law of Armed Conflicts' 8 *Israel Law Review* (1973) 7–9.

[21] Articles 34 and 147 Fourth Geneva Convention 1949. See also Article 2 ICTY Statute 1993; Article 8(2)(a)(viii) ICC Statute 1998.

[22] Article 46 First Geneva Convention 1949; Article 47 Second Geneva Convention 1949; Article 13 Third Geneva Conventions 1949; Article 33 Fourth Geneva Convention 1949.

[23] Articles 20, 51(6), 53(c), 54(4), 55(2), 56(4) AP I 1977.

case.[24] In both these cases humanitarian considerations outweighed reciprocal enforcement. A further mechanism provided for in the Geneva Conventions is a commission of enquiry.[25] Additional Protocol I provides for an independent fact-finding commission and this was established in 1991, though its jurisdiction depends on the consent of the belligerent states.[26]

A prominent mechanism in the implementation of the Geneva Conventions has been the appointment of neutral states as protecting powers to safeguard the interests of the parties to the conflict.[27] This role was first taken by Switzerland in the Franco-Prussian War, 1870, which it continued, along with Sweden, in the Second World War. If a state is unwilling to perform this role it can also be undertaken by an impartial organisation, notably the ICRC.[28] However, this system depends on the consent of the parties. In hostilities such as the China–India conflict, 1962–3 or the India–Pakistan war over Bangladesh in 1971, the role of a protecting power was rejected by belligerent states.[29]

Looking at international bodies, international criminal institutions have played a prominent role in upholding the laws of war through the punishment of war crimes. In particular, the International Criminal Tribunal for the former Yugoslavia (ICTY), as well as trying individual war criminals, has significantly developed different areas of IHL. Nonetheless, there are limitations. War crimes involve breaches of the laws of war that entail individual criminal responsibility.[30] Moreover, they straddle both international humanitarian and international criminal law, which may pose questions over their source. International

[24] *Prosecutor* v. *Kupreškić*, IT-95-16-T, 14 January 2000, paras 527–36; see also T. Meron, 'The Humanization of Humanitarian Law', 94 *AJIL* (2000) 249–51; G. B. Roberts, 'The New Rules for Waging War: The Case against Ratification of Additional Protocol I', 26 *VJIL* (1985) 141–5.

[25] Article 52 First Geneva Convention 1949; Article 53 Second Geneva Convention 1949; Article 132 Third Geneva Convention 1949; Article 149 Fourth Geneva Convention 1949.

[26] Article 90 AP I 1977. See R. Wolfrum and D. Fleck, 'Enforcement of International Humanitarian Law', in D. Fleck (eds), *The Handbook of International Humanitarian Law*, 2nd edn (Oxford: Oxford University Press, 2008), 711–12.

[27] Article 8 First, Second and Third Geneva Conventions 1949; Article 9 Fourth Geneva Convention 1949.

[28] Article 10 First, Second and Third Geneva Conventions 1949; Article 11 Fourth Geneva Convention 1949.

[29] Draper, 'The Implementation of the Modern Law of Armed Conflicts', 14.

[30] *Prosecutor* v. *Dusko Tadić* (Interlocutory Appeal on Jurisdiction) IT-94-1-AR, 2 October 1995, para. 94.

criminal bodies derive their jurisdiction from their statutes, which contain specific lists of war crimes for that institution that may differ in their formulation from those in IHL instruments. As Robert Cryer outlines in Chapter 6, there is an internal tension within these tribunals as to whether their crimes are a self-contained regime, or whether they draw from the laws of war. The bodies also pose important questions in terms of their jurisdiction, which are examined by Alex Batesmith in Chapter 13 on corporate criminal responsibility, and their procedure, as explored by Caroline Harvey in Chapter 15 on self-representation before the ICTY.

The enforcement of a specific type of war crime, grave breaches of the Geneva Conventions, is based on the states parties to those conventions, who can, if their domestic law permits, exercise jurisdiction over them in their national courts. These include: killing, torture, inhuman treatment, wilfully causing great suffering or serious injury, unlawful deportation, transfer or confinement, and hostage-taking against protected persons; wilfully depriving a prisoner of war or other protected person of the right to a fair and regular trial and compelling them to serve in the forces of a hostile power; and extensive, unlawful and wanton destruction or appropriation of property, not justified by military necessity. States parties have a legislative obligation to provide effective sanctions for those offences and can try suspects in their national courts. The ICTY and International Criminal Court (ICC) can also exercise jurisdiction over these crimes, within the terms of their statutes.[31] States also have the right to hand over the suspect to another state party that has made a prima facie case against the accused, though, significantly, they do not have an obligation to do so.[32] A limitation in grave breaches is that they are restricted to international armed conflicts – there is no equivalent for non-international armed conflicts.

Human rights bodies have also played a significant and growing role in the interpretation of the law relating to military operations. This has been particularly significant for the law regarding international armed conflict through occupation.[33] Human rights bodies have extended their jurisdiction in situations where an occupier has control over a population, such as in the US invasion of Grenada[34] and the Israeli-occupied

[31] Article 2 ICTY Statute 1993; Articles 5 and 8(2)(a)(viii) ICC Statute 1998.

[32] Draper, 'The Implementation of the Modern Law of Armed Conflicts', 11.

[33] See P. Rowe, *The Impact of Human Rights Law on Armed Forces* (Cambridge: Cambridge University Press, 2006), 122–33.

[34] *Coard et al.* v. *United States*, Report No. 109/99, Case 10.951 (1999), para. 37.

Palestinian territories.[35] The European Court of Human Rights considered that an occupying power in effective control of an area has 'the responsibility . . . to secure, within the area under its control, the entire range of substantive rights set out in the Convention and those additional protocols which it has ratified'.[36] Internal conflicts fall within state territory and, therefore, also within the traditional scope of human rights jurisdiction. In this instance, though, states have been more reluctant to apply the laws of war. Neither the United Kingdom, in relation to Northern Ireland, nor Russia, regarding Chechnya, designated the violence in those regions as a non-international armed conflict, with the result that they were only addressed under human rights law.[37] However, human rights bodies have made the designation themselves. The Inter-American Commission of Human Rights in *Abella* v. *Argentina* (1997) considered an attack on a military barracks to amount to a brief non-international armed conflict.[38]

The practice of human rights bodies has raised questions on interpretation of the relationship between human rights and IHL. A notable example is the *Al-Jedda* v. *UK* (2011) case in which the European Court considered that the internment of civilians was incompatible with the liberty and security of the person under Article 5(1) of the European Convention. In its view, the Fourth Geneva Convention, which, in Article 42, allows for internment based on 'absolutely necessary' security grounds, did not create an obligation that conflicted with this right.[39] However, in Chapter 8, Charles Garraway argues that this interpretation of the Convention, in terms of obligations, is to misread it.

The status of a conflict

The application of IHL depends on the existence of an 'armed conflict'. These, in turn, come in two types: international, which involves two or more states, and non-international, which does not. The distinction is

[35] Concluding Observations of the Human Rights Committee, Israel, CCPR/CO/78/ISR (2003), para. 11; *Wall in Occupied Palestinian Territory* (Advisory Opinion), ICJ Reports 2004, paras 109–11.

[36] *Al-Skeini* v. *United Kingdom*, Application No. 55721/07 (2011), para. 138; *Cyprus* v. *Turkey*, Application No. 25781/94 (2001), para. 77.

[37] See W. Abresch, 'A Human Rights Law of Internal Armed Conflict: The European Court of Human Rights in Chechnya' 16 *EJIL* (2005) 754.

[38] *Juan Carlos Abella* v. *Argentina*, Report No. 55/97, Case 11.137 (1997), paras 149–56, 160–61.

[39] *Al-Jedda* v. *United Kingdom*, Application No. 27021/08 (2011), para.107.

crucial as the two types of armed conflict correspond to different sets of legal provisions. Custom has softened this distinction,[40] but prisoner of war status and grave breaches of provisions of the Geneva Conventions, in particular, only apply in an international armed conflict.[41] The two designations are not necessarily exclusive and can coexist within the same war.[42] This was recognised by the International Court in *Nicaragua* (1986), which concerned hostilities between the Nicaraguan government and the Contra rebels within the country and external intervention by the USA. The Court found that both an international and a non-international conflict were simultaneously taking place.[43] Similarly, in *Thomas Lubanga Dyilo* (2012), the ICC considered that, while Uganda's occupation of Bunia airport in the Democratic Republic of the Congo created an international armed conflict, this existed alongside a separate non-international conflict involving rebel groups in the region.[44] This coexistence can highlight the sharp legal differences in the two conflicts so that captured soldiers from an intervening state could be entitled to prisoner of war status, but captured rebels would not.[45]

The term 'armed conflict' is not defined in the Geneva Conventions, though it has been described by the ICTY as 'a resort to armed force between States or protracted armed violence between governmental authorities and organized armed groups or between such groups within a State'.[46] It should be noted, however, that the deployment of one country's military forces in another does not necessarily mean that an armed conflict is taking place. Peacekeeping missions, stationed with the consent of the receiving state, do not create an armed conflict. As Nigel D. White explores in Chapter 5, these armed forces are generally

[40] *Prosecutor* v. *Dusko Tadić* (Interlocutory Appeal on Jurisdiction) IT-94-1-AR, 5 October 1995, paras 96–127 (1995). See also L. Moir, *The Law of Internal Armed Conflict* (Cambridge: Cambridge University Press, 2002), 134–60; T. Meron, 'The Continuing Role of Custom in the Formation of International Humanitarian Law', 90 *AJIL* (1996) 239–49.

[41] J. Pejic, 'Status of Armed Conflicts', in E. Wilmshurst and S. Breau (eds), *Perspectives on the ICRC Study on Customary International Humanitarian Law* (Cambridge: Cambridge University Press, 2007), 77–8.

[42] Y. Dinstein, *War, Aggression and Self-Defence*, 5th edn (Cambridge: Cambridge University Press, 2012), 6–7.

[43] *Case concerning Military and Paramilitary Activities in and against Nicaragua (Nicaragua* v. *US)*, ICJ Reports 1986, para. 219.

[44] *Prosecutor* v. *Thomas Lubanga Dyilo*, ICC-01/04-01/06, 14 March 2012, paras 563–7.

[45] Pejic, 'Status of Armed Conflicts', 93.

[46] *Prosecutor* v. *Dusko Tadić* (Interlocutory Appeal on Jurisdiction) IT-94-1-AR, 5 October 1995, para. 70.

governed by international human rights law, rather than the laws of war, except where they have been given a coercive enforcement mandate. Common Article 2 of the Geneva Conventions also provides that the existence of an armed conflict does not depend on recognition by its parties. As Dieter Fleck notes in Chapter 3, states have often been reluctant to make this characterisation, especially in relation to non-international conflicts. The term points to a loss of control over a territory and they have preferred designations such as law enforcement or action against terrorism.

International armed conflict

An international armed conflict involves hostilities between two or more states and legally is the more substantial of the two types of conflict, activating the provisions of both the Hague and Geneva Conventions. An international armed conflict can arise in several ways and, once it has, the laws of war will operate in the whole territory of the warring states.[47]

The first way is for two states to engage in hostilities, even if one of them does not recognise the existence of the state of war.[48] Second, a state's territory may be partially or totally occupied.[49] Occupation, as defined in Article 42 of Hague Regulation IV 1907 and custom, involves the placing of territory under the actual authority of a hostile army.[50] The reasons for the occupation are irrelevant.[51] Nor does it have to meet with armed resistance.[52] The ICJ, in *D. R. Congo* v. *Uganda* (2005), considered that the crucial element was not simply the presence of troops, but the substitution of authority, and an occupation only extends to where this can be exercised. This authority is accompanied by a duty to maintain law and order while respecting the territory's existing laws.[53] These powers of occupation, though, are not the same thing as sovereignty. An attempt by an occupier to assert this could violate the prohibition on the threat or use of force against the territorial integrity of a state,[54] the non-acquisition of territory by the threat or use of force[55] and the right of self-determination.[56]

[47] *Ibid.*, para. 70. [48] Common Article 2 Geneva Conventions 1949. [49] *Ibid.*

[50] *Democratic Republic of Congo* v. *Uganda*, ICJ Reports 2005, para. 172.

[51] *Ibid.*, para. 173. [52] Article 2(2) Fourth Geneva Convention 1949.

[53] Article 43 Hague Regulation IV 1907.

[54] *Wall in Occupied Palestinian Territory*, ICJ Reports 2004, para. 87. See UNSC Res. 662 (1990): '*Decides* that annexation of Kuwait by Iraq under any form and whatever pretext has no legal validity, and is considered null and void.'

[55] ICJ Reports 2004, paras 87, 121. See UNSC Res. 298 (1971) and UNSC Res. 478 (1980) on the invalidity of Israeli measures to change the legal status of Jerusalem.

[56] ICJ Reports 2004, paras 88, 122.

Third, a state could directly intervene in another state's internal conflict,[57] though the conflict is not internationalised if those forces have been invited by that state.[58] Fourth, external intervention by a state in an internal conflict may be less direct and take the form of support for rebels. If this assistance creates a situation where a state is in overall control of a movement, the ICTY and ICC have taken the view that this could internationalise the conflict, whilst the ICJ has not taken a definite stance.[59] Fifth, if an internal conflict within a state results in its dissolution or the secession of part of its territory, the continuing conflict between the new states will be international.[60] Sixth, Article 1(4) of Additional Protocol I to the Geneva Conventions provides that armed conflicts in which peoples are fighting colonial domination, alien occupation and racist regimes are international armed conflicts.

Non-international armed conflict

The law in a non-international armed conflict can be found in Common Article 3 of the Geneva Conventions and Additional Protocol II. As Lindsay Moir notes in Chapter 4, the non-international armed conflict, though normally understood as a civil war, in fact reflects a default position whereby a conflict has not met the criteria for an international armed conflict. This means that non-international armed conflicts do not have to be internal but can cross state borders, as long they do not have the sufficient involvement of two states.[61] The so-called 'War on Terror' is certainly international, but not an armed conflict between states. An ambiguous example was the 2006 conflict between Israel and the Shia militia Hezbollah, which was conducted on Lebanese territory but did not involve active participation by that state's armed forces. A UN Commission of Enquiry recognised this as a novel situation for the laws of war, though it favoured characterising the conflict as international based on Hezbollah's political ties to the Lebanese state and the

[57] *Prosecutor* v. *Tadic* (Appeals), IT-94-1-A, 15 July 1999, para. 84.

[58] Pejic, 'Status of Armed Conflicts', 92; Dinstein, *The Conduct of Hostilities*, 27–8; L. Moir, *The Law of Internal Armed Conflict* (Cambridge: Cambridge University Press, 2002), 50–1.

[59] *Tadic* (Appeals), para. 145; *Prosecutor* v. *Thomas Lubanga Dyilo*, para. 541; *Case concerning the Application of the Convention on the Prevention and Punishment of the Crime of Genocide (Bosnia and Herzegovina* v. *Serbia and Montenegro)*, ICJ Reports 2007, paras 404–5.

[60] *Prosecutor* v. *Tadic* (Trial), para. 569.

[61] *Prosecutor* v. *Thomas Lubanga Dyilo*, para. 541.

occupation of Lebanese territory.[62] This has led some writers to argue for a new hybrid category of the 'transnational armed conflict',[63] though Moir is sceptical of this, arguing that the non-international armed conflict provides an appropriate regime for cross-border conflicts involving non-state actors.

Even if the non-international armed conflict reflects a default position, it also constitutes a legal threshold in hostilities. This can be seen explicitly in Article 1(2) of Protocol II, which specifies that internal disturbances and tensions, such as riots and isolated and sporadic acts of violence, do not amount to an armed conflict. Article 1(1) details the level of organisation and control needed for this type of conflict. The dissident groups covered by the Protocol have five particular features. First, they are organised armed groups. Second, they are under responsible command. Third, they control part of a state's territory. Fourth, this control enables them to carry out sustained and concerted military operations. Fifth, they have a capacity to implement the Protocol, which indicates structure and internal discipline. Common Article 3 does not specify the criteria for a non-international armed conflict and could potentially represent a lower threshold. Commentary for the article, however, notes the need to distinguish such conflicts from banditry or unorganised and short-lived insurrections and contains non-binding criteria that match those in Article 1(2).[64] An example from the Inter-American Commission was the attack on the La Talbada military base in Argentina in 1989. Even though it lasted just thirty hours, it was found to fall within Common Article 3 due to its nature and level: that it was carefully planned and coordinated and executed as a military operation against government forces.[65] The definition adopted by the ICTY in

[62] The UN Commission of Enquiry described it as 'sui generis'. Report of the Commission of Inquiry, A/HRC/3/2 (2006), para. 53. The Commission, however, characterised the conflict as an international armed conflict based on: (1) the participation of Hezbollah in the constitutional organs of the Lebanese state; (2) the role of Hezbollah as a resistance movement against the Israeli occupation of Lebanese territory; and (3) the state of Lebanon was the object of direct hostilities by Israel. Significantly, the Commission also found that Article 2 of the Geneva Conventions was activated by occupation, even if met by no resistance. *Ibid.*, paras 55–9.

[63] See G. S. Corn, 'Making the Case for Conflict Bifurcation in Afghanistan: Transnational Armed Conflict, al Qaida and the Limits of the Associated Militia Concept', in M.N. Schmitt (ed.), *The War in Afghanistan: A Legal Analysis*, International Law Studies, vol. 85 (Newport, RI: US Naval War College, 2009), 184–5.

[64] Commentary to Common Article 3, First Geneva Convention, 49–50.

[65] *Juan Carlos Abella* v. *Argentina*, Report No. 55/97, Case 11.137 (1997), paras 154–6.

Tadić (see above), and echoed by the ICC,[66] is based on protracted armed violence (interpreted as its intensity)[67] and a sufficient degree of organisation, with the involvement of a government and/or organised armed groups. This again is intended to distinguish acts such as banditry and (more questionably) terrorism and draws from the Commentary to Common Article 3.[68]

Common Article 3 offers a minimum standard of protection in armed conflict. This includes humane treatment and non-discrimination for persons taking no active part in the hostilities, including members of armed forces who have laid down their arms, and care for the sick and wounded. It also protects those persons from violence, hostage-taking, outrages upon their personal dignity, in particular humiliating and degrading treatment, and punishment without an internationally recognised judicial process. Protocol II provides a more extensive range of protections for persons who have been detained and the wounded, sick and shipwrecked. It also protects civilians from attack and the destruction of objects indispensable for their survival, such as crops,[69] as well as forced movement, unless for their security or imperative military reasons.[70] It prevents attacks on cultural objects and installations containing dangerous forces, such as dams and nuclear power stations.[71] However, while Protocol II is binding on its 167 parties, it is not considered to represent custom, unlike Common Article 3.[72] Moreover, it does not provide for prisoner of war status. Captured

66 Article 8(2)(f) ICC Statute 1998: 'armed conflicts that take place in the territory of a State when there is protracted armed conflict between governmental authorities and organized armed groups or between such groups'.

67 'The criterion of protracted armed violence has therefore been interpreted in practice, including by the *Tadić* Trial Chamber itself, as referring more to the intensity of the armed violence than to its duration. Trial Chambers have relied on indicative factors relevant for assessing the "intensity" criterion, none of which are, in themselves, essential to establish that the criterion is satisfied. These indicative factors include the number, duration and intensity of individual confrontations; the type of weapons and other military equipment used; the number and calibre of munitions fired; the number of persons and type of forces partaking in the fighting; the number of casualties; the extent of material destruction; and the number of civilians fleeing combat zones. The involvement of the UN Security Council may also be a reflection of the intensity of a conflict.' *Prosecutor* v. *Haradinaj, Balaj and Brahimaj* (Trial) IT-04-84-T, 3 April 2008, para. 49. See also Report of the Commission of Inquiry on Lebanon, A/HRC/3/2 (2006), para. 51.

68 *Tadić* (Trial), para. 562. 69 Articles 13–14 AP II 1977. 70 Article 17 AP II.

71 Articles 15–16 AP II.

72 *Prosecutor* v. *Dusko Tadić* (Interlocutory Appeal on Jurisdiction), para. 89.

members of armed opposition groups are answerable for their actions under the domestic law of the state in which they are fighting.[73]

Protections for civilians

The protection of civilians is one of the principal aims of the laws of war. This is underlined in Article 51(2) of Additional Protocol I, which declares that: 'The civilian population as such, as well as individual civilians, shall not be the object of attack.' The concept of a civilian, however, is essentially a negative one, as a non-combatant.[74] This makes it extremely broad and it can include, for example, the environment. Combatants, by contrast, are members of the armed forces or armed groups of a party to a conflict, with the exception of the medical personnel and chaplains attached to that force.[75] These individuals have the right to participate directly in hostilities and so can also be targeted.

This division is encapsulated in Hague Law by the principle of distinction. In Article 48 of Additional Protocol I, 'Parties to the conflict shall at all times distinguish between the civilian population and combatants and between civilian objects and military objectives and accordingly shall direct their operations only against military objectives.' Article 52(2) adds that attacks shall be strictly limited to military objectives, which are objects that by their nature, location, purpose or use make an effective contribution to military action. By their total or partial destruction, capture or neutralisation, in the circumstances ruling at the time, they offer a definite military advantage. Beyond this, the use of force could be a violation of the principle. Thus, Croat forces burning houses in Bosnian Muslim towns, after they had been captured, was found by the ICTY to be a violation of the laws of war.[76]

This, however, assumes that two classes of individual – combatants and civilians – can be easily separated. Members of regular armed forces can be identified by their uniforms, allowing them to be targeted but also

[73] A. Rogers, 'Combatant Status', in E. Wilmshurst and S. Breau (eds), *Perspectives on the ICRC Study on Customary International Humanitarian Law* (Cambridge: Cambridge University Press, 2007), 125.

[74] Article 50(1) AP I. See also A. Cullen, *The Concept of Non-International Armed Conflict in International Humanitarian Law* (Cambridge: Cambridge University Press, 2010), 49–61.

[75] Article 43(2) AP I.

[76] *Prosecutor* v. *Naletilić and Martinović* (Trial), IT-98-34-T, 31 March 2003, paras 583–5, 589. A broad view of military advantage can be found in *Eritrea Ethiopia Claims Commission*, Partial Award (2005), 45 *ILM* (2006) 418–20.

to enjoy protections, such as prisoner of war status, if captured. This trade-off also applies to irregular forces, like militias, if they follow a chain of command, can be identified by their distinctive insignia, carry their arms openly and conduct operations following the laws and customs of war.[77] The only identifiable fighters who do not enjoy protection are mercenaries, whose destructive involvement in conflicts, especially in Africa, led to their denial of prisoner of war status in Additional Protocol I.[78] This need for soldiers to identify themselves in order to enjoy protection underlines one of the aims of the laws of war, to eliminate certain forms of perfidy in combat. It also stems from the historical background to the laws of war in the nineteenth century, where defined armies would meet on the battlefield away from civilians.

Modern warfare, however, has seen the combat zone become much larger and more diffuse and guerrilla warfare, in particular, blurs the line between civilians and combatants. The classic example is the proverbial farmer who by day works in the fields, but at night exchanges farming tools for a rifle. Under the Geneva Conventions these fighters do not fit the profile of identified combatants, and the protections accorded to them, but are instead 'unlawful combatants'[79] liable to prosecution, though they must still receive humane treatment and a fair trial.[80] Additional Protocol I created a presumption for prisoner of war status that can only be overturned by a competent tribunal.[81] The only instance of civilians immediately turning into protected combatants is the *levée en masse*, in which the inhabitants of a previously unoccupied territory spontaneously take up arms to resist an invading enemy force. Provided that they carry their arms openly and respect the laws and customs of war, they enjoy the same protections accorded to regular combatants.[82]

Additional Protocol I in 1977 controversially narrowed the distinction between combatants and civilians. Article 44(3) provides that:

77 Article 4(A)(2) Third Geneva Convention 1949. 78 Article 47 AP I 1977.

79 E. Crawford, *The Treatment of Combatants and Insurgents under the Law of Armed Conflict* (Oxford: Oxford University Press, 2010), 53–5; Dinstein, *The Conduct of Hostilities*, 34–9; K. Ipsen, 'Combatants and Non-Combatants', in Fleck, *Handbook of International Humanitarian Law*, 83.

80 Article 5 Fourth Geneva Convention 1949; Article 45(3) AP I. See J. Callen, 'Unlawful Combatants and the Geneva Conventions', 44 *VJIL* (2004) 1025–72.

81 Article 45(1) AP I 1977.

82 Article 2 Hague Regulations annexed to Convention IV 1907; Article 13(6) First and Second Geneva Conventions 1949; Article 4(6) Third Geneva Convention 1949.

> owing to the nature of the hostilities an armed combatant cannot so distinguish himself, he shall retain his status as a combatant, provided that, in such situations, he carries his arms openly: (a) during each military engagement, and (b) during such time as he is visible to the adversary while he is engaged in a military deployment preceding the launching of an attack in which he is to participate.

This has proved to be one of the most controversial provisions in the Protocol. The speed of the transition from civilian to combatant, by simply producing a weapon, has been criticised for shifting the balance between regular and irregular forces too much to the latter's advantage. It also means that civilians are more likely to be targeted.[83]

Additional Protocol I only allows such individuals to be targeted while they are actively engaged in hostilities. However, as Charles Garraway explores in Chapter 8, the ICRC Assembly has effectively disposed of this with the proposal that members of organised armed groups have a continuous combat function and can be targeted as such.[84] This designation is based on a lasting integration into that group with involvement in the preparation, execution or command of acts that amount to direct participation in hostilities. A person recruited, trained and equipped by the group for direct participation in a conflict can be assumed to have this function, even if not actively engaged in hostilities. However, this does not extend to more peripheral, but still essential, participants, such as financiers, trainers and weapons manufacturers.[85] The ICRC has considered that direct participation depends on three principles: (1) the threshold of harm involved (acts that cause death, injury and destruction); (2) a direct causal link between an act and this harm (which excludes persons in a supporting role); and (3) a belligerent nexus (the act is in support and to the detriment of parties in a conflict).[86]

A further complication with this distinction is that military action will draw from civilian support and infrastructure. Destroying an enemy munitions factory provides a clear military advantage, but its workers may be civilians. Roads, railways, bridges, telecommunications, broadcasting and electricity supplies are essential both for civilians and the military, with a corresponding risk of civilian casualties when attacked.[87] A tragic example of this took place in the Kosovo air campaign in

[83] 'Interpretive Guidance on the Notion of Direct Participation in Hostilities under International Humanitarian Law', 90 *IRRC* (2008) 991.

[84] *Ibid.*, 1002–9. [85] *Ibid.*, 1007–8. [86] *Ibid.*, 1016–33.

[87] M. Lippman, 'Aerial Attacks on Civilians and the Humanitarian Law of War: Technology and Terror from World War I to Afghanistan', 33 *California Western*

April 1999. One target in this campaign was the bridge over the Grdelica Gorge in Serbia, which provided a resupply route for Serb forces in Kosovo. A NATO aircraft attacked the bridge, releasing two laser-guided missiles, at which point a passenger train crossed it. The train was hit with at least ten fatalities.[88] Industry also creates problems for targeting. Some industrial facilities, such as refineries, port facilities, metal works and chemical plants that make explosives, can clearly support military action. But a broad targeting of industry, with attendant civilian casualties, may go beyond military objectives to broader goals of weakening a state's economy or civilian morale. However, production in most industries could be redirected to military ends[89] and this creates a difficult balance. Lastly, civilian buildings, including schools and private dwellings, can be used to accommodate troops or for military headquarters and may correspondingly be targeted, though with obvious dangers if information is inaccurate.[90]

These ambiguities are managed with the principle of proportionality.[91] This is not explicitly provided for in international instruments, but has nevertheless informed them and is strongly implied in Additional Protocol I[92] with the notion of an 'indiscriminate' attack.[93] Proportionality does not exclude the possibility of civilian casualties, but relates them to the importance of the military objectives pursued.[94] Thus, an investigation by the ICTY into the Kosovo air campaign concluded that the death of around 500 civilians in relation to the release of 23,614 munitions did not indicate an intention to target civilians. The casualties were in proportion to attacks on military objectives.[95] Article 51(5) in Protocol I gives an outline of a clearly disproportionate attack: one that treats

International Law Journal (2002) 43–4; A. P. V. Rogers, *Law on the Battlefield* (Manchester: Manchester University Press, 1996), 43–6.

88 Final Report to the Prosecutor by the Committee Established to Review the NATO Bombing Campaign against the Federal Republic of Yugoslavia: www.icty.org/x/file/Press/nato061300.pdf.

89 Dinstein, *The Conduct of Hostilities*, 104; S. Oeter, 'Methods and Means of Combat', in Fleck, *Handbook of International Humanitarian Law*, 184–5.

90 Article 52(3) AP I 1977 provides that if there is doubt as to whether a building is being used in this way, it will be presumed not to be.

91 J.-M. Henckaerts and L. Doswald-Beck, *Customary International Humanitarian Law*, 3 vols (Cambridge: Cambridge University Press, 2005), vol. 1, *Rules*, 46–9; J. G. Gardam, 'Proportionality and Force in International Law', 87 *AJIL* (1993) 410.

92 See Judge Higgins, Dissenting Opinion, *Nuclear Weapons* (n. 4, above), ICJ Reports 1996, 587, para. 20.

93 Article 51(4) AP I 1977.

94 W. J. Fenrick, 'The Rule of Proportionality and Protocol I in Conventional Warfare', 98 *Military Law Review* (1982) 93–4.

95 Final Report to the Prosecutor, para. 54.

distinct military objectives in a village, town or city as a single objective or which is expected to cause excessive civilian casualties and damage to civilian objects in relation to the concrete and direct military advantage anticipated.[96] An example of this is provided by *Blaškić* (2000) in which the ICTY found that: 'By advocating the vigorous use of heavy weapons to seize villages inhabited mainly by civilians, General Blaškić gave orders which had consequences out of all proportion to military necessity and knew that many civilians would inevitably be killed and their homes destroyed.'[97] This was found to constitute a war crime.[98]

Protocol I provides further guidance with provisions on a precautionary approach to attack preparation. Under Article 57, planners should do everything feasible to verify that the objects of an attack are not civilian, that their choice of means and methods minimise civilian casualties or damage to civilian objects and should refrain from attacks that cause excessive casualties and damage in relation to the concrete and direct military advantage anticipated. When a choice is possible between several military objectives, the object should be selected that causes least damage to civilians and civilian objects.

Nonetheless, the principle remains essentially subjective and, in less clear-cut circumstances, the line between a proportionate and an indiscriminate attack can be harder to make. In *Gotovina*, which concerned the Croat assault on the Serb town of Knin, the ICTY Trial Chamber adopted a 200-metre rule, whereby an artillery strike more than this distance from a legitimate target was presumed not to be in error but indiscriminate.[99] However, as Maya Brehm notes in Chapter 11, the ICTY Appeals Chamber rejected this, recognising that different experts took a range of positions on the accuracy of those weapons.[100]

The crucial feature of proportionality is that the elements in an attack are relative to one another. The importance of the target can be weighed against its effect on civilians. Destroying a strategically vital bridge may

[96] See Article 51(5) AP I 1977.

[97] *ICTY Prosecutor* v. *Tihomir Blaškić*, IT-95-14-T, 3 March 2000, para. 651.

[98] See also Article 8(2)(b)(iv) Rome Statute of the International Criminal Court (1998): 'Intentionally launching an attack in the knowledge that such attack will cause incidental loss of life or injury to civilians or damage to civilian objects or widespread, long-term and severe damage to the natural environment which would be clearly excessive in relation to the concrete and direct overall military advantage anticipated.'

[99] *Prosecutor* v. *Gotovina* (Trial), IT-06-90-T, 15 April 2011, para. 1898. For criticism of this, see W. B. Huffman, 'Margin of Error: Potential Pitfalls of the Ruling in *Prosecutor* v. *Ante Gotovina*', 211 *Military Law Review* (2012) 1–56.

[100] *Prosecutor* v. *Gotovina* (Appeal), IT-06-90-A, 16 November 2012, paras 51–67.

justify higher civilian casualties than a less significant one. This balance could change again with the weapons available (e.g., precision-guided munitions) or the tactics used (e.g., night-time raids). Moreover, as Charles Garraway notes in Chapter 8, civilians themselves are a diverse group: casualties sustained by workers in a munitions factory or mothers and children have different impacts. The balance is also evolving as new weapons and tactics emerge.[101] These technologies bring different perspectives. Aerial drones physically detach their operators from the battlefield, though in Chapter 9 David Turns considers that this does not fundamentally differ from the decisions of pilots in the air. Bill Boothby, in Chapter 10, looks at an even greater degree of detachment: whether targeting could be performed by autonomous systems rather than human decision-makers. This, he considers, could be legal in remote locations away from civilian populations. This balance of different elements may be a realistic legal response to pressures of the battlefield, but it is less satisfactory for soldiers themselves who want clear guidance on when they can use weapons without facing criminal charges.

Geneva Law has a more complex approach to civilians, with a range of protected persons. Article 4 of the Fourth Geneva Convention states that these are persons: 'who, at a given moment and in any manner whatsoever, find themselves, in case of a conflict or occupation, in the hands of a Party to the conflict or Occupying Power of which they are not nationals'.[102] Significantly, this does not encompass all civilians. The focus is on the nationals who find themselves under the control of a hostile state. Correspondingly, Article 4 excludes nationals of the occupying or belligerent state and allied states, as well as nationals of neutral states with normal diplomatic relations. The assumption is that those individuals can be legally protected by their state.[103]

The ICTY in *Tadić* (Appeals) (1999) challenged this assumption by considering that refugees from a belligerent state who no longer owe allegiance to it or benefit from its protection (e.g., German Jews in occupied France) and stateless people should also be protected under Article 4.[104] The *Tadić* case further unpicked the equation of nationality and loyalty. Its context was the Bosnia conflict in which the lines of

[101] M. N. Schmitt, 'The Principle of Discrimination in 21st Century Warfare', 2 *Yale Human Rights and Development Law Journal* (1999) 167.
[102] Article 4 Fourth Geneva Convention 1949.
[103] Article 4(2) Fourth Geneva Convention 1949.
[104] *ICTY Prosecutor* v. *Duško Tadić* (Appeals), para. 164.

belligerency were drawn ethnically between Serbs, Croats and Bosniacs (Muslims), who, at least initially, shared the same nationality (Yugoslav). The Tribunal defined protected persons by ethnicity, arguing that it was justified by the object and purpose of the Fourth Geneva Convention in providing the maximum protection for civilians.[105] The Tribunal later also questioned the exclusion of co-belligerents. Croats and Bosniacs in Bosnia were allies against the Serbs, but also fought each other. The Tribunal in *Blaškić* (2000) emphasised the importance of 'actual relations [rather] than formal ties' and found that Bosnian Muslim civilians could be protected against Croat attacks.[106]

Civilians who fall under the power of an enemy belligerent state are extremely vulnerable and the Fourth Geneva Convention gives them security, whilst allowing the occupier to establish an administration. Property is protected, except in cases of absolute military necessity,[107] and the population cannot be compelled to serve in the occupier's armed forces, though labour can be requisitioned for limited purposes and in exchange for fair remuneration.[108] The occupier must respect much of the existing infrastructure, maintaining educational institutions and health services, allowing the work of religious ministers[109] and paying due regard to the status of public officials and judges, though the latter two can also be removed.[110] To pay for this administrative burden, it is allowed to collect taxes according to existing laws.[111] The penal laws of the territory remain in force and may be repealed or suspended only if they pose a threat to security or prevent the application of the Convention. The occupier cannot introduce retroactive criminal offences or disproportionate penalties.[112] If protected civilians are charged with offences, they are entitled to a fair trial[113] and to serve their sentences in the territory. If the occupation ends, the occupying power cannot retain them.[114] Forced population transfers, the deportation of protected persons from occupied territory and the transfer of parts of its own civilian population to the territory are prohibited under

[105] *Ibid.*, paras 166–9. [106] *Prosecutor* v. *Tihomir Blaškić*, para. 146.
[107] Article 53 Fourth Geneva Convention 1949.
[108] Articles 51–2 Fourth Geneva Convention 1949.
[109] Articles 50, 55–63 Fourth Geneva Convention 1949.
[110] Article 54 Fourth Geneva Convention 1949.
[111] Article 48 Hague Regulations annexed to Convention IV 1970.
[112] Articles 64, 65 and 67 Fourth Geneva Convention 1949.
[113] Articles 71–4 Fourth Geneva Convention 1949.
[114] Articles 76–7 Fourth Geneva Convention 1949.

Article 49 and are a war crime under Article 8(2)(b)(viii) of the Rome Statute. Correspondingly, Israeli settlement on territory occupied in the Arab–Israeli conflict in 1967 was described by the Security Council as a 'flagrant violation' of the Fourth Geneva Convention.[115]

Combatants

As seen in the previous section, combatants constitute the armed forces of a belligerent state or organised armed groups. They enjoy combat immunity whereby they may legally engage in acts of violence within the laws of war[116] and, in turn, can be legitimately targeted. They are also protected if unable to participate in the conflict through injury, illness or capture.

Sick and wounded

Combatants who become wounded or sick are covered by the first two Geneva Conventions. The First Geneva Convention concerns them on the battlefield, while the Second covers them at sea, as well as the shipwrecked. Persons in those circumstances become prisoners of war and entitled to care and humane treatment without discrimination. They should not be wilfully left without medical assistance or in conditions that expose them to risks of contagion or infection. Additional Protocol I further specifies that they should not be subjected to any medical procedure inconsistent with generally accepted medical standards.[117] Priority in treatment can only be for urgent medical reasons.[118]

Belligerents have a duty after engagements to take all possible measures to search for the wounded and sick, without delay, and to protect and collect them and ensure their care. They also have an obligation to search for the dead and prevent them from being despoiled. Both Conventions call on belligerents to conclude local arrangements to allow for medical access and the removal of the sick and wounded.[119] They must also protect and support local volunteers who want to perform this

115 SC Res. 465 (1980). See also ICJ Reports 2004, paras 120–1, 137.

116 Crawford, *The Treatment of Combatants and Insurgents*, 52.

117 Article 11(1) AP I. See L. C. Green, *The Contemporary Law of Armed Conflict*, 2nd edn (Manchester: Manchester University Press, 2000), 219.

118 Article 12 First Geneva Convention 1949; Article 12 Second Geneva Convention 1949.

119 Article 15 First Geneva Convention 1949; Article 18 Second Geneva Convention 1949.

task.[120] Medical units attached to armed forces cannot be attacked, unless they commit harmful acts outside their humanitarian duties, and the fact that they are armed or have armed guards does not deprive them of their protected status.[121] Likewise, hospital ships are not to be attacked.[122] Parties are to make records of the sick, wounded and dead enemy personnel in their hands and transmit this to the Information Bureau provided for by the Third Geneva Convention. The dead are not to be disposed of, as far as circumstances permit, without a medical examination to confirm death and an attempt to establish their identity.[123]

Prisoners of war

Combatants in an international armed conflict who are captured by the enemy become prisoners of war under the Third Geneva Convention and retain this status until released and repatriated.[124] These prisoners become the responsibility of the detaining state, which has a range of obligations for them. They must be treated humanely, without discrimination and protected from violence, disease, insults and public curiosity,[125] with women given due regard to their sex.[126] When prisoners are questioned, they are only bound to give their surname, first names, rank, date of birth and number, or equivalent information, and cannot be coerced to provide more.[127] They must be removed from the conflict zone, as soon as possible, unless their wounds or health make this too risky.[128] The transfer process, however, has often been the period in which prisoners have come to most harm, such as with the 'death marches' of the Korean War and Second World War. Sufficient transport should be provided or if the transfer is on foot, twelve miles (twenty

[120] Article 18 First Geneva Convention 1949; Article 21 Second Geneva Convention 1949.

[121] Articles 19, 21 and 22 First Geneva Convention 1949.

[122] Article 20 First Geneva Convention 1949; Article 22 Second Geneva Convention 1949.

[123] Articles 16–17 First Geneva Convention 1949; Articles 19–20 Second Geneva Convention 1949.

[124] Article 5 Third Geneva Convention 1949.

[125] Articles 13 and 16 Third Geneva Convention 1949. See P. Rowe, 'Prisoners of War in the Gulf Area', in P. Rowe (ed.), *The Gulf War 1990–91 in International and English Law* (London: Routledge, 1993), 195.

[126] Article 14 Third Geneva Convention 1949.

[127] Article 17 Third Geneva Convention 1949.

[128] Articles 19 and 23 Third Geneva Convention 1949.

kilometres) a day is considered reasonable, though this is not specified in the Third Geneva Convention.[129]

The Third Convention allows prisoners to be interned in camps, as long as they provide a healthy environment.[130] The detaining power has an obligation to establish an infirmary, maintain proper washing, toilet and laundry facilities and conduct medical inspections at least once a month.[131] Those held should receive sufficient food and water, clothing appropriate to the climate and accommodation no less favourable than the detaining power's own troops in the same area.[132] They are entitled to keep personal items and money, though these can be removed for security reasons,[133] send letters and receive parcels with food, clothing, medicine and materials, such as books, musical instruments and sporting equipment.[134] Prisoners are subject to the military laws and regulations of the detaining power, which can take disciplinary or judicial measures against those who breach them.[135] Attempting to escape is only a disciplinary offence,[136] but prisoners can be tried for offences committed before their capture, in particular war crimes, under the laws of the detaining power.[137]

The conditions for the trial of prisoners are examined by Peter Rowe in Chapter 14. Article 84 provides that prisoners shall be tried in a military court, unless the detaining power's own laws provide for its armed forces to be tried in a civil court. Such a court must be independent and impartial and provide a fair and regular trial. Rowe argues that many states' military courts are not fully capable of providing these guarantees and could face challenges from human rights bodies, or even commit a grave breach of the Third Geneva Convention.[138] A particular problem has been that the personnel within a military court can operate within a chain of command, which has been found to undermine their independence and impartiality.[139]

129 H. Fischer, 'Protection of Prisoners of War', in Fleck, *Handbook of International Humanitarian Law*, 391–3.
130 Articles 21–2 Third Geneva Convention 1949.
131 Articles 15, 29, 30 and 31 Third Geneva Convention 1949.
132 Articles 25, 26 and 27 Third Geneva Convention 1949.
133 Article 18 Third Geneva Convention 1949.
134 Articles 71–2 Third Geneva Convention 1949.
135 Article 82 Third Geneva Convention 1949.
136 Article 92 Third Geneva Convention 1949.
137 Article 85 Third Geneva Convention 1949.
138 Article 130 Third Geneva Convention 1949.
139 See *Findlay* v. *United Kingdom*, Application No. 22107/93 (1997), paras 72–80.

Methods of warfare and prohibited weapons

A basic principle of the laws of war is that methods and means of warfare are not unlimited. Three principles inform the choice of weapons used in a conflict. First, the principle of distinction prohibits weapons that are completely incapable of distinguishing military targets from civilians. Thus, biological weapons are inherently indiscriminate as the release of a pathogen could not be limited to military objectives.[140] Other weapons are indiscriminate depending on how and where they are used – for example, cluster bombs in urban areas.

Second, there is the prevention of superfluous injury and unnecessary suffering.[141] These are, of course, relative concepts, as conventional weapons are quite capable of inflicting appalling injuries and agonising deaths in a manner proportionate to military objectives. The International Court of Justice (ICJ) described 'unnecessary suffering' as 'harm greater than that unavoidable to achieve legitimate military objectives' and 'uselessly aggravating' the suffering of combatants.[142]

Third, there is the protection of the environment. The ICJ in *Nuclear Weapons* considered that the environment was an element in determining the necessity and proportionality of military action.[143] Article 35(3) of Additional Protocol I prohibits methods of warfare intended or expected to cause widespread, long-term and severe damage to the natural environment,[144] though the ICJ considered that this obligation existed only in treaty law.[145] This prohibition was repeated in the ENMOD Convention of the same year.[146] It was also accompanied by an understanding of those terms: 'widespread' meant 'encompassing an area on the scale of several hundred square kilometres', 'long-lasting' denoted 'lasting for a period of months, or approximately a season' and 'severe' was 'involving serious or significant disruption or harm to human life, natural and economic resources or other assets'. This formula was also used in Article 8(2)(b)(iv) of the International Criminal Court (ICC) Statute.

Drawing from these general principles, specific types of weapon are prohibited under particular treaty regimes. As Maya Brehm outlines in

[140] Schmitt, 'The Principle of Discrimination in 21st Century Warfare', 147.

[141] Article 35(2) AP I. Article 8(2)(b)(xx) Rome Statute 1998.

[142] ICJ Reports 1996, para. 78. [143] *Ibid.*, paras 30 and 33.

[144] Article 35(3) AP I 1977. [145] ICJ Reports 1996, para. 31.

[146] Article 1 Convention on the Prohibition of Military or any Hostile Use of Environmental Modification Techniques 1977.

Chapter 11, this started with the St Petersburg Declaration 1868, which banned explosive bullets (explosive projectiles under 400 grammes). The range of prohibited projectiles increased with the Hague Declaration IV, 3 1899, which addressed bullets that expand or flatten easily in the human body (so-called dumdum bullets).[147] This is repeated in the ICC Statute, though such bullets, due their greater stopping power, are used by law-enforcement agencies in anti-terrorist and hostage situations. Protocol I to the Convention on Certain Conventional Weapons (CCW) 1981 bans weapons whose primary effect is to injure by fragments that escape detection by X-rays. Protocol II (amended in 1996)[148] prohibits booby-traps that take the form of an apparently harmless object, but which detonate when disturbed or approached, or are associated with a range of objects from internationally recognised protective emblems to children's toys and food or drink.[149] Protocol III prohibits the use of incendiary weapons against civilians or military objectives within a concentration of civilians. Protocol IV 1995 prohibits blinding laser weapons. Protocol V 2003 created obligations on parties to mark and clear or destroy explosive war remnants.

The use of mines has posed a serious challenge under the principle of distinction. As hidden dangers they create particular risks for civilians, especially if mine fields are not identified, the mines are scattered or if they remain active after hostilities have ended. CCW Protocol II provided that mined areas should be recorded and the information provided to civilians on the cessation of active hostilities.[150] It prohibited remotely delivered mines whose location could not be accurately recorded and which could not be rendered harmless once they no longer served a military purpose. Amendments to the Protocol in 1996 banned

[147] Declaration (IV, 3) Concerning Expanding Bullets 1899.

[148] Protocol on Prohibitions or Restrictions on the Use of Mines, Booby-Traps and Other Devices as Amended on 3 May 1996.

[149] Article 7(1): 'Without prejudice to the rules of international law applicable in armed conflict relating to treachery and perfidy, it is prohibited in all circumstances to use booby-traps and other devices which are in any way attached to or associated with: (a) internationally recognized protective emblems, signs or signals; (b) sick, wounded or dead persons; (c) burial or cremation sites or graves; (d) medical facilities, medical equipment, medical supplies or medical transportation; (e) children's toys or other portable objects or products specially designed for the feeding, health, hygiene, clothing or education of children; (f) food or drink; (g) kitchen utensils or appliances except in military establishments, military locations or military supply depots; (h) objects clearly of a religious nature; (i) historic monuments, works of art or places of worship which constitute the cultural or spiritual heritage of peoples; or (j) animals or their carcasses'.

[150] Article 9 Amended Protocol II.

features that endangered mine clearance: mines that detonated in the presence of commonly available mine detectors and anti-handling devices that operated after the mine itself had ceased to function.[151] However, the Protocol was still widely seen inadequately to protect civilians and a full ban on the use, manufacture and stockpiling of anti-personnel mines was established in the Ottawa Convention 1997.[152] A similar concern with civilian casualties caused by scattered unexploded ordnance underlay the Cluster Munitions Convention 2008, which prohibits such weapons. Nonetheless, this ban has divided states[153] and the treaty currently has only eighty-three parties.[154]

Chemical, biological and nuclear weapons (weapons of mass destruction) run against the principle of distinction on account of their indiscriminate effects as well as the prohibition of unnecessary suffering. However, they are also governed by specific treaty regimes.

The first instrument to outlaw chemical weapons was the Hague Declaration IV, 2 1899, which prohibited the use of projectiles whose sole object was to diffuse asphyxiating or deleterious gases.[155] Despite these obligations, poison gas was used extensively in the First World War and a ban on those weapons was reiterated in the peace treaties that concluded it in 1919.[156] The Geneva Protocol 1925, with 137 parties, recognised that a prohibition on such weapons applied to the majority of the world's powers, but sought to make it universal. This ambition can be seen to have been realised with evidence of a customary ban from, at least, the late 1960s.[157] This is supported by the Chemical Weapons Convention (CWC) 1993, which, with 189 parties, binds almost all the world's states and establishes a system of reporting and inspection. Nonetheless, chemical weapons have been used by Iraq in the Iran–Iraq

151 Article 3(5–6) Amended Protocol II.

152 Article 1 Convention on the Prohibition of the Use, Stockpiling, Production and Transfer of Anti-Personnel Mines and on their Destruction 1997 (161 states parties).

153 Dinstein, *The Conduct of Hostilities*, 80.

154 See www.clusterconvention.org/the-convention/convention-status/ (accessed 31 July 2013).

155 Declaration (IV, 2) concerning Asphyxiating Gases 1899 (32 states parties).

156 Article 171 Treaty of Versailles (Germany) 1919; Article 135 Treaty of St Germain (Austria) 1919; Article 82 Neuilly-sur-Seine 1919 (Bulgaria) 1919; Article 119 Treaty of Trianon (Hungary) 1919; Article 176 Treaty of Sèvres (Turkey) 1919.

157 See UNGA Res. 2603A (XXIV) 1969: 'the Geneva Protocol embodies the generally recognized rules of international law prohibiting the use in international armed conflicts of all biological and chemical methods of warfare, regardless of any technical developments'. See also R. R. Baxter and T. Buergenthal, 'Legal Aspects of the Geneva Protocol of 1925', 64 *AJIL* (1970) 853–4, 865.

War 1980–8 and against its own civilians[158] and in the Syrian civil war in 2013.[159]

The Geneva Protocol also prohibited biological weapons and a separate Biological Weapons Convention (BWC) was concluded in 1972 and has 169 state parties. This bans the development, acquisition, retention and stockpiling of biological weapons.[160] It does not have an inspection element and has not been seen as being as effective as the CWC, although the ban it helped establish is likewise considered part of custom.[161] The use of chemical weapons is specifically a war crime under the ICC Statute,[162] though curiously this is not the case for biological weapons. This discrepancy can be explained by the brinkmanship of states pressing for nuclear weapons to be included in the Statute, who argued that if those weapons were not added then neither should biological ones. Unfortunately, the result of these tactics was a serious and glaring omission in the Statute.[163]

Nuclear weapons, unlike chemical and biological ones, are not subject to a comprehensive treaty-based prohibition. The Nuclear Non-Proliferation Treaty (NPT) 1968 prevents the transfer of nuclear weapons or assistance in manufacturing them.[164] Some treaties prohibit the deployment of nuclear weapons in certain areas, such as the Antarctic or outer space, while others prevent the testing of such weapons.[165] These, though, do not amount to a general ban.[166] The NPT only imposes a duty on nuclear weapons states to pursue good faith negotiations on disarmament and on a treaty on complete disarmament.[167] A series of UN General Assembly resolutions have divisively proclaimed the

[158] Report of the Mission Dispatched by the Secretary-General to Investigate Allegations of the Use of Chemical Weapons in the Conflict between the Islamic Republic of Iran and Iraq, S/19823 (1988).

[159] United Nations Mission to Investigate Allegations of the Use of Chemical Weapons in the Syrian Arab Republic, Report on the Alleged Use of Chemical Weapons in the Ghouta Area of Damascus on 21 August 2013 www.un.org/disarmament/content/slideshow/Secretary_General_Report_of_CW_Investigation.pdf.

[160] Article 1 Convention on the Prohibition of the Development, Production and Stockpiling of Bacteriological (Biological) and Toxin Weapons and on their Destruction 1972.

[161] Dinstein, *The Conduct of Hostilities*, 83.

[162] Article 8(2)(b)(xviii) Rome Statute 1998; Resolution RC/Res. 5 (2010) and amended Article 8(2)(e)(xiii–xiv).

[163] R. Cryer, *Prosecuting International Crimes: Selectivity and the International Criminal Law Regime* (Cambridge: Cambridge University Press, 2005), 279–80.

[164] Article I Treaty on the Non-Proliferation of Nuclear Weapons 1968.

[165] ICJ Reports 1996, para. 58. [166] *Ibid.*, para. 63.

[167] Article VI Treaty on the Non-Proliferation of Nuclear Weapons 1968.

illegality of nuclear weapons.[168] However, the International Court in *Nuclear Weapons* considered that they did not establish a customary prohibition.[169] The Court found that the use of nuclear weapons seemed scarcely reconcilable with the principles of distinction and the prohibition of unnecessary suffering,[170] whilst not commenting on whether it inevitably affected the neutrality of other states.[171] Nevertheless, it was unable to find with certainty that the use of nuclear weapons would be at variance with the principles of armed conflict in any circumstance, especially in extreme cases of self-defence.[172] Correspondingly, the Court came to the politically nuanced conclusion,[173] considering the marked division between states on this issue, that 'it cannot reach a definitive conclusion as to the legality or illegality of the use of nuclear weapons by a State in an extreme circumstance of self-defence, in which its very survival would be at stake'.[174]

The contemporary challenges to the laws of war

The chapters in this book expand on some of the contemporary challenges to the laws of war touched on here. The laws of war exist in the same state of evolution as their subject matter. They have at their heart simple and just ideas: the protection of civilians, the sick and wounded and prisoners. But, implementation can often involve difficult and complex balances. The challenges to the laws of war broadly fall into three types. The first relate to the structure of IHL itself. There has always been a dichotomy between Geneva and Hague Law, but today the laws of war have been stretched further across international criminal law and human rights law. These, in turn, bring their own procedures and cultures. Second, the division between international and non-international armed conflicts, essential for unlocking the various provisions of the laws of war, has continued to develop with different actors and within different contexts. Third, the basic principle of distinction still raises questions over the nature of combatants, the use of weapons and new methods for delivering them. These issues will be explored more fully in the subsequent chapters.

168 See, e.g., UNGA Res. 1653 (XVI) (1961) (55 in favour, 20 against, with 26 abstentions).
169 ICJ Reports 1996, paras 68–73. 170 *Ibid.*, para. 95. 171 *Ibid.*, para. 93.
172 *Ibid.*, paras 95–6.
173 See K. Kulovesi, 'Legality or Otherwise?: Nuclear Weapons and the Strategy of Non Liquet', 10 *Finnish Yearbook of International Law* (1999) 55–89.
174 ICJ Reports 1996, para. 97.

2

Army Legal Services and academia

A. P. V. ROGERS AND GORDON RISIUS

Introduction

This chapter is intended to provide a short history of the relationship between serving or retired officers of the Army Legal Services (ALS) and academic lawyers, together with some reflections from the ALS point of view on the usefulness of the relationship and suggestions as to how it might be developed. Although ALS officers are sometimes described as military lawyers in this chapter, many of the experiences described have been shared by legal officers from the Royal Navy and Royal Air Force. Those from all three services are usually referred to as 'service lawyers'.

The areas of law that provide the main work for military lawyers are, first of all, those providing for the recruitment, terms of service, discipline and discharge of military personnel. Most of this used to be found in the Army Act of 1955, but much of it has now been incorporated, on a tri-service basis, in the Armed Forces Act 2006. Subject to jurisdictional arrangements, the statutes also apply English criminal law to Army personnel; so military lawyers also need to be familiar with that body of law. Additionally, there is other legislation relating to the reserve forces; to activities of the armed forces that impinge on the civilian population, such as billeting and requisitioning, assisting the civil authorities with natural disasters, or in dealing with riots and civil unrest; and in relation to the stationing of foreign forces or headquarters in the United Kingdom. In recent years there has been an increasing tendency not to exempt the Armed Forces from what might be termed social legislation, which considerably broadens the field for military lawyers,

The authors' thanks go to Professor Elihu Lauterpacht, Professor Peter Rowe, Professor Françoise Hampson, Major-General (retired) David Selwood, Mr Michael Meyer, Brigadier Stuart Lythgoe, Professor Colonel Charles Garraway and Ms Karen Fachechi for their valuable comments, suggestions and assistance.

and, of course, the Human Rights Act 1998 has had a considerable impact on Army legal work, resulting in litigation in several cases.

Apart from domestic law, military lawyers are also concerned with elements of international law, such as the law of armed conflict, international human rights law and with treaties and other international agreements, usually known as status of forces agreements, governing the rights and duties of Army personnel operating abroad in situations short of armed conflict. In this chapter, the expressions 'military law' or 'service law' are used in a broad sense to cover all these areas of law.

Apart from the law of armed conflict[1] and human rights law, academic lawyers, with some notable exceptions in the field of constitutional law,[2] have tended not to include military law in their writings. However, some military lawyers and civilians associated with the Army, whether as legal advisers or teachers, along with academic lawyers, have joined forces to publish books, manuals and articles on the law of armed conflict and other aspects of military operations and the stationing of forces.[3]

Historical background

Military manuals

The 1914 edition of the *Manual of Military Law*, inspired by the Hague Convention IV of 1907, contained a chapter devoted to the law of war (chapter 14). It was the joint work of a leading international lawyer, Professor Lassa Oppenheim, and Colonel, later Brigadier-General, Sir James Edmonds. He was an officer of the Royal Engineers and a military historian who was secretary to the United Kingdom delegation at the diplomatic conferences that ended with the Geneva Convention of 1906, and at the Red Cross Conference of 1907. He may have become interested in the law of war as a result of his experience, hence his participation in the preparation of the chapter in question. At the time

[1] The classic academic textbook used for many years to supplement their own manuals was L. Oppenheim, *International Law*, ed. H. Lauterpacht, 7th edn (London: Longmans, 1952), vol. 2.

[2] For example, R. F. V. Heuston, *Essays in Constitutional Law*, 2nd edn (London: Stevens, 1964), which contains useful essays on the royal prerogative and on civil disorder or the book by Peter Rowe, *Defence: The Legal Implications* (London: Brassey's, 1987).

[3] Examples of such manuals include D. Fleck (ed.), *The Handbook of the Law of Visiting Forces* (Oxford: Oxford University Press, 2001) and T. D. Gill and D. Fleck (eds), *The Handbook of the International Law of Military Operations* (Oxford: Oxford University Press, 2010). Tony Rogers contributed to both of these

the chapter was written, Edmonds was an officer in the directorate of military intelligence.

The 1958 *Manual of Military Law, Part III*, subtitled 'The Law of War on Land', was intended to bring the law up to date following the experience of the Second World War and the subsequent war crimes trials, as well as the new Geneva Conventions of 1949. It was a collaborative effort involving Professor Hersch Lauterpacht and Colonel Gerald Draper, with much of the text drawn from Lauterpacht's revision of Oppenheim's *International Law* for its seventh edition (1952).[4] Lauterpacht found Draper a meticulous lawyer, who had seen active service in the Second World War, with whom it was a pleasure to work.[5] After studying law at King's College, University of London, Draper was admitted as a solicitor in 1936, but in 1946 was called to the Bar. He served in the Irish Guards from 1941 to 1944, when he was seconded to the Judge Advocate General's office as a military prosecutor for the war crimes trials in Germany until 1949. He served in the ALS from then until his retirement from the Army in 1956 in the rank of colonel. He then entered the academic world, eventually becoming professor of law.[6]

Draper was keen to maintain the association with academic lawyers that had begun with chapter 14, and it was he who suggested that the services of Professor Lauterpacht, then Whewell Professor of Public International Law in the University of Cambridge, should be requested 'as the overall gubernator, mentor, inspirer and first drafter of the broad principles' underlying the manual. Indeed, Draper had previously approached Lauterpacht, when dealing with war crimes shortly after the Second World War, for a reading list on international law to supplement the old chapter 14.[7] Both Lauterpacht and Draper valued the collaboration they had with the American Professor, Richard Baxter, who had seen military service during the Second World War and later became a judge of the International Court of Justice.

The changes brought about by the Geneva Protocols of 1977 and the Conventional Weapons Convention of 1980 necessitated a new manual.

4 E. Lauterpacht, *The Life of Hersch Lauterpacht* (Cambridge: Cambridge University Press, 2010), 360.

5 *Ibid.*

6 A fuller biography by the Count de Salis appears in M. Meyer and H. McCoubrey (eds), *Reflections on Law and Armed Conflicts* (The Hague: Kluwer Law International, 1998), pp. xvii–xxvii.

7 G. I. A. D. Draper, 'Comments on Military Manuals', reproduced *ibid.*, 115–16.

It was decided that, unlike its predecessor, which dealt only with the law of war on land, this should be a joint service manual also covering naval and air warfare. Although the original intention was that it should be less of a legal textbook than its predecessor and more of a practical guide for military personnel, it gradually developed to resemble the 1958 Manual. There is still a need for such practical guidance, and this is often to be found in service doctrine, training or instructional publications, and in orders issued for a particular operation.

Work on the new Manual started in 1978 under the auspices of the Aimed Forces legal services. Some twenty-one chapters were then envisaged. The Director of Army Legal Services (DALS) was to be responsible for fourteen general and land chapters and the Director of Legal Services (RAF) and the Chief Naval Judge Advocate for the remaining air and naval chapters respectively. An Army lawyer in the rank of colonel was appointed the editor and, under his direction, the many land warfare chapters were drafted in the period 1979–82. Separate authors, or author teams, were appointed to deal with the naval and air chapters. By the time of the military operations in the South Atlantic in 1982, much of the Manual had been written in first draft.

From the outset there was dissension over the type of manual required. Some liked a more informal style, not following the treaty wording too closely; others preferred a more scholarly approach, paying close attention to treaty language. Some saw it as a handbook for military personnel; others as a legal textbook. Some saw no need to depart from the text of the 1958 Manual unless it was necessary to do so; for example, because the law had changed,[8] or because there was new law,[9] or there was another need to update that particular text.

When work began, it was hoped that NATO states would move towards ratification of the Additional Protocols together, would make common statements of interpretation and, as far as possible, and certainly on key or controversial issues, adopt common language in their respective manuals. However, these good intentions were undermined by the differing speeds at which NATO states moved towards ratification.[10] Nevertheless, representatives of a number of

[8] Owing, for example, to the impact of Part II of Protocol I on the treatment of the wounded, sick and shipwrecked.

[9] For example, the new provisions of Protocol I on the conduct of hostilities in Part IV.

[10] For example, Italy ratified the protocol in 1986, Germany in 1991, the United Kingdom in 1998 and the USA has still to ratify.

English-speaking nations[11] did exchange correspondence and met periodically over a number of years to discuss problem areas and drafting issues.

By 1986, a complete work in draft form with index had been produced and awaited a decision on ratification of the protocols. By then, the USA had publicly declared that it would not ratify them. It was at about this time that Mr (later Professor, now Sir) Christopher Greenwood, currently a judge of the International Court of Justice, became involved in the project, having been asked by Mr Franklin Berman, of the legal advisers' department at the Foreign and Commonwealth Office (later Sir Franklin Berman, the legal adviser), to read and comment on the drafts so far produced. That began the long and fruitful association between the service lawyers and a leading Cambridge academic international lawyer, which reflected the service and academic association that had been so important in the 1958 Manual, as well as in the 1914 chapter, in ensuring the necessary academic rigour.

In 1987, the draft was revised with the intention of getting closer to the earlier manual and to the treaty language. One shortcoming of the 1958 Manual was the tendency of the authors to summarise or paraphrase the treaty language, so, when it seemed necessary or desirable to do so, the revised draft departed from the 1958 text by including the relevant treaty language as a quotation.

In the period from 1994 to 1997, and following the experience of military operations in the Iraq conflict of 1991, the text was revised once again, especially the early chapters. Additionally, chapters 5 and 6, on the conduct of hostilities and on weapons, were completely rewritten.

A decision on ratification of the Protocols was still awaited. Ratification took place after the election of the Blair government, at rather short notice, in 1998. Ratification at last made production of the manual a high priority. The Director-General Joint Doctrine and Concepts took over responsibility for the manual from the service lawyers and appointed a project officer, an editorial board and a general editor to bring the work to a final conclusion. Professor Greenwood was at last formally appointed the academic consultant and there were many contributors. In the end, it was decided to maintain the combined academic and military approach adopted in the earlier works. Experience of military operations in Kosovo and Afghanistan was taken into account. A draft of

11 Australia, Canada, New Zealand, United Kingdom and USA. We were joined at some of the meetings by the late Birgitte Juul of Denmark.

the manual was issued and tested during the Iraq war of 2003, and the final version was finally adopted and published in 2004.

Problem areas that had faced the editorial team were naval warfare, neutrality and human rights law. In the end, it was decided to adopt the San Remo Manual[12] for the naval chapter and this, with some commentary, replaced the earlier draft naval chapters. A chapter on neutrality law, though drafted, was not included, mainly because it would have meant holding back publication while further research was carried out – though there are references to neutrality law drawn from the San Remo text. Similarly, it was considered that to include human rights law would be to go beyond the scope of the manual, although, again, there are some cross-references to that body of law.

Diplomatic conferences

Professor Draper was a member of the UK delegation at the Red Cross Conferences between 1957 and 1973, but the real stimuli for ALS/ academic relations were the Diplomatic Conference of 1974–7 and the Conventional Weapons Conference of 1979–80. Many states included both academic and service lawyers in their delegations at these negotiations and they found much common ground. The UK delegations included diplomats, non-legal service personnel with special expertise, such as medical or weaponry knowledge, but also military lawyers, including Draper, Colonel (later Major General) Sir David Hughes-Morgan[13] and Tony Rogers. The resulting protocols and conventions added substantially to the existing body of the law of war. Of particular interest in this context is Article 82 of Protocol I of 1977, which introduced a requirement for the armed forces to have legal advisers to advise commanders on the application of the Geneva Conventions of 1949 and the Protocol and about the instruction to be given on this subject to members of the armed forces. Article 83 of the Protocol required states to encourage the study of the subject by the civilian population. The effect of these two articles was to increase the involvement of lawyers in law of war training, both in the armed forces and at universities.

The involvement of ALS officers in diplomatic conferences continued into the present millennium. Among others, Colonel (later Professor)

[12] L. Doswald-Beck, *San Remo Manual on International Law Applicable to Armed Conflicts at Sea* (Cambridge: Cambridge University Press, 1995).

[13] After retirement from the Army he became a Circuit Judge.

Charles Garraway worked on the 1996 Review Conference on the Conventional Weapons Convention (Amended Protocol II and Protocol IV); the International Criminal Court from 1996 to 2001; the Second Protocol to The Hague Cultural Property Convention in 1999; and his office also looked after the Anti-Personnel Landmines (Ottawa) negotiations.

Courses of study

It was not uncommon for ALS officers to be sent on short courses at universities. These included the Law Society's advocacy training courses for solicitors. Tony Rogers attended a course on modern German law at the London School of Economics in 1973.

By at least the late 1980s, and probably earlier, the Ministry of Defence had established a scheme whereby officers could be sent to universities to study full-time for higher degrees, usually at master's level. In about 1989, Tony Rogers requested permission to attend an LLM degree course. The request was refused. However, it was agreed to authorise the allocation of, presumably, continuing education funds to cover tuition fees for an external studentship, on the understanding that all the work would be done in private time.[14] That course of study, at Liverpool University, under the tutelage of Professor Peter Rowe over a period of five years, brought contacts with many academics. The attendance of ALS officers on full-time LLM degree courses subsequently became regular practice, subject to budget restraints.

ALS has also sent officers to universities to attend specially arranged courses on the law of armed conflict. In about 1987, Professor Rowe visited DALS about offering a course for ALS officers on the laws of war. The first course for ALS officers took place at Liverpool University in September 1988. Indeed, Gordon Risius was on the first cohort. The course lasted one month. It gradually widened its participation to

[14] Authority had been given some years earlier to releasing officers to sit as Recorders. It is not known whether there was a fear that additionally releasing officers to undertake academic study might be a step too far at that stage; it was probably just a very cautious reaction. Gordon Risius followed the Recorder route and gained much from the training provided by the Judicial Studies Board (now transforming into the Judicial College), which consists of a healthy balance between experienced judges and academics. However, it appears that the proposal in the 1980s of continuation training for judges was met with hostility, based on the perception that judicial independence was under threat, to the extent that some judges refused outright to participate. Happily, that hostility has long since evaporated.

include RAF Legal Branch officers and, subsequently, military lawyers from one or two other states. Professor Rowe led the course until he left the university in 1995, but it has continued to the present day, although somewhat shortened. The present scheme is for officers to attend a basic course at the University of Hull, or, more recently, Sheffield University, and then a more advanced course at Liverpool University and now Nottingham University. The idea of joint ALS and academic study or research in particulars areas of interest is also being explored.

In recent years, ALS has frequently brought in academic lawyers to lecture at its own conferences and seminars. This may have begun when Law Society rules requiring solicitors to undergo continuation training were extended to ALS officers and they attended Law Society-approved courses, where experts such as Professors Sir John Smith and Diane Birch lectured on criminal law and evidence. Eventually, ALS was given its own budget for such courses and engaged leading academics, including Professor Birch, to take part. These were extended beyond criminal law to cover the law of armed conflict and, for those stationed in Germany, elements of German law. It is pleasing to note that this tradition has continued, with legal training days at the Defence Academy, Shrivenham, including both professional legal and academic presentations; and the annual conference of the Service Prosecuting Authority at RAF Northolt, which has leading members of the Bar, as well as academics, such as Professor David Ormerod, talking about developments in criminal law.[15]

International conferences, expert meetings, discussion groups and other academic contacts

The International Committee of the Red Cross (ICRC) has organised many international meetings of experts, including both academic and military lawyers, to discuss difficult law of armed conflict issues. In recent years these have included meetings relating to anti-personnel landmines, laser weapons and to the meaning of the term 'civilians taking a direct part in hostilities', in all of which Tony Rogers participated. The International Review of the Red Cross contains many articles by academic and military lawyers, as well as members of the ICRC.

The British Red Cross Society, too, has been very active in encouraging the dissemination and discussion of the law of armed conflict and has

[15] Major Hannah Giles, *Adjutant General's Corps Journal*, 21 (2012), 26–7.

arranged short courses for trainee journalists, civil servants and health professionals, as well as seminars or conferences, to coincide with important events, such as the Gulf War of 1991 and the anniversaries of the Geneva Conventions and Protocols, or relating to specific issues, such as the control of anti-personnel landmines. Academic and service lawyers have regularly been speakers on such issues.[16]

The Lauterpacht Centre for International Law in Cambridge has, for many years, held courses on international law for civil servants, and Tony Rogers felt privileged to join the eminent academics and practitioners as a speaker on these courses.

An important, perhaps unique, society that combines expertise in academic, as well as applied, law is the International Society for Military Law and the Law of War, which was established in Strasbourg in 1956 and now has its seat in Brussels. The aim of the society is to study and disseminate military law and IHL. It publishes a review and arranges courses and meetings, as well as triennial international congresses to discuss current issues. These congresses are usually organised by one of the society's twenty-two national groups. Its nearly 750 members come from approximately fifty states and include university professors, military or civilian judges or magistrates, and general and field officers of the armed forces, including legal officers. Professor Draper was an active member of the society for many years and his collection of copies of the review, with his valuable, and often acerbic, handwritten marginal comments, are now to be found at the Lauterpacht Centre.

Academic and practising lawyers also come together at the International Institute of Humanitarian Law, which was founded in 1970 with its seat at San Remo in Italy, to promote IHL, human rights and refugee law. One of its activities is to conduct basic law of war courses, in various languages, for non-legally qualified officers of armed forces from all over the world. Given that participants were not expected to have much knowledge of the subject, the first director of these courses, the late Colonel Frédéric de Mulinen, preferred not to include academics on the teaching staff, and most teaching was done in classes devoted to dealing with practical exercises.[17] In more recent years, however, more

[16] Gordon Risius took part in a number of British Red Cross Society summer schools and gatherings for journalists.

[17] His approach tended to be upset by the fact that many states, lacking at the time their own courses on the law of armed conflict, tended to send legal officers as participants. Gordon Risius acted as one of the class leaders for a number of years and recently an ALS officer has been stationed in San Remo on a full-time basis.

formal lectures have been included in the programme. Of course, academic participation is strong in the institute's more advanced courses and periodic roundtable meetings.

In the United Kingdom, a law of armed conflict discussion group, chaired by Lady Fox and attended by both academic and practising lawyers, met regularly over many years at the British Institute of International and Comparative Law in London, and was instrumental in publishing two collections of essays on the law of armed conflict.[18]

The United Kingdom National Group of the International Society, which was founded in 1988 under the chairmanship of Professor Peter Rowe, has continued to hold similar meetings to the present day. Although personnel change from time to time, the chairman has tended to be an academic lawyer and the secretary a military lawyer. The Group could be a suitable forum for developing further contact and exchange of ideas between academic and practising lawyers. The Group holds periodic meetings to discuss topics of military law or the law of armed conflict, but has not published any papers, though any important contribution can be offered to the editors of the parent society's review. There has been criticism of the Group from the academic community on the basis of a lack of consistent quality, which has been partly due, in recent years, to the precedence given to the requirements of military operations and the lack of participation by lawyers from the Royal Navy and Royal Air Force. It has been suggested that an annual weekend conference might attract academic involvement, though in times of budget restraint this may not be possible. It has also attracted criticism from the operational law side as being too 'rooted in the twentieth century'. In addition, owing to the scattered locations of its members, the nature of military postings and financial restraints, not many members are able to attend its meetings, so the possibility of video-conferencing is now being explored.

The contacts built up at these institutions and discussion groups have led to the publication of several collections of essays by both academic and service lawyers.[19]

[18] M. A. Meyer (ed.), *Armed Conflict and the New Law* (London: British Institute of International and Comparative Law, 1989) and H. Fox and M. A. Meyer, *Effecting Compliance* (London: British Institute of International and Comparative Law, 1993).

[19] For example, P. Rowe (ed.), *The Gulf War 1990–91 in International and English Law* (London: Routledge, 1993); R. Burchill, N. D. White and J. Morris, *International Conflict and Security Law* (Cambridge: Cambridge University Press, 2005); and E. Wilmshurst and S. Breau, *Perspectives on the ICRC Study on Customary International Humanitarian Law*

Transition to the concept of operational law

The developments noted above might suggest that many ALS officers were routinely involved in operational law issues from 1948 onwards, when some of them had been detached from the Military Department of the Judge Advocate General's Office and transferred to the new Army Legal Services Staff List.[20] However, their involvement with practical operational legal issues was, for many years thereafter, sporadic and minimal.[21]

Despite the publication in 1958 of Part III of the *Manual of Military Law*, which might have been expected to stimulate some military interest in legal issues, during the early stages of the cold war it was still almost unheard of for ALS officers to be asked legal questions about the conduct of military operations. The lack of interest does not appear to have been confined to the Army, as the authors recall Professor Adam (later Sir Adam) Roberts mentioning that not a single Defence White Paper published for more than forty years after the end of the Second World War mentioned law of war issues. The reasons may initially have included the same general weariness with such topics that had resulted in the post-Second World War prosecutions for war crimes being ended before all those awaiting trial had been brought to court. Nevertheless, an associated reason was undoubtedly the widespread view that British soldiers instinctively knew how to behave properly on operations and that the international rules introduced following the Second World War were primarily for the benefit of other states, and so had little to do with the task of defending Western Europe against an attack by Warsaw Pact forces.

Even the negotiations that resulted in the Additional Protocols of 1977 did little to stimulate military interest. The need for legal advice for soldiers on operational duty came to be recognised not from conventional

(Cambridge: Cambridge University Press, 2007). The last was a joint project involving Chatham House and the British Institute of International and Comparative Law.

20 Following the recommendations of the Oliver and Lewis Committees, in 1948, the Office of the Judge Advocate General was transferred from the War Office to the Lord Chancellor's Department, leaving army lawyers under the new Director of Army Legal Services (DALS) in the rank of brigadier, while air force legal officers formed the new Royal Air Force Legal Services.

21 When Gordon Risius was commissioned into ALS in 1973, his initial training lacked even the customary attachment to a teeth arm unit, and consisted solely of being told to read the *Manual of Military Law*, Part I, and, later, attending a short, practical military law course. Experienced ALS officers provided the instruction, but there was no academic input and nothing at all on the law of armed conflict.

operational law considerations but owing to the 'Troubles' in Northern Ireland, once military shooting incidents began to give rise to murder prosecutions in the civil courts there. This led to the establishment of the ALS 'flying lawyer service', with a legal officer on permanent standby to deploy immediately, by helicopter if necessary, to the scene of any shooting incident to ensure that the soldier concerned understood his rights under Royal Ulster Constabulary questioning. However, the issues calling for consideration were always governed by domestic law – it was never seriously considered that a state of internal armed conflict had been reached – thus, military lawyers came to be acknowledged as having an internal security operational role, but not yet one relevant to conventional armed conflict.

The Falklands War of 1982 might have been expected to alter significantly this perception, with a host of legal questions at every level being generated from the outset. However, although the requirement for a deployed military lawyer was quickly recognised, the arrival of the designated ALS officer was repeatedly delayed by freight requirements, which were regarded as a higher priority, with the result that he did not reach Port Stanley until just after the surrender. This was, perhaps, surprising, given the serious initial Whitehall legal error in briefing the Prime Minister to tell the House of Commons that captured Argentinian forces were not being treated as prisoners of war, '*because there had been no declaration of war*'. However, there was still a military mindset that operations and the law had little to do with each other.

Before the 1980s, there had been little specialisation within ALS. Most officers were stationed in large legal branches at the major command headquarters of the day[22] and were expected to cover all the main duties, such as providing disciplinary advice to commanders and staff officers, prosecuting at courts martial, and occasionally acting as military law instructors. At the beginning of the 1980s, however, it was decided to deploy ALS officers to smaller offices at divisional headquarters level, initially in Germany. This was partly to reduce the time officers spent travelling across the North German Plain, but, more importantly, also to establish more effective relationships with military units, commanders and their staff officers. One of the effects was to involve legal officers, for the first time, in routine divisional exercises, though to begin with

[22] United Kingdom Land Forces (Wilton, near Salisbury), Northern Ireland (Lisburn), British Army of the Rhine (Rheindahlen, near Mönchengladbach, Germany), Land Forces Cyprus (Episkopi) and Far East Land Forces (Hong Kong).

questions designed to raise practical legal issues tended to be ignored and resolved on the basis of common sense, without any legal input. In consequence, many ALS officers were rarely tested on operational matters.[23]

The belated arrival of the ALS officer in the Falklands in 1982 resulted in an immediate demand for advice on such matters as prisoner of war handling and repatriation, but he was still not seen as having a role to perform in battlefield operations.

The Falklands campaign did, however, generate some awareness of the law of armed conflict, an interest common to both military and academic lawyers. The experience of military operations there, as well as in Iraq in 1991, served to demonstrate its usefulness, as did the air campaign against Serbia in connection with Kosovo later in the decade, the war-fighting operations in Iraq in 2003 and the bombing campaign against Libya in 2011. During this period there was a steady broadening of the scope of interest of military lawyers, beyond the law of armed conflict, encompassing legal issues arising during military deployments that were unrelated to armed conflict as such.

The trend began with the UNPROFOR operations in Bosnia in the 1990s, when British troops took part in peace support operations, but were not involved in the conflict there until force had to be used against Serbian forces in order to protect the safe areas. Those peace support operations brought with them their own legal problems, not addressed in the law of armed conflict treaties, ranging from issues of local law about status of forces, to the use of force by peacekeeping troops in the treatment of those arrested. Similarly, operations in Kosovo, in Iraq after the end of the occupation, and the continuing operations in Afghanistan, have involved military lawyers in a broad palette of legal issues.

[23] At the end of one exercise in Germany in 1981 a complaint that the staff had failed to seek any ALS advice whatsoever, despite the inclusion of more than 100 scenarios designed to raise legal issues, elicited the worrying response that it had not been appreciated that the law might have any bearing on any of them, and they had, therefore, been dealt with on the basis of common sense. This was coupled with the even more worrying and unrealistic suggestion that on future exercises it would be helpful if such scenarios could be accompanied by a note flagging up the need for legal advice. Of course, a lot depended, and still depends, on the attitude of commanders. Some were more attuned to the importance of legal issues. Tony Rogers particularly remembers in the 1980s being the legal staff officer to Major General David Ramsbotham, then commander of the 3rd Armoured Division, who was interested in the law of war and was keen to involve legal officers both as players and in exercising control. He later became General Sir David Ramsbotham, commander of the UK Field Army, and subsequently the Adjutant General, and after his retirement a very effective Chief Inspector of Prisons for England and Wales. He now sits in the House of Lords as Lord Ramsbotham.

Thus, the increased demand for legal advice, on what is nowadays referred to as operational law, covers not just the law of armed conflict, but also a much broader spectrum, some of it relating to the applicability of international human rights law, British domestic human rights law and the actions of British forces operating abroad.

By the late 1990s, ALS had reorganised and expanded, partly as a result of the court martial and summary dealing reforms required to ensure compliance with the European Convention on Human Rights,[24] but also because of the increased demand for operational legal advice.[25] However, it was soon found that the demands for such advice were becoming too great for ALS advisory branches to meet on their own, even with the assistance of officers borrowed from the Prosecuting Authority, and there was accordingly a need for a dedicated operational law branch. Building on the experience of a small operational law cell created in the early 1990s, a much more substantial Operational Law Branch, under a third ALS brigadier, was eventually established in 2003, with a headquarters alongside the Directorate of Land Warfare at Warminster. Numbers in any branch are never static, but about 30 per cent of ALS's strength (currently approximately thirty-two officers) is expected to be serving in the Operational Law Branch.[26] It is regarded primarily as a training organisation and among its highest profile courses currently are its Brigade Lawyers' Operational Law Courses, which now regularly involve academic instructors and the attendance of military lawyers from overseas. The Branch now deals with a wide variety of issues covering the law of armed conflict and international criminal law, targeting, the use of force, the status of forces and memoranda of understanding, the Regulation of Investigatory Powers Act 2000, interrogation,

[24] This involved the creation of the Army Prosecuting Authority, staffed by ALS officers, and its formal separation from ALS Advisory branches, where ALS officers continue to provide commanders with initial disciplinary advice on the summary disposal of cases not justifying a court martial, or on referring the more serious cases to the Prosecuting Authority.

[25] Having been excluded during a divisional exercise in Germany in 1981 from the commander's first planning group, on the ground that his operation plans needed no legal advice, Gordon Risius was gratified, soon after taking over as DALS in 1997, to be told by a young ALS captain, just back from the Balkans, that when he had attended his divisional commander's first meeting the commander had opened the discussion by asking where his lawyer was. He had then made it clear that from then on the officer was to be seated next to him.

[26] They serve not only in Warminster but also at locations such as the Primary Joint Headquarters at Northwood, the Allied Rapid Reaction Corps, in the USA and Australia, and have been deployed to countries such as East Timor and Sierra Leone, as well as more familiar places like Iraq and Afghanistan.

counter intelligence and public interest immunity. Problems tend to be of a practical nature and, of course, the situation in each area of operations is different. This broader concept of operational law has received less attention in academic circles except, possibly, in relation to human rights law.[27]

Involvement of retired ALS officers in academic life

While it is not uncommon for retired officers of the armed forces to make the transition to academia, only a few ALS officers have done so. The most celebrated of these was undoubtedly Professor Draper, who was a lecturer at King's College London in 1956 and reader in 1964. In 1967, he became a reader at the University of Sussex and from 1976 to 1979 a professor of law there. Since then, Tony Rogers and Professor Charles Garraway[28] have made their own contributions to academic life.

ALS and academic collaboration in practice

The benefits to ALS of collaboration with academics should be evident from the previous sections of this chapter. Practitioners tend to be busy with their day-to-day work and rarely have time for in-depth research, unless they can be spared for courses of study or they can call on academic experts for training and assistance. The advantages for academic lawyers are less obvious. Indeed, academics working for the services are sometimes irked by comments on, or decisions taken for policy reasons about, their work.[29] They probably consider that this compromises their academic independence.

On the other hand, contacts with service lawyers can be beneficial. For example, Professor Françoise Hampson has written to express the view that, proportionately, there are more people teaching and studying the

[27] See, e.g., P. Rowe, *The Impact of Human Rights Law on Armed Forces* (Cambridge: Cambridge University Press, 2006).

[28] Charles Garraway has been a visiting professor at King's College London from 2002 to 2008; a senior fellow of the British Institute of International and Comparative Law since 2004; the Stockton Professor of International Law at the US Naval War College, Newport, Rhode Island in 2004–5; an associate fellow, International Security Programme, Royal Institute of International Affairs (Chatham House) from 2005 to 2012; a visiting professor at the London School of Economics in 2006; and since 2006 he has been a fellow of the Human Rights Centre at the University of Essex. He was awarded the degree of Doctor of the University of Essex on 19 July 2012.

[29] See Lauterpacht, *Life*, 362–4 about the compromise in the 1958 Manual over the issue of nuclear weapons.

law of armed conflict in the United Kingdom (not including the military) than in other European states, or the USA, and that, to a significant extent, this was down to a climate created in ALS, which has continued since.[30] She also said that the ready contact and joint projects involving military lawyers and academics, such as the book on the ICRC customary law study,[31] keep the latter 'grounded' and prevents them from misinterpreting the law of armed conflict and coming up with unrealistic solutions. She added that, in relation to some academics, 'they have no reality check. That is particularly important in relation to Hague law issues and in relation to the fact that some of them appear to confuse human rights in armed conflict with the law of armed conflict'.[32]

In her oration on the occasion of the award of a doctor's degree to Professor Garraway on 19 July 2012, Professor Hampson said:

> The ALS has always been very open to academics who are interested in the practical application of the law [...] I would like to emphasise the huge value that we in the Law School and Human Rights Centre place on our contact with the ALS and how much we appreciate their openness and willingness to discuss issues with us.

Military lawyers, of course, tend to be more concerned about the practical implementation of the law of armed conflict and are often under time pressure, so, when faced with a problem, they will generally start with the treaty texts and commentaries, only turning to academic works if they still cannot find the answers. With some notable exceptions,[33] however, they find that academic writers lack practical expertise and, therefore, fail to discuss, or provide appropriate guidance for dealing with, actual legal problems encountered in military operations. This means that academic works tend to be used more as background reading to assist military lawyers in preparing training programmes, manuals and other work of less urgency. Some military lawyers have, therefore, tried, in their own writing, teaching and academic contacts, to provide guidance to military personnel, whilst simultaneously producing material giving academics a glimpse of operational reality.[34] The International

[30] Letter to Tony Rogers dated 31 March 2008.

[31] Wilmshurst and Breau, *Perspectives on the ICRC Study on Customary International Humanitarian Law* (n. 19, above).

[32] Email to Tony Rogers dated 22 December 2012.

[33] See, e.g., Rowe, *Defence: The Legal Implications.*

[34] Practical guidance is contained in, for example, G. Risius and M. A. Meyer, 'The Protection of Prisoners of War against Insults and Public Curiosity', 295 *International*

Society for Military Law and the Law of War has, for decades, striven to bridge the gap with its many conferences and publications involving both military and academic lawyers.

Conversely, academics tend to be more interested in the philosophical aspects of the law. For example, postgraduate student feedback indicates that many of them find that looking at, and discussing, nuts and bolts issues, even the detailed examination of treaty texts, does not provide them with a sufficient intellectual challenge. For that reason, military lawyers might find it difficult to be taken seriously in an academic environment. Professor Rowe has commented:

> I think academic lawyers can be broadly separated into those more interested in the theoretical side and those who try to combine theory with the practical side in which I would include operational law. The difficulties that academics of the latter group face are fact-finding as to operational law and a knowledge of national law and military law. Of these two, fact-finding is the more difficult. I have often thought that it would be a really good idea for (selected) academics to be brought into the loop (probably with ALS) at some stage when actual operational law is being thought through. It is likely that they might throw up some issues which otherwise might not, but should, be addressed.[35]

The future

It seems to the authors that collaboration between ALS officers and academic lawyers over many years has been fruitful and beneficial for both sides, for ALS in deepening knowledge of relevant areas of law, and for academia in providing the 'operational reality' that enhances their academic research and writing. In times of financial restraint it may be difficult to improve much on the ad hoc contacts in place already, but there may a case for establishing more formally a circle of academic and military lawyers who can meet when the need arises to discuss problems of interpretation and practice. As Professor Garraway has commented:

> Françoise [Hampson] has, in the past, suggested that DGALS[[36]] should have a small group of academics whom he could consult – and even host a half day meeting like the [Foreign and Commonwealth Office] meeting for academics to discuss current issues [. . .] With the demise of the old

Review of the Red Cross (1993) 288 or A. P. V. Rogers, 'Zero-Casualty Warfare', 82 *International Review of the Red Cross* (2000) 165.

35 Email to Tony Rogers dated 20 December 2012.

36 Director General Army Legal Services, the new title for the officer formerly known as DALS.

> international law specialism, we need to ensure that ALS maintains its academic contacts.[37]

This seems to be confirmed by the comments of Peter Rowe quoted at the end of the previous section.

However, there is another area where academic and military lawyers could cooperate to advance informed discussion and debate, before decisions are made that are regretted later. The authors have noted what they consider to be a worrying trend in recent years for both military law and the law of armed conflict to be ignored by policy-makers, judicial bodies, human rights and criminal law practitioners, and lobbyists.[38] In some quarters there is, understandably, overt hostility towards military institutions.[39] In the United Kingdom too, and notwithstanding major reforms in recent years, questions are still being asked about the desirability of entrusting the military justice system to the military.[40] The authors begin to wonder whether these bodies of law are in danger of becoming redundant in view of the fact that most cases come either before human rights tribunals, which apply human rights law, or are dealt with in war crimes tribunals, where the judges tend to be criminal lawyers, in either case with little knowledge of the law of armed conflict or experience or understanding of military operations. The authors consider that this is an undesirable development, because the human rights law approach, by its nature, tends to focus on the rights of the individual rather than on the interests, or duties

[37] Email to Tony Rogers dated 15 December 2012.

[38] Mr William Fenrick, former legal adviser to the International Criminal Tribunal for the former Yugoslavia, has put it thus, in an email to Tony Rogers dated 16 July 2012: 'ever since I began working at ICTY, one of my main intellectual concerns has been trying to bridge the gap between the law as applied before the event by military legal practitioners and operators, and the law as assessed by outside scholars and as applied after the event by criminal lawyers before various tribunals'.

[39] Tony Rogers remembers an international human rights conference in Geneva some years ago when this antagonism was palpable. However, it thawed as the conference proceeded and the delegates, many of whom were from states which had suffered at the hands of military regimes, realised that at least the military lawyers present at the conference shared many of their concerns and equally wanted to work towards eliminating arbitrary actions by those in authority.

[40] See, e.g., the article entitled 'Army Told to Open up its System of Justice' in *The Times* on 3 January 2013 by its Defence Editor, Deborah Haynes, and the letters in reply, published in the same newspaper on 7 January 2013, from Ann Lyon on the parallels between Army disciplinary procedures and employers' disciplinary proceedings in civilian life, and from Admiral Jenkin urging those seeking change to be exceedingly careful not to diminish the ability of a fighting force to succeed.

towards their population, of states, so that a proper balance of conflicting interests is not achieved – something that the law of armed conflict has been developed over centuries to do. Also, whilst criminal law safeguards the interests of the person on trial, as well as those of society as a whole, it may not take account of operational reality – something that military law has been developed over centuries to achieve.[41]

While it is important that these issues be properly debated, the debate must be fully informed, as Alexander Pope famously remarked of critics in his heroic couplet:

> A little learning is a dangerous thing;
> Drink deep, or taste not the Pierian spring.[42]

It follows that those involved in the debate must take account of the knowledge and experience of experts, and must not be quick to dismantle an edifice that has been carefully constructed to deal with the specific situation of armed conflict. This might be where academic and military lawyers, working together, could make a useful contribution.

The authors consider that the law of armed conflict continues to be important and relevant in the twenty-first century as a body of law specially designed to meet wartime needs, the importance of which is well understood by members of the armed forces. It has been carefully developed to reach a balance between military necessity and humanity, it provides realistic and practical guidance that can be readily applied in the heat of battle and, furthermore, it now contains effective sanctions that can be applied to transgressors. It has been modified and improved over a long period of time and this process will, no doubt, continue in the future. Society ignores this body of law at its peril and to the detriment of humanity. No wholesale revision is necessary; modification should continue to be done slowly, carefully and expertly, as the need arises.

[41] Part of the problem is that judges nowadays have little or no experience of military service. This was not the case a few years ago, when military matters were afforded sympathetic treatment by judges such as Lord Bingham, Lord Justice Lawton and Lord Justice Watkins who had had military experience. Lawton and Watkins both saw active military service during the Second World War. Indeed, Watkins won the United Kingdom's highest award for gallantry in action, the Victoria Cross, in Normandy, in 1944.

[42] *An Essay on Criticism*, published in 1711.

PART I

Structural and systemic aspects of the laws of war

3

Development of new rules or application of more than one legal regime?

DIETER FLECK

Introduction

It is for more than three decades now that I have gratefully profited from Peter Rowe's contributions to the law applicable in military operations. His famous textbook on military law and the laws of war,[1] which mirrors Peter's broad perspective on operational issues, had a convenient place on my office bookshelf over many years. His historical perspective, even on more specified legal issues, was extremely helpful for my own research.[2]

The question whether the laws of war are 'fit for purpose' has intrigued me to first consider that purpose: is it broadly peace as a common goal in our ever imperfect world? Is it litigating military necessities? Is it protecting the fate of the victims? Is it balancing the rules of fair play in situations of danger and combat stress? Should there be more than one purpose (and in fact for each of these different goals we could think of specific principles and rules of the *jus in bello*): could the laws of war then be characterised as a multi-purpose set of rules? Is this particular branch – to adopt Rosalyn Higgins's widely appreciated characterisation of international law – more than a simple set of rules, but rather a process that might serve such various purposes? Open for dynamic development, but nevertheless serving as an appropriate tool for authoritative decision-making 'by the use of analogy, by reference to context, by analysis of the alternative consequences'?[3]

1 P. Rowe, *Defence: The Legal Implications* (London: Brassey's, 1987).

2 P. Rowe, 'Historical Developments Influencing the Present Law of Visiting Forces', in D. Fleck (ed.), *The Handbook of the Law of Visiting Forces* (Oxford: Oxford University Press, 2001), 11–32.

3 R. Higgins, *Problems and Process: International Law and How We Use It* (Oxford: Clarendon Press, 1994) 10.

Any serious assessment will be influenced by a number of different elements: the facts determining the application of the laws of war; the relationship between that legal branch and other disciplines that continue to be relevant during armed conflict; the influence armed conflict may have on the application of those rules of international law that were designed for normal peacetime, but continue to be relevant for actors and victims in an armed conflict; the role of national law in military operations; and the interaction of various national contingents, which may be bound to different obligations, but are tasked to cooperate nevertheless. I will address these different issues in turn and also try to present some conclusions.

Problems of acceptance of a state of armed conflict

Legal discussions over the last decades have produced a wealth of arguments on the notion of armed conflict, a legal term that marks the applicability threshold for IHL. As a matter of abstract definition the issue seems to be settled. For international armed conflicts it is confirmed in common Article 2 to the Geneva Conventions that any resort to armed force between states would suffice for the Conventions' application, whether or not a state of war is recognised by the parties. For internal conflicts there is general support today for the formula used in *Tadić* that:

> an armed conflict exists whenever there is a resort to armed force between States or protracted armed violence between governmental authorities and organised armed groups or between such groups within a State.[4]

While this definition does not really seem controversial today, it appears that states are reluctant formally to apply it to current conflicts. The existence of an armed conflict was confirmed neither by the United Kingdom in Northern Ireland[5] nor by the Russian Federation in Chechnya,[6] with the forensic effect that in both conflicts *lex specialis*

[4] ICTY, *Prosecutor* v. *Tadić*, Appeals Chamber Decision on Defence Motion for Interlocutory Appeal on Jurisdiction of 2 October 1995, para. 70. See also International Law Association, Committee on the Use of Force, 'Final Report on the Meaning of Armed Conflict in International Law', *Report of the Seventy-Fourth Conference* (The Hague: ILA, 2010), 676–721.

[5] See www.bbc.co.uk/history/recent/troubles/#conflict_in_context (accessed 14 January 2013).

[6] Despite an early decision taken by the Constitutional Court of the Russian Federation (No. 10-P of 31 July 1995 on the constitutionality of the Russian Federation Presidential

rules of IHL remained unconsidered by the European Court of Human Rights.[7] States participating in the International Security Assistance Force (ISAF) had insisted, over several years, on characterising their mission in Afghanistan as a form of post-conflict peacebuilding, and had referred to occasional hostilities as either law enforcement or part of a global, i.e., international, war on terror. Conversely, the International Committee of the Red Cross (ICRC) had officially stated that, following the convening of the *Loya Jirga* in Kabul in June 2002 and the subsequent establishment of an Afghan transitional government on 19 June 2002, armed hostilities conducted by allied forces against groups such as the Taliban and Al-Qaeda in Afghanistan are governed by the rules applicable in non-international armed conflict.[8] That conclusion was finally shared by Western states after a difficult process of controversial political debate and decision-making. The military operation *Unified Protector* in Libya, which was authorised by the Security Council as a necessary measure 'to establish a ban on all flights in the airspace of the Libyan Arab Jamahiriya in order to help protect civilians',[9] had never been referred to by participating states as being part of an international armed conflict, although it had led to effectively wiping out Gaddafi's air capability. In Syria the legal character of the still ongoing conflict remained undefined for quite a long time, even though the ICRC was active from the beginning assisting victims and negotiating with both the Syrian authorities and the opposition groups in an attempt to arrange for appropriate conditions needed to get access to civilians and detainees, or to arrange for a two-hour cessation in the fighting every day.

edicts and decrees of the Russian government on restoring law and order in the Chechen Republic, CLRF.1995. No.33.CT.3424); see W. Abresch, 'A Human Rights Law of Internal Armed Conflict: The European Court of Human Rights in Chechnya', 16 *EJIL* (2005) 741–67.

[7] See, e.g., ECtHR, *Case of Ireland* v. *United Kingdom*, Application No. 5319/71, Judgment of 18 January 1978 concerning a series of extrajudicial powers of arrest, detention and internment on what has been described by the responding government as 'the longest and most violent terrorist campaign witnessed in either part of the island of Ireland'; and ECtHR, *Case of Isayeva* v. *Russia*, Application No. 57950/00, Judgment of 24 February 2005 concerning the bombardment of Katyr-Yurt in the Achkhoy-Martan district. While these cases are clearly related to the conduct of hostilities, others show that law enforcement, however robust, may also be required within the same armed conflict; see ECtHR, *Finogenov and others* v. *Russia*, Application Nos 18299/03, 27311/03, Judgment of 20 December 2011 on the siege in October 2002 of the *Dubrovka* theatre in Moscow by Chechen separatists and the decision to overcome the terrorists and liberate the hostages using gas.

[8] ICRC, *aide-mémoire* submitted on 18 November 2002 to Permanent Missions in Geneva.

[9] SC Res. 1973 (2011), paras 6–12.

In 2008, the ICRC had reminded states that in accordance with a strong and prevailing legal opinion:

1. International armed conflicts exist whenever there is *resort to armed force between two or more States.*
2. Non-international armed conflicts are *protracted armed confrontations* occurring between governmental armed forces and the forces of one or more armed groups, or between such groups arising on the territory of a State [party to the Geneva Conventions]. The armed confrontation must reach *a minimum level of intensity* and the parties involved in the conflict must show *a minimum of organisation.*[10]

Is formal acceptance of such situations by the parties to the conflict in any sense constitutive for the contents and quality of their legal obligations? Certainly not, as this would reverse the meaning and purpose of the principle underlying common Article 2 to the Geneva Conventions. However, in practical terms the acceptance that a state of war exists will be highly relevant for humanitarian protection. It triggers operational and administrative efforts to implement wartime obligations under IHL and facilitates any claiming of existing rights for the victims. This situation exists in international and non-international armed conflicts likewise.

For states involved in a non-international armed conflict a realistic acceptance of the existing situation is particularly difficult as it implies that law enforcement operations are no longer sufficient to maintain, or re-establish, national security under the rule of law. Specific obligations under national emergency laws may be triggered by the existence of an armed conflict, but the political leadership, considering the disadvantages connected with emergency rule, will hesitate to cross this threshold. Certain human rights may be derogated in a time of 'public emergency which threatens the life of the nation and the existence of which is officially proclaimed' (Article 4, para. 1, ICCPR),[11] yet there is little state practice for such derogation and even declared derogations may

[10] ICRC (2008) 'How is the Term "Armed Conflict" Defined in International Humanitarian Law?', opinion paper (March 2008): www.icrc.org/eng/resources/documents/article/other/armed-conflict-article-170308.htm (accessed 14 January 2013) (emphasis in original).

[11] International Covenant on Civil and Political Rights (ICCPR) (19 December 1966) 999 UNTS 171; see also Article 15 European Convention on Human Rights (ECHR) (4 November 1950) 213 UNTS 221; Article 27 American Convention on Human Rights (ACHR) (22 November 1969) 1144 UNTS 123, Article 4 Arab Charter on Human Rights (22 May 2004) 12 *International Human Rights Reports* (2005) 893.

become a matter of dispute.[12] Opposition groups fighting according to the law of armed conflict may become candidates for an amnesty at the end of hostilities (Article 6, para. 5, Additional Protocol II to the Geneva Conventions) rather than prosecuted under national criminal law for their participation in hostilities.

The legal protection of those fighters under the *jus in bello* should, however, be clear. Any unnecessary suffering and superfluous injury must be avoided and a distinction is to be made between fighters and civilians, as long, and for such time, as the latter do not directly participate in hostilities. The principles of distinction, avoidance of unnecessary suffering, and humanity are not confined to armed conflicts. They also apply to law enforcement operations in peacetime. Decades ago, Jean Pictet held it important enough to stress:

> What Government would dare to claim before the world, in a case of civil disturbances which could justly be described as mere acts of banditry, that, Article 3 not being applicable, it was entitled to leave the wounded uncared for, to torture and mutilate prisoners and take hostages?[13]

That statement is still relevant today. There are, indeed, standards of behaviour that deserve and require full respect in any situation. The principle of proportionality is inherent in all legal branches and differences in its application in the conduct of hostilities, as opposed to law enforcement operations, are often exaggerated. A recent example is the unfortunate dispute on restraints on the use of force in direct attack, which penetrated discussions on the ICRC's *Interpretive Guidance on the Notion of Direct Participation in Hostilities.*[14] Those criticising the

[12] It remains questionable, for example, whether the material conditions for derogation under Article 15 ECHR and Article 4 ICCPR were met in the case of the British Anti-Terrorism, Crime and Security Act (2001). See J. Black-Branch, 'Powers of Detention of Suspected International Terrorists under the United Kingdom Anti-Terrorism, Crime and Security Act 2001: Dismantling the Cornerstones of a Civil Society', 27 *European Law Review Human Rights Survey* (2002) 26; V. H. Henning, 'Anti-terrorism, Crime and Security Act 2001: Has the United Kingdom Made a Valid Derogation from the European Convention on Human Rights?', 17 *American University Law Review* (2002) 1277.

[13] J. S. Pictet (ed.), *The Geneva Conventions of 12 August 1949, Commentary* (Geneva: ICRC, 1958), 35–6, with reference to the Final Record of the Diplomatic Conference of Geneva of 1949, vol. 2, sect. B, at 121.

[14] N. Melzer, *Interpretive Guidance on the Notion of Direct Participation in Hostilities under International Humanitarian Law* (Geneva: ICRC, 2009). See, e.g., W. Hays Parks, 'Part IX of the ICRC "Direct Participation in Hostilities" Study: No Mandate, No Expertise, and Legally Incorrect', 42 *New York University Journal of International Law and Politics* (2010) 769 and the patient and comprehensive response by N. Melzer,

approach taken by the ICRC have widely ignored the fact that the relevant Section IX requires no more and no less than restraining the use of force to 'what is actually necessary to accomplish a legitimate military purpose in the prevailing circumstances'. This is, indeed, a rule of common sense no military commander is free to ignore. Section IX of the *Interpretive Guidance* is far from introducing a general 'capture rather than kill' principle into the conduct of hostilities in armed conflict, as purposely alleged by some of its critics.[15] Yet it addresses similarities in conduct for military and police personnel, whilst fully accepting what is necessary under the different paradigms of war fighting and law enforcement, as required in the circumstances prevailing at the time. Indeed, 'it would defy basic notions of humanity to kill an adversary or to refrain from giving him or her an opportunity to surrender where there manifestly is no necessity for the use of lethal force'.[16] As expressly stated in the *Interpretive Guidance*, this analysis and interpretation is based on IHL only, yet its conclusions remain 'without prejudice to additional restrictions on the use of force, which may arise under other applicable frameworks of international law such as, most notably, international human rights law or the law governing the use of force (*jus ad bellum*)'.[17] Section IX should caution those advocating different approaches to combat and to police operations. The latter may also be extremely robust. The applicable principles and rules of conduct in those different situations are often similar and the standards of protection used mutually influence each other.

Persons who are in the power of a party to the conflict and who do not benefit from more favourable treatment under the Geneva Conventions or Additional Protocol I are to be treated humanely in all circumstances and enjoy minimum protections as confirmed in Article 75 Additional Protocol I, protections that derive from human rights law applicable both in peacetime and times of armed conflict. This leads me to conclude that parties to a conflict cannot effectively insist on an applicability threshold for compliance with their obligations under IHL as its principles and rules also influence peacetime behaviour. Nor should states be expected formally to recognise a state of armed conflict when they are engaged in

'Keeping the Balance between Military Necessity and Humanity: A Response to Four Critiques of the ICRC's Interpretive Guidance on the Notion of Direct Participation in Hostilities', 42 *New York University Journal of International Law and Politics* (2010) 892–913.

15 Parks, 'Part IX of the ICRC "Direct Participation in Hostilities" Study', 815.

16 Melzer, *Interpretive Guidance*, 82. 17 *Ibid.*

robust law enforcement or self-defence operations. Even before the beginning of an armed conflict, and particularly post-conflict, peace-building principles and rules of IHL provide guiding standards for any use of force. The principles of necessity, proportionality and humanity are generally as relevant for law enforcement operations in peacetime as for the conduct of hostilities during armed conflict, notwithstanding certain differences in their application. Where different legal paradigms apply for law enforcement, robust peacekeeping and the conduct of hostilities, these should be approached in light of the practical requirements of conducting military operations, regardless of how the conflict is characterised.

Problems of fragmentation versus integration of different branches of international law

While the notion of armed conflict has become a matter of uncertainty and even controversy today, there is increasing consensus on the relevance of various branches of international law, well beyond the *jus in bello*, during the conduct of hostilities. The role of IHL and its relationship with other relevant legal branches needs to be further explored in this context. Armed forces are operating today in situations that are not well defined and that are subject to continuous change. They are not only confronted with states and state organs, but also with individuals. The role of non-state actors has changed since 1907 when the Hague Regulations were adopted. The rights and obligations of these individuals, as well as the legal foundations for compliance and control, deserve and require further discussion.

It seems to be common coinage for contemporary armed forces that the principles and provisions of IHL must be applied in context with other relevant branches of international law. This consideration starts with the definition of armed conflicts, which determines the formal field of application, and it likewise applies to the protection of victims and to issues of counter-measures and reparations. Any party to an armed conflict will be interested to avoid allegations of acting in breach of the prohibition of the use of force under Article 2 (4) of the UN Charter. No military operation will remain unaffected by the progressive development of jurisprudence on human rights in times of conflict and terrorism.[18] In particular peacekeepers, including those acting under a

[18] See P. Rowe, *The Impact of Human Rights Law on Armed Forces* (Cambridge: Cambridge University Press, 2006); J. K. Kleffner, 'Human Rights and International Humanitarian

Chapter VII mandate, must consider the post-conflict effects of their mission and conduct even the most robust operations accordingly.

There are, however, *lex specialis* rules for the conduct of hostilities. Parties to an armed conflict may kill enemy fighters without warning and detain them without trial, although in principle the right to life, the right to a trial, and other fundamental rights continue to apply in armed conflict. This was acknowledged by the ICJ in its Advisory Opinion on *Nuclear Weapons*:

> In principle, the right not arbitrarily to be deprived of one's life applies also in hostilities. The test of what is an arbitrary deprivation of life, however, then falls to be determined by the applicable *lex specialis*, namely, the law applicable in armed conflict that is designed to regulate the conduct of hostilities. Thus whether a particular loss of life, through the use of a certain weapon in warfare, is to be considered an arbitrary deprivation of life contrary to Article 6 of the [International Covenant on Civil and Political Rights], can only be decided by reference to the law applicable in armed conflict and not deduced from the terms of the Covenant itself.[19]

A few years later, in its Advisory Opinion on the *Wall in the Occupied Palestinian Territory*, the Court asserted that in armed conflicts international human rights instruments are applicable in respect of acts performed by a state in the exercise of its jurisdiction outside its own country, particularly in occupied territories.[20] It also explained that there are three possible situations as regards the relationship between IHL and human rights law:

> some rights may be exclusively matters of international humanitarian law; others may be exclusively matters of human rights law; yet others may be matters of both these branches of international law.[21]

This jurisprudence was confirmed in *Democratic Republic of the Congo* v. *Uganda*.[22] It was again relevant in the case of *Georgia* v. *Russian*

Law: General Issues', in T. D. Gill and D. Fleck (eds), *The Handbook of the International Law in Military Operations* (Oxford: Oxford University Press, 2010), 51–77; L. Doswald-Beck, *Human Rights in Times of Conflict and Terrorism* (Oxford: Oxford University Press, 2011).

19 ICJ, *Legality of the Threat or Use of Nuclear Weapons* (Advisory Opinion of 8 July 1996), ICJ Reports 1996, 226, para. 25.

20 ICJ, *Legal Consequences of the Construction of a Wall in the Occupied Palestinian Territory* (Advisory Opinion of 9 July 2004), ICJ Reports 2004, 178, paras 107–13.

21 *Ibid.*, para. 106.

22 ICJ, *Case Concerning Armed Activities on the Territory of the Congo (Dem. Rep. Congo* v. *Uganda)*, Judgment of 19 December 2005, ICJ Reports 2005, 168, paras 215–20.

Federation, in which the Court, in preliminary proceedings, confirmed the application of the International Convention on the Elimination of All Forms of Racial Discrimination (CERD)[23] during an armed conflict, stating:

> the acts alleged by Georgia appear to be capable of contravening rights, provided for by CERD, even if certain of these alleged acts might also be covered by other rules of international law, including humanitarian law.[24]

Yet for procedural reasons no judgment was handed down on the merits of this case, as the conditions under Article 22 of CERD for seizing the Court had not been fulfilled:

> accusations and replies by both Parties on the issues of 'extermination' and 'ethnic cleansing' attest to the existence of a dispute between them on a subject-matter capable of falling under CERD. However, they fail to demonstrate an attempt at negotiating these matters.[25]

While pending cases of the Court do not provide an opportunity for further developing this jurisprudence, there may be possibilities to do this in future.

The former Foreign Office Legal Adviser Sir Daniel Bethlehem has recently concluded that the Court had addressed the inter-relationship between IHL and human rights law:

> with the broadest of brushes – there are two bodies of law; this suggests that there are three possible ways of interaction: either one applies or the other applies or they both apply. But when you sit in the kind of seat that I was sitting in until recently, you have to make sense of this, and statements of this kind hardly give any guidance at all for the practical purpose of advising a state.[26]

I may submit that more substantive guidance can be drawn from this jurisprudence, so that it does offer more than 'precautionary advice', to use Daniel Bethlehem's words.[27] In each of the three cases the Court

[23] International Convention on the Elimination of All Forms of Racial Discrimination (21 December 1965) 660 UNTS 195.

[24] ICJ, *Georgia* v. *Russian Federation*, Order of 15 October 2008, ICJ Reports 2008, 353, para. 112

[25] ICJ, *Georgia* v. *Russian Federation*, Judgment on Preliminary Objections of 1 April 2011, ICJ Reports 2011, para. 181.

[26] Daniel Bethlehem, 'The Secret Life of International Law', 1 *Cambridge Journal of International and Comparative Law* (2012) 32.

[27] *Ibid.*, 33.

refrained from characterising the relationship between the two branches of law themselves. Instead, it dealt with the application of specific rights during armed conflict. In *Nuclear Weapons* the Court referred to the prohibition of an 'arbitrary deprivation of life'. In the *Wall* case it expressively referred to 'some' rights that may be governed by both branches of international law, while others are exclusively governed by one of the two branches. In *Democratic Republic of the Congo* v. *Uganda* the Court pronounced on the relationship between human rights and IHL in broader terms, but did so in the clear context of the right to life (Article 6, para. 1, ICCPR), the prohibition of torture (Article 7 ICCPR), and the protection of children in armed conflict (Article 38, paras. 2 and 3 of the Convention on the Rights of the Child). While the ICJ has asserted that in armed conflicts some rights are exclusively governed by IHL, whereas others are governed exclusively by human rights, and still others are governed by both bodies of law, it expressly confirmed that, in the latter case, 'both these branches of international law, namely human rights law and, as *lex specialis*, international humanitarian law' must be considered.[28] Hence it is fully consistent with the Court's jurisprudence to conclude that while IHL and human rights law are complementary the *lex specialis* concept should be used to determine whether, and to what extent, the application of a specific human rights provision is limited in a particular situation of armed conflict.[29]

It should be noted that this jurisprudence is, first and foremost, relevant for the obligation of states as it may still be disputed whether, and to what extent, non-state actors bear obligations under human rights law.[30] Consequently, any resulting *lex specialis* obligation under IHL

[28] Cf. the *Wall* case (n. 20, above), para. 106.

[29] See J. A. Frowein, 'The Relationship between Human Rights Regimes and Regimes of Belligerent Occupation', 28 *Israel Yearbook on Human Rights* (1999) 12, where the author convincingly argues that the *lex specialis* argument cannot solve all situations, as it cannot be inferred from the *Nuclear Weapons* Opinion that human rights treaties in general would have to be interpreted in the light of international humanitarian law. He also underlines that certain human rights, such as the prohibition of torture or slavery, or the right to legal personality, are not open to derogation and are formulated in absolute terms without any limitations in times of armed conflict. This does not exclude, however, that obligations deriving from human rights norms will be informed by armed conflict situations and applicable standards of protection are shaped by relevant *lex specialis* norms of international humanitarian law.

[30] But see C. Tomuschat, 'The Applicability of Human Rights Law to Insurgent Movements', in H. Fischer, U. Froissart, W. H. von Heinegg and C. Raap (eds), *Krisensicherung und Humanitärer Schutz – Crisis Management and Humanitarian Protection* (Berlin: Berliner Wissenschafts-Verlag, 2004), 573–91 drawing on a coherent practice of the General

would be one of states. Obligations of non-state actors (which appear to be less disputed under IHL than under human rights law) may deserve additional considerations.

The relationship between human rights and IHL has specifically been dealt with in the jurisprudence of the Inter-American Commission on Human Rights. In the *Avilán* case,[31] in which extra-judicial executions during the non-international armed conflict in Colombia had to be investigated, the Commission held that the non-derogable guarantee of the right to life set forth in the American Convention on Human Rights applies along with, and is informed by, the provisions of IHL for internal hostilities. Common Article 3 of the Geneva Conventions obliges the parties to internal armed conflicts to afford humane treatment to those persons who do not take part, or who no longer take active part, in the hostilities. In *Coard*, the Commission confirmed that both systems of international law – humanitarian law and human rights – were applicable in the armed conflict between Grenadian nationals and US military forces in 1983. The Commission held that the concurrent application of the two systems of protection is inevitable and that it was therefore competent to investigate the procedures taken by the parties involved in the conflict.[32] In the *Tablada* case,[33] owing to the lack of sufficient evidence establishing that state agents had used illegal methods and means of combat, the Commission concluded that the killing or wounding of the attackers, which occurred during the non-international armed conflict and internal disturbances prior to the cessation of combat in January 1989, were legitimately combat-related and thus did not constitute violations of the ACHR. However, it also underlined that it was in clear violation of Article 5 ACHR that all survivors of the attack and seven persons convicted as accomplices were tortured *hors de combat* and executed extra-judicially.

Assembly and the Security Council to make insurgent movements responsible for respecting human rights.

[31] Inter-American Commission on Human Rights (IACHR), Report No. 26/97, Case 11.142, *Colombia*, 30 September 1997: www.cidh.oas.org/annualrep/97eng/Colombia11142.htm (accessed 14 January 2013).

[32] IACHR, Report No. 109/99, Case 10.951, *Coard et al.* v. *United States*, 29 September 1999, paras 39, 42: www.cidh.oas.org/annualrep/99eng/Merits/UnitedStates10.951.htm (accessed 14 January 2013).

[33] IACHR, Case 11.137, *Juan Carlos Abella*, Report No. 55/97, *Argentina*, OEA/Ser/L/V/II.97, Doc. 38 (30 October 1997), paras 188, 379, 381 www.cidh.oas.org/annualrep/97eng/Argentina11137.htm (accessed 14 January 2013); see L. Zegveld, 'The Interamerican Commission on Human Rights and International Humanitarian Law: A Comment on the Tablada Case', 324 *IRRC* (1998) 505.

In *Las Palmeras* the Inter-American Court on Human Rights specified that although the Inter-American Commission has broad faculties as an organ for the promotion and protection of human rights it can clearly be inferred from the ACHR that the procedure initiated in contentious cases before the Commission, which culminates in an application before the Court, should refer to rights protected by that Convention[34] and that the Commission and the Court did not have competence to determine whether a given act was in violation of the 1949 Geneva Conventions or treaties other than the ACHR.[35] As the Court had confirmed in *Bamaca-Velásquez*,[36] this does not preclude taking into consideration provisions of IHL in order to interpret the ACHR. In this context it should also be considered that human rights bodies have a responsibility to investigate those limitations of human rights in armed conflicts, which may apply under the *lex specialis* role of IHL. It is for this reason that IHL must be dealt with, even by human rights organs, which may thus provide support to ensure respect for IHL.

The relevant jurisprudence of the ECtHR is not as dense as yet. Although military operations of various kinds have been reviewed in its jurisprudence, the Court, as exemplified above,[37] for decades did not see a requirement of identifying *lex specialis* rules of IHL. However, more recently the Grand Chamber has revisited contentious issues of the inter-relationship between IHL and international human rights law; underlined extraterritorial obligations of states under international human rights law; and confirmed positive human rights obligations in occupied territory.[38]

Typical examples for human rights obligations that appear to be limited under *lex specialis* rules of IHL are detention (its purposes,

[34] IACHR, *Case of Las Palmeras* v. *Colombia*, Preliminary Objections, Judgment of 4 February 2000, Series C No. 67, para. 34 http://international.lawsociety.org.uk/files/case%20of%20las%20palmeras%20v%20colombia%202000.pdf (accessed 14 January 2013); see F. Kalshoven, 'State Sovereignty Versus International Concern in Some Recent Cases of the Inter-American Court of Human Rights', in G. Kreijen (ed.), *State, Sovereignty, and International Governance* (Oxford: Oxford University Press, 2002), 259; L. Zegveld, 'Remedies for Victims of Violations of International Humanitarian Law', 851 *IRRC* (2003) 516.

[35] IACtHR, *Las Palmeras Case*, Judgment of 6 December 2001, paras 17 n.1, 24 n. 2.

[36] IACtHR, *Bámaca-Velásquez*, Ser. C No. 70 (2000), Judgment of 16 November 2000, paras 205–9: www1.umn.edu/humanrts/iachr/C/70-ing.html (accessed 14 January 2013).

[37] See nn. 5–6, and accompanying text, above.

[38] ECtHR, *Al-Jedda* v. *United Kingdom* (application no. 27021/08), Judgment of 7 July 2011, paras 63–181; ECtHR, *Al-Skeini and Others* v. *United Kingdom* (application no. 55721/07), Judgment of 7 July 2011, paras 130–86.

control and duration) and investigations into the reasons of any loss of life as a result of force. During armed conflict *habeas corpus* cannot be guaranteed in the same way as in peacetime, although the legal protection of detainees remains important. Also, the way in which investigations on the use of deadly force are to be conducted will be different under battlefield conditions. While full application of Article 6 (1) ICCPR and relevant regional human rights conventions, such as Article 2 ECHR, requires, in peacetime, an independent formal investigation to be conducted in each individual case, this may be inapplicable in armed conflict. Whereas a Detaining Power would be under an obligation to conduct official enquiries in cases of death or serious injury of a prisoner of war (Article 121 GC III) or civilian internee (Article 131 GC IV), such obligation does not exist in cases of death or serious injury on the battlefield.

Thus, the *lex specialis* principle remains important for the conduct of hostilities, but it should also be acknowledged that in armed conflict there is frequently a need to apply rules and procedures deriving from other branches of international law in situations where no specific rule of IHL applies. Activities to ensure compliance are a case in point. Article 1 common to the Geneva Conventions and Article 1 (1) of Additional Protocol I stipulate an obligation not only to respect but also to ensure respect of IHL. This obligation has now developed into customary international law.[39] States and international organisations acting under this obligation are not limited to measures specifically designated by IHL. Rather, they will use procedures regulated under diplomatic law and will also base their initiatives on other legal branches and on the Charter itself.

The practical relevance of human rights for military operations is underlined by the fact that some subject-areas are dealt with more fully in human rights law than in the norms of humanitarian law. Indeed, important provisions of the ICCPR, the ECHR, the ACHR, the African

[39] See J.-M. Henckaerts and L. Doswald-Beck (eds), *Customary International Humanitarian Law* (Cambridge: Cambridge University Press, 2005). While the commentary to Rule 139 only refers to a state's obligation 'to ensuring respect by other persons or groups acting in fact on its instructions' (vol. 1, p. 496), Rule 144 stipulates that states 'must exert their influence, to the degree possible, to stop violations of international humanitarian law' and the commentary underlines that 'the ICRC has repeatedly stated that the obligation to "ensure respect" is not limited to behavior by parties to a conflict, but includes the requirement that States do all in their power to ensure that international humanitarian law is respected universally' (509–10).

Charter on Human and Peoples' Rights (ACHPR) and the Arab Charter on Human Rights are applicable in times of armed conflict, without being reflected in specific rules of IHL. Among other provisions, the prohibition of slavery (Article 8 ICCPR, Article 4 ECHR), the prohibition of racial discrimination (CERD); the freedom of opinion (Article 18 ICCPR, Article 9, 10 ECHR, Article 27 Arab Charter), the right to recognition as a person before law (Article 16 ICCPR, Article 3 ACHR), the right to be free from imprisonment for failure to fulfil a contractual obligation (non-derogable under ICCPR, derogable under Article 1 of Protocol 4 to the ECHR, Article 7 ACHR, Article 14 Arab Charter), the right to a nationality (Article 20 ACHR), the right to participate in government (Article 23 ACHR), the right to existence and self-determination (Article 20 ACHPR), legal protections against disappearances and against destruction of homes are of clear significance in military operations, particularly in non-international armed conflicts.[40] The fact that certain human rights obligations may be derogated in times of emergency[41] is of minor importance in this respect. While derogation may provide clarity, and thus support the rule of law, practice has shown that derogations have hardly been declared in times of armed conflict.[42] Cases of derogation remained singularised and, at the same time, highly controversial.[43]

In the same vein, optional rules of IHL, such as Article 90 of Additional Protocol I on the International Humanitarian Fact-Finding Commission, do not prevent states and international organisations from using other fact-finding mechanisms, such as those available under human rights law or international criminal law, for investigating alleged breaches of IHL. Hence, IHL cannot be separated from human rights law and other legal branches. This must be considered when sound rules are to be developed for the conduct of military operations in practice.

[40] See. L. Moir, *The Law of Internal Armed Conflict* (Cambridge: Cambridge University Press 2002), 208–10.

[41] See Article 4 ICCPR, Article 15 ECHR, Article 27 ACHR, Article 4 Arab Charter on Human Rights. There is no derogation clause in the ACHPR.

[42] T. Buergenthal, 'To Respect and to Ensure: State Obligations and Permissible Derogations', in L. Henkin (ed.), *The International Bill of Human Rights* (New York: Columbia University Press, 1981), 72; R Higgins, 'Derogations under the Human Rights Treaties', 48 *BYBIL* (1976–7) 281; Rowe, *The Impact of Human Rights Law on Armed Forces*, 118–21.

[43] See n. 12, above; Rowe, *The Impact of Human Rights Law on Armed Forces*, 159–61.

The effect of armed conflict on treaties

It is in this context that the continuing validity of peacetime obligations in armed conflicts deserves particular attention. The Draft Articles on the Effects of Armed Conflicts on Treaties adopted by the International Law Commission[44] provide in Article 7 (which is still expository in character) that an implication that treaties continue in operation, in whole or in part, during armed conflict may be seen in their subject matter. An indicative list of relevant categories of treaties is provided in the Annex of the Draft Articles, which still needs to be explored in light of state practice and jurisprudence. In the dispute between *Georgia* v. *Russia* the ICJ did not hesitate to confirm the applicability of CERD, without limitation, during an armed conflict.[45] The same may be said of treaties protecting the natural environment or treaties on international criminal justice. Appropriate consequences need to be drawn for military planning and for the development of rules of engagement. If it is correct to state that the Draft Articles do promote a 'general principle of legal stability and continuity' in armed conflict,[46] this may apply not only to treaties but also to other sources of international law, customary rules in particular. Pertinent examples may be found in the law of the sea. There are newly emerged norms on the continental shelf and on the exclusive economic zone that are yet to be reaffirmed under current treaty law. There is also an exclusive right of exploitation by coastal states, codified first in the 1958 Convention on the Continental Shelf[47] and reaffirmed in the 1982 Law of the Sea Convention,[48] which has long been a part of customary law and is to be respected even where a coastal state has not ratified these treaties. The same applies to the exclusive power of states to exploit fishing and natural resources in an Exclusive Economic Zone reaching out 200 nautical miles from their coasts. While such zones are not prohibited for naval operations in an international armed conflict, the parties to the conflict shall 'in addition to observing

[44] ILC Draft Articles on Effects of Armed Conflicts on Treaties: http://untreaty.un.org/ilc/texts/instruments/english/commentaries/1_10_2011.pdf (accessed 14 January 2013); see also Official Records of the General Assembly, Sixty-Sixth Session, Supplement No. 10 (A/66/10), ch. 6, sect. E; *Yearbook of the International Law Commission* (2011), vol. 2, pt. 2; Report of the Sixth Committee (A/66/473); UNGA Res. 66/98 (13 January 2012).

[45] See nn. 24–5, above. [46] See nn. 24–5, above; Commentary (1) to Article 3.

[47] Convention on the Continental Shelf (29 April 1958) 499 UNTS 311.

[48] Law of the Sea Convention (10 December 1982) 1833 UNTS 397.

the other applicable rules of the law of armed conflict at sea, have due regard for the rights and duties of the coastal State'.[49]

There may be practical consequences stemming from these principles, and it is practice itself that may facilitate implementation. Numerous military operations are conducted in unclear, yet critical, situations between peace and armed conflict, where clear decisions on the applicability of the *jus in bello* and its *lex specialis* effect may hardly be expected and there may be a need for actors to comply with peacetime modes of application as part of their operational objective. It should be made part of military operational planning to identify relevant legal parameters deriving from peacetime obligations and to develop rules of engagement accordingly.

The role of national law in military operations

Regular military forces, as organs of their sending state, are bound to comply with the constitutional order and national laws and regulations of that state. This has consequences not only for the decision to send military forces abroad, but also for their cooperation with the receiving state. It may even affect the conduct of hostilities. As national law may include rights and obligations in addition to those deriving from international law, there may be national operational rules in addition to those deriving from international law. As a consequence, a comprehensive study into applicable national law relevant for the conduct of military operations must include pertinent rules of the law of sending states and, at least to a certain extent, also of the receiving state.

National laws, regulations and orders may supplement international rights and obligations. In such cases states will issue national directives to ensure compliance with relevant national and international law. They may also declare *caveats* to delineate participation of their military contingents in international cooperation, or see to it that international rules of engagement will be in harmony with their relevant national requirements.

A topical case in point, which is of distinct practical relevance for international military cooperation, is related to an issue that is apparently not regulated by international law at all: what is the consequence of an order that was given in breach of international law? Is the recipient

[49] L. Doswald-Beck (ed.), *San Remo Manual on International Law Applicable to Armed Conflict at Sea* (Cambridge: Cambridge University Press, 1995), para. 34.

of that order obliged to obey? Or is the unlawful order null and void? Under what circumstances is the recipient entitled, or even obliged, to refuse execution of that order? As these questions are of obvious relevance for the maintenance of discipline in any multinational unit, it might be argued that a convincing solution should be found, in unified form, at the international level. This matter is yet to be discussed at the political level. Some years ago, a comparative study into ten European military law systems, which are relevant for national contingents of multinational units in Central Europe (Belgium, Denmark, France, Germany, Italy, Luxembourg, The Netherlands, Poland, Spain and the United Kingdom), investigated the issue, found certain divergences and recommended the following solution *de lege ferenda*:

> The soldier is obliged to obey his superior. The soldier is obliged to refuse to obey a command, if that command manifestly requires the soldier to commit a punishable offence. The soldier is not obliged to obey illegal orders.[50]

Such a formula would require a change of the present national laws in some European member states, e.g., in Germany where even unlawful orders are binding, unless they were given for no official purpose, offend human dignity or constitute a criminal offence.[51] Not every unlawful military order, however, will meet these exceptional conditions and in

[50] G. Nolte and H. Krieger, 'European Military Law Systems – Summary and Recommendations', in G. Nolte (ed.), *European Military Systems* (Berlin: de Gruyter, 2003), 10.

[51] § 11(1) and (2) Soldatengesetz [Soldiers Law]: Gehorsam [Obedience]: (1) Der Soldat muss seinen Vorgesetzten gehorchen. Er hat ihre Befehle nach besten Kräften vollständig, gewissenhaft und unverzüglich auszuführen. Ungehorsam liegt nicht vor, wenn ein Befehl nicht befolgt wird, der die Menschenwürde verletzt oder der nicht zu dienstlichen Zwecken erteilt worden ist; die irrige Annahme, es handele sich um einen solchen Befehl, befreit den Soldaten nur dann von der Verantwortung, wenn er den Irrtum nicht vermeiden konnte und ihm nach den ihm bekannten Umständen nicht zuzumuten war, sich mit Rechtsbehelfen gegen den Befehl zu wehren. (2) Ein Befehl darf nicht befolgt werden, wenn dadurch eine Straftat begangen würde. Befolgt der Untergebene den Befehl trotzdem, so trifft ihn eine Schuld nur, wenn er erkennt oder wenn es nach den ihm bekannten Umständen offensichtlich ist, dass dadurch eine Straftat begangen wird. [(1) The soldier shall obey his/her superiors. He/she shall carry out their orders completely, conscientiously and immediately, to the best of his/her ability. It shall not be deemed disobedience to ignore an order that violates human dignity or that is not given for service purposes. The erroneous assumption that an order of this kind has been given relieves him/her of the responsibility only if the error could not be avoided, or if it could not be expected of him/her, under the circumstances known to him/her, to reject the order by resorting to legal remedies. (2) An order must not be obeyed if a crime or offence would thereby be committed. Should the subordinate, nevertheless, comply with the order, he is found guilty only if he realises that a crime or

practice the order will then be binding under the law of one state, but not necessarily under the law of other states participating in the same military operation.

To consider the matter in all its complexities, directives issued by a commander to members of a foreign contingent of his or her multinational unit will, in many cases, not be military orders in the technical sense; they may rather be equated to directives issued outside the military system, as is the case under German law.[52] A multinational commander will then be unable to ensure execution of such directives and to maintain implementation in good order and discipline, so the assistance and support of the relevant national commander will be required,[53] but again the binding effect has to be determined.

Within military and political bodies of the European Union and its member states no action has yet been taken on this issue. It would be a challenging task to broaden the study mentioned above[54] to include all European States cooperating in multinational units. Even more effort would be required to cover peace operations conducted or authorised by the United Nations, which, even after fifty years' experience, has not yet formally adopted general policy rules on command and control.[55] In any event, the final recommendations should include situations in which orders are given in breach of legal norms but must still be considered as binding, as no peremptory norm nor criminal law is affected and it is the commanding officer who bears responsibility for compliance with the law and the effective performance of the mission.

Interoperability in multinational contingents

States engaged in military cooperation should ensure legal interoperability in the event of any difference in legal obligations that may

offence is committed thereby, or if it is obvious from the circumstances known to him that such is the case.]

[52] § 11(3) Soldatengesetz [Soldiers Law]: (3) Im Verhältnis zu Personen, die befugt sind, dienstliche Anordnungen zu erteilen, die keinen Befehl darstellen, gelten § 62 Absatz 1 und § 63 des Bundesbeamtengesetzes entsprechend. [(3) In relation to persons authorised to give official directions other than military orders, sections 62 (1) and 63 of the Federal Civil Service Act apply *mutatis mutandis*.] The latter provisions require civil servants to support their superiors and follow their directives without subjecting them to military discipline.

[53] See D. Fleck, *The Handbook of the Law of Visiting Forces* (Oxford: Oxford University Press, 2001), 39–43.

[54] Nolte and Krieger, 'European Military Law Systems'.

[55] Gill and Fleck, *The Handbook of the International Law in Military Operations*, 572.

become relevant. This is, in the first case, a practical requirement in order to avoid conflicting orders or behaviour and ensure the effectiveness of their cooperation. Differences in legal obligations will not exclude military cooperation as such. Yet, it is to be considered that no state may request any act or omission which would contravene any legal obligation of the requesting state, or even the requested state. Hence contingent commanders should be aware of relevant legal differences and ensure smooth performance of their mission according to the rules.

In cases of different legal obligations, interoperability will not be reached by simply applying the lowest common denominator. On the contrary, policy considerations may well call for the highest common denominator. As mentioned by the late Professor Leslie Green, during the 1991 war in the Gulf, which was fought by the United States alongside a coalition of twenty-six states in which no common legal obligations as to Additional Protocol I existed, White House press releases on aerial bombardments extensively used language of Article 51 (5) of that Protocol – one of the more controversial provisions in the perception of the US Administration that had been used as one of its arguments against ratification of the Protocol – to explain how precision strikes in Iraq had been planned and executed. The Chairman of the US Joint Chiefs of Staff, General Colin Powell, in his Report to Congress on Coalition Operations in the Gulf, had gone even further in stating that the provisions of Additional Protocol I were, for the main part, applied as if they constituted customary law.[56]

In addition to policy considerations there may be legal obligations to support higher standards in the behaviour of states. Article 21 of the 2008 Convention on Cluster Munitions requires states parties not only to inform non-parties with whom they engage in military operations on relevant obligations under this Convention, but also to encourage them to ratify, accept, approve or accede to it with the goal of attracting the adherence of all states to this Convention. This is more than a hortative clause. It is a very useful formula that should also be considered in other areas of cooperation and deserves to be implemented by the United Nations and regional organisations as well.

[56] L. C. Green, *The Contemporary Law of Armed Conflict*, 2nd edn (Manchester: Manchester University Press, 2000), xv; Department of Defense, 'Conduct of the Persian Gulf War: Final Report to Congress' (1992), 696, 700–3.

Conclusions

Summing up my comments on the question whether the laws of war are fit for purpose, I think that a positive answer will be possible as long as this branch of international law is properly understood, is applied in context with other relevant branches, and existing gaps are closed by cooperation. There are, however, specific challenges to be met:

1. Parties to an internal conflict cannot effectively insist on an applicability threshold for compliance with their obligations under IHL as its principles and rules are influencing peacetime behaviour as well. Nor should states be expected formally to recognise a state of armed conflict when they are engaged in robust law enforcement or post-conflict peacebuilding.
2. International humanitarian law cannot be convincingly applied without regard to human rights law and other relevant legal disciplines.
3. For the conduct of military operations, similar effects apply to general principles and customary rules of international law as to international treaties.
4. National laws and regulations may require *caveats* in military cooperation. They may also supplement international law in areas not (yet) regulated at the international level. To support interoperability, states and international organisations should endeavour to harmonise relevant rights and obligations.
5. Harmonisation of military laws should be developed further within the European Union. One example is the still open issue of when a soldier is entitled, or even obliged, to refuse execution of an unlawful order and what is the consequence as to the order's effectiveness.
6. International cooperation offers incentives to increase interoperability between different national contingents.
7. Considering that the laws of war are serving more than one purpose, the process of joint application and further development of its rules continues to include a variety of considerations and even opposing legal interests. Where *lex lata* rules are not expected to be changed, informal solutions must be envisaged.

4

'It's a bird! It's a plane! It's a non-international armed conflict!': cross-border hostilities between states and non-state actors

LINDSAY MOIR

> A contention may, of course, arise between armed forces of a State and a body of armed individuals, but this is not war.[1]
>
> [M]odern conflict often does not appear to fit nicely into the strict traditional legal concepts of what constitutes international or non-international 'armed conflict'.[2]

Introduction

Key to the effective legal regulation of any armed conflict is the identification of precisely what the nature of that armed conflict is. Only by disposing of the question as to whether a particular armed conflict is to be classified as either international or non-international in character can the applicable set of IHL rules be determined. This has important consequences both for the regulation of hostilities and for the imposition of individual criminal responsibility for breaches of the relevant law in that – despite a growing tendency to see both as subject to many of the same humanitarian norms[3] – clear

[1] L. Oppenheim, *International Law*, vol. 2, *Disputes, War and Neutrality*, ed. H. Lauterpacht, 7th edn (London: Longman, 1952), 203.

[2] K. Watkin, '21st Century Conflict and International Humanitarian Law: Status Quo or Change?', in M. Schmitt and J. Pejić (eds), *International Law and Armed Conflict: Exploring the Faultlines* (Leiden: Martinus Nijhoff, 2007), 273.

[3] See L. Moir, 'Towards the Unification of International Humanitarian Law?', in R. Burchill, N. D. White and J. Morris (eds), *International Conflict and Security Law: Essays in Memory of Hilaire McCoubrey* (Cambridge: Cambridge University Press, 2005), 108–28; J. K. Kleffner, 'Human Rights and International Humanitarian Law: General Issues', in T. D. Gill and D. Fleck (eds), *The Handbook of the International Law of Military Operations* (Oxford: Oxford University Press, 2010), 56–7.

(and important) differences still exist, perhaps especially in terms of the absence of combatant status for insurgent forces in non-international armed conflicts.[4] Accordingly, international and non-international armed conflicts remain subject to separate legal regimes, a position amply illustrated by their separate treatment in the Rome Statute of the International Criminal Court. International armed conflicts are governed by the full range of IHL, whereas non-international armed conflicts are regulated by the much more limited provisions of common Article 3 of the 1949 Geneva Conventions, possibly also by Additional Protocol II 1977 (depending on the circumstances),[5] as well as by an apparently burgeoning set of customary IHL rules.[6] Thus, despite occasional suggestions to the contrary,[7] the accurate classification of any given armed conflict as either international or non-international retains its importance, and it is necessary critically to assess recent assertions that these two categories are no longer sufficient.

[4] Similarly, the law of occupation applies only to international armed conflicts. Some uncertainty remains regarding the applicability to non-international armed conflict of some rules regulating methods and means of combat. See Kleffner, 'Human Rights and International Humanitarian Law', 57.

[5] Article 1(1) AP II provides a much higher threshold than that required for the application of common Article 3 (and, indeed, customary international law), thereby regulating only a (rather small) sub-set of non-international armed conflicts. See L. Moir, *The Law of Internal Armed Conflict* (Cambridge: Cambridge University Press, 2002), 100–3.

[6] See J.-M. Henckaerts and L. Doswald-Beck, *Customary International Humanitarian Law*, 3 vols (Cambridge: Cambridge University Press, 2005), vol. 1, *Rules*, where the vast majority of the 161 customary rules identified are stated to be equally applicable to non-international armed conflict.

[7] See, e.g., HCJ 769/02, *Public Committee against Torture in Israel* v. *Government of Israel* [2006], para. 11, referring to Israeli claims that there was no need to decide the character of its conflict with Palestinian groups in the Gaza Strip and West Bank because, 'according to all of the classifications, the laws of armed conflict will apply to the acts of the State. These laws allow striking at persons who are party to the armed conflict and take an active part in it, whether it is [...] international or non-international'. The ICJ, in its *Case Concerning Military and Paramilitary Operations in and against Nicaragua (Nicaragua* v. *United States of America) (Merits)*, Judgment, 27 June 1986, para. 218, described common Article 3 as a 'minimum yardstick', even in the event of international armed conflict, in that its provisions represent 'elementary considerations of humanity'. As such, it suggested in para. 219 that 'Because the minimum rules applicable to international and to non-international conflicts are identical, there is no need to address the question whether those actions must be looked at in the context of the rules which operate for the one or for the other category of conflict.'

The basic framework: international versus non-international armed conflict

Prima facie, it seems obvious that hostilities between two or more states are international in character, whereas hostilities between a state and a non-state party are non-international. Article 2 of Hague Convention IV 1907 states that the annexed Regulations 'do not apply except between contracting Powers', whilst Article 2 common to the 1949 Geneva Conventions provides that those Conventions are applicable to 'all cases of declared war or of any other armed conflict which may arise between two or more of the High Contracting Parties'. Only states can be High Contracting Parties, and it therefore seems clear that the Conventions as a whole apply only to armed conflicts between two or more states.[8] This position is confirmed by the International Committee of the Red Cross (ICRC) in its Commentaries to the Conventions, which indicate that '[a]ny difference arising between two States and leading to the intervention of armed forces is an armed conflict within the meaning of Article 2',[9] and by Article 1(3) of 1977 Additional Protocol I, which explicitly relates to the protection of victims of *international* armed conflict and indicates its applicability to those 'situations referred to in [common] Article 2'. More recently, the International Criminal Tribunal for the former Yugoslavia (ICTY) has also reaffirmed that an international armed conflict exists whenever there is 'resort to armed force between States'.[10]

Such international armed conflicts tend to be easily recognised as the use of force by one state against another is fairly unusual. That is not to say, of course, that there cannot be situations in which the existence (or otherwise) of an international armed conflict is difficult to determine. Thus, whilst the ICRC Commentaries suggest that 'It makes no difference how long the conflict lasts, or how much slaughter takes place',[11] the reality is that a relatively minor resort to force between states – usually discussed in terms of 'border incidents' – need not

[8] Although parties to a non-international armed conflict can agree to apply the Conventions as a whole, rather than the provisions of common Article 3 alone. See Moir, *The Law of Internal Armed Conflict*, 63–5.

[9] J. S. Pictet (ed.), *Commentary on Geneva Convention I* (Geneva: ICRC, 1952), 32.

[10] *Prosecutor* v. *Tadić*, Appeal on Jurisdiction, IT-94-1-AR72, 2 October 1995, para. 70.

[11] Pictet, *Commentary on Geneva Convention I*, 32, a position described as the 'first-shot theory', whereby international humanitarian law 'applies from the first moment that force is used by one State against another State'. See Kleffner, 'Human Rights and International Humanitarian Law', 54.

necessarily be seen as constituting an armed conflict.[12] As Yoram Dinstein explains:

> Incidents involving the use of force, without reaching the threshold of war, occur quite often in the relations between States. Border patrols of neighbouring countries may exchange fire; naval units may torpedo vessels flying another flag; interceptor planes may shoot down aircraft belonging to another State; and so forth.
>
> [. . .]
>
> in large measure, [the classification of military action as either war or a closed incident ('short of war')] depends on the way in which the two antagonists appraise the situation. As long as both Parties choose to consider what transpired as a mere incident, and provided that the incident is rapidly closed, it is hard to gainsay that view. Once, however, one of them elects to engage in war, the other side is incapable of preventing that development.[13]

The existence of international armed conflict accordingly requires an analysis of the situation, including factors such as the intention of the states involved,[14] and whether or not hostilities can be perceived as 'comprehensive'.[15]

On the basis that the formal difference between international and non-international armed conflicts is that the former 'requires there to be at least two State parties to the conflict',[16] it might have been thought that any armed conflict involving participants other than states cannot be international in character, and so must be non-international. Geoffrey Corn, for example, argues that IHL has developed according to the

[12] See, e.g., G. D. Solis, *The Law of Armed Conflict: International Humanitarian Law in War* (Cambridge: Cambridge University Press, 2010), 151–2.

[13] Y. Dinstein, *War, Aggression and Self-Defence*, 5th edn (Cambridge: Cambridge University Press, 2011), 11.

[14] Solis, *The Law of Armed Conflict*, 152.

[15] Dinstein, *War, Aggression and Self-Defence*, 12. The *UK Manual of the Law of Armed Conflict* (Oxford: Oxford University Press, 2004), 29 suggests that 'Whether any particular intervention crosses the threshold so as to become an armed conflict will depend on all the surrounding circumstances', whilst Kleffner, 'Human Rights and International Humanitarian Law', 54 indicates that 'the factual circumstances of a military operation amounting to an international armed conflict will determine which of the rules are practically relevant and, as a consequence, the extent to which the law applies'.

[16] D. Turns, 'The "War on Terror" through British and International Humanitarian Law Eyes: Comparative Perspectives on Selected Legal Issues', 10 *New York City Law Review* (2007) 435, at 456. See also Kleffner, 'Human Rights and International Humanitarian Law', 58: 'Decisive for the characterization of an armed conflict as international is that the violent confrontation is one between two or more States.'

assumption that there are only two types of armed conflict, leading to 'the evolution of an "either/or" law-triggering paradigm: either the conflict was between two states, satisfying the triggering criteria of Common Article 2, or the conflict was between a state and a non-state armed entity within the territory of the state, satisfying the triggering criteria of Common Article 3'.[17] For reasons that will be outlined below, his characterisation of the scope of common Article 3 appears overly restrictive. The applicability of an 'either/or paradigm', whereby an armed conflict that is not inter-state, and so falls outside the scope of common Article 2, must instead be a non-international armed conflict within the ambit of common Article 3, nonetheless seems entirely accurate. Indeed, the ICRC has indicated that, in its view, 'Legally speaking, no other type of armed conflict exists.'[18]

Granted, Article 1(4) Additional Protocol I 1977 muddies the waters somewhat by providing that the situations referred to in common Article 2, and thereby regulated by the Protocol by means of Article 1(3), include those armed conflicts 'in which peoples are fighting against colonial domination and alien occupation and against racist regimes in the exercise of their right of self-determination'. This has the effect of transforming what would previously have constituted a category of non-international armed conflicts into international armed conflicts for the purposes of IHL. It is, however, an extremely limited exception and, moreover, one which has had very little practical impact.[19] Thus, the general framework of classification seems straightforward: an armed conflict must be either international or non-international in character, and any armed conflict that does not fall within the scope of common Article 2 or Additional Protocol I (i.e., which is neither a conflict involving two or more states, or else a war of national liberation) must be characterised as non-international.

[17] G. S. Corn, 'Making the Case for Conflict Bifurcation in Afghanistan: Transnational Armed Conflict, al Qaida and the Limits of the Associated Militia Concept', in M. N. Schmitt (ed.), *The War in Afghanistan: A Legal Analysis*, International Law Studies, vol. 85 (Newport, RI: US Naval War College, 2009), 209.

[18] ICRC, 'How is the Term "Armed Conflict" Defined in International Humanitarian Law?', opinion paper, March 2008: www.icrc.org/eng/assets/files/other/opinion-paper-armed-conflict.pdf, 1.

[19] See C. Greenwood, 'Customary Law Status of the 1977 Geneva Protocols', in A. J. M Delissen and G. J. Tanja (eds), *Humanitarian Law of Armed Conflict – Challenges Ahead: Essays in Honour of Frits Kalshoven* (Dordrecht: Martinus Nijhoff, 1991), 111–12.

Complications?

Despite the apparent simplicity of the position outlined above, the accurate classification of armed conflict is not always a straightforward exercise, for a variety of reasons. Initially, for example, there may be some debate regarding the lower threshold and whether an armed conflict exists at all. Reference has already been made to minor border incidents and the question as to whether or not these necessarily constitute an international armed conflict. However, the relevant threshold for international armed conflict is not necessarily a high one,[20] and the question is even more problematic in the context of non-international armed conflict where the dividing line between internal disturbances and tensions, which fall short of the relevant threshold, and armed conflict *per se* can be especially difficult to identify. Thus, in addition to a certain level of organisation on the part of non-states parties,[21] the ICTY's *Tadić* formula for the existence of non-international armed conflict also requires 'protracted armed violence' – a test that, despite the ordinary meaning of the word 'protracted', has come to be regarded as 'referring more to the intensity of the armed violence than to its duration'.[22]

Equally, the characterisation of an armed conflict as either international or non-international can be problematic at the upper threshold, where, for example, there may be active involvement on the part of one or more third states, of the UN, or of other multinational forces. The generally accepted position is that intervention on behalf of a non-state armed group against the government party serves to internationalise an armed conflict, whereas intervention on behalf of the government does not.[23]

[20] Indeed, it would appear that the threshold for non-international armed conflict is actually higher. See, e.g., N. Lubell, *Extraterritorial Use of Force against Non-State Actors* (Oxford: Oxford University Press, 2010), 94; Turns, 'The "War on Terror"', 442: 'Legally [. . .] an armed attack that leads to self-defense will normally involve a resulting armed conflict, even if very limited in scope and of very short duration.'

[21] For a detailed survey of how the ICTY has assessed the criterion of organisation, and indicative factors, see *Prosecutor* v. *Boškoski and Tarčulovski*, Trial Chamber Judgment, IT-04-82-T, 10 July 2008, paras 199–203.

[22] *Prosecutor* v. *Haradinaj, Balaj and Brahimaj*, Trial Chamber Judgment, IT-04-84-T, 3 April 2008, para. 49. As it did in relation to the organisation element, the Trial Chamber in *Prosecutor* v. *Boškoski* (n. 21, above) undertook a survey of how the ICTY had approached the question of the threshold of intensity (paras 177–8).

[23] See, e.g., Kleffner, 'Human Rights and International Humanitarian Law', 57–8; Y. Dinstein, *The Conduct of Hostilities under the Law of International Armed Conflict*, 2nd edn (Cambridge: Cambridge University Press, 2010), 27–8; Moir, *The Law of Internal Armed Conflict*, 50–1; J. Pejić, 'Status of Armed Conflicts', in E. Wilmshurst

Furthermore, there would appear to be a growing tendency for contemporary armed conflicts to be 'mixed' in character, incorporating both international and non-international aspects. In such situations, the international and non-international armed conflicts are seen as existing simultaneously yet separately, with the applicable humanitarian law regime determined by the nature of the parties to the particular hostilities in question. As Dinstein indicates:

> The fact that a State (or rather its central Government) is beset by enemies from both inside and outside its territory does not mean that the international and the internal armed conflicts necessarily merge. Some hostilities may be waged exclusively between the domestic foes (i.e. between the central Government and rebel groups), whereas other hostilities may take place on the inter-State plane (*viz.* between the central Government and a foreign State). [The law of international armed conflict] governs only the international military operations.[24]

The result is that 'within one area of fighting, there may be three or more parties fighting side by side and with each other – each combination of two parties fighting under a different set of rules'.[25] Thus, in 1986, the International Court of Justice (ICJ) determined that the situation in Nicaragua comprised elements of both types of hostilities, and that:

> The conflict between the *contras*' forces and those of the Government of Nicaragua is an armed conflict which is 'not of an international character'. The acts of the *contras* towards the Nicaraguan Government are therefore governed by the law applicable to conflicts of that character; whereas the actions of the United States in and against Nicaragua fall under the legal rules relating to international conflicts.[26]

Cross-border hostilities between states and non-state actors

This contribution has as its focus another situation in which the accurate characterisation of an armed conflict may be problematic, namely, where

and S. Breau (eds), *Perspectives on the ICRC Study on Customary International Humanitarian Law* (Cambridge: Cambridge University Press, 2007), 92.

24 Dinstein, *The Conduct of Hostilities*, 27. 25 Lubell, *Extraterritorial Use of Force*, 93.

26 *Nicaragua* Case (n. 7, above), para. 219. See also more recent confirmation in *Prosecutor* v. *Tadić*, Appeals Chamber Judgment, IT-94-1-A, 15 July 1999, para. 84; Report of the Independent International Fact-Finding Mission on the Conflict in Georgia, vol. 2, p. 300; Report of the International Commission of Inquiry to Investigate All Alleged Violations of International Human Rights Law in the Libyan Arab Jamahiriya, 1 June 2011 (UN Doc. A/HRC/17/44), paras 62–6; *Prosecutor* v. *Lubanga*, ICC Trial Chamber Judgment Pursuant to Article 74 of the Statute, ICC-01/04-01/06, 14 March 2012, para. 540.

hostilities occur between a state (or, indeed, more than one state) on the one hand and a non-state actor on the other – but where hostilities involve military operations on the territory of another state, thereby crossing international frontiers. Although not an entirely new phenomenon,[27] such situations do seem to be becoming more prevalent and have certainly been high on the international legal agenda since the events of 11 September 2001.[28]

Behind the apparently increased concern with military action of this type lies what would appear to be a growing acceptance of the possibility of self-defence against non-state actors (at least in circumstances where the host state is either unable or unwilling to prevent their activities).[29] Clearly, action taken in self-defence does not occur in a legal vacuum and – to the extent that such operations can be said to constitute an armed conflict, as outlined above – is regulated by the relevant rules of IHL. Of course, this serves only to underline the point that the relevant body of IHL must be determined according to the classification of hostilities as either international or non-international. However, there is a particular problem in this context that has been expressed as follows:

> A conflict between a state and a transnational network operating in and from numerous other states, but not necessarily with their support, is anything but an exact match for the traditional concepts of international and non-international armed conflicts. Not being a conflict between states creates difficulties in defining it as international, while the fact that borders are crossed raises questions of whether it is non-international.[30]

In light of this apparent quandary, and arising largely, although not exclusively, in the context of military action against the Taliban and

[27] See, e.g., the 1837 *Caroline* incident, involving the use of force by Great Britain against Canadian rebels operating from within the United States: 29 *British and Foreign State Papers* 1137–8; 30 *British and Foreign State Papers*, 195–6.

[28] See, e.g., A. Paulus and M. Vashakmadze, 'Asymmetrical War and the Notion of Armed Conflict – A Tentative Conceptualization', 91 *International Review of the Red Cross* (2009) 95, at 110; and H. Duffy, *The 'War on Terror' and the Framework of International Law* (Cambridge: Cambridge University Press, 2005), 254 noting that 'traditional concepts of armed conflict are increasingly subject to question post 11 September 2001'.

[29] As discussed below, more active involvement on the part of the host state may well lead to a military response against governmental forces and infrastructure, thereby rendering hostilities international in character. For further discussion, see L. Moir, *Reappraising the Resort to Force: International Law, Jus ad Bellum and the War on Terror* (Oxford: Hart Publishing, 2010), 22–31 and 147–53; P. Rowe, 'Responses to Terror: The New "War"' 3 *Melbourne Journal of International Law* (2002) 301.

[30] Lubell, *Extraterritorial Use of Force*, 93–4.

Al-Qaeda in Afghanistan (exacerbated by the unhelpful political terminology of a 'global war on terror'), some scholars have sought to suggest that the traditional international legal regime for the classification of armed conflict is no longer appropriate or satisfactory, in that neither category truly reflects these situations. As such, it has been asserted that they should be seen as representing a new, 'hybrid' category of '*transnational* armed conflict'.[31] To what extent, however, is this true?

The importance of 'host state' consent and/or participation

The first point to note is that any consideration of this subject must be properly framed by a consideration of the attitude, and activities, of the state in whose territory the non-state actor is located (i.e., the 'host state'). It may be, for example, that the host state chooses actively to resist military operations on its territory. Whilst this would clearly lead to inter-state hostilities, it would not necessarily transform the nature of any separate hostilities between the non-host state and the non-state actors – at least in the absence of the requisite link between the host state and the armed group. Yet, it is often suggested that the very exercise of force by one state on the territory of another must be considered an international conflict.[32] Jan Kleffner, for example, has asserted that, 'Even if there is no military activity of the territorial State in support of the organized armed group, an invasion by one State into another State's territory should [. . .] be seen as triggering the law of international armed

[31] Corn, 'Making the Case for Conflict Bifurcation in Afghanistan', 184. See also, e.g., W. K. Lietzau, 'Combating Terrorism: The Consequences of Moving from Law Enforcement to War', in D. Wippman and M. Evangelista (eds), *New Wars, New Laws? Applying the Laws of War in 21st Century Conflicts* (Ardsley, NY: Transnational, 2005), 42 suggesting that, in terms of classifying conflict as either international or non-international, the 'new era of terrorist activity ill fits either category'.

[32] See, e.g., F. Kalshoven and L. Zegveld, *Constraints on the Waging of War*, 4th edn (Cambridge: ICRC/Cambridge University Press, 2011), 221: 'When it comes to determining what law to apply to the extraterritorial operations of a state engaging in armed conflict with a non-state armed group on another state's territory, one situation is beyond question: when the first state directs its military operations against the territorial state as well, the situation indubitably constitutes an international armed conflict. For all other situations, the main consideration should be one of law of war policy: any significant fighting on another state's territory requires the most complete, most solidly established set of principles and rules, that is, the law of international armed conflict'.

conflict.'[33] Of course, the same author has also argued that 'triggering the application' of the law of international armed conflict is not quite the same as its practical application based upon factual circumstances.[34] Thus, the relevant rules would in fact only become applicable where hostilities between the two states actually occur, either through armed resistance on the part of the host state, or through attacks upon governmental targets and infrastructure rather than operations strictly limited to non-state targets.[35]

As Noam Lubell indicates, 'the only way extraterritorial forcible measures against non-state actors could be governed by the laws of international armed conflict would be in cases where the apparent non-state actor was in fact a state agent or assimilated into the forces of another state'.[36] Thus, in order for hostilities not *prima facie* involving the forces of the host state to be international, it would be necessary to demonstrate an element of state control over the non-state actor, such that their activities can be equated with those of the host state itself.[37] This can certainly be 'challenging on a factual basis',[38] especially as the necessary level of state control remains a question of some controversy in international law. Thus, whilst the ICJ required the rather exacting threshold of 'effective control' in order to attribute armed activities to a state,[39] the ICTY subsequently held that a lower threshold of 'overall control' was sufficient for the determination of the nature of an armed conflict.[40] The latter approach, satisfied by a state not only 'equipping and financing the group, but also by coordinating or helping in the general planning of its military activity',[41] has recently found favour in

33 Kleffner, 'Human Rights and International Humanitarian Law', 59.

34 *Ibid.*, 54: 'If, during [an international armed conflict] no member of the opposing armed forces is captured the law pertaining to prisoners of war is not applicable.'

35 Kleffner accepts that, 'if and to the extent that the nature of the operation is such that it is not limited to engaging the organized armed group, but is also directed against the armed forces and infrastructure of the territorial State, the law of international armed conflict applies': *ibid.*, 60.

36 Lubell, *Extraterritorial Use of Force*, 98–9.

37 See, e.g., Kleffner, 'Human Rights and International Humanitarian Law', 57: 'A *prima facie* non-international armed conflict in State A will have to be treated as an international armed conflict by virtue of the fact that State B exercises control over an organized armed group which fights against the government of State A.'

38 Lubell, *Extraterritorial Use of Force*, 110.

39 *Nicaragua* Case (n. 7, above), para. 115. See also the discussion in A. Cassese, 'The *Nicaragua* and *Tadić* Tests Revisited in Light of the ICJ Judgment on Genocide in Bosnia', 18 *European Journal of International Law* (2007) 649.

40 *Prosecutor* v. *Tadić* (n. 26, above), para. 120.

41 *Ibid.*, para. 131.

the jurisprudence of the International Criminal Court,[42] although whether this will dispose of the question remains to be seen.[43]

Equally, it may be that the host state has provided its consent in relation to military operations against the non-state group. In such situations there is clearly no inter-state, common Article 2 conflict and the situation must be characterised as non-international.[44] It will be recalled that intervention by a third state on behalf of a state engaged in armed conflict against an organised armed group operating within its own territory does not, of itself, transform the conflict into an international one.[45] Host state consent should, then, render the situation analogous, 'in as much as the territorial State allies itself with the other State in the latter's fight against an organized armed group. Such an alliance does not necessarily have to manifest itself in military support by the territorial State, but can consist of the mere permission to let the other state operate on its territory'.[46]

States are, of course, understandably reluctant to accept the use of force by other states on their territory. Much more problematic, then, are situations in which a non-state armed group acts independently of the host state (or at least where any involvement by the host state is insufficient to cross the relevant 'control' threshold), but where the host state is not prepared to consent to cross-border military activity aimed at the armed group. Dinstein describes such activity as 'extra-territorial law enforcement', whilst nevertheless maintaining that it falls under the auspices of legitimate self-defence.[47] As already indicated, it is difficult to conceive of actions taken in self-defence (and met with armed force)

42 *Prosecutor* v. *Lubanga*, para. 541: 'As regards the necessary degree of control of another State over an armed group acting on its behalf, the Trial Chamber has concluded that the "overall control" test is the correct approach. This will determine whether an armed conflict not of an international character may have become internationalised' (see n. 26, above).

43 Especially in light of the ICJ's entrenchment of its *Nicaragua* position. See Cassese, 'The *Nicaragua* and *Tadić* Tests Revisited'; L. Moir, 'Action against Host States of Terrorist Groups', in M. Weller (ed.), *The Oxford Handbook of the Use of Force in International Law* (Oxford: Oxford University Press, forthcoming 2014); Y. Dinstein, 'Terrorism and Afghanistan', in Schmitt, *The War in Afghanistan*, 47–8.

44 See, e.g., S. Vité, 'Typology of Armed Conflicts in International Humanitarian Law: Legal Concepts and Actual Situations', 91 *International Review of the Red Cross* (2009) 69, at 89.

45 See n. 23, above.

46 Kleffner, 'Human Rights and International Humanitarian Law', 59. See also Dinstein, 'Terrorism and Afghanistan', 46–7.

47 Dinstein, 'Terrorism and Afghanistan', 48–9; although he also insists that 'the nomenclature is not of major import: it is the normative substance that counts'.

as not amounting to armed conflict of some sort, and one in which it is the character of the belligerents, rather than the territorial reach of the conflict, that determines the applicable rules. In this respect, 'so long as the non-state actor remains independent of the territorial state, the armed conflict between it and the outside state should be considered a non-international armed conflict'.[48] Why, then, do problems still seem to persist in terms of characterising these situations for the purposes of IHL?

Common Article 3 conflict, and the confusion between 'non-international' and 'internal'

The answer is that a possible impediment to this straightforward conclusion can, in fact, be found in the text of common Article 3 itself, which states that it is applicable where there is an 'armed conflict not of an international character occurring in the territory of one of the High Contracting Parties'. The phrase 'not of an international character' ought simply to be taken to mean those armed conflicts falling outside the scope of common Article 2, which is not particularly problematic for the categorisation of the type of cross-border operations in question. The subsequent, geographical requirement may, however, be the source of greater difficulty.

Granted, for the 'archetypal' non-international armed conflict – i.e., an internal conflict between the forces of a state and an organised armed group (or groups) operating within its borders – this is hardly a testing condition. Indeed, given that ratification of the 1949 Geneva Conventions is now universal, it may well be the case that this particular requirement has lost any practical significance. As the ICRC has suggested, 'any armed conflict between governmental armed forces and armed groups or between such groups cannot but take place on the territory of one of the Parties to the Convention'.[49] That may be true, but it does not

[48] Lubell, *Extraterritorial Use of Force*, 110. See also, e.g., Duffy, *The 'War on Terror'*, 251: 'Armed groups [. . .] may of course act under the authority of a state or states. But they cannot themselves constitute a party to an international conflict absent such state involvement'; Kleffner, 'Human Rights and International Humanitarian Law', 58: 'If one side of the armed conflict consists of an organized armed group whose actions cannot be attributed to another State [. . .] the armed conflict remains of a non-international nature.'

[49] ICRC, 'How is the Term "Armed Conflict" Defined in International Humanitarian Law?', 3.

necessarily avoid the difficulties that arise in terms of legal classification caused by an understanding of non-international armed conflict whereby it is considered to entail only those hostilities that are, in fact, *limited* to the territory of a High Contracting Party.

The drafting history of common Article 3 might seem to suggest that this is what was intended. Indeed, as Anthony Cullen indicates, the *travaux préparatoires* demonstrate that the 'delegates involved in drafting the provision understood "armed conflict not of an international character" as having essentially the same meaning as "civil war"'.[50] Corn further explains that, because common Article 3 was included largely in response to 'the brutal civil wars that ravaged Spain, Russia, and other states during the years between the two world wars, the trigger for this baseline humanitarian provision came to be understood as conflicts that were primarily intra-state, or internal armed conflicts'.[51] This is certainly the position expressed by the ICRC Commentaries, with Commentary IV, for example, providing that those 'conflicts referred to in Article 3 are armed conflicts, with armed forces on either side engaged in hostilities – conflicts, in short, which are in many respects similar to an international war, but take place *within the confines of a single country*'.[52]

This would clearly exclude armed conflicts between a state and a non-state armed group occurring on the territory of a third state – as, indeed, does Article 1(1) Additional Protocol II, which expressly limits its applicability to those armed conflicts 'which take place in the territory of a High Contracting Party between *its armed forces* and

[50] A. Cullen, *The Concept of Non-International Armed Conflict in International Humanitarian Law* (Cambridge: Cambridge University Press, 2010), 49.

[51] G. S. Corn, '*Hamdan*, Lebanon, and the Regulation of Hostilities: The Need to Recognize a Hybrid Category of Armed Conflict', 40 *Vanderbilt Journal of Transnational Law* (2007) 295, at 307. See also S. Murphy, 'Evolving Geneva Convention Paradigms in the "War on Terrorism": Applying the Core Rules to the Release of Persons Deemed "Unprivileged Combatants"', 75 *George Washington Law Review* (2007) 1105, at 1115–16: 'A fair reading of the negotiating history suggests that this Common Article 3 paradigm was principally designed to address the situation of an armed conflict *internal* to a single state. [...] Common Article 3 contemplates an armed conflict between a state and nonstate actor, but does so largely in the context of the classic civil war.'

[52] J. S. Pictet (ed.), *Commentary on Geneva Convention IV* (Geneva: ICRC, 1958), 36 (emphasis added). See also J. S. Pictet (ed.), *Commentary on Geneva Convention III* (Geneva: ICRC, 1960), 37 and *Commentary on Geneva Convention II* (Geneva: ICRC, 1960), 33.

dissident armed forces or other organised armed groups', and which additionally requires that the non-state actor 'exercise [...] control over a part of *its territory*'. There can be no doubt that both instances of the word 'its' refer to the state and that it is, accordingly, necessary for the non-state group to be engaged in hostilities with the territorial state and controlling a part of that state's territory. Such conflict is, by its nature, *internal* and, as such, Additional Protocol II would seem to be inapplicable to cross-border hostilities.[53] However, it must be recalled[54] that Additional Protocol II has a much narrower scope than common Article 3, and the non-applicability of the former does not mean that the type of armed conflict in question cannot be considered non-international according to the latter's more flexible threshold.

There has, however, been a relatively widespread – and more general – tendency to equate the concept of *non-international* armed conflict with that of *internal* armed conflict.[55] Derek Jinks, for example, has asserted that 'the Geneva Conventions, in Article 3 common to the four conventions, explicitly regulate *internal* armed conflicts';[56] William Lietzau has asserted that the Geneva Conventions 'speak to the circumstances of "international armed conflict" and "*internal* armed conflict" or "conflict not of an international character"', and that conflicts crossing international borders are thereby excepted 'from designation as an "internal armed conflict"';[57] whilst David Turns has argued that, 'If the British and Iraqi States are not at war with each other, but there is a conflict going on in Iraq, it cannot be international according to the definitions in the Geneva Conventions or Additional Protocol I. Therefore, by default almost, it must be *not international*, or effectively *internal*.'[58]

Similarly, a Resolution adopted by the Institute of International Law in 1999 provides in Article I that:

[53] See also Lubell, *Extraterritorial Use of Force*, 100. [54] See n. 5, above.

[55] Including the current author. See Moir, *The Law of Internal Armed Conflict*.

[56] D. Jinks, 'September 11 and the Laws of War', 28 *Yale Journal of International Law* (2003) 1, at 10 (emphasis added).

[57] Lietzau, 'Combating Terrorism', 42 (emphasis added).

[58] Turns, 'The "War on Terror"', 473 (emphasis added). There are numerous other examples in academic writing. See, e.g., L. C. Green, *The Contemporary Law of Armed Conflict*, 3rd edn (Manchester: Manchester University Press, 2008), 343: 'A non-international armed conflict has traditionally been one in which the governmental authorities of a state are opposed by armed groups *within that state* seeking to overthrow those authorities by force of arms' (emphasis added).

For the purposes of this Resolution:

- the expression 'armed conflicts in which non-State entities are parties' means *internal* armed conflicts between a government's armed forces and those of one or several non-State entities, or between several non-State entities; also included are *internal* armed conflicts in which peacekeeping forces intervene;
- the expression 'non-State entities' means the parties to *internal* armed conflicts who oppose the government's armed forces or are fighting entities of a similar nature and who fulfil the conditions set forth in Article 3 common to the Geneva Conventions of 1949 on the Protection of Victims of War or in Article 1 of the 1977 Protocol Additional to the Geneva Conventions and relating to the Protection of Victims of Non-International Armed Conflicts (Protocol II).[59]

Likewise, the *UK Manual of the Law of Armed Conflict* discusses the application of common Article 3, Additional Protocol II and customary international law in the context of *internal*, rather than non-international, armed conflict.[60] Additionally, the *Manual on the Law of Non-International Armed Conflict* (the San Remo Manual) has recently asserted that 'Non-international armed conflicts are armed confrontations occurring *within the territory of a single State* and in which the armed forces of no other State are engaged against the central government', explaining that they 'do not include conflicts in which two or more States are engaged against each other. Nor do they encompass conflicts extending to the territory of two or more States'.[61]

Further, the Israeli Supreme Court held, in *Public Committee against Torture in Israel* v. *Israel*,[62] that the Israeli Defence Force action against militant Palestinian organisations in the Occupied Palestinian Territories was an international armed conflict – in large part because the conflict crossed the frontiers of the state.[63] It expressed the view that:

[59] Resolution on the Application of International Humanitarian Law and Fundamental Human Rights in Armed Conflicts in which Non-State Entities are Parties: www.idi-iil.org/idiE/resolutionsE/1999_ber_03_en.PDF (emphasis added).

[60] *UK Manual of the Law of Armed Conflict*, 31–3.

[61] International Institute of Humanitarian Law (drafting committee M. N. Schmitt, C. H. B. Garraway and Y. Dinstein), *The Manual on the Law of Non-International Armed Conflict, with Commentary* (2006): www.iihl.org/iihl/Documents/The%20Manual%20on%20the%20Law%20of%20NIAC.pdf, 2 (emphasis added).

[62] See n. 7, above.

[63] *Ibid.*, para. 18. The Court also asserted, however, that the hostilities occurred in the context of belligerent occupation, by definition constituting an international armed conflict, and that they should also be seen as international in character due to the massive capability possessed by contemporary terrorist organisations.

> the fact that the terrorist organizations and their members do not act in the name of a state does not turn the struggle against them into a purely *internal* state conflict. Indeed, in today's reality, a terrorist organization is likely to have considerable military capabilities. At times they have military capabilities that exceed those of states. Confrontation with those dangers cannot be restricted within the state and its penal law. Confronting the dangers of terrorism constitutes a part of the international law dealing with armed conflicts of international character.[64]

Thus, it is perhaps fair to say that common Article 3 armed conflicts 'have generally become synonymous with *internal* conflicts',[65] based on an underlying assumption (i.e., that non-international conflicts take place within the engaged state's territory) that is certainly 'not out of place'.[66] Clearly, cross-border military operations against non-state actors cannot be described as *internal*. Nor, in the absence of hostilities between two or more states, are they *international*. Given the emergence of non-state actors capable of inflicting significant damage on foreign states,[67] the growing acceptance of self-defence in such situations, and the consequent increase in the number of such contemporary conflicts, the importance of identifying the appropriate humanitarian law regime – if, indeed, there is one – cannot be overstated. It may well be true that such scenarios were not contemplated by the drafters of the Geneva Conventions. However, to maintain in the face of their increasing prevalence that only inter-state hostilities constitute international armed conflict, whereas only wholly internal hostilities are non-international armed conflicts, would leave those armed conflicts between a state and a foreign-based or transnational armed group – or, indeed, a non-international armed conflict that, whilst initially internal, spills over into the territory of a neighbouring state – as neither one type nor the other and so beyond the scope of IHL.

Just such an approach was taken by the US Court of Appeals. It determined that the Geneva Conventions 'contemplate only two types of armed conflicts', but that the conflict existing between the United States and Al-Qaeda came within the scope of neither common Article 2 (since Al-Qaeda was neither a state nor a High Contracting Party) nor common Article 3 (since it applies only to conflicts confined to a single

[64] *Ibid.*, para. 21 (emphasis added).

[65] Corn, 'Making the Case for Conflict Bifurcation in Afghanistan', 184.

[66] Lubell, *Extraterritorial Use of Force*, 100.

[67] See, e.g., Lietzau, 'Combating Terrorism', 41: 'Where nation-states dominated previous conflicts, private organizations such as al Qaeda now possess the capability to wage war.'

country, whereas 'the war against terrorism in general and the war against al Qaeda in particular' was not).[68] This approach leads to an entirely unacceptable 'regulatory gap' in relation to cross-border hostilities, for which there is 'no principled (or pragmatic) rationale'.[69] As Marco Sassòli has explained:

> If [the provisions of common Article 3] meant that conflicts opposing states and organized armed groups and spreading over the territory of several states were not 'non-international armed conflicts', there would be a gap in protection, which could not be explained by states' concerns about their sovereignty. Those concerns made the law of non-international armed conflict more rudimentary. Yet concerns about state sovereignty could not explain why victims of conflicts spilling over the territory of several states should benefit from less protection than those affected by conflicts limited to the territory of only one state.[70]

In fact, and despite suggestions to the contrary, common Article 3 does not limit its applicability to *internal* conflict. Even Corn accepts that, irrespective of the historical context in which it was drafted and adopted, 'nowhere does the article expressly use "internal" as the indication of the type of armed conflict triggering its humanitarian mandate. Instead, Common Article 3 expressly indicates that its substantive protections are applicable to all non-international armed conflicts'.[71] It may be true that the Conventions had initially envisaged situations of civil war in the classic sense, and that 'between 1949 and 2001, the term "non-international" evolved to become synonymous with internal'.[72] However, based on a straightforward reading of common Article 3, 'there is no inherent reason of principle why that should be the case'.[73] Indeed, 'the essential point about the concept of non-international armed conflict is that it refers to military contests that are not fought between the armed forces of nation states, which alone under international law have the authority to go to war'.[74]

[68] *Hamdan* v. *Rumsfeld*, 415 F.3d 33 (2005), 41.
[69] Jinks, 'September 11 and the Laws of War', 41.
[70] M. Sassòli, 'Transnational Armed Groups and International Humanitarian Law', Harvard University Program on Humanitarian Policy and Conflict Research, Occasional Paper Series, 6 (2006), 9.
[71] Corn, '*Hamdan*, Lebanon, and the Regulation of Hostilities', 307. [72] *Ibid.*
[73] A. Dworkin, 'Military Necessity and Due Process: The Place of Human Rights in the War on Terror', in Wippman and Evangelista, *New Wars, New Laws?*, 60.
[74] *Ibid.*

Jinks further recalls that common Article 3 was seen as revolutionary at the time of its adoption, due to the introduction of international legal regulation in the context of what had previously been considered domestic matters, and has argued that if it governs wholly internal armed conflicts, which it assuredly does, it must, therefore, apply '*a fortiori* to armed conflicts with international or transnational dimensions'.[75] As a result, 'the best reading of Common Article 3 is that it applies to all armed conflicts not covered by Common Article 2 of the Geneva Conventions'.[76]

Thus, returning to Corn's 'either/or law-triggering paradigm' (according to which IHL has evolved 'with an almost exclusive focus' on whether conflicts are either inter-state or intra-state,[77] but which results in a regulatory gap through its failure 'to acknowledge the possibility that an extraterritorial non inter-state combat operation launched by a state using regular armed forces could qualify as an armed conflict triggering law of war regulation'),[78] this author prefers an either/or law-triggering paradigm that sees an armed conflict as being either *international* (i.e., inter-state, as per common Article 2) or else *non-international* (i.e., not inter-state – but not necessarily intra-state – as per common Article 3). This was the approach eventually adopted by the US Supreme Court in *Hamdan* v. *Rumsfeld*, where it held that 'the phrase "not of an international character" bears its literal meaning'; i.e., not between sovereign states.[79]

This viewpoint is entirely consistent with the approach of the ICRC Commentaries, which, despite their apparent strictness on the issue, insist that 'the Article should be applied as widely as possible'.[80] Admittedly, the customary international law definition of armed conflict, as developed by the ICTY, is slightly more ambiguous. It will be recalled that this requires the 'resort to armed force between States or protracted armed violence between governmental authorities and organized armed groups or between such groups within a State',[81] which might, on one reading, indicate that an armed conflict exists where there is: (a) the resort to armed force between states, or (b) protracted armed violence between governmental authorities and organised armed groups or between such groups *within a state*. As such, the geographical element (i.e., of hostilities occurring 'within a State') might seem applicable

[75] Jinks, 'September 11 and the Laws of War', 10. [76] *Ibid.*, 39.
[77] See Corn, 'Making the Case for Conflict Bifurcation in Afghanistan' (n. 17, and accompanying text, above).
[78] Corn, '*Hamdan*, Lebanon, and the Regulation of Hostilities', 309.
[79] 548 US 557 (2006), 628–31. [80] Pictet, *Commentary on Geneva Convention I*, 50.
[81] *Prosecutor* v. *Tadić* Appeal on Jurisdiction, para. 70.

to hostilities between states and armed groups. Nonetheless, an alternative reading requires: (a) the resort to armed force between states, or (b) protracted armed violence between governmental authorities and organised armed groups, or (c) between such groups within a state, and means that non-international hostilities between a state and an organised armed group could therefore extend beyond a single territory. This seems preferable, especially in light of the congruent applicability of common Article 3 and the customary humanitarian law rules of non-international armed conflict.[82]

To further buttress this proposition, it will be recalled that the intervention of a third state at the request of a government engaged in internal hostilities against a non-state party does not serve to internationalise the conflict. The third state is certainly using armed force extraterritorially, but it is nonetheless considered to be a party to a non-international armed conflict.[83] Moreover, in relation to a non-international armed conflict originally confined to the territory of a single state, but subsequently extending onto the territory of another (or, indeed, others),[84] there is a degree of consensus that:

> When the armed forces of a State party to a non-international armed conflict temporarily pursue an organized armed group into the territory of a neighbouring State in the course of an uninterrupted military operation which commenced in the territory of the former State, [...] the applicable law does not change by the mere fact that an international border is being crossed in the process.[85]

[82] See Cullen, *The Concept of Non-International Armed Conflict in International Humanitarian Law*, 174–85 for an excellent discussion of the threshold for the application of customary law and common Article 3 in the context of Article 8(2) of the ICC Statute. Indeed, the question as to whether even a non-international armed conflict between non-state armed groups must be limited to the territory of a single state, as would appear to be the case according to the *Tadić* test, is an interesting one, although beyond the scope of this chapter.

[83] See, e.g., Lubell, *Extraterritorial Use of Force*, 101. He continues: 'to be absolutely precise, the Common Article 3 requirement does not actually require that the state in which it occurs should be involved in the conflict. Theoretically, one could read it to mean that state A could be involved in an armed conflict not of an international character, occurring in the territory of state B, which is a high contracting party to the Conventions, without state B having a part in the conflict' (102). Far from being theoretical, however, this is precisely the type of situation in question.

[84] Described as an 'exported' non-international armed conflict by Vité, 'Typology of Armed Conflicts in International Humanitarian Law', 89.

[85] Kleffner, 'Human Rights and International Humanitarian Law', 59–60. See also Dinstein, *The Conduct of Hostilities*, 27; Lubell, *Extraterritorial Use of Force*, 103: 'A primary reason for states creating and maintaining two separate categories of conflict has been to avoid giving

In this context, it should be noted that the Statute of the International Criminal Tribunal for Rwanda – clearly concerned with non-international, rather than international, armed conflict in that Article 4 (regarding violations of the relevant laws of war) is limited to violations of common Article 3 and Additional Protocol II – asserts the jurisdiction of the Tribunal not only over those violations of IHL committed on Rwandan territory, but also over those 'Rwandan citizens responsible for such violations committed in the territory of neighbouring States'.[86]

As such, the textual reference in common Article 3 to conflicts occurring on the territory of a High Contracting Party should be seen as a general geographical requirement, which is very easily fulfilled, and recalling simply that common Article 3 applies only in the territory of those states that have ratified the Geneva Conventions. It does not require that hostilities be limited geographically to the territory of a single, engaged state.[87]

Conclusion

There is no need to adjust the traditional categorisation of armed conflict in IHL, which remains entirely fit for purpose. The position is clear: international and non-international armed conflicts can, and should, be 'distinguished [. . .] by the parties involved rather than by the territorial scope of the conflict'.[88] Cross-border hostilities occurring between a state and an independent non-state party are, therefore, non-international in character.

This conclusion cannot, of course, dispose of every conceivable issue and some difficulties remain. There are, for example, those that would

any recognized status or right to fight to rebels and insurgents. Armed conflicts that begin as internal can lead to some of the fighting spilling over borders, and it cannot be the case that by stepping across the border a rebel would suddenly be entitled to claim elevation to prisoner of war status and subsequent immunity for attacks against state forces.'

86 ICTR Statute, Article 1. See also Article 7, indicating that the territorial jurisdiction of the Tribunal extended not only to the territory of Rwanda itself but also 'to the territory of neighbouring States in respect of serious violations of international humanitarian law committed by Rwandan citizens'.

87 Sassòli, 'Transnational Armed Groups and International Humanitarian Law', 9; Jinks, 'September 11 and the Laws of War', 41.

88 L. Zegveld, *Accountability of Armed Opposition Groups in International Law* (Cambridge: Cambridge University Press, 2002), 136; Y. Sandoz, C. Swinarski and B. Zimmerman (eds), *Commentary on the Additional Protocols of 8 June 1977 to the Geneva Conventions of 12 August 1949* (Geneva: ICRC, 1987), para. 4458.

strongly dispute the relevance, and/or appropriateness, of IHL *per se* in such situations. As Adam Roberts explains:

> For at least 25 years, the United States has expressed a concern, shared to some degree by certain other states, regarding the whole principle of thinking about terrorists and other irregular forces in a laws-of-war framework. To refer to such a framework, which recognizes rights and duties, might seem to imply a degree of moral acceptance of the right of any particular group to resort to acts of violence, at least against military targets.[89]

Yet, if the hostilities in question are deemed to be non-international armed conflicts, such concerns are unnecessary in that the relevant rules of humanitarian law do not grant any formal combatant status to non-state actors:

> If the call for a new model of conflict is based upon a concern that the current armed conflict framework forces states to recognize that groups [. . .] would have the right to attack state forces with impunity, then these worries can be alleviated by applying the non-international model. The rules of non-international armed conflict do not give legal status to groups and do not contain any provisions allowing for individual combat status, while at the same time – depending on certain interpretations – they may allow state forces to target active members of armed groups. Moreover, since the rules of non-international armed conflict do not grant combatant status an individual who attacks state soldiers does not have immunity from prosecution by that state.[90]

Thus, the laws of non-international armed conflict are far more suitable for such situations than those of international armed conflict – not only in terms of guarding against any perceived status for non-state (or 'terrorist') groups, but also in light of the increased likelihood that the non-state group will be able to comply with their humanitarian

[89] A. Roberts, 'The Laws of War in the War on Terror', in F. L. Borch and P. S. Wilson (eds), *International Law and the War on Terror*, International Law Studies, vol. 79 (Newport, RI: US Naval War College, 2003), 186. See also, e.g., V. Lowe, '"Clear and Present Danger": Responses to Terrorism', 54 *International and Comparative Law Quarterly* (2005) 185, 187–8; Lubell, *Extraterritorial Use of Force*, 123, referring to the 'perception that the existing armed conflict paradigm automatically entitles the non-state group to belligerent rights and combatant status for its members. On the one hand, allowing states to attack group members anywhere, while denying group members the right to use force against the state, is said to be "extreme and unconvincing" and "hard to accept". On the other hand, providing the full benefits to members of these groups is said by others to be equally problematic'.

[90] Lubell, *Extraterritorial Use of Force*, 123–4.

obligations.[91] Of course, it also remains for any non-state group to clearly cross the threshold of organisation required for a non-international armed conflict to exist in the first place – and according to this measure it is unlikely that a *terrorist* group would be able to be considered a *party* to an armed conflict at all.[92] In terms of Al-Qaeda, for example, it seems fairly certain that its lack of organisation, allied with its methods of operation, mean that it could not be party to an armed conflict with the USA, or indeed anybody else.[93]

The conclusion that cross-border hostilities between states and non-state actors are non-international in nature does not avoid the inevitable difficulties involved in applying this framework to what can be extremely complex – and rapidly changing – factual situations,[94] potentially leading to different characterisations of the same scenario. In the context of Israel's 2006 military operations against Hezbollah within Lebanon, for example, Marco Sassòli suggested that the situation should be seen as a common Article 2 international armed conflict, in light of the absence of

[91] See *ibid.*, 124, discussing this issue of, and the link between, capacity and incentive to comply.

[92] See, e.g., Solis, *The Law of Armed Conflict*, 157: 'Terrorist attacks, if the terrorists have a sufficient organization and if the attacks are sufficiently violent and protracted, may be instances of non-international common Article 3 conflicts. If not sufficiently organized, and if the attacks are not lengthy in nature, they are simply criminal events.'

[93] See Duffy, *The 'War on Terror'*, 252: 'A particular problem, at least in the light of current understandings of the nature of al-Qaeda, relates to the difficulty in defining what is variously described as an organisation, a movement or a "series of loosely connected operational and support cells" as an identifiable and distinct party to a conflict.' See also Vité, 'Typology of Armed Conflicts in International Humanitarian Law', 93; Pejić, 'Status of Armed Conflicts', 85; Sassòli, 'Transnational Armed Groups and International Humanitarian Law', 10–11.

[94] See the numerous differing interpretations of hostilities in Afghanistan from 7 October 2001 onwards in, e.g., Green, *The Contemporary Law of Armed Conflict*, 74; Duffy, *The 'War on Terror'*, 255–6; Dinstein, 'Terrorism and Afghanistan', 51–2; M. Sassòli, 'The International Legal Framework for Stability Operations: When May International Forces Attack or Detain Someone in Afghanistan?' in Schmitt, *The War in Afghanistan*, 432–3; Dworkin, 'Military Necessity and Due Process', 60–1; Lubell, *Extraterritorial Use of Force*, 112–21; D. Jinks, 'The Temporal Scope of Application of International Humanitarian Law in Contemporary Conflicts', Harvard University Program on Humanitarian Policy and Conflict Research, Background Paper prepared for the Informal High-Level Expert Meeting on the Reaffirmation and Development of International Humanitarian Law, Cambridge, 27–29 January 2003: www.hpcrresearch.org/sites/default/files/publications/Session3.pdf, 9; F. J. Hampson, 'Afghanistan 2001–2010', in E. Wilmshurst (ed.), *International Law and the Classification of Conflicts* (Oxford: Oxford University Press, 2012), 242.

Lebanese consent.[95] The UN Human Rights Council Commission of Inquiry similarly considered the situation to constitute an international armed conflict, despite accepting that the hostilities were carried out only between Israel and Hezbollah,[96] owing to its decision to characterise Hezbollah as agents of Lebanon. To the extent that Lebanon itself had been a direct target of Israeli action,[97] it was considered by the Commission to be a party to the conflict, and Hezbollah was accordingly a group 'belonging to a Party to the conflict' in terms of Article 4A(2) Geneva Convention III. As such, the hostilities were deemed international in character.[98] Others, however, saw the link between Hezbollah and Lebanon as being much less certain, with no clear relationship of agency or control, so that combat operations between Israel and Hezbollah – although carried out on Lebanese territory – represented an armed conflict that was instead non-international in character.[99]

Of course, the precise nature of the relationship between a host state and a non-state group is likely to be difficult to establish conclusively in many cases. Nonetheless, arguments as to how the specific facts of any particular situation can be accommodated within the relevant normative framework are a feature of all legal systems, and must not be confused with arguments as to what the law actually provides. As far as cross-border hostilities between states and non-state actors are concerned, and avoiding the confusion caused by an overly narrow interpretation of

[95] See Sassòli, 'Transnational Armed Groups and International Humanitarian Law', 5. Paulus and Vashakmadze, 'Asymmetrical War', 112, agree: 'If the Lebanese government had consented to Israel's intervention on its territory, the conflict would have constituted a non-international armed conflict between the state of Israel and Hezbollah. However, the Israeli military intervention occurred without Lebanon's consent and resulted in large-scale destruction of the Lebanese infrastructure.' As is, I hope, clear from the discussion above, this author does not, however, believe that a lack of state consent alone is sufficient to transform the nature of hostilities.

[96] Report of the Commission of Inquiry on Lebanon Pursuant to Human Rights Council Resolution S-2/1*, 23 November 2006 (UN Doc. A/HRC/3/2), para. 53.

[97] *Ibid.*, para. 58. [98] *Ibid.*, paras 50–62 and 65–8.

[99] See, e.g., Solis, *The Law of Armed Conflict*, 162: 'Given that the fighting in the Israel–Lebanon example – the armed conflict – does not directly involve the State of Lebanon or its armed forces, or those of any second state, it is reasonable to view the conflict as a common Article 3 conflict'. Vité, 'Typology of Armed Conflicts in International Humanitarian Law', 91–2 asserted that the non-international armed conflict between Israel and Hezbollah existed alongside a separate international armed conflict between Israel and Lebanon. See also Green, *The Contemporary Law of Armed Conflict*, 345; I. Scobbie, 'Lebanon 2006', in Wilmshurst, *International Law and the Classification of Conflicts*, 387.

common Article 3, the legal framework itself actually benefits from both clarity and simplicity:

> when a State enters into a conflict with a non-governmental armed group located in the territory of a neighbouring State and the armed group is acting under the control of its own State, 'the fighting falls within the definition of an international armed conflict between the two States'. However, if the armed group is not acting on behalf of a government, in the absence of two States opposing each other, there is no international armed conflict.[100]

[100] *Prosecutor* v. *Lubanga* (n. 26, above), para. 541.

5

Security Council mandates and the use of lethal force by peacekeepers: what place for the laws of war?

NIGEL D. WHITE

Introduction

Since the turn of the twenty-first century, peacekeepers have been under pressure to protect civilians and to protect the peace process. Peacekeepers have been criticised for being inactive in the face of violence when the mandates given to them by the Security Council clearly enable them, arguably require them, to use necessary measures against those who would undermine the peace or threaten civilians.[1]

The chapter will explore the gap between the Security Council's mandate and the use of lethal weapons by peacekeepers and its implications for the law applicable to the use of force by peacekeepers. The argument is that the more coercive the mandate becomes, the more it might be expected that peacekeepers use force in accordance with the laws of war. However, the reality is that, unless they (exceptionally) become combatants in an armed conflict, they remain bound by human rights law, specifically, to respect the right to life. The question then becomes whether the human rights legal framework is sufficient to allow peacekeepers to carry out their mandate or whether it is possible to identify a new legal framework as part of an emerging *jus post bellum*?

The focus of the chapter is on the military component of peace operations acting under the mandate, command and control of the United Nations (UN) – the blue helmets; although reference is also made to the police element of UN peace operations. The chapter will

[1] Especially in relation to the conflict in Darfur; for example, A. de Waal, 'Darfur and the Failure of the Responsibility to Protect', 83 *International Affairs* (2009) 1039; C. G. Badescu and L. Bergholm, 'The Responsibility to Protect and the Conflict in Darfur: The Big Let Down', 40 *Security Dialogue* (2009) 287.

trace the development of peace operations from their inception as limited military forces in the 1950s to their modern form, which is not only multifaceted but appears, from the mandates given by the Security Council to such operations over the last decade, to be more belligerent than their predecessors.

Peacekeepers, even at their inception, have been given functions that are less than those of combat yet more than those of law enforcement, but it is argued that this does not somehow place them in a legal no-man's-land. Instead, it is asserted that, despite increasingly coercive Security Council mandates, peacekeepers remain subject to international human rights law standards when using weapons and, only exceptionally, when actively engaged as combatants within an armed conflict situation, to international humanitarian law (IHL) standards – where the right to life is qualified by those laws of war that allow 'enemy' combatants to be engaged with lethal force.[2] There is, as yet, no intermediate position that might emerge as part of a developing *jus post bellum* regime.

Support for this position is drawn from two resources that feature in this book – the perspectives of the military lawyer and of Peter Rowe himself. First of all, support for the position adopted in this chapter is drawn from the argument of Rob McLaughlin of the Royal Australian Navy, who reasoned that there are only two legitimate paradigms for multinational peace operations acting under a Chapter VII mandate, one of armed conflict and another of law enforcement, and that the default position is that of law enforcement governed by human rights law.[3] This chapter adopts a similar position, although it approaches the subject through considering the nature, doctrine and practice of

[2] P. Rowe, *The Impact of Human Rights Law on Armed Forces* (Cambridge: Cambridge University Press, 2006), 135: The '*lex specialis* (international humanitarian law) *permits* a lawful combatant to kill another lawful combatant providing that the means of doing so are not, themselves, prohibited under that law'. See further, the International Court of Justice in *Legality of the Threat or Use of Nuclear Weapons*, ICJ Reports 1996, 240, para. 25: 'The protection of the International Covenant of Civil and Political Rights does not cease in times of war, except by operation of Article 4 of the Covenant whereby certain provisions may be derogated from in a time of national emergency. Respect for the right to life is not, however, such a provision. In principle, the right not arbitrarily to be deprived of one's life applies also in hostilities. The test of what is an arbitrary deprivation of life, however, then falls to be determined by the applicable *lex specialis*, namely, the law applicable in armed conflict which is designed to regulate the conduct of hostilities.'

[3] R. McLaughlin, 'The Legal Regime Applicable to the Use of Lethal Force When Operating under a United Nations Security Council Chapter VII Mandate Authorising All Necessary Means', 12 *JCSL* (2007) 389–417.

UN peacekeeping operations, and argues that the concept of self-defence, as developed by that doctrine and practice, is both wide enough to allow peacekeepers to perform their functions and specific enough to remain compliant with human rights law.

Further support is drawn from Peter Rowe, who convincingly reasoned that there are many operational, as well as legal, reasons why military contingents contributing to peacekeeping forces will not be combatants in an armed conflict, not least that it is very unlikely that 'participating states will wish to accept that they are engaged in an armed conflict and thereby lose' their legal protection 'even where their national contingents come under intense fire and a number are killed or wounded'.[4] For Rowe, the legal framework governing the use of lethal force by peacekeepers will be 'compiled from the national, military law and any human rights obligations' of the troop-contributing nations (TCNs).[5]

The nature and development of peacekeeping

Peacekeeping was essentially a development of the stifling and ubiquitous effects of the cold war and, as such, was not envisaged in the UN Charter. Nevertheless, it was vital in securing the basic goal of the UN, namely, a minimum level of peace and security in trouble spots around the world. This initially resulted in very small UN unarmed observer forces in colonial and post-colonial conflict zones in Indonesia, Kashmir and Palestine in the late 1940s, dispatched to provide the Security Council with a reliable account of the facts. This led, in 1956, to a fully fledged, lightly armed, but several-thousand-strong force (the UN Emergency Force – UNEF I) deployed to secure the peace by acting as a buffer between formerly hostile nations following the British/French/Israeli intervention in Sucz.

Although new in its day, this now 'traditional' type of peacekeeping, embodied in UNEF I, reflected classical principles of international law in that it was based on the consent of the host state or states and, even though it appeared to constitute military intervention, its respect for sovereignty was reflected in the neutrality of such forces. The restrictions on the use of force to defend peacekeepers or their equipment meant that

[4] P. Rowe, 'Maintaining Discipline in United Nations Peace Support Operations: The Legal Quagmire for Military Contingents', 5 *JCSL* (2000) 45, 52. See also Rowe, *The Impact of Human Rights Law on Armed Forces*, 227.

[5] Rowe, *The Impact of Human Rights Law on Armed Forces*, 233.

the trinity of peacekeeping principles (consent, impartiality and non-use of force)[6] reflected the fundamental principles of international law of sovereignty, non-intervention and non-use of force found in Article 2 of the UN Charter.[7]

The fact that the UN General Assembly mandated the original force (UNEF I) is no coincidence[8] in that its functions reflected the views of the Non Aligned majority, as well as traditional principles of international law that gave such states protection from intervention. However, peacekeeping subsequently crossed into the domain of the Security Council as part of its primary responsibility for peace and security under Article 24 of the UN Charter. This has led to the possibility of a more coercive peacekeeping force empowered, in whole or in part, under Chapter VII of the UN Charter.

The dialectic between consensual peacekeeping and its more belligerent variant was established as early as the second full peacekeeping force in the Congo in 1960–4 and was repeated, with less success, in the force in Somalia in 1993–5.[9] It is currently back on the agenda as the UN struggles to implement the 'responsibility to protect',[10] 'protection of civilians in armed conflict',[11] and 'human security' agendas,[12] through, *inter alia*, 'protection' mandates given to UN forces by the Security Council.[13] These mandates typically authorise the UN force under Chapter VII 'to use all necessary means to carry out its mandate, within its capabilities and its areas of deployment', including 'to protect civilians under imminent threat of physical violence'.[14]

In general, the orthodoxy is that such mandates are compatible with the traditional principles of international law and peacekeeping[15] and, therefore, do not constitute full-blown military enforcement action against a state on a par with the UN-authorised actions in Korea in 1950–3 and the Gulf in 1991 (whose constitutional base is Article 42 of

[6] Report of the Special Committee on Peacekeeping Operations, GAOR 66th Session, supplement no. 19 (New York: United Nations, 2012), para. 25.

[7] *Ibid.* [8] UNGA Res. 998–1001 (1956). [9] UNSC Res. 814 (1993), 897 (1994).

[10] As formulated at the UN's World Summit Outcome Document of 2005 in UNGA Res. 60/1 (2005) paras 139–9.

[11] See, e.g., UNSC Res. 1674 (2006) on the protection of civilians.

[12] Human security was first posited in the UNDP's Human Development Report, New Dimension in Human Security (New York: United Nations, 1994).

[13] N. D. White, 'Empowering Peace Operations to Protect Civilians: Form Over Substance', 13 *Journal of International Peacekeeping* (2009) 327.

[14] UNSC Res. 1528 (2004) establishing UNOCI in the Ivory Coast.

[15] *Certain Expenses of the United Nations*, ICJ Reports 1962, 163–4.

Chapter VII of the UN Charter).[16] The late 1980s and early 1990s saw the end of the cold war and a change in UN interventions, with operations in Namibia, Nicaragua, El Salvador, Cambodia and Mozambique becoming multi-functional by combining peacekeeping with limited peace-building. The latter was usually centred on the holding of elections as the pivotal event between conflict and a stable state. Such operations were a mixed success, with a number failing because the electoral process did not engage factions sufficiently to prevent a fresh outbreak of fighting (for instance, in Angola in the 1990s).[17] Furthermore, these developments did not prevent the occurrence of egregious human rights violations under the noses of peacekeepers, most shockingly the genocides in Rwanda and Srebrenica.[18]

More integrated extensive peace operations have emerged since the 2000 Brahimi Report.[19] Such operations combine peacekeeping with more ambitious peace-building; the latter consisting of much more than the crude introduction of Western-style democracy to an often alien environment. Given that such operations are often conducted in fragile or failed states, there has been a trend towards enabling the military element of such operations to use force beyond the traditional limited form of self-defence possessed by peacekeepers.

The increasing complexity of peace operations that followed the recommendations of the 2000 Brahimi Report has been described as a process of 'civilianisation' of peace operations, whereby the still large military peacekeeping component is matched by the inclusion of 'civil administration, humanitarian assistance, policing, electoral, human rights monitoring, economic revival functions and personnel'.[20] In some ways this disguises the changes that have been wrought, at least at the level of the mandate, in the military element.

Arguably, the developing nature and function of modern complex peace operations reflect changes in international law in which the

16 UNSC Res. 83 (1950); UNSC Res. 678 (1990).

17 V. P. Fortna, 'United Nations Angola Verification Mission', in W. J. Durch (ed.), *The Evolution of UN Peacekeeping* (Basingstoke: Macmillan, 1994), 353.

18 See Report of the Independent Inquiry into the Actions of the United Nations during the 1994 Genocide in Rwanda, 15 Dec 1999 (UN Doc. S/1999/1257); Report of the Secretary-General Pursuant to General Assembly Resolution, the Fall of Srebrenica, 15 November 1999 (UN Doc. A/54/549).

19 Report of the Panel on United Nations Peace Operations, 21 August 2000 (UN Doc. A/55/305 and S/2000/809) (hereinafter Brahimi Report).

20 J. Cockayne and D. Malone, 'United Nations Peace Operations: Then and Now', 9 *International Peacekeeping: The Yearbook of International Peace Operations* (2005) 18.

prominence of external self-determination in the period of decolonisation and independence of new states has, to a large extent, been replaced by concerns for internal self-determination within existing states, while the protection and enhancement of human rights and human security (of individuals and groups) have supplemented the traditional concern for security between states. This has led to twenty-first-century peace operations being furnished, as a matter of course, with Chapter VII elements in their mandates empowering them to protect the peace process and civilians under threat of attack, while still being based on the consent of the host state.

The move towards greater coercion by UN peace operations has continued apace. Although they remain distinct from military enforcement action taken by a coalition of the willing (CoW), this is often more in composition and command and control than in the mandates. The NATO-led IFOR and KFOR operations in Bosnia and Kosovo, although under UN mandates,[21] operate under delegated command and control and, moreover, are equipped and, at least at their inception, were mandated to undertake potentially much deadlier levels of force than UN-commanded and controlled blue-helmeted forces.[22] That distinction has become somewhat eroded. The NATO-led forces are authorised to operate against states and non-state actors alike,[23] while UN operations generally operate against non-state actors (spoilers), those that threaten civilians and, exceptionally, organised rebel and insurgent armed groups.[24] This means that although UN peace operations do not undertake peace enforcement against a state potentially in

[21] UNSC Res. 1031 (1995) re IFOR in Bosnia; UNSC Res. 1244 (1999) re KFOR in Kosovo.

[22] See, e.g., para. 9(a) of UNSC Res. 1244 (1999), which decided that KFOR's responsibilities included 'deterring renewed hostilities, maintaining and where necessary enforcing a ceasefire, and ensuring the withdrawal and preventing the return into Kosovo of Federal and Republic military, police and paramilitary forces'.

[23] See, e.g., para. 15 of UNSC Res. 1031 (1995), which authorised IFOR to 'take all necessary measures to affect the implementation of and to ensure compliance with Annex 1-A of the peace agreement', stressed that 'all parties shall be held equally responsible for compliance, and shall be equally subject to such enforcement action by IFOR as may be necessary to ensure implementation of that Annex'.

[24] See, e.g., UNSC Res. 1925 (2010), which established United Nations Organisation Stabilisation Mission in the Democratic Republic of the Congo (MONUSCO) in the Democratic Republic of the Congo (DRC) (to replace the United Nations Organisation Mission in the Democratic Republic of the Congo (MONUC)), and emphasised the primary responsibility of the government for security, but stated that MONUSCO and the government should, *inter alia*, secure the 'completion of the ongoing military

an international armed conflict, they may become engaged as combatants in a non-international armed conflict involving non-state actors.[25]

Thus, increasingly coercive mandates would suggest that peacekeepers can cross the line to become war-fighters, or 'combatants' in the language of the laws of war (IHL), sometimes causing confusion as to the legal status of peacekeepers, who are traditionally not seen as legitimate targets. Indeed, attacks on them remain prohibited under the 1994 UN Safety Convention.[26] In 1999, the UN Secretary-General attempted to clarify the non-combatant status of peacekeepers, even in situations of armed conflict, by declaring that they are to be viewed as civilians under IHL unless, and until, they actively engage as combatants in an armed conflict.[27]

It is in this complex, constantly shifting and often dangerous environment that armed UN peacekeepers and police operate, with the potential to (mis)use lethal weapons.

Widening of defensive use of force

Over the lifetime of peacekeeping operations there has been confusion as to the nature and level of force that peacekeepers are permitted to use. Sitting somewhere between a military combat operation and an armed police operation,[28] this confusion is unsurprising, even though the UN has had plenty of practice in which to develop clear norms on the use of force.

At its core, the limited use of force available to peacekeepers means self-defence, which is normally interpreted narrowly to cover a peacekeeper using force in defence of his own life, his 'comrades and any person entrusted in [his] care, as well as defending [his] post, convoy,

operations in the Kivus and Orientale Province, resulting in minimizing the threat of armed groups and restoring security in sensitive areas'.

[25] In either case there is enforcement action requiring the authority of the Security Council. See UNSC Res. 1744 (2007) re African Union (AU) force (AMISOM) mandated to fight alongside government forces against al-Shabaab.

[26] 1994 UN Convention on the Safety of United Nations and Associated Personnel, Articles 7–9.

[27] UN Secretary-General's Bulletin, 'Observance by United Nations Forces of International Humanitarian Law' (UN Doc. ST/SGB/1999/13), 1999, sect. 1.2. On the difficulty of reconciling the Bulletin with the 1994 Convention, see Rowe, 'Maintaining Discipline in United Nations Peace Support Operations', 52–3.

[28] A position that has become even more acute with the end of the cold war, see M. Kaldor, *New and Old Wars: Organized Violence in a Global Era* (Stanford, CA: Stanford University Press, 1999), 125.

vehicle or rifle'.[29] Beyond this there has been a continuing lack of clarity as to whether the force could also 'defend' that force's mandate.

While UNEF stuck to a narrow interpretation of self-defence by using light arms to defend itself, by 1960 there was an alternative version of peacekeeping in the Congo. ONUC used a variety of weapons: mortars, fighter and bomber aircraft, light armoured vehicles, as well as rifles, light automatic weapons and bayonets and anti-tank and anti-aircraft weapons.[30] ONUC initially confined its use of force to self-defence when overseeing the withdrawal of Belgian troops, but that proved inadequate when its task became the elimination of the mercenaries supporting the Katangese secession.[31] In reality, in 1961, ONUC had ceased to act in a defensive way and began to take the initiative and enforce the peace by engaging the forces of non-state actors in combat.[32]

This has also occurred in more recent operations; for example, in July 2012, the United Nations Organisation Stabilisation Mission in the Democratic Republic of the Congo (MONUSCO) used offensive force, including attack helicopters, against M23 rebels in the Democratic Republic of the Congo (DRC); and in April 2011, United Nations Operation in the Ivory Coast (UNOCI) used attack helicopters against the heavy weapons of the forces of former President Laurent Gbagbo in the Ivory Coast.

Despite a post-cold war trend towards allowing more offensive action to be taken by peacekeepers, there remains reluctance, especially from TCNs, to move away from self-defence as this makes the force less acceptable to the host state and the parties within it. Thus, narrow self-defence remains the norm for modern peacekeeping, even those peace operations having Chapter VII elements to their mandates, requiring them to protect the peace process and civilians.

However, despite this reticence in practice, the UN has expanded the concept of self-defence at the doctrinal level. The Brahimi Report of 2000 did this by extending the language of self-defence from individual self-defence to defence of the mission.[33] This forms part of the doctrinal development of when legitimate force can be used by peacekeepers

[29] 'General Guidelines for Peace-Keeping Operations' (UN Doc. UN/210/TC/CG95) (1995).

[30] G. I. A. D. Draper, 'The Legal Limitations Upon the Employment of Weapons by the United Nations Force in the Congo', 12 *ICLQ* (1963) 396.

[31] UNSC Res. 169 (1961). [32] UNSC Res. 161 (1961). [33] Brahimi Report, paras 48–51.

through the 'gradual expansion of the meaning of self-defense in PKOs, from individual self-defense inherent to military personnel, to freedom of movement and defense of positions, to the defense of the mandate and the protection of third parties'.[34]

This development is reflected in the UN's latest statement of peacekeeping doctrine in the 2008 Principles and Guidelines document (sometimes known as the Capstone Document) – which, while still distinguishing peacekeeping from enforcement action, states that it is 'widely understood that peacekeeping forces may use force at the tactical level, with the authorization of the Security Council, if acting in self-defense and defense of the mandate'.[35] However, the reality is that once self-defence is so expanded it is no longer individual self-defence but is a mandate permitting a certain level of enforcement (of measures of the type envisaged by Article 40 of Chapter VII), though short of full peace-enforcement under Article 42 of Chapter VII.

Thus, increasing pressure is on peacekeepers to use force to protect civilians under attack or under threat of attack and to protect the peace agreement and process from 'spoilers' wishing to undermine it. With the greater use of weapons that this potentially entails, the problem becomes the choice as to which legal regime should be applicable to modern peace operations – that applicable in armed conflict (IHL) or international human rights law norms.

Applicable law: international humanitarian law or international human rights law?

Increasingly coercive mandates mean that peacekeepers can potentially cross the line to become 'combatants', in the language of the laws of war (IHL), sometimes causing confusion as to the legal status of peacekeepers who are traditionally not seen as legitimate targets.[36] In 1999, UN

[34] N. Tsagourias, 'Consent, Neutrality/Impartiality and the Use of Force in Peacekeeping Operations: Their Constitutional Dimension', 11 *JCSL* (2006) 465, 473.

[35] United Nations Peacekeeping Operations: Principles and Guidelines (UN, 2008), 31 (hereinafter Capstone Document).

[36] See judgment of the Special Court for Sierra Leone in *Prosecutor* v. *Issa Hassan Sesay, Morris Kallon and Augustine Gbao* (Case No. SCSL-04-15-A: Special Court for Sierra Leone (Appeals Chamber), 26 October 2009) (*RUF* case), which was concerned with the criminality of attacks by RUF rebel forces against UNAMSIL in Sierra Leone. For discussion, see J. Sloan, 'Peacekeepers under Fire: Prosecuting the RUF for Attacks against the UN Assistance Mission for Sierra Leone', 9 *Law and Practice of International Courts and Tribunals* (2010) 243.

Secretary-General Kofi Annan, in a piece of internal UN law, reasserted the civilian status of peacekeepers, even in situations of armed conflict, by declaring that they are to be viewed as civilians under IHL unless and until they actively engage as combatants in an armed conflict.[37] This establishes the default position of a peacekeeper as a non-combatant, with him or her only becoming a combatant in exceptional circumstances.[38] This should be contrasted with the legal status of US and other soldiers sent to fight against Iraqi forces in Kuwait, under a UN enforcement mandate,[39] who were clearly instructed to engage the enemy,[40] thereby recognising that they were lawful combatants and also legitimate targets in an armed conflict.

IHL is applicable during an armed conflict, and thus is primarily applicable to the *in bello*, rather than the *post bellum*, stage (with the exception of the law of occupation). If, however, violence persists or flares up in the post-war phase and reaches the level of an armed conflict of a non-international character (defined by the International Criminal Tribunal for the former Yugoslavia as protracted armed violence between governmental authorities and organized armed groups within a state),[41] then IHL applies to the parties to that conflict and also to a UN peacekeeping operation should it engage, as a party to a conflict, against organised armed groups. Being based in the host state with the consent of that government signifies that a peacekeeping force would not become engaged against the forces of the host state in an international armed conflict. Indeed, if it

[37] UN Secretary-General's Bulletin, 'Observance by United Nations Forces of International Humanitarian Law', sect. 1.2.

[38] However, see Peter Rowe's point that the Bulletin's assumption is that the UN may become a party to a non-international armed conflict does not accord with Article 2(2) of the 1994 Convention, under which peacekeepers remain protected until they are 'engaged as combatants against organized armed forces and to which the law of international armed conflict applies': Rowe, 'Maintaining Discipline in United Nations Peace Support Operations', 52. Thus, Rowe concludes that the 'protection of the 1994 Convention would continue to apply to UN and associated personnel as long as they are not engaged in an *international* armed conflict as a party to the conflict. Thus, even if they are, technically, parties to a *non-international* armed conflict, the protection of the 1994 Convention would apply. The Secretary-General's Bulletin, however, produces a different result. It leads to the conclusion that all combatants in whatever type of armed conflict are equal in the eyes of international humanitarian law and that those who attack UN forces have a "right" to do so providing they also comply with the fundamental principles and rules of that law': *ibid.*, 53–4.

[39] UNSC Res. 678 (1990).

[40] See Pocket Card in A. Roberts and R. Guelff (eds), *Documents on the Laws of War* (Oxford: Oxford University Press, 2000), 561.

[41] *Prosecutor* v. *Tadić* (1996) 105 *ILR* 488.

were to, the peacekeeping force would cease to be a peacekeeping operation and would become a non-consensual enforcement action requiring authorisation under Article 42 of the UN Charter.

All this suggests that IHL does not play a significant role in a post-war situation to which peacekeepers are deployed and it is the *jus post bellum*, more accurately, those aspects of general international law, human rights law, refugee law and international criminal law, as well as the national criminal and military laws of the TCNs and national law of the host state, that together frame the work of a peace operation.

This doctrinal position is reflected in practice. A review of a sample of current UN operations shows that peacekeepers will only exceptionally become engaged as a party in a non-international armed conflict. An examination of documentation (UN force press briefings and other documents, as well as the Secretary-General's reports and Security Council resolutions) of three different types of UN peacekeeping force over the last five years – in Cyprus (a traditional force), in Liberia (in a dangerous but stable state) and in the DRC (where protracted armed violence regularly breaks out) – reveals that while the force in Cyprus has not used any significant force in the last five years and the Liberian force has only used force in relatively narrow circumstances of self-defence and in dealing with riots, the Congo force has regularly used both defensive force to protect itself and civilians and, occasionally, alongside government forces, offensive force against armed groups who undermine the peace and threaten civilians.[42] It is only in the latter situation, when fighting alongside government forces against organised armed groups, that the peacekeepers should be applying the laws of war.

It follows that for most peacekeepers the relevant international laws will be those governing human rights. The existence of human rights obligations on peacekeepers flows from two main sources. The first source for peacekeepers is as state agents and comes from the human rights obligations of their sending states under human rights treaties,[43] which attach to them, even when acting extraterritorially, in circumstances where they exercise control over areas or individuals. Although human rights jurisprudence is mixed, there is some indirect support,

[42] Data on file with the author, who would like to thank Auriane Botte, PhD student in the School of Law at the University of Nottingham, for painstakingly gathering this data.

[43] Consider also the human rights obligations of the host states to ensure that human rights within its jurisdiction are protected: Rowe, *The Impact of Human Rights Law on Armed Forces*, 234.

from the Inter-American Commission on Human Rights, for making a further argument that when peacekeepers fire weapons at individuals they are, in effect, asserting jurisdiction over them for the purposes of human rights law.[44] However, the orthodox view is that found in the General Comment of the Human Rights Committee in 2004 where it stated that parties to the International Covenant on Civil and Political Rights must ensure the human rights of persons 'within the power or effective control of the forces of a State Party acting outside its territory [. . .] such as forces constituting a national contingent of a State Party assigned to an international peace-keeping or peace-enforcement operation'.[45]

The second source of human rights obligation applies to peacekeepers as members of a UN force, given the UN's obligations under customary international law that attach to it as an international legal person.[46] The International Law Commission (ILC) 2011 Articles on the Responsibility of International Organizations clearly show that it is possible to attribute wrongful acts to the UN;[47] such responsibility is based on it having duties under customary international law, including ones to uphold and protect human rights.

The use of lethal force and the right to life

Having established that human rights law is normally applicable to peacekeepers[48] and that even a more belligerent force will only

[44] L. Doswald-Beck, *Human Rights in Times of Conflict and Terrorism* (Oxford: Oxford University Press, 2011), 19–21 citing cases where the state has been held to be in breach of the right to life when firing at a person from a distance; for example, *Armando Alejandre Jr, Carlos Costa, Mario de la Pena and Pablo Morales* v. *Cuba (Brothers to the Rescue case)*, Case 11.589, Report No. 86/99, 29 September 1999, para. 25. But, see the European Court of Human Rights decision in *Banković and others* v. *17 NATO States*, Admissibility Decision (Grand Chamber), 12 December 2001, paras 52–3.

[45] Human Rights Committee, General Comment 31, 'Nature of the General Legal Obligation on States Parties to the Covenant', UN Doc CCPR/C/21/Rev.1/Add.13 (2004), para. 10.

[46] *Reparation for Injuries Suffered in the Service of the United Nations*, ICJ Reports 1949, 174–8; *Interpretation of the Agreement of 25 March 1951 between the WHO and Egypt*, ICJ Reports 1980, 73, 89–90.

[47] ILC, Draft Articles on the Responsibility of International Organizations, Articles 3–7 (UN Doc. A/66/10) (2011); taken note of in UNGA Res. 66/100 (2011).

[48] See further, N. D. White, 'Use of Weapons in Peace Operations', in Stuart Casey-Maslen (ed.), *Weapons under International Human Rights Law* (Cambridge: Cambridge University Press, 2014); D. Stephens, 'The Lawful Use of Force by Peacekeeping Forces: The Tactical Imperative', 12 *International Peacekeeping* (2005) 163.

occasionally become engaged as combatants, and so subject to humanitarian law, it would appear that modern peacekeepers are placed between the rock of human rights constraints and the hard place of a Security Council mandate that appears to require them to use lethal force in a range of circumstances.

The fact that UN peacekeepers and armed police carry weapons, the use of which may cause deaths, seems at first glance to be incompatible with the right to life. When, if at all, is the taking of life by UN peacekeepers and police justified? Major human rights treaties make it clear that the right to life, though fundamental, is not absolute. The basic principle is that life cannot be taken arbitrarily.[49] Louise Doswald-Beck suggests that in order to understand when life is not taken arbitrarily a good starting place is Article 2(2) of the European Convention on Human Rights, which, in contrast to Article 6 of the International Covenant on Civil and Political Rights, details when lethal force is permitted.

Drawing on this, essentially, during peacetime and situations short of armed conflict, lethal force can only be used when absolutely necessary for self-defence (including defence of third parties), to effect an arrest or prevent escape of a detainee, or in action taken to quell a riot or insurrection; while during an armed conflict IHL applies to those engaged in it as combatants, when the right to life is further qualified, although civilians and those *hors de combat* remain protected. This provides a relatively clear legal framework within which peacekeepers should operate.

A more detailed examination of UN policy and guidelines on when peacekeepers can use force, including lethal force, shows that the UN largely acts within this legal framework, indeed, that the UN frames its policies and directives largely within the parameters of international human rights law, rather than IHL. For example, the Department of Peacekeeping Operations' *Handbook on United Nations Multidimensional Peacekeeping Operations* of 2003 provides that self-defence includes the 'right to protect oneself, other UN personnel, UN property and other persons under UN protection', though it does recognise that the Security Council can, exceptionally, authorise an operation to use armed force in situations other than self-defence, which might suggest going beyond the human rights standard. Beyond that the Handbook leaves it to the mission-specific Rules of Engagement (RoE) to 'clarify the different

49 Doswald-Beck, *Human Rights in Times of Conflict and Terrorism*, 161.

levels of the use of force that can be used in various circumstances, how each level of force should be used and any authorizations that may need to be obtained from commanders'.[50]

RoE perform a mediatory role between the mandate and the actual use of force by peacekeepers. They 'specify the circumstances in which armed force may be used by a military unit and its permissible extent and degree'.[51] RoE 'provide as clearly as possible the parameters within which armed military personnel assigned to a peacekeeping operation may use force'.[52] In this way, it has been argued that RoE are more important than the Security Council's mandate in determining the actual level and extent of force used by a peacekeeping component.[53] RoE are usually not 'regarded as legal instruments in their own right, but rather they reflect the law and thus are intended to ensure that military forces act within the law. The "law" in question may comprise both national and international law'.[54]

Each mission's RoE govern the use of force by military peacekeepers and directives on the use of force (DUFs) govern the use of force by any police contingent to the mission. Both are developed by the UN Department of Peacekeeping Operations (DPKO) in New York. In 2002, the UN produced draft RoE,[55] though their current status is unclear. Oswald, Durham and Bates assert that the 'legal foundation for DUF is primarily' international human rights law, whereas the 'legal framework for RoE is a combination of' IHL and international human rights law.[56] This analysis of the legal framework for the RoE of the peacekeeping

[50] DPKO, 'Handbook on United Nations Multidimensional Peacekeeping Operations' (New York: United Nations, 2003), 57.

[51] H. McCoubrey and N. D. White, *The Blue Helmets: Legal Regulation of United Nations Military Operations* (Aldershot: Dartmouth, 1996), 146.

[52] R. Zacklin, 'The Use of Force in Peacekeeping Operations' in N. M. Blokker and N. Schrijver (eds), *The Security Council and the Use of Force* (Leiden: Martinus Nijhoff, 2005), 100.

[53] P. Rowe, 'The United Nations Rules of Engagement and the British Soldier in Bosnia', 43 *ICLQ* (1994), 947.

[54] D. Stephens, 'The Lawful Use of Force by Peacekeeping Forces: The Tactical Imperative', 12 *International Peacekeeping* (2005), 163.

[55] UNDPKO, 'Guidelines for the Development of Rules of Engagement (ROE) for United Nations Peace-Keeping Operations', May 2002 (UN Doc. MD/FGS/0220.0001), in C. K. Penny, 'Drop That or I'll Shoot ... Maybe: International Law and the Use of Deadly Force to Defend Property in UN Peace Operations', 14 *International Peacekeeping* (2007), 365.

[56] B. Oswald, H. Durham and A. Bates (eds), *Documents on the Law of UN Peace Operations* (Oxford: Oxford University Press, 2010), 562.

component raises some concerns. The RoE of such forces should only reflect IHL if, and only to the extent that, they exceptionally become engaged as combatants within an armed conflict and, therefore, should normally be framed by international human rights law not a 'mixture' of the two.

Although a systematic review of RoE is not possible, materials that reflect the RoE, such as soldiers' pocket cards, training materials, standards and rules, all suggest that it is the case that RoE are largely framed by human rights law and, indeed, should be framed by such law and only exceptionally by the laws of war.[57] Of course, if the mandate is for military enforcement action wherein the force will be engaged as combatants in an armed conflict, then the framework for the RoE will largely be the laws of war,[58] although it must not be forgotten that human rights law continues to apply during armed conflict.

As mentioned above, the 2008 Capstone Document expands somewhat on when potentially lethal force may be used, stating that peacekeeping operations may 'use force at the tactical level, with the authorization of the Security Council, if acting in self-defense and defense of the mandate'. Again, the latter seems open-ended, but the Capstone Document goes on to explain that 'all necessary means', which would include lethal force where necessary, may be used against 'militias, criminal gangs, and other spoilers who may actively seek to undermine the peace process or pose a threat to the civilian population' in order to 'deter forceful attempts to disrupt the political process, protect civilians under imminent threat of physical attack, and/or assist the national authorities in maintaining law and order'.[59]

It is possible to interpret these guidelines as being compatible with human rights standards if the provisions recognising that potentially lethal force may be used when absolutely necessary to effect an arrest or in tackling riots and insurrections is applied to include these, and analogous, situations faced by peacekeepers when force is absolutely necessary to tackle militias, criminal gangs and other armed spoilers who undermine the peace or threaten civilians. If this purposive interpretation is adopted, then it follows that there is sufficient leeway in

57 McLaughlin, 'The Legal Regime Applicable to the Use of Lethal Force', 411.

58 As in UNSC Res. 678 (1990), which authorised the use of force to expel Iraq from Kuwait, and reflected in the RoE given to Coalition forces to engage the enemy.

59 Capstone Document, 34–5.

human rights law to enable peacekeepers to perform their functions using potentially lethal force where absolutely necessary.

There remains the problem of ensuring that peacekeepers do not exceed these standards under the guise of a Chapter VII mandate that authorises 'necessary measures', for necessary measures in a situation short of armed conflict are those absolutely necessary to defend civilians or to defend peacekeepers when tackling those who undermine the peace.[60] There also remains the problem, found in many UN documents, of peacekeepers being permitted to use deadly force to protect UN property, which is generally difficult to reconcile with human rights law,[61] although it is permissible in some circumstances under IHL.

Article 103 of the UN Charter, which states that obligations derived from the Charter prevail over those in any other international treaty, does not affect the analysis given above for a number of reasons, two of which will be mentioned. First, Article 103 does not affect customary obligations under human rights law and protecting the right to life is one of those. Second, Security Council obligations cannot override human rights treaty obligations unless the Security Council expressly states that this is the case. Drawing upon the European Court of Human Rights judgment in the case *Al-Jedda* of 2011, it is for TCNs to interpret Security Council mandates to peacekeepers to use necessary measures in line with their human rights obligations unless, and until, the Security Council clearly exempts states from these obligations.[62]

[60] Labelled 'active' self-defence by McLaughlin, 'The Legal Regime Applicable to the Use of Lethal Force', 410.

[61] It may be possible, in certain limited circumstances, to reconcile defence of property with human rights law if, for example, lethal force is used to prevent insurgents acquiring and using UN weapons against peacekeepers or civilians – K. M. Larsen, *Human Rights Treaty Obligations of Peacekeepers* (Cambridge: Cambridge University Press, 2012), 376–7, 379–80. See further, the UN Special Rapporteur on extrajudicial summary or arbitrary executions who stated that 'protection of property cannot be invoked as a justification for the use of potentially lethal force unless it is somehow linked to the defence of life': Report of the Special Rapporteur annexed to UN Doc. A/66/330, 30 August 2011, para. 43.

[62] 'The Court does not consider that the language used in this Resolution indicates unambiguously that the Security Council intended to place Member States within the Multi-National Force under an obligation to use measures of indefinite internment without charge and without judicial guarantees, in breach of their undertakings under international human rights instrument including the Convention': *Al Jedda* v. *The United Kingdom*, Application No. 27021/08, Judgment, 7 July 2011, para. 105. But see Larsen, *Human Rights Treaty Obligations of Peacekeepers*, 380.

Positive obligations to prevent the arbitrary deprivation of life

The argument so far has been that while human rights law allows peacekeepers to use lethal force where absolutely necessary and proportionate in self-defence, in defence of third parties and to deal with armed spoilers, they cannot go beyond that by adopting some of the more generous rules of IHL unless, and until, they become engaged as combatants in an armed conflict. There is no halfway house between human rights law and IHL and this should be borne in mind by the Security Council, the Secretary-General and the UNDPKO when mandating, assembling and directing the activities of a peacekeeping force.

The UN's interpretation of when peacekeepers can use force seems to accord, with some exceptions, with the obligation on TCNs and the UN not to take life arbitrarily, but pressure will increase on peacekeepers to use lethal force more extensively. Thus, care must be taken to ensure that policies and guidelines do not broaden the circumstances of when force can be used beyond the frameworks provided by international law.

Furthermore, as the Human Rights Committee points out, the obligation on states, and by analogy the UN, is not only to ensure that their agents do not arbitrarily take life, but also to take positive measures to protect that right.[63] Those positive obligations, drawn from treaty body practice on both law enforcement and military activities, are: first, the presence of clear laws prohibiting the 'arbitrary use of potentially lethal force'; second, adequate training of military, security and police personnel to ensure they respect the law; third, adequate planning of any peace operation to prevent arbitrary loss of life as much as possible;[64] and, finally, provision for independent investigation and, if necessary, criminal prosecution of violators.[65] Access to justice for victims should also be included in the last obligation, including non-judicial avenues of redress.

Looking at the UN's doctrine and practice in this regard there are a number of deficiencies that will be pointed out.

63 Human Rights Committee, 'General Comment 6 on Article 6', 30 April 1982, §5.

64 Drawing upon the European Court of Human Rights, *McCann* v. *United Kingdom*, Judgment, Application No. 18984/91, 27 September 1995.

65 Doswald-Beck, *Human Rights in Times of Conflict and Terrorism*, 162, 167.

Whether there is UN law governing when lethal force may be used by peace operations

While there are a number of UN documents (more for UN police than for peacekeepers) specifying when lethal force can be used, they are primarily concerned with redefining the notion of self-defence. The detail is left to RoE for the military component of peace operations and DUF for the police element, arguably leaving a gap in which the UN should provide more precise, but generally applicable, regulations on when lethal force can be used. The key document is the 1990 Basic Principles on the Use of Force and Firearms by Law Enforcement Officials,[66] which is viewed in the UN system as normative.[67] Although it may well have become custom, its terms are limited to police enforcement. While some of its principles are also applicable to peacekeepers, there is a need for an equivalent document for UN peacekeepers. This document should still be based on human rights law, but should clarify when lethal force can be used against spoilers and other armed groups. It should also clarify the UN's position on protection of UN property, which is inconsistent with human rights standards.[68]

Whether there is adequate training of personnel in respect for the law

Analysis of UN documents on training reveals that, for peacekeepers, the responsibility to ensure that soldiers are properly trained, presumably including basic weapons training, falls on member states, though the Secretary-General is requested to prepare training materials to assist those states in this regard.[69]

The development of training materials at UN level and ensuring that TCNs use them are both essential if the UN is to reduce the unevenness of training within TCNs, where it can be envisaged that, left to their own devices, there will be contingents with little or no training, a number that

[66] Endorsed in UNGA Res. 45/166 (1990) para. 4.

[67] Policy on Formed Police Units in United Nations Peacekeeping Operations (UNDPKO2009.32), para. 21.

[68] For efforts to promote a 'human rights' revision of the UN's standard SOFA, see the project based at Essex University: www.essex.ac.uk/plrp/documents/model_sofa_peliminay_report_august_2010.pdf.

[69] UNGA Res. 49/37 (1995).

are well trained in IHL, but not in human rights law, and others that have comprehensive training programmes.

Pre-Deployment Training Standards are, since 2007, now being produced by the UNDKO. However, they are not encouraging when considered against the applicable laws that have been identified thus far. For example, the 'Human Rights Standard in the Use of Force', produced in 2009, does not contain a 'standard' as such, but simply states that the training module on this issue will 'provide participants with a clear understanding of the human rights implications relating to the use of force and firearms by law enforcement officials'.[70]

Even more worryingly, in 2011, the DPKO produced the 'UN Protection of Civilian PDT Standards' that, on the one hand, restate the rules on self-defence that have been identified since 1956 and, on the other, then go much further than this when contemplating mandates with Chapter VII elements. The document provides that all UN peacekeepers have an inherent right to defend themselves by using force, up to and including deadly force if necessary. In addition, peacekeepers, authorised under Chapter VII, can use such force 'to prevent, pre-empt, and respond effectively to acts of, or imminent threat of, violence against civilians from any source, including host-state bodies or authorities'.[71]

As a 'standard' this leaves a great deal to be desired, potentially encouraging broad interpretations of when deadly force can be used and when weapons can be fired, for instance, 'pre-emptively'. Furthermore, though it is true to say that the impartial enforcement of a protection mandate should not distinguish between states and non-state actors who threaten civilians, the fact is that action against the government will constitute enforcement action rather than peacekeeping.

Whether there is adequate planning of peace operations in terms of mandate, size and equipment (including weapons) to limit to the greatest degree loss of life (including the lives of UN peacekeepers, UN police and civilians)

Training, no matter how comprehensive, will only be effective if there has been adequate planning so that the force deployed is capable of meeting the exigencies of the situation and environment it is deployed to. This is recognised by the 2008 Capstone Document:

[70] ITS/DPET, 'Police STM: Human Rights Standard in the Use of Force', 4/2009, 9.
[71] DPKO, 'UN Protection of Civilian PDT Standards' (UNDPKO, 2011), 20.

> The Secretariat has a responsibility to provide the Security Council with an accurate assessment of the risks associated with its decision to deploy a United Nations peacekeeping operation, and ensure that its mandate and capabilities are tailored to the requirements of the situation.[72]

However, the realities of putting a peace operation together often result in peace operations that are, at least initially, inadequate for the task. An examination of the UN Secretary-General's initial reports to the UN Security Council, advising on the nature and extent of the operation for a particular situation, often reveals this as he struggles to put in place a force that is sufficient in size and adequately equipped and supported.

The reality is that in the deployment period up to full complement, the greatest danger is to civilians and to the peace process, not from the arbitrary use of force by UN personnel, but from ongoing violence committed by non-state actors.

Whether there is automatic investigation into when life is arbitrarily taken by a UN peacekeeper and into provision for access to justice for victims

Arguably, even in the exceptional circumstances of armed conflict, independent investigation of uses of lethal force by UN peacekeepers or police, as well as when the lives of UN personnel are themselves lost, is required. In conditions short of armed conflict such investigation is clearly required under human rights law. Within the UN system, this function is performed by the Office of Internal Oversight Services (OIOS),[73] though its 'Investigations Manual' of 2009[74] makes it clear that each TCN has 'sovereign rights and primary responsibility' to investigate allegations of misconduct by its military personnel. Nevertheless, OIOS investigators may play a role if the TCN so requests, or if the TCN has failed to respond to a complaint, but such an investigation is subject to the national and military law of the TCN.[75]

In terms of access to justice for victims, there are a number of UN laws and practices providing remedies, though they tend not to be specifically human rights focused, yet the reality is that many abuses will go unpunished and victims will remain without redress. The 1946 Convention on the Privileges and Immunities of the United Nations, which grants the

[72] Capstone Document, 49. [73] UNGA Res. 48/218B (1994).
[74] Available at www.un.org/Depts/oios/pages/id_manual_mar2009.pdf.
[75] *Ibid.*, para. 6.5.5.

UN and its agents legal immunities, still requires that the UN 'shall make provisions for appropriate modes of settlement' for contractual disputes or disputes of a private law character to which the UN is a party (in Article VIII, sect. 29). The 1990 model UN SOFA provides for the establishment of a standing claims commission for disputes or claims of a private law character,[76] though in practice such commissions have not been created and claims have been settled through internal claims review boards.[77] Furthermore, there has been considerable practice by the UN, dating back to the first forces in 1956 and 1960, by which the UN has paid compensation to injured third parties.[78] None of these, however, provides for a systematic system of access to justice for victims of human rights violation at the hands of UN peacekeepers or police.

Conclusion

Throughout the history of peacekeeping, there has been a gap between the mandates agreed at the political level in the UN – in the Security Council, General Assembly and Secretariat – and the actions of peacekeepers on the ground. One only has to go back to Bosnia, during the dark days of UNPROFOR, when Chapter VII resolutions spoke of safe areas protected by UNPROFOR contingents that were wholly inadequate in military terms; or back to the mid-1970s, when SG Waldheim stated that peacekeepers could use force to protect their mandate at a time when they were clearly restricted to a narrow concept of self-defence.

While the Security Council may feel that it has discharged its primary responsibility for peace and security by introducing Chapter VII into modern peace operations, it leaves the situation on the ground unclear.[79] Peacekeepers are required to use lethal force to protect civilians and the peace process. However, this chapter has argued that, in so doing, they

76 UNGA Res. 45/594, Annex (1990), para. 51.

77 B. Oswald, H. Durham and A. Bates (eds), *Documents on the Law of UN Peace Operations* (Oxford: Oxford University Press, 2010), 324.

78 *Ibid.*, 323.

79 Rowe, 'Maintaining Discipline in United Nations Peace Support Operations', 47, where he eloquently explains that 'The starting point will be the mandate. This is likely to be expressed in rather general terms, telling states where the pitch is, who the players are and the objective of the operation, but providing no clear rules to when a yellow or red card should be shown to the players.'

are primarily bound by the principles of human rights law, and principles of IHL are the exception.[80]

While it is possible to reconcile the 'protection mandates' given to modern peace operations with the restrictions on the arbitrary deprivation of life contained in human rights law, care must be taken, as mandates produced by the Security Council increase pressure on peacekeepers and TCNs, not to stray into a legal no-man's-land between human rights law and humanitarian law. In this zone individuals would have neither clear rights under human rights law nor protection under the laws of war, meaning that the use of lethal force is unaccountable and open to abuse.

Any arguments for a middle ground between human rights law and the laws of war would have to be based on a conceptualisation of a *jus post bellum*, which might claim that a special regime for the use of force is necessary to secure the peace in a post-conflict, but still violent and volatile, situation.[81] As yet, no such sustained arguments have been made and, even when they are, it will require a further process of international negotiation and law-making to elaborate such standards. This author would argue against any underlying justification for such a development given that human rights laws, especially non-derogable ones, such as the right to life,[82] were framed precisely with violent situations in mind. Furthermore, human rights law is sufficiently flexible to allow peacekeepers to do their jobs within the strictures of the law. It is not human rights law that prevents peacekeepers fulfilling their functions, rather it is often a lack of military capability. Of course, there is great concern that peacekeepers use force when necessary to protect civilians under existential threat, but care must be taken to ensure that while more is done to achieve this laudable aim, the excessive use of force by peacekeepers, which may itself lead to the arbitrary deprivation of life, is not encouraged.

[80] See also McLaughlin, 'The Legal Regime Applicable to the Use of Lethal Force', 417. 'Any assumption that a SC Chapter VII "all necessary means" mandate either creates its own "third paradigm" in relation to the use of lethal force, or is by default to be understood as invoking the IHL paradigm, runs the high risk of offending what is arguably the actual international and domestic default legal paradigm – the law enforcement paradigm, with its focus on human rights, criminal law and limiting the use of lethal force to (essentially) self-defence situations.'

[81] T. Weiss, 'The Blurring Border between the Police and the Military: A Debate without Foundations', 49 *Cooperation and Conflict* (2011) 396, 397. See generally, C. Stahn, 'Jus ad Bellum, Jus in Bello, Jus post Bellum?', 17 *EJIL* (2006) 921.

[82] Article 4 International Covenant on Civil and Political Rights 1966.

6

The relationship of international humanitarian law and war crimes: international criminal tribunals and their statutes

ROBERT CRYER

Introduction

In this contribution, I shall attempt to link some of the areas in which Peter Rowe has worked discussing the interplay of international humanitarian law (IHL) and the law of war crimes. The interrelationship of international human rights law and IHL has been the subject of a great deal of attention. Some might say a little too much and perhaps, at the risk of seeming to be a hypocrite, I would too.[1] However, the interrelationship of IHL and international criminal law has not been the subject

It is a pleasure to write in honour of Professor Peter Rowe for a number of reasons. The first is respect. Professor Rowe is a genuinely eminent figure in the worlds of the law of armed conflict, military law, human rights law, international criminal law and the interrelationship between domestic and international law in all of these fields. The second reason is collegial. Professor Rowe has always been a stalwart of the UK international law 'scene', always willing to contribute to ongoing debates and present at conferences in addition to the genuinely extraordinary administrative burdens he has shouldered for his universities. The third, which I flatter myself to separate from the foregoing, is personal. As well as being an esteemed international law colleague, Peter has always been an immensely supportive mentor and friend. Suffice it to say, when, after half past four on a Friday afternoon, owing to snafus on both my and a human resources department's parts, I wrote to Peter to ask a favour (I did not elucidate about what, as it was precisely what traditionally irritates academics when done by students, never mind colleagues: provide a reference at very short notice). Having done so, I received a very generous response at one minute past nine on Monday morning, asking how he could help. Suffice it to say the reference was written, sent and received before the deadline (first thing Tuesday). I have worked with Peter on a number of projects, and examined with him, and it has always been a pleasure. His knowledge, judgment, intellect and warmth have always been a source of inspiration.

[1] R. Cryer 'The Interplay of Human Rights and Humanitarian Law: The Approach of the ICTY', 14 *JCSL* (2009) 511.

of such frequent investigation.[2] Only very recently has there been any systematic study of the interplay between these two closely related areas of law.[3]

The law of war crimes is not the same as IHL *per se*, although, the two have large overlaps. There are differences, on both sides, which ought to be borne in mind. Therefore, this contribution will look at how IHL and the law of war crimes have been seen to relate and how one has contributed to the other, with specific reference to the approach of international criminal tribunals to the issue. It will do so, after some initial comments about the conceptual relationship between the two, by looking at the extent to which international criminal tribunals have considered themselves to apply their Statutes as determinative of the substantive law they are to apply, or as at least a partial *renvoi* to IHL (and within that, what version of IHL), and thus, the extent to which their judgments can contribute to our understanding of the latter body of law.

War crimes and international humanitarian law

Back in the early twentieth century, it might have been enough to say that 'it is not necessary to enumerate exactly what may now be considered war crimes or violations of the laws of war. The list will change from time to time, by the addition of new offences and the omission of those now so considered'.[4] However, this comment was made at a time when the relationship between the law of war crimes, domestic law and IHL was not clear. It is certainly no longer enough to be so lackadaisical. For various reasons (partly political, partly conceptual and partly related to human rights concerns), a more in-depth analysis of the question is needed.

It is absolutely correct to say that the law of war crimes and IHL have a very close relationship. There are, for example, no war crimes that are

[2] Although Peter has looked into the matter; see P. Rowe, 'War Crimes', in P. Rowe, D. McGoldrick and E. Donnelly (eds), *The Permanent International Criminal Court: Legal and Policy Issues* (Oxford: Hart, 2004), 203, 217–19.

[3] For such recent discussions though, see R. Bartels, 'Discrepancies between International Humanitarian Law on the Battlefield and in the Courtroom: The Challenges of Applying International Humanitarian Law during Criminal Trials', in M. Matthee et al. (eds)., *Armed Conflict and International Law: In Search of the Human Face. Lieber Amoricum in Memory of Avril McDonald* (The Hague: Asser Press, 2013), 339; R. Bartels, 'Dealing with the Principle of Proportionality in Armed Conflict in Retrospect: The Application of the Principle in International Criminal Trials', 46 *Israel Law Review* (2013) 271.

[4] E. Colby, 'War Crimes', 23 *Michigan Law Review* (1924–5) 482, 482.

not violations of IHL[5] and, as Gerhard Werle has said, 'war crimes law always makes reference to IHL. The substantive law is not autonomous that happens to be based on IHL, but is accessorial to this body of law'.[6] Still, this does not mean that the relationship is one of unity. Aspects of the theoretical aspects of this discussion have been dealt with elsewhere;[7] what this contribution seeks to do is to investigate the approach to the interplay of IHL and war crimes law by the international criminal tribunals. In particular, it seeks to investigate the authority that international criminal tribunals have to apply and interpret IHL as an aspect of their subject matter jurisdiction.

The extent to which international tribunals' interpretation of international law is structured by its substantive/material jurisdiction is one that is perhaps not always investigated in detail.[8] This may be for a number of reasons, the first being an inappropriate and inaccurate analogy to the ICJ. This relates to the general perception that the ICJ is the model for international courts and that it has plenary jurisdiction, i.e., whatever dispute is sent to that Court can be determined on whatever the applicable international law on point is.

This misunderstanding has perhaps arisen owing to the fact that most international lawyers follow their teaching and believe, as a default position, that the sources of international law are, for the most part, those in Article 38(1) of the ICJ Statute.[9] As a matter of the substantive jurisdiction of the ICJ, this is not strictly true, its jurisdiction to adjudicate on a particular dispute is not necessarily all the possible law applicable to that dispute. For example, in one case the ICJ may have jurisdiction to apply customary law, but not treaty law, or *vice versa* in another.[10] The ICJ understands this, but it tends to do its level best to ensure that the

[5] G. Werle, *Principles of International Criminal Law*, 2nd edn (The Hague: T.M.C. Asser Press, 2009), 358.

[6] *Ibid.*

[7] R. Cryer, 'War Crimes', in N. D. White and C. Henderson (eds), *Research Handbook on Conflict and Security Law* (Cheltenham: Edward Elgar, 2013), 467, 474–5 and R. Cryer, 'Individual Liability in International Law', in T. L. H. McCormack and R. Liivoja (eds), *Routledge Handbook on the Law of Armed Conflict* (London: Routledge, 2014).

[8] The relationship of such jurisdiction to personal/temporal jurisdiction is discussed in R. Cryer, *Prosecuting International Crimes: Selectivity and the International Criminal Law Regime* (Cambridge: Cambridge University Press, 2005), chs 5–6.

[9] See, e.g., J. Crawford, *Brownlie's Principles of Public International Law*, 8th edn (Oxford: Oxford University Press, 2012), 20.

[10] An example of the former case is *Case Concerning Military and Paramilitary Activities in and against Nicaragua* (*Nicaragua* v. *USA*), ICJ Reports 1984, 4. One of the latter is *Case Concerning the Application of the Convention Concerning the Prevention and*

substantive outcome on the facts is the same[11] and upon occasion has used limited jurisdictional provisions to expound issues of general international law.[12]

The approach of international tribunals outside the criminal sphere to general international law and other specialised areas of international law is very interesting, as is the approach of the ICJ to the determinations of international criminal tribunals,[13] but beyond the scope of this chapter.[14] It is raised, however, to make the point that this narrow issue is, in fact, indicative of a more general issue relating to international tribunals, that is not always sufficiently appreciated – the limits of their material jurisdiction. In the end, international courts and tribunals are only expressly entitled to apply the law that their founding document(s) warrant(s) them to do so. Hence, for example, the European Court of Human Rights is no more entitled directly to apply the Inter-American Convention on Human Rights than its Inter-American counterpart is entitled to apply the European Convention on Human Rights (ECHR).

This is not to say that courts do, or ought to, avoid looking at other aspects of international law; in particular, in the context of treaty interpretation, Article 31(3)(c) of the Vienna Convention on the Law of Treaties more than encourages it.[15] Also, direct and indirect judicial dialogue can work very strongly to ensure that their output at least avoids any gross instances of *per incuriam* decisions.[16] However, although this can help, when understood in context, to contribute to

Punishment of the Crime of Genocide (*Bosnia* v. *Serbia*) ICJ General List no. 91, 26 February 2006.

11 See, e.g., *Nicaragua* (n. 10, above), paras 92–7.

12 *Case Concerning Oil Platforms* (*Iran* v. *USA*), ICJ Reports 2003, 161. For critique, see F. Berman, 'Treaty Interpretation in a Judicial Context', 29 *Yale Journal of International Law* (2004) 315.

13 See, e.g., R. Cryer 'Neither Here nor There? The Status of International Criminal Jurisprudence in the International and UK Legal Orders', in M. Bohlander and K. Kaikobad (eds) *International Law and Power: Perspectives on Legal Order and Justice: Essays in Honour of Colin Warbrick* (The Hague: Brill, 2008) 183, 189–91.

14 For a useful study on one court's approach, see M. Forowicz, *The Reception of International Law in the European Court of Human Rights* (Oxford: Oxford University Press, 2010).

15 See R. Gardiner, *Treaty Interpretation* (Oxford: Oxford University Press, 2008), ch. 7; J.-M. Sorel and V. Boré Eveno, 'Article 31', in O. Corten and P. Klein, *The Vienna Convention on the Law of Treaties: A Commentary* (Oxford: Oxford University Press, 2011), 804, 828–9.

16 A.-M. Slaughter, 'Judicial Globalization', 40 *Virginia Journal of International Law* (1999) 1103.

the overall corpus of international law, it is always important also to understand the foundational documents of the tribunals which define their material jurisdiction.[17]

Nuremberg, Tokyo and the cold war era

Prior to the creation of direct individual liability under international law for war crimes, the ambit of the law of war crimes and its relation to IHL was largely left to domestic law and, if truth be told, confusion about the issue abounded. Hence, it was only really with the international criminal tribunals established after the Second World War that the interrelationship of IHL and war crimes became a significant issue.[18] The first two provisions on point, which granted the Nuremberg and Tokyo International Military Tribunals (IMTs) jurisdiction over war crimes, were, according to your perspective, either deeply telling or question begging. Article 6(b) of the Nuremberg IMT's constituent Statute granted that tribunal jurisdiction over 'violations of the wars and customs of war' followed by a non-exhaustive list. In addition to the fact that it considered its Charter to be 'decisive and binding' on it,[19] and the clear, manifest, violations of IHL committed by the Nazis, the Nuremberg IMT had little to add to the question of the interrelationship of the law of war (as it was then called) and the law of war crimes.

Hence, responding to the claim that there might not be direct criminal responsibility for violations of IHL, the Tribunal issued a simple rebuttal; asserting that the question of criminality of violations of the Regulations attached to the Fourth Hague Convention of 1907 and Geneva Convention of 1929 (or, strictly speaking, in the case of the Hague Convention, and at times for the Geneva Convention, of their customary concomitants) was beyond doubt.[20] Custom, it ought to be said, had to come to the rescue in relation to the Hague Regulations owing to the IV Convention's *si omnes* clause that rendered the Hague Regulations, as a matter of treaty law, inapplicable as the Soviet Union was not a party to that Treaty.[21] This could be seen as an implicit acceptance on point by the Nuremberg IMT that Article 6(b) of its Charter referred to the *applicable* humanitarian

[17] Sadly there is no space to deal in detail with the *nullum crimem sine lege* issues that this issue raises. See generally, K. Gallant *The Principle of Legality in International and Comparative Criminal Law* (Cambridge: Cambridge University Press, 2009).

[18] Cryer, 'Individual Liability'.

[19] 'Nuremberg IMT: Judgment and Sentence', 41 *AJIL* (1947) 171, 248.

[20] *Ibid.*

[21] *Ibid.*

law, rather than creating an autonomous head of jurisdiction cast adrift of the conditions of applicability of the underlying law. Whether or not the authors of the judgment thought about it so clearly is, however, unclear, although it is notable that, despite generally referring to the 1929 Geneva Convention, when discussing crimes against Soviet prisoners of war, who were not protected by that convention, they noted that customary law still protected them.[22]

The Tokyo IMT's Statute, on the other hand, simply granted jurisdiction to the Tribunal over 'violations of the laws and customs of war', a provision that implied that the Tokyo IMT could prosecute all violations of IHL without further discussion.[23] Owing to the discussion that the Tribunal engaged in about Japan's agreement to apply the 1929 Geneva Convention to prisoners of war, and the extent to which that agreement brought it into force, we can see a fairly clear example of a Tribunal considering its Statute to contain a reference to the applicable IHL, rather than a regime cut off from the underlying treaties and custom and their conditions of applicability.[24] On the secondary question of the relationship between IHL and the law of war crimes, following the Nuremberg IMT's lead, the majority in the Tokyo IMT adopted the view that there was criminal liability for seemingly all such violations.[25] Only the (in)famous dissentient, Judge Pal, questioned this, declaring that some (frankly, serious) violations of the laws of armed conflict were not criminal, although his reasons for doing so were not necessarily solely legalistic.[26]

Whatever the position was then, after that the development of IHL and the law of war crimes, to the controversial extent to which they overlapped, tended to focus on the Geneva Conventions in the post-war era and, in particular, and in some ways inaccurately, on the grave breaches provisions of those conventions and their domestic prosecution.[27] This was understandable, given that, by the 1950s, the chances of an international criminal court being created were, to be optimistic, remote.[28] The International Law Commission may have spent a great

[22] *Ibid.*, 228–9.

[23] N. Boister and R. Cryer, *The Tokyo International Military Tribunal: A Reappraisal* (Oxford: Oxford University Press, 2008), ch. 7.

[24] *Ibid.*, 183–7. [25] *Ibid.*, 188–9. [26] *Ibid.*

[27] J. Stewart, 'The Future of the Grave Breaches Regime: Segregate, Assimilate, or Abandon?', 7 *JICJ* (2009) 855.

[28] I. Brownlie, *Principles of Public International Law*, 4th edn (Oxford: Clarendon Press, 1990), 563–4.

deal of time working on international criminal law, on and off, in the post-war era, but there was little discussion of the interplay between substantive IHL and war criminality. Indeed, it was only in 1977 that Additional Protocol I went 'even' as far as to declare that grave breaches were, in fact, 'war crimes'.[29]

The 'modern' era of war crimes prosecutions: the International Criminal Tribunal for the former Yugoslavia (ICTY), International Criminal Tribunal for Rwanda (ICTR) and the integrationist ideal

The ICTY

Against this background, probably the biggest development in the fifty years after the Nuremberg IMT's judgment was the creation of the ICTY in 1993. Article 2 of the ICTY's Statute granted the tribunal jurisdiction over grave breaches of the Geneva Conventions and Article 3 over a non-exhaustive list of 'serious violations of the laws and customs of war', that list essentially tracing those included in Article 6(b) of the Nuremberg IMT's statute.[30]

Article 2

The possibility of there being a significant disjuncture between international criminal law and IHL could not be excluded as initially, with respect to Article 2 of the ICTY Statute, the Trial Chamber in the *Tadić* case argued that the Statute, rather than 'referring out' to IHL for its applicability criteria, was, in essence, an autopoetic system. Hence, rather than requiring an international armed conflict for the applicability of the grave breaches provisions (which remains, as a matter of general international law, the accepted position),[31] the Trial Chamber determined that they could prosecute grave breaches of those conventions irrespective of the nature of the conflict. This was because it was included in the Statute, and the Chamber opined that it:

[29] AP I, Article 85(5).

[30] For early interpretations of this, see V. Morris and M. P. Scharf, *The International Criminal Tribunal for Former Yugoslavia: An Insider's Guide* (Irvington-on-Hudson, NY: Transnational, 1995), 63–73.

[31] J.-M. Henckaerts, 'The Grave Breaches Regime as Customary International Law', 7 *JICJ* (2009) 683, although see S. Boelaert-Suominen, 'Grave Breaches, Universal Jurisdiction and Internal Armed Conflicts: Is Customary Law Moving Towards a Uniform Enforcement Mechanism for all Armed Conflicts?', 5 *JCSL* (2000) 63.

> [H]as been so drafted as to be self-contained rather than referential, save for the identification of the victims of enumerated acts; that identification and that alone involves going to the Conventions themselves for the definition of 'persons or property protected' [. . .] [T]he requirement of international conflict does not appear on the face of Article 2. Certainly, nothing in the words of the Article expressly require its existence; once one of the specified acts is allegedly committed upon a protected person the power of the International Tribunal to prosecute arises if the spatial and temporal requirements of Article 1 are met [. . .] [T]here is no ground for treating Article 2 as in effect importing into the Statute the whole of the terms of the Conventions, including the reference in common Article 2 of the Geneva Convention [*sic*] to international conflicts. As stated, Article 2 of the Statute is on its face, self-contained, save in relation to the definition of protected persons and things.[32]

This, in and of itself, does not convince. It would require considerable discussion to explain why Article 2 imports aspects of the conditions of applicability; that persons or property be 'protected' by the relevant Convention, whilst not importing the conditions of applicability of the Convention, which includes those criteria and the conditions for their application. Sadly, the Chamber provided no such reasoning, proceeding instead by way of assertion on point.

Had this been accepted, the law of war crimes, at least in some contexts, would have been cast adrift from its underlying norms – those of IHL. For the purposes of the consistency of IHL and international criminal law, it would have been deeply problematic. Therefore, at least two cheers are owed to the Appeals Chamber who took a firm (and firmly expressed) line against the autopoetic argument in the relevant *Tadić* appeal,[33] reasserting the centrality (in this regard) of the applicability of the Conventions as a whole to the interpretation of the Statute, stating that:

> With all due respect, the Trial Chamber's reasoning is based on a misconception of the grave breaches provisions and the extent of their incorporation into the Statute of the International Tribunal. The grave breaches system of the Geneva Conventions establishes a twofold system: there is on the one hand an enumeration of offences that are regarded so serious as to constitute 'grave breaches'; closely bound up with th[e relevant] [. . .] enforcement mechanism [i.e., universal jurisdiction] [. . .] The international armed conflict requirement was a necessary limitation on the grave breaches

[32] Trial Chamber Decision, paras 49–51 as cited in *Prosecutor* v. *Tadić*, Decision on Interlocutory Appeal on Jurisdiction (Case No. IT-94-1-AR72), ICTY Appeals Chamber, 2 October 1995, para. 79.

[33] As we will see, there has been more than one.

> system in light of the intrusion on State sovereignty that such mandatory universal jurisdiction represents [. . .] The Trial Chamber is right in implying that the enforcement mechanism has of course not been imported into the Statute of the International Tribunal, for the obvious reason that the International Tribunal itself constitutes a mechanism for the prosecution and punishment of the perpetrators of 'grave breaches.' However, the Trial Chamber has misinterpreted the reference to the Geneva Conventions contained in the sentence of Article 2: 'persons or property protected under the provisions of the relevant Geneva Conventions.' [. . .] For the reasons set out above, this reference is clearly intended to indicate that the offences listed under Article 2 can only be prosecuted when perpetrated against persons or property regarded as 'protected' by the Geneva Conventions under the strict conditions set out by the Conventions themselves.[34]

In his (sadly overlooked) opinion in *Tadić*, Judge Sidhwa summed the matter up, both eloquently and with admirable clarity and brevity:

> Article 2 is not self contained. Its meaning only becomes clear by reference to the Conventions. This is a case of legislation by reference. The offences, therefore, listed under Article 2 are those that specifically fall under and are treated as 'grave breaches' in the Geneva Conventions of 1949 and are those that can be committed only in an international armed conflict. This is the interpretation on a straight evaluation of the Article.[35]

In spite of the Appeals Chamber's clear rejection of the Trial Chamber's idea, it had a surprising (albeit brief) afterlife. Some four years after the *Tadić* Appeal Decision, Judge Rodrigues, in the *Aleksovski* decision,[36] attempted to reassert the independent nature of the ICTY statute, cutting it free from the tethers of the applicability provisions of the Conventions themselves. It cannot be said that Rodrigues was working *per incuriam*, he responded, quite directly, to the *Tadić* Appeal Chamber's view that the international armed conflict requirement applied to the Geneva Conventions, and thus to Article 2 too. He asserted that:

> Article 2 of the Statute is autonomous in relation to the Geneva Conventions from which it is inspired and, a fortiori, from the conditions required for them to apply. The argument is based on the interpretation that the Security Council was the appropriate organ to characterise the

34 *Prosecutor v. Tadić* (n. 32, above), paras 80–1.

35 *Ibid.*, Separate Opinion of Judge Sidhwa, para. 110.

36 *Prosecutor* v. *Aleksovski*, Judgment, IT-95-14-T, 25 June 1999, Dissenting Opinion of Judge Rodrigues.

> conflict in the former Yugoslavia as internal or international and did not intend to make such a characterisation; concomitantly, the Security Council established the Tribunal under Chapter VII of the United Nations Charter and conferred on it definite and specific judicial powers defined by the Statute so that they might be applied as such, irrespective of issues of State sovereignty, protected under the Geneva Convention by the international character condition.[37]

His argument, which deserves detailed consideration, proceeded along the following lines. First, that the Security Council did not identify the nature of the conflict, but intended that all persons responsible for serious violations of IHL were to be prosecuted.[38] He then attempted to turn the reasoning of the *Tadić* Appeals Chamber decision against itself, noting that it asserted that the grave breaches provisions related to the jurisdiction of foreign domestic courts, and pointed to the impact that the granting of such courts' universal jurisdiction has on sovereignty. Rodrigues said that this was all very well, but irrelevant. This was an international tribunal, set up by the Security Council under Chapter VII to prosecute offences accepted not to be simply a matter of domestic concern; therefore, for him the sovereignty concerns were simply inapplicable.[39] He bolstered this, relying on the ideas of Allain Pellet, by asserting that 'it would be "something of a paradox for the violation of treaty-based rules, which moreover have their own control mechanism, to be punished by a court created by non treaty-based means"'.[40]

He then moved on to argue that the Secretary-General's report had intended the Tribunal to prosecute all violations of IHL in former Yugoslavia and therefore, by including grave breaches in the jurisdiction of the ICTY, the Security Council intended for the grave breaches to apply to the conflict in former Yugoslavia, irrespective of its classification. This, in his view, did not violate the *nullum crimen sine lege* principle owing to the fact that customary law had developed, as Judge Abi-Saab had argued (in dissent) in *Tadić*, to apply the grave breaches provisions to both types of conflict.[41] He followed this up with a literal argument based on the idea that, owing to the fact that Article 2 refers to persons and property protected by the Geneva Conventions, when the Statute sought to incorporate external standards

[37] *Ibid.*, para. 32. [38] *Ibid.*, paras 32–6. [39] *Ibid.*, para. 38. [40] *Ibid.*

[41] *Ibid.*, paras 39–41, 44–6. This argument was discussed at n. 31, and accompanying text, above.

(such as the applicability provisions of the Geneva Conventions) it specifically mentioned them.[42]

He finished, not without flourish, by arguing that his:

> approach presents the undeniable advantage of being consistent with regard to the objectives which resulted in the establishment of the Tribunal, namely, the prosecution of persons accused of serious violations of IHL committed in the territory of the former Yugoslavia since 1991 in accordance with the provisions imposed upon it by the Statute and not by any other legislative instrument. It may also claim to be operational since it permits Article 2 to be applied more soundly and with greater certainty and unconditional respect for the dignity of the humankind as a universal value. One must also bear in mind that any differences in the characterization of the conflict could jeopardize or even run directly counter to the objectives of the Tribunal which are to administer justice and to contribute to the restoration of peace and peacekeeping – especially to the extent that the conflict, at least in part, can be viewed as having been motivated by cultural, religious or ethnic reasons.[43]

Let us leave aside the question of precedent within the Tribunal[44] and deal with his arguments in turn. The first is that the Security Council did not determine the nature of the conflict, but determined that the ICTY should prosecute all violations of IHL in the territory of former Yugoslavia. The former, factual, issue is accurate as, if nothing else, the fact that Article 4 of the ICTY's Statute on crimes against humanity refers to both international and non-international armed conflict is good evidence of this.

The legal conclusion he draws from it, however, is far less convincing. The Security Council can equally, and less problematically, be read as granting the ICTY jurisdiction over all violations of IHL applicable in the former Yugoslavia. This is more convincing in that the Security Council would not have the mandate retrospectively to apply otherwise inapplicable law to a situation. For example, it would not be plausible that the Security Council applied IHL to a non-conflict situation, but this would

[42] *Prosecutor* v. *Aleksovski*, Judgment, IT-95-14-T, 25 June 1999, Dissenting Opinion of Judge Rodrigues, para. 42.

[43] *Ibid.*, para. 43.

[44] Which, to be fair, was only clearly set up on the Appeal from this decision, *Prosecutor* v. *Aleksovski*, Judgment, IT-95-14-A, 24 March 2000, para. 113. Equally, where there is an Appeals Chamber decision, even in the absence of a formal doctrine of precedent, it is a 'brave' Trial Chamber that ignores an Appeals Chamber decision on point. See Cryer, 'Neither Here nor There?', 192.

be the outcome of applying Judge Rodrigues's argument to its (il)logical conclusion. This could be accused of being an argument *reductio ad absurdum*, and to some extent it is. However, what it shows is that a simpler solution is available: the Security Council only intended for the Tribunal to prosecute violations of the applicable law. This would also deal with any claims of a violation of the *nullum crimen* principle.

To be fair, Judge Rodrigues deals with this in a later part of his argument where he argues that this aspect is dealt with by the fact that, in his view, customary law had developed to extend the grave breaches provisions to non-international armed conflicts. That view has found little support in state practice (including, as we will see, with all due caveats, in the Rome Statute) and was discussed above. There is, outside of one US statement,[45] which would be unlikely to be reiterated today,[46] and was not agreed with by others, no evidence that the Security Council sought to apply the grave breaches provisions outside of their traditional applicability provisions.[47] It could be argued that the Security Council members voting for it were just doing so in the specific circumstances of former Yugoslavia, but it is unlikely that, given the practical likelihood that it would be taken as a precedent, they would have done so; and certainly not *sub silentio*.

The second argument, that the grave breaches regime is inherently linked to the fact that they grant universal jurisdiction to national courts, a position which is distinguishable from international tribunals, has some merit, but fails to take sufficient account of the fact that an international tribunal is also seen by states as a considerable limitation on their sovereignty, as, for example, early US opposition to the ICC showed.[48]

45 See *Prosecutor* v. *Tadić* (n. 32, above), para. 83.

46 Given that US hostility to aspects of AP I centres, *inter alia*, on its expansion of privileged belligerency and prisoner of war status in Article 44 of that Protocol and the extension of the concept of international armed conflicts to wars of national liberation (see Letter of Transmittal from President Ronald Reagan, AP II, 81 *AJIL* (1987) 910, 911). See generally, T. Meron, 'The Time Has Come for the United States to Ratify Protocol I', 88 *AJIL* (1994) 678. It is extremely unlikely that any post-9/11 US administration would adopt such a view.

47 Still less would any of the Security Council members voting for Resolution 827, which brought the ICTY into being and adopted its Statute, be assumed to have applied, for example, the concept of privileged belligerency and occupation to non-international armed conflicts, the two areas upon which the law of international and non-international armed conflict has been resolutely kept separate by states, without very clear evidence that that was the intention.

48 See, e.g., J. Gurule, 'United States Opposition to the 1998 Rome Statute Establishing an International Criminal Court: Is the Court's Jurisdiction Truly Complementary to National Criminal Jurisdictions?, 36 *Cornell International Law Journal* (2001–2) 1.

This is, admittedly, not a complete answer to Judge Rodrigues's point, in that the Security Council, when acting under Chapter VII, is entitled to ignore sovereignty issues, a position that Article 2(7) of the UN Charter makes clear,[49] and indeed the *Tadić* Appeals Chamber itself relied upon.[50] However, when adopting the ICTY's Statute the Security Council did not, on all the available evidence, address its mind to that point and certainly not to the extent to which Judge Rodrigues reads their hypothetical intent. It could be thought that the Secretary-General's report could provide some evidence of their intent; however, that report itself is by no means clear that the intention was to sever the grave breaches provisions from their conditions of applicability.

Furthermore, Judge Rodrigues's position fails to take into account the argument of the *Tadić* Appeals Chamber referred to above, i.e., that the reference to persons or property protected by the Geneva Conventions makes clear that it refers to those who are protected by the Conventions, where they are applicable.[51] The concept of 'protected person' and 'property' is parasitic on the applicability of the Geneva Conventions as a whole, i.e., that there is an international armed conflict. The fact that common Article 3 to the 1949 Geneva Conventions protects, at one level, certain persons in non-international armed conflicts has never been interpreted as meaning those so protected by that article come under the grave breaches provisions. Hence, as the *Tadić* Appeals Chamber argued, the reference to protected persons or property necessarily includes the applicability of those concepts, which, in turn, rely on the applicability provisions of the 1949 Geneva Conventions as a whole – that there is an international armed conflict. If there is not an international armed conflict, then, as the Appeals Chamber argued, there are no protected persons or property; that status relies upon, and is created by, those aspects of those Conventions.

This is not to say that the ICTY has not developed those concepts (in particular in the context of 'protected persons' for the purposes of the Fourth Geneva Convention of 1949 (GC IV)),[52] but such developments have been argued, and presented, as interpretation of the Conventions,

[49] Whether it ought in a particular situation or not, however, is a different question.

[50] See *Prosecutor* v. *Tadić* (n. 32, above), paras 56–60.

[51] *Ibid.* This also deals with his penultimate (literal) argument, mentioned above.

[52] *Prosecutor* v. *Tadić*, Judgment, IT-94-1-A, 15 July 1999, paras 164–6. Although the Appeals Chamber does not refer to it, a Trial Chamber previously took such a view; however, this was based less directly on the Conventions: *Prosecutor* v. *Delalić, Mucić, Delić and Landžo*, Judgment, IT-96-21-T, 16 November 1998, paras 244–66. For a piece

rather than statements about hermetically sealed (ICTY) Statutory interpretation. It is on this basis that the ICTY has defended itself against charges of violating the *nullum crimen sine lege* principle, explaining that its expansive interpretation of 'protected persons' in GC IV:[53]

> is consistent with the rules of treaty interpretation set out in the Vienna Convention. Further, the Appeals Chamber in Tadić only relied on the travaux préparatoires to reinforce its conclusion reached upon an examination of the overall context of the Geneva Conventions. The Appeals Chamber is thus unconvinced by the appellants' argument and finds that the interpretation of the nationality requirement of Article 4 in the Tadić Appeals Judgement does not constitute a rewriting of Geneva Convention IV or a 're-creation' of the law. [. . .] The Appeals Chamber finds that this interpretative approach is consistent with the rules of treaty interpretation set out in the Vienna Convention.[54]

To turn next to Rodrigues's assertion that that it would be paradoxical for a tribunal to enforce treaty-based rules whilst having not been created by a treaty itself, this is legally unconvincing, for a number of reasons. First, briefly, paradox is not illegality. Second, there is no inherent paradox in a body of law based on one source of international law being enforced by one created by another. The ICJ, for example, adjudicates on the basis of customary international law and this is considered unexceptionable, or, at the very least, not paradoxical, even though it does so on the basis of a treaty.[55] Additionally, there have always been non-treaty-based methods of enforcing IHL, such as reprisals (to the extent to which they are still accepted),[56] so this does not seem sufficiently important to be used to reach substantive conclusions such as Rodrigues's.

Admittedly, it is difficult to imagine general principles or customary international law creating a court, but, at least since the *Effect of Awards*

presaging the decision, see B. Brown, 'Nationality and Internationality in International Humanitarian Law', 34 *Stanford Journal of International Law* (1998) 347.

53 *Prosecutor* v. *Delalić, Mucić, Delić and Landžo*, Judgment, IT-96-21-A, 20 February 2001, paras 73 ff. See W. Schabas, *The Rome Statute of the International Criminal Court: A Commentary* (Oxford: Oxford University Press, 2010), 212.

54 *Prosecutor* v. *Delalić, Mucić, Delić and Landžo* (n. 53, above), para. 73.

55 Article 38(1)(b)(c) ICJ Statute. See A. Pellet, 'Article 38', in Andreas Zimmermann et al. (eds), *The Statute of the International Court of Justice: A Commentary*, 2nd edn (Oxford: Oxford University Press, 2012), 731, 759–60.

56 On which, see F. Kalshoven, 'Reprisals and the Protection of Civilians: Two Recent Decisions of the Yugoslavia Tribunal', in L. C. Vohrah et al. (eds), *Man's Inhumanity to Man: Essays in International Law in Honour of Antonio Cassese* (The Hague: Kluwer, 2003), 481.

opinion, notably relied upon by the Appeals Chamber in *Tadić*, it has been accepted that a resolution of an international organisation can create a tribunal.[57] It might be argued that criminal tribunals are different, but this would have applied similarly to the Tokyo IMT, which was created by a declaration of General MacArthur. Although the legality of that tribunal was the subject of considerable debate by the prosecution, defence and judges, even if not detailed in the final set of opinions, none of those protagonists even considered that the matter of treaties and custom being enforced by a Tribunal created by a resolution as being awkward.[58]

Next, strictly speaking, the ICTY finds its legal authority in the UN Charter (a treaty), i.e., the powers granted to the Security Council under Chapter VII and the obligation of states to carry out its decisions under Article 25.[59] Pellet counters that just because something finds its basis in a treaty that does not make it a treaty, and '[m]oreover, it is terribly abstract and does not square with reality: certainly, a State against which an action is taken by, e.g. the Security Council under Article 41 or 42 of the Charter, cannot be deemed to have "agreed" to the measure'.[60] This is true, but does not make the point in that, as a matter of treaty law, the consequence is the same – they are so bound. Furthermore, given the nature of the ICTY's Statute, and the fact that, for the most part, it has treated its Statute (an annex to a Security Council Resolution) as a treaty for the purposes of interpretation,[61] the distinction hardly seems fatal, not least because the ICJ has tended to apply the rules of the Vienna Convention on the Law of Treaties, *mutatis mutandis*, to Security Council Resolutions that are far less like treaties than the ICTY's Statute.[62]

It is true that his final argument – that his interpretation was more consistent with ensuring human dignity – is not outside the naturalistic bent of many pronouncements of international criminal tribunals

57 *Prosecutor* v. *Tadić* (n. 32, above), para. 38.

58 On the nature of the Tribunal, see Boister and Cryer, *The Tokyo International Military Tribunal*, ch. 2.

59 *Prosecutor* v. *Tadić* (n. 32, above), paras 28 ff. See also R. Cryer, H. Friman, D. Robinson and E. Wilmshurst, *An Introduction to International Criminal Law and Procedure*, 3rd edn (Cambridge: Cambridge University Press, 2014), 9.

60 Pellet, 'Article 38', 767–78.

61 See W. Schabas, 'Interpreting the Statutes of the Ad Hoc Tribunals', in Vohrah et al., *Man's Inhumanity to Man*, 847.

62 *Accordance With International Law of the Unilateral Declaration of Independence in Respect of Kosovo*, ICJ List 141, Opinion of 22 July 2010, para. 94.

(including the ICTY).[63] However, such pronouncements do not, in themselves, make strong legal arguments and beg the question of what 'human dignity', a deeply controversial concept, actually is.[64]

Article 3

The interpretation that the ICTY took of Article 2, however, cannot be entirely separated off from its approach to Article 3, which it took to be a residual clause covering all other violations of applicable IHL to the international and/or non-international conflict(s) in former Yugoslavia, subject to the following conditions:

(i) the violation must constitute an infringement of a rule of international humanitarian law;
(ii) the rule must be customary in nature or, if it belongs to treaty law, the required conditions must be met;
(iii) the violation must be 'serious,' that is to say, it must constitute a breach of a rule protecting important values, and the breach must involve grave consequences for the victim; and
(iv) the violation must entail, under customary or conventional law, the individual criminal responsibility of the person breaching the rule.[65]

In spite of condition (iv), which is controversial and has perhaps led to some of the ICTY's least-convincing 'proofs' of customary international law, this interpretation has had an enormous impact on the jurisdiction of the ICTY. It has meant that the ICTY has considered itself to have jurisdiction over all the treaties in force for the various conflicts, be they international or non-international, and the customary law applicable to both types of conflict. This has allowed it to concentrate on the content of the norms (which they frequently consider to be the same) in both treaty and custom, and between both types of conflict. Owing to this, the ICTY has been able to bypass the issue of the type of conflict and the issue of applicability criteria contained in the treaties (and custom). However, this is only because they have the backdrop of custom, which the ICTY has taken Article 3 to allow them to apply, in the (frequent)

[63] See R. Cryer, 'International Criminal Tribunals and the Sources of International Law: Antonio Cassese's Contribution to the Canon', 10 *JICJ* (2012) 1045.
[64] G. Fitzmaurice, '*Vae Victis* or Woe to the Negotiators: Your Treaty or Our Interpretation of It', 65 *AJIL* (1971) 358.
[65] *Prosecutor* v. *Tadić* (n. 32, above), para. 94.

instances in which they determine it to be identical in both types of conflict, without regard for the applicability provisions that would otherwise have to be fulfilled from the point of view of treaty law.[66]

On substantive issues, the ICTY has taken a strong line on the parasitic nature of the law of war crimes on IHL and this has, to a very great extent, permitted it to make very considerable contributions to IHL through its pronouncements on the law of war crimes, which have necessitated it to pronounce on issues of IHL. They are far too numerous to elucidate upon here.[67] To take but one example, related to the vexed issue of the applicability of the law of non-international armed conflict, the test set in *Tadić*, that of protracted armed violence between governmental armed forces and organised armed groups or between such groups, was, to all intents and purposes (linguistic infelicity aside), adopted in the Rome Statute.[68]

The ICTY's contribution to the law of war crimes and IHL cannot be overestimated. However, it is not always appreciated that Article 3 allowed the ICTY to circumvent formal criteria of applicability via the escape-route of custom. This, though, was probably the high point of authority granted to a specialised court/tribunal to determine the ambit of the relevant international law. Since then, or at least after the creation of the ICTR, the manner in which international criminal tribunals have been given material jurisdiction over war crimes has reflected a desire on the part of states to retain control over the substantive content of international criminal law and, given the reflexive nature of the relationship between IHL and the law of war crimes, IHL too.

[66] S. Boelaert-Suominen, 'The Yugoslavia Tribunal and the Common Law Applicable to all Armed Conflicts', 13 *LJIL* (2000) 619.

[67] See, e.g., C. Greenwood, 'The Development of International Humanitarian Law by The International Criminal Tribunal for the Former Yugoslavia' (1998) 2 *Max Planck Yearbook of United Nations Law* 97. When it comes to the development of individual liability for violations in non-international armed conflict, Peter, at the time, expressed some surprise (although not unhappiness): C. Warbrick and P. Rowe 'The International Criminal Tribunal for Yugoslavia: The Decision of the Appeals Chamber on the Interlocutory Appeal on Jurisdiction in the *Tadic* Case', 45 *ICLQ* (1996) 691, 698.

[68] *Prosecutor* v. *Tadić* (n. 32, above), para. 70; Rome Statute, Article 8(2)(f). See S. Sivakumaran, 'Identifying an Armed Conflict not of an International Character', in C. Stahn and G. Sluiter (eds), *The Emerging Practice of the International Criminal Court* (Leiden: Brill, 2009) 363, 380. S. Sivakumaran, *The Law of Non-International Armed Conflict* (Oxford: Oxford University Press, 2012), ch. 5.

The ICTR

The ICTR, by virtue of Articles 3 and 4 of its Statute, was granted jurisdiction over serious violations of common Article 3 of the 1949 Geneva Conventions and Additional Protocol II, the latter in spite of questions over its customary status, owing to the fact that Rwanda was a party to that treaty,[69] and of the doubt expressed by some at the time as to whether or not there was, as a matter of law, a criminal law side to the law of non-international armed conflict.[70] Rather like in Nuremberg, the question of whether or not the conduct of the accused lay at the edges of IHL has not really arisen due to the clear breaches that have been at issue before that Tribunal. Hence, in a variation of the axiom that hard cases make bad law, the ICTR has made little law on point at all. When it comes to international crimes, generally speaking the ICTR has, rightly or wrongly, considered itself to have bigger crimes (genocide and crimes against humanity) to fry (to mix a metaphor). It has not always got the law of war crimes right,[71] but it has always treated the law of war crimes as reliant on IHL and has therefore contributed, to a more limited, but still real extent, to our understanding of IHL, perhaps most notably on the conditions of applicability of Additional Protocol II. This is because, although the Statute treated the conflict as non-international, the ICTR has determined the applicability of IHL itself.[72]

The Special Court for Sierra Leone: a mixed/muddled approach

One of the very helpful decisions made by the drafters of the ICTY Statute was to take a studiously ecumenical approach to the nature of the conflict(s) in former Yugoslavia, i.e., whether they were international

[69] Report of the Secretary-General Pursuant to Paragraph 5 of Security Council Resolution 955, 13 February 1995 (UN Doc. S/1995/134), paras 11–12.

[70] P. Rowe, 'War Crimes and the Former Yugoslavia: The Legal Difficulties', 32 *Revue de Droit Militaire et le Droit de la Guerre* (1993) 317, 328–33. Peter was not alone: D. Plattner, 'The Penal Repression of Violations of International Humanitarian Law Applicable in Non-International Armed Conflicts', 278 *IRRC* (1990) 409, 414; Final Report of the Commission Established Pursuant to Security Council Resolution 780, Annex to Letter dated 24 May 1994 from the Secretary-General to the President of the Security Council (UN Doc. S/1994/674), para. 42. Report of the Secretary-General Pursuant to Paragraph 5 of Security Council Resolution 955, 13 February 1995 (UN Doc. S/1995/134), para. 12.

[71] See generally, L. J. van den Herik, *The Contribution of the Rwanda Tribunal to the Development of International Law* (Leiden: Martinus Nijhoff, 2005), ch. 5.

[72] *Ibid.*, 217.

or non-international. This, when it came to the applicable IHL, may have been accidental or based on an unstated assumption that, if the conflict was non-international, crimes against humanity (and perhaps genocide) would pick up the slack left by any lacunae in the law of war crimes.[73] The *Tadić* decision's approach to Article 3 of its Statute, which it took to grant it jurisdiction over all serious violations of the applicable IHL (i.e., that applicable to the relevant international or non-international armed conflicts at issue in any one case), rendered the decision somewhat moot. Furthermore, there is little question that the armed conflict in Rwanda was non-international. Hence, to frame the war crimes jurisdiction of that Tribunal in terms of the IHL applicable to non-international armed conflict, and its focus on genocide and crimes against humanity,[74] has not caused that Tribunal any legal difficulty, not least as the conflict in Rwanda in the early part of 1994 was undoubtedly an armed conflict and there was no reason to believe that the conflict had been internationalised.[75]

Nonetheless, the issue of the nature of a conflict, and thus the substantive law applicable to it, being settled by a stroke of the drafter's pen, prior to a detailed analysis of the conflict and the relevant applicable law, is a problem, as can be seen from the Statute of the Special Court for Sierra Leone (SCSL). Here, the Secretary-General did not grant the SCSL jurisdiction over genocide as there was no evidence that it had occurred in Sierra Leone.[76] This may be the case, but it raises the issue of whether the possibility of a genocide charge ought to have been excluded from the beginning.[77] There is, however, no evidence that this absence had any significant impact on the practice of the Prosecutor or the Court.[78]

73 On the importance of crimes against humanity in international tribunals, see L. N. Sadat, 'Crimes against Humanity in the Modern Era', 107 *AJIL* (2013) 334.

74 *Ibid.*, 346–9. 75 See van den Herik, *The Contribution of the Rwanda Tribunal*, 226.

76 Report of the Secretary-General on the establishment of a Special Court for Sierra Leone, 4 October 2000 (UN Doc. S/2000/915), para. 13.

77 This is particularly so as genocide, under customary law, does not require a plan or policy, and the relevant elements of crimes for the ICC do not themselves exclude the possibility of an individual perpetrator acting in the context of, for example, crimes against humanity. See, e.g., V. Oosterveld, 'Context of Genocide', in R. S. Lee et al. (eds), *The International Criminal Court: Elements of Crimes and Rules of Procedure and Evidence* (Ardsley, NY: Transnational, 2001), 44, 47–8.

78 For a discussion from the ex-prosecutor, see D. Crane, 'The Bright Red Thread: The Politics of International Criminal Law – Do We Want Peace or Justice? The West African Experience', in L. N. Sadat (ed.), *Forging a Convention on Crimes against Humanity* (Cambridge: Cambridge University Press, 2011), 59.

The same cannot be said when it comes to the war crimes jurisdiction of the Special Court. Although its Statute grants it jurisdiction over violations of common Article 3, Additional Protocol II and three named violations of IHL, in Articles 3 and 4 of its Statute, these, in accordance with the assumption of the drafters of the Statute, reflected the idea that the conflict in Sierra Leone was non-international.[79] The question of whether or not the activities of Liberia and other actors served to internationalise the conflict, however, became relevant when the defence in the *Fofana* case sought to argue that the Tribunal only granted the SCSL jurisdiction over offences in non-international armed conflicts, and the relevant conflict in Sierra Leone was not of that nature.

The Tribunal responded that, for the applicability of Article 3, which granted the SCSL jurisdiction over violations of common Article 3 and Additional Protocol II, the relevant norms were, essentially on the basis of custom, applicable to both types of armed conflicts.[80] This may be true, but does not quite answer the question of whether or not the SCSL has been granted jurisdiction over those violations under its Statute. It may be true, as the ICTY Appeals Chamber said in the *Čelebići* case (picking up on language in *Tadić*), that what is prohibited in non-international armed conflict must be prohibited in their international cousins.[81] But the ICTY could make this move as Article 3 of its Statute, as interpreted in *Tadić*, was considered to give it plenary jurisdiction over all treaty and customary law applicable to the conflict (other than grave breaches – the subject of Article 2). This is not the case for the SCSL. It is also notable that the ICC, even where the prohibitions are identical in international and non-international conflicts, has insisted on charges being on the basis of the appropriate applicable law.[82] The SCSL has responded to this type of claim by saying that:

[79] C. Byron, 'Commentary', in G. Sluiter and A. Klip (eds), *Leading Cases of the International Criminal Tribunals*, vol. 9 (Antwerp: Intersentia, 2006), 142.

[80] *Prosecutor* v. *Fofana*, Decision on Challenge to Jurisdiction *Materiae*: Nature of the Armed Conflict, SCSL-2004-14-AR72, 25 May 2004, paras 2–25.

[81] *Prosecutor* v. *Delalić, Mucić, Delić and Landžo* (n. 52, above), paras 147, 150.

[82] *Prosecutor* v. *Lubanga*, Judgment, ICC-01/04-01/06, 14 March 2012, para. 525, referring to the Pre-Trial Chamber's views, and, at para. 539, averring that 'In the view of the Chamber, for the purposes of the present trial the international/non-international distinction is not only an established part of the international law of armed conflict, but more importantly it is enshrined in the relevant statutory provisions of the Rome Statute framework, which under Article 21 must be applied. The Chamber does not have the power to reformulate the Court's statutory framework.'

> where the rules are identical in respect of both internal and international armed conflict it cannot follow that because the provision of the Statute is framed in the terms of the treaty provision applicable to internal armed conflicts, the Tribunal has no jurisdiction to apply the provision in the context of an international armed conflict.[83]

Precisely why this is the case is not elaborated upon. The SCSL, it must be remembered, did not have the luxury of a provision akin to Article 3 of the ICTY Statute that it could fall back on. Article 3 of the SCSL's Statute is far more like Article 2 of the ICTY Statute and cannot be 'liberated' from the applicability of the treaty provisions it granted the SCSL jurisdiction over violations of.

Admittedly, Article 4 of the SCSL Statute grants it jurisdiction over three named violations of IHL, which could be read as applicable to either type of armed conflict as it does not identify its criteria of applicability.[84] However, Article 3 of the SCSL Statute does by referring to common Article 3 and Additional Protocol II. Following the *Tadić* type reasoning, as that Tribunal applied it to its Article 2 (on grave breaches), the reference would include the conditions of applicability. The SCSL was not granted jurisdiction separately over customary offences and so the customary way around this was not, in law, available to the SCSL in the way it was to the ICTY. Nonetheless, the Tribunal has not considered this aspect in any detail since then and has confined its discussion of the applicability of common Article 3 and Additional Protocol II by virtue of the conditions and threshold set in the latter treaty.[85] This is somewhat paradoxical as it has never been claimed that the conditions in the second Additional Protocol apply to international armed conflicts and, as a matter of treaty law, Additional Protocol II only applies to non-international conflicts.

In the case in which the issue of the nature of the armed conflict would have been most germane, the *Taylor* case,[86] the Trial Chamber simply

[83] *Prosecutor* v. *Fofana* (n. 81, above), para. 26.

[84] *Ibid.*, para. 30. The reasoning is not entirely unassailable (as the language is drawn from parts of the Rome Statute dealing with non-international armed conflicts), but far stronger than the comments it made on Article 3.

[85] At one level this is understandable, in that AP II has a higher threshold of applicability than common Article 3, hence if AP II does, then so will common Article 3 (in non-international conflicts).

[86] *Prosecutor* v. *Taylor*, Judgment, SCSL-03-01-T, 18 May 2012. The reason it could have been relevant was that the essence of the Prosecution's case was that Liberia, through Taylor, had a hand in the conflict in Sierra Leone. This could have internationalised the conflict.

followed *Fofana* and said that all that was required was an armed conflict of either type.[87] However, given that the defence had not argued that the conflict was internationalised in *Taylor*, little practical effect can be laid at the door of this problem. What it does show, however, is that the pre-determination (even implicitly) by a drafter of the nature of a conflict is ill-advised.

That said, on the substance of IHL, the Special Court has, to all intents and purposes, adopted the view that IHL is the appropriate law to apply as the predicate for war crimes. Whilst it may (again) be the case that it has not always got the law right,[88] it has made some important and influential strides with respect to, for example, the protection of peacekeepers under the law of war crimes and IHL.[89] For our purposes, the point is that, applicability aside, it has not struck out on its own on the substantive norms of IHL that it has applied.

The Rome Statute: a semi-autonomous regime

As William Schabas has said, the Rome Statute was the first time that the question of the applicable law was expressly dealt with in the Statute of an international criminal tribunal (at least in a similar manner to, for example, the ICJ Statute). The other tribunals' statutes were not intended, in many ways, to be self-contained regimes.[90] Nor entirely is the Rome Statute. Article 21 provides that:

1. The Court shall apply:
   (a) In the first place, this Statute, Elements of Crimes and its Rules of Procedure and Evidence;
   (b) In the second place, where appropriate, applicable treaties and the principles and rules of international law, including the established principles of the international law of armed conflict;
   (c) Failing that, general principles of law derived by the Court from national laws of legal systems of the world including, as appropriate, the national laws of States that would normally exercise jurisdiction over the crime, provided that those principles are not

87 *Ibid.*, para. 563.
88 See, e.g., J. K. Kleffner, 'Friend or Foe? On the Protective Reach of the Law of Armed Conflict', in Matthee et al., *Armed Conflict and International Law*, 285.
89 For a useful survey, see S. Sivakumaran, 'War Crimes before the Special Court for Sierra Leone', 8 *JICJ* (2010) 1009.
90 Schabas, *The Rome Statute of the International Criminal Court*, 281–2.

inconsistent with this Statute and with international law and internationally recognized norms and standards.

2. The Court may apply principles and rules of law as interpreted in its previous decisions.[91]

What is notable, though, is that Article 21 creates a hierarchy with the Statute at the top.[92] Only if there is a lacuna in the Statute, Rules of Procedure and Evidence and Elements of Crimes that cannot be resolved by the application of the usual canons of treaty interpretation is the ICC entitled to go outside of them to custom or general principles.[93] This is important as the Rome Statute exhaustively defines the war crimes subject to its jurisdiction and, indeed, goes further in that the elements of crimes (which the ICC has decided to apply unless there is an 'irreconcilable contradiction' between them and the Statute)[94] provide even further elaboration of the road the drafters wanted the ICC Chambers to take.[95] It is the case that a number of war crimes in the Rome Statute are defined more narrowly than their IHL counterparts.[96] For an example, it is useful to compare the provisions on collateral damage in IHL and the Rome Statute.[97] The standard definition of an indiscriminate attack, contrary to IHL in international armed conflict, is contained in the (customary) Article 57(2)(iii) of Additional Protocol I, which requires belligerents to:

> refrain from deciding to launch any attack which may be expected to cause incidental loss of civilian life, injury to civilians, damage to civilian objects, or a combination thereof, which would be excessive in relation to the concrete and direct military advantage anticipated.[98]

[91] See generally, G. Bitti, 'Article 21 of the Statute of the International Criminal Court and the Treatment of Sources of Law in the Jurisprudence of the ICC', in Stahn and Sluiter, *The Emerging Practice of the International Criminal Court*, 285.

[92] See generally, R. Cryer, 'Royalism and the King: Article 21 and the Politics of Sources', 12 *New Criminal Law Review* (2009) 390.

[93] *Prosecutor* v. *al-Bashir*, Decision on the Prosecutor's Application for a Warrant of Arrest, ICC-02/05-01/09, 4 March 2009, para. 126. For critique, see Cryer, 'Royalism and the King', 397–8.

[94] *Prosecutor* v. *al-Bashir* (n. 92, above), paras 127–8.

[95] Schabas, for example, describes them as an 'obsessive exercise in legal positivism', 'Interpreting the Statutes of the Ad Hoc Tribunals', 887.

[96] See Cryer, *Prosecuting International Crimes*, 268–83.

[97] I am grateful for discussions with Dapo Akande on this point.

[98] See generally, Y. Sandoz, C. Swiniarski and B. Zimmerman (eds), *Commentary on the Additional Protocols* (Geneva: ICRC, 1987), 683–5. On its customary status, see *Prosecutor* v. *Galić*, Judgment, IT-98-29-T, 5 December 2003, paras 57–8.

The relevant grave breach (of Article 85(3)(b)(iii)) of Additional Protocol I is defined as follows:

> (b) launching an indiscriminate attack affecting the civilian population or civilian objects in the knowledge that such attack will cause excessive loss of life, injury to civilians or damage to civilian objects, as defined in Article 57, paragraph 2 (a)(iii).[99]

The addition of a knowledge requirement can be understood as responding to the issue that the general definitions are not created with criminal liability (in particular *mens rea* requirements) in mind. However, the relevant part of the Rome Statute (Article 8(2)(b)(iv)) grants the ICC jurisdiction over offences related to this principle in the following terms, criminalising:

> Intentionally launching an attack in the knowledge that such attack will cause incidental loss of life or injury to civilians or damage to civilian objects [. . .] which would be *clearly* excessive in relation to the concrete and direct *overall* military advantage anticipated.[100]

Note that instead of the damage being 'excessive in relation to the concrete and direct military advantage', Article 8(2)(b)(iv) requires a higher threshold of '*clearly* excessive in relation to the concrete and direct *overall* military advantage' (emphasis added). There are arguments about whether this was for the understandable reason of parsing obligations designed with state, rather than criminal, liability in mind.[101] That does not explain the raising of the threshold (by the addition of the italicised words) that is not customary.[102] However, owing to Article 21, the ICC will have to apply it. Therefore, when looking at the jurisprudence of the ICC when prosecuting this and certain other crimes,[103] the statutory background (i.e., the Rome Statute) must be borne in mind. They cannot be read as straightforward applications of IHL. To do so would risk narrowing

[99] See Sandoz, Swiniarski and Zimmerman, *Commentary on the Additional Protocols*, 995–6.

[100] Emphasis added. See generally, R. Arnold, 'Article 8(2)(b)(iv)', in O. Triffterer (ed.), *Commentary on the Rome Statute of the International Criminal Court*, 2nd edn (Oxford: Hart, 2008), 338.

[101] H. von Hebel and D. Robinson, 'Crimes within the Jurisdiction of the Court', in R. S. Lee (ed.), *The International Criminal Court: The Making of the Rome Statute* (The Hague: Kluwer, 1999), 79, 111.

[102] Cryer, *Prosecuting International Crimes*, 277–9.

[103] For example, Article 8(2)(b)(i), where the customary *mens rea* is probably recklessness, not knowledge. See A. Cassese, 'The Statute of the International Criminal Court: Some Preliminary Reflections', 10 *EJIL* (1999) 144, 154.

the protection under IHL by reading a controversial definition of a war crime (which is narrower than the relevant grave breach of the underlying treaty).

However, the situation is not quite as bleak for those (myself included)[104] who prefer coherence over fragmentation in international criminal law, at the very least where international criminal tribunals, or courts acting on the basis of universal jurisdiction, are interpreting international crimes. There are a number of reasons for this. The first is that the Rome Statute itself suggests a recourse to general IHL in Article 21(1)(b), which refers to '[i]n the second place, where appropriate, applicable treaties and the principles and rules of international law, including the established principles of the international law of armed conflict'. This does, admittedly, render such reference secondary, but, in the context of war crimes, general IHL is likely to be a fairly frequent source of reference.

There are two aspects to this. The first relates to Articles 8(2)(a) and 8(2)(e). These grant the ICC jurisdiction over grave breaches of the 1949 Geneva Conventions and violations of common Article 3. It was clear in the drafting and terminology of both of these provisions that they were intended, *pace Tadić*, to refer to the conditions of applicability and the ambit of protections provided for in those Conventions. Not least, Article 8(2)(a) refers to grave breaches of the Conventions and to 'persons and property protected' by the relevant convention and the Elements of Crimes (drafted, as was the Rome Statute, after *Tadić*) require an international armed conflict for the application of that provision.[105]

For the other two provisions granting the ICC jurisdiction over war crimes, both Article 8(2)(b) and (e) (on international and non-international armed conflicts respectively) condition the jurisdiction of the court 'within the established framework of international law'. This seems quite directly to give a *renvoi* to IHL when the ICC is prosecuting war crimes. It may be the case that this condition was imposed to ensure that the Tribunal does not become too 'progressive' in its interpretations of IHL,[106] and the Elements of Crimes do not always dispel this

[104] Cryer, 'Royalism and the King', 394–5.

[105] For example, K. Dörmann et al., 'The Context of War Crimes', in Lee et al., *The International Criminal Court*, 112, 114–15. It was assumed that this means the same thing in the context of Articles 8(2)(a) and (b).

[106] M. Cottier, 'Article 8(2)(b)', in Triffterer, *Commentary on the Rome Statute*, 332, 323.

suspicion.[107] Still, this is, in fact, a useful clarification for the Court, tying its interpretations to IHL. Some time ago Peter noted that a number of the terms in the Rome Statute, such as 'attack', are defined *inter alia* in Additional Protocol I and this was a way for the ICC to apply those definitions to ensure consistency.[108] This has proved prophetic, in that the ICC has, for the most part, kept to the definitions found in existing IHL treaties[109] and the jurisprudence of the *ad hoc* tribunals. For example,[110] in the *abu Garda* case, while interpreting the crime of attacking peacekeepers in Article 8(2)(e)(iii) of the Rome Statute (which was, to all intents and purposes, cut and pasted into Article 4(b) of the SCSL Statute), the relevant Pre-Trial Chamber drew upon both Additional Protocol I and the SCSL's decision in the *RUF* case to interpret the relevant terms in accordance with IHL.[111]

Looking to international armed conflicts the ICC has noted that the Rome Statute and the Elements of Crimes do not define the concept themselves.[112] Therefore, the ICC has looked to the jurisprudence of the ICTY, in particular, to determine the existence and nature of an armed conflict.[113] In addition to this, when looking at the criteria for an international armed conflict, taking into account that the requirement that Article 8(2)(b) needs to be interpreted in accordance with existing IHL, the Trial Chamber in *Lubanga* looked specifically to the Geneva Conventions and Additional Protocol I, and its acceptance that it applies in situations of occupation, to delineate whether Article 8(2)(b) did apply (finding that it does).[114] Perhaps more controversially it adopted the ICTY's test of 'overall' control over armed groups, for the purposes of internationalising conflicts, over the ICJ's preferred 'effective control' test.[115] Given the controversy on point,[116] the ICC in *Lubanga* might have addressed that particular issue further.

[107] See Elements of Crimes for Article 8(2)(b)(viii) and H. von Hebel, 'Article 8(2)(b)(viii)', in Lee et al., *The International Criminal Court*, 158, 159–62.

[108] Rowe, 'War Crimes', 219.

[109] Although, as Peter has written, the issue of reservations here may cause difficulties, although this has not, as yet, been an issue: Rowe, 'War Crimes', 218–19.

[110] For discussion, see Schabas, *The Rome Statute of the International Criminal Court*, 396–7.

[111] *Prosecutor* v. *abu Garda*, Decision on the Confirmation of Charges, ICC-02/05-02/09, 8 February 2010, paras 64–5, as they noted, *ibid.*, attacks in international and non-international armed conflicts mean the same thing in this context.

[112] *Prosecutor* v. *Lubanga* (n. 82, above), para. 531. [113] *Ibid.*, para. 541.

[114] *Ibid.*, para. 542. [115] *Ibid.*, para. 541.

[116] See J. Crawford, *State Responsibility* (Cambridge: Cambridge University Press 2013), 146–56.

Turning to non-international armed conflicts, Article 8(2)(f) of the Rome Statute does provide a definition:

> Paragraph 2 (e) applies to armed conflicts not of an international character and thus does not apply to situations of internal disturbances and tensions, such as riots, isolated and sporadic acts of violence or other acts of a similar nature. It applies to armed conflicts that take place in the territory of a State when there is protracted armed conflict between governmental authorities and organized armed groups or between such groups.[117]

This, of course, pursuant to Article 21, is the controlling definition for the ICC. That said, the language is intentionally almost identical to the test developed by the ICTY in the *Tadić* case.[118] Therefore, it is notable that, in setting out the test applicable before the ICC, the Trial Chamber in *Lubanga* looked at Additional Protocol II's conditions of applicability but drew heavily on the jurisprudence of the ICTY. It preferred the standards the ICTY set for the application of the customary law of non-international armed conflict, as well as the factors that it had identified as being relevant, to the (higher) threshold that was set as a matter of treaty law for its applicability, in Additional Protocol II.[119] In doing so the Trial Chamber in *Lubanga* tied the interpretation of the Statute (back?) to the general standard set in IHL. This, for our purposes, is welcome. It avoids fragmentation between tribunals and the law of war crimes and its parent law: IHL.

The fact that earlier tribunals have, when it has come to substantive norms, based themselves on IHL (and, in doing so, contributed to that law too) assists greatly, as Peter has noted, with an important caveat:

> The International Criminal Tribunals for the Former Yugoslavia and for Rwanda have produced a number of decisions of great authority on issues relating to war crimes [. . .] These Tribunals have acted under their respective Statutes, the wording of which differs from that of Article 8

[117] The ICC has also seemingly applied this to Article 8(2)(c) of the Rome Statute, which grants it jurisdiction over violations of Common Article 3 of the Geneva Conventions. This is probably unexceptionable. See Schabas, *The Rome Statute of the International Criminal Court*, 205–6.

[118] See *Prosecutor* v. *Tadić* (n. 32, above), para. 70. The slight discrepancy is most probably the result of a *lapsus calami* rather than an intention to change the test.

[119] *Prosecutor* v. *Lubanga* (n. 82, above), paras 535–8. It is interesting that they did not discuss in any depth the practice of the ICTR or SCSL, although this is probably because they tended to deal with the (higher) threshold in AP II.

> of the Rome Statute [. . .] when discussing war crimes these differences should be borne in mind. It may be that the Court would take a different view.[120]

This links back to what was said above, that the ICC must, in the final analysis, apply its Statute first. The risk of fragmentation therefore cannot be entirely discounted. It ought to be said, on the other hand, that on the issue on which we have concentrated most attention, the applicability of IHL and which type, the ICC has done a great deal to ensure consistency between its Statute, the jurisprudence of the tribunals and pre-existing IHL, as seen above.[121]

Conclusion

As this, necessarily partial, survey attempts to show, the relationship between the law of war crimes and IHL is a close one and, for the most part, international criminal tribunals have done their best to tie their interpretations back to the relevant applicable IHL, although there are some exceptions. Additionally, they have attempted to be, so far as possible, consistent between themselves. As Nerlich has said, though, the first duty of each tribunal is to apply its Statute first and general international law (including as interpreted by the *ad hoc* tribunals) second.[122] In some ways the practice of the ICTY in particular has proven to be exceptionally important, but cannot be divorced, any more than the decisions of the other courts and tribunals discussed above, from the Statute it was called upon to interpret and apply. It is simply that the tribunal in the *Tadić* case interpreted Article 3 of that Statute to grant it jurisdiction over all criminal violations of the applicable treaty and customary law (other than the grave breaches provisions, covered by Article 2) applicable in former Yugoslavia. The other tribunals in the post-Nuremberg/Tokyo world have not had that luxury (although they have done their best to avoid too many consequences to flow from this – occasionally (step forward the SCSL) on somewhat stretched legal grounds).

[120] Rowe, 'War Crimes', 219.

[121] On this see also V. Nerlich, 'The Status of ICTY and ICTR Precedent in Proceedings before the ICC', in Stahn and Sluiter, *The Emerging Practice of the International Criminal Court*, 305. Procedure may be a different matter, but it is far outside the scope of this contribution.

[122] *Ibid.*, 325.

The tying of war crimes law so closely to IHL has enabled the *ad hoc* tribunals (and, to the extent to which it has built up jurisprudence on point, the ICC) to contribute back to IHL, which is a law that rarely receives detailed judicial consideration – particularly in relation to battlefield conduct. Nonetheless, it is true that the practice of the criminal tribunals, particularly with respect to 'Hague' law, has been criticised, especially from the point of view of the level of expertise, difficulty of finding facts and the complexity of the law.[123] Furthermore, some have said that the tribunals have been too willing to put their thumb on the scale on the side of humanity rather than military necessity.[124] Some of these critiques may have purchase, although it ought to be said that their interpretation of military necessity has tended to be not too bad[125] and, for the most part, their jurisprudence, whilst often open to criticism,[126] bears up fairly well when compared to other national and international tribunals' work on point.[127]

Detailed evaluation of the specific decisions on point would render this piece a monograph rather than a chapter in a book. Suffice it to say that the way in which the tribunals have attempted, albeit imperfectly, to reconcile treaties, custom and their constituent documents has contributed strongly to the detail and corpus of IHL, even if occasionally by negative example. Twenty years ago, works on IHL tended to speak of specific incidents and pronounce, from an academic Olympian height, whether they were lawful or not, often without providing reasons. The tribunals have worked quite hard to be coherent on point, at times (step forward again the SCSL) at the risk of ignoring their founding documents' jurisdictional provisions, perhaps on the basis of inapposite inferences drawn from the ICTY's, perhaps Lauterpachtian,

123 Bartels, 'Dealing with the Principle of Proportionality'.

124 M. Schmitt, 'Military Necessity and Humanity in International Humanitarian Law: Preserving the Delicate Balance', 50 *VJIL* (2010) 795.

125 N. Hayashi, 'Requirements of Military Necessity in International Humanitarian Law and International Criminal Law', 28 *Boston University International Law Journal* (2010) 39, 139–40.

126 Some recent decisions have few defenders. See, e.g., J. N. Clark, 'Courting Controversy: The ICTY's Acquittal of Croatian Generals Gotovina and Markač', 11 *JICJ* (2013) 399.

127 For critical views of national courts on point, see Y. Ronen '*Silent Enim Leges Inter Arma* – but Beware the Background Noise: Domestic Courts as Agents of Development of the Law on the Conduct of Hostilities', 26 *LJIL* 599 (2013); E. Benvenisti, 'Judicial Misgivings regarding the Application of International Norms: An Analysis of Attitudes of National Courts', 4 *EJIL* (1993) 159.

interpretation of its Article 3.[128] Whether the ICC will be able to do so is more complex in that the drafters of its Statute took care to prevent it being too 'progressive'.[129] Its jurisprudence ought therefore, as with those of its siblings, to be read carefully and with appropriate reference to the jurisdictional provisions that govern its action.

[128] On Lauterpacht's influence on international criminal law, see M. Koskenniemi, 'Hersch Lauterpacht and the Development of International Criminal Law', 2 *JICJ* (2004) 810.

[129] The role of Article 10 of the Rome Statute here is important, but its nuance is, unfortunately, often lost in the maelstrom that often characterises debate on custom or treaty interpretation.

PART II

Effective protection?

7

The future of Article 5 tribunals in the light of experiences in the Iraq War 2003

NICHOLAS MERCER

> Should any doubt arise as to whether persons, having committed a belligerent act and having fallen into the hands of the enemy, belong to any of the categories enumerated in Article 4, such persons shall enjoy the protection of the present Convention until such time as their status has been determined by a competent tribunal.[1]

When I joined the British Army in 1991 I was sent to Liverpool University, early in my career, to be tutored in the laws of war by Professor Dominic McGoldrick and Professor Peter Rowe. It was unforeseeable that a decade later I would be the Command Legal Adviser for Headquarters 1st (UK) Armoured Division in the Iraq War 2003 – a war in which the British Army put an armoured division into the field for the last time, which became one of the most complex and controversial wars in which the United Kingdom has ever been involved and which reverberates today both politically and legally. The legal problems were immense and, for the first time in a generation, all four Geneva Conventions (GC) came into play along with the vexed question as to whether human rights law applied on the battlefield. However, it seems very fitting to be writing a chapter as a tribute to Professor Rowe who prepared me and many of my contemporaries in the British Army for the numerous conflicts that arose over the next twenty years.[2]

The conference which led to this book being written was a conference for both academics and military lawyers and it seems particularly appropriate that the views of military lawyers are heard alongside academics because they have had the (often) awkward task of trying to apply the laws of war to the battlefield. This is not simply an academic exercise, but

[1] Article 5 GC III 1949.

[2] Legal officers prepared by Professor Peter Rowe and Professor Dominic McGoldrick at the University of Liverpool in 1994 went on to serve in Northern Ireland, Bosnia and Herzegovina, Iraq and Afghanistan.

also involves the complex task of interpretation and implementation of the law of armed conflict in the context of a real-time battle rhythm – sometimes under fire – where there are strategic, political and tactical considerations simultaneously to take into account. It can also require decisions to be taken with some haste and without the comfort of either research or the facilities for research, or indeed even the ability to seek the opinions of others owing to communications problems or radio silence. This can, of course, sometimes be a blessing. However, the conditions under which the law of armed conflict can sometimes be practised should not be underestimated. Furthermore, the relationship between a military commander and his/her legal adviser can also play a significant role in any legal issue, in both its acceptance and its implementation. As with so many situations in life, the difference between theory and practice is immense, but this dynamic makes the law of armed conflict such a fascinating and challenging area of the law.

Prior to the Iraq War in 2003, the laws of war had had a comfortable existence in the British Army. They did not apply in Northern Ireland and, although the laws of war applied in both the Falklands War and the first Iraq War in 1991,[3] not only were those wars mercifully short, but sovereign territory was restored almost immediately once the ground war was over. In the Iraq War 2003,[4] however, the UK found itself in belligerent occupation with the myriad of legal problems that GC III and IV present in such a situation. Added to the mix was the fact that the battlefield had changed immeasurably by 2003. Whereas in the Falklands War and the first Iraq War combatants generally complied with the provisions of Article 4 GC III,[5] in the Iraq War 2003 over half of the prisoners captured by Coalition forces in the UK area of operations (AO) were in civilian clothing. It was this dramatic change on the battlefield that was to make Article 5 tribunals such a problem. Almost as soon as the prisoners were conveyed to the prisoner of war (POW) facility at Um Qsar, not only was it noticeable that a vast number were not in uniform but, predictably, a sizeable number insisted that they were not combatants at all but were civilians innocently caught up in the conflict. As the word spread that detention could be challenged, so too did the numbers seeking to challenge their detention. The United Kingdom suddenly found itself having, potentially, to conduct well in excess of 1,500

[3] Operation Desert Storm 1991. [4] Known as Op Telic 2003.

[5] See Article 4 (1) and (2) and the requirements for members of the armed forces and militias generally.

Article 5 tribunals[6] as well as coping with all the other immeasurably difficult tasks that the British Army was encountering as an Army of Occupation, and for which it was so ill-prepared.[7]

The legal framework for determining the status of prisoners at the time of the Iraq War 2003 was found in the 'Prisoner of War Determination of Status Regulations 1958' made by Royal Warrant. Under the regulations, a board of inquiry (BOI), normally used for domestic military inquiries, would be convened by an officer of at least the rank of Major to determine the status of anyone about whom there was any doubt. In theory this should have worked relatively well as BOIs are routinely convened both under the Army Act 1955 and now under the Armed Forces Act 2006.[8] In simple terms, a Board of Officers is assembled[9] to investigate and determine anything that falls within the regulations and the officers simply hear the relevant evidence and then make their determination. The rules of evidence are relatively relaxed, though the Board can seek the assistance of a legal officer should the need arise. However, although a BOI generally works well in the routine business of the Armed Forces, it proved far more problematic on the battlefield.

Once it became apparent that Article 5 tribunals were going to be necessary to determine status, the first issue was deciding how such claims were to be investigated and, in particular, how evidence and witnesses were going to be obtained to determine any claim. The Military Police were overstretched for the task. The breakdown in law and order in southern Iraq, together with some enormously complicated investigations into alleged war crimes,[10] a major helicopter crash[11] and

[6] It was estimated that something in the region of 1,500 Article 5 tribunals were required.

[7] See *Daily Mirror*, 'Desert Sham: Officer Admits Iraq Occupation Shambles', 18 May 2006: www.mirror.co.uk/news/uk-news/desert-sham-officer-admits-iraq-625512.

[8] The Armed Forces Act 2006 came into force on 31 October 2009.

[9] Normally three in number with a Major as the senior officer, although the rank can vary depending on the seriousness and complexity of the matter under investigation.

[10] For instance, the investigation into the deaths of Spr Allsop and SSgt Cunningham at Az Zubayr was to prove particularly difficult and complex. The investigation resulted in the detention of Faisal al Sadoon and Khalef Hussain Mufdhi who were transferred to the Iraqi High Tribunal in breach of a European Court injunction. See *Al-Sadoon and Mufdhi* v. *The United Kingdom*, 61498 (2010) ECHR (4 October 2010). See http://news.bbc.co.uk/1/hi/uk/5399052.stm.

[11] 12 March 2003. The servicemen were on board a US Marine CH-46 Sea Knight helicopter as part of the invading force of allied troops involved in seizing oilfields on the al Faw peninsula.

other deaths[12] meant that the Military Police were already heavily over-committed. Through the good offices of the Provost Marshal,[13] four men, commanded by a senior non-commissioned officer (SNCO), were made available to begin the task of conducting the investigations. However, given the potential for over 1,500 investigations, the number of investigators fell hopelessly short of what was required. In an attempt to make the task more palatable, the Military Police were first tasked to investigate just ten cases so that a start could be made on convening and hearing the Article 5 tribunals, with investigations and tribunals then, it was hoped, running concurrently. At least that was the theory. However, the investigations ran into problems almost immediately and after the first week not one case had been investigated and indeed *all* attempts at investigation had floundered.

The reasons for the failure, in the first instance, were largely due to the problems connected with obtaining the relevant evidence. The obvious place for any investigation to start was the circumstances of capture, together with any property that had been seized from the prisoner. This, in theory, would give a very good indication of whether the individual was taking part in hostilities or was otherwise entitled to POW status.[14] A number of measures had been put in place to record the circumstances of capture, but all were to prove problematic. In the first instance, a prisoner was meant to have a capture tag attached to him by the capturing unit that gave relevant details, including time and place of capture. However, over 90 per cent of prisoners captured did not have completed capture tags and, of the 10 per cent who did have the tags, the information was so sketchy or illegible as to be bordering on useless.[15] Capture tags were a requirement for all capturing units to complete but, in practice, this did not happen. The same applied to battlefield reports, known as COMCAPREPS.[16] These were rarely completed but were

[12] See evidence of the Baha Mousa Inquiry where it was acknowledged that the British Army was investigating 'a number of deaths in UK custody' www.bahamousainquiry.org/.

[13] Lieutenant Colonel E. O. Forster-Knight OBE, later Provost Marshal for the British Army.

[14] See Article 4 GC III 1949 and Article 44 AP I 1977 for those entitled to POW status.

[15] It should be remembered that the average reading/writing age of an infantry soldier is eleven years old and that, in any event, battlefield conditions make the completion of such documents very difficult. See BBC News, 18 July 2013: 'Almost 40% of army recruits have reading age of 11': www.bbc.co.uk/news/education-23346693.

[16] Common Capture Reports (COMCAPREPS). These were reports from the battlefield that were meant to be completed by the capturing unit and accompany the prisoners to the POW facility.

meant to be reports from the capturing units of the circumstances of capture. The battlefield is far from ideal for staff work and this was borne out in practice. In addition to the capture tags and the COMCAPREPS, the prisoners were also meant to be given a POW identity bracelet showing which nation had captured a particular prisoner.[17] However, these bracelets were routinely altered, swapped or discarded[18] and there were also cultural reasons which made prisoners averse to wearing a bracelet. The number of prisoners captured, the chaos of the battlefield, fighting in urban areas and the corralling of prisoners on the battlefield meant that it was often impossible to identify where, and in what circumstances, a prisoner was captured. Furthermore, the United Kingdom acted as relief in place[19] for the USA, which added an additional layer of complexity as prisoners would often be passed to UK forces by an American unit with little formal handover. Obtaining the relevant evidence regarding capture was a very difficult exercise.

Another important source of evidence was the property that was taken from the prisoner on capture as this could provide evidence of their name, rank, unit or, indeed, if they had weapons or military equipment, whether or not they were taking an active part in hostilities.[20] However, this also proved equally problematic. The property of the POWs was hopelessly chaotic and 'identifying particular property to an individual PW proved difficult verging on the impossible'.[21] The prisoners had been captured by both UK and US forces and, more often than not, the prisoner had been separated from both their weapons and their personal possessions. It was not uncommon to see a bus or helicopter coming into the POW camp with kit being brought in separately, and often at a later date. This was not in accordance with the instructions given to units prior to the commencement of hostilities, but was an unfortunate consequence of both a lack of adequate training as well as the pressure of military operations. All this was further compounded by the fact that the

[17] See Article 12 GC III 1949, which states that 'the Detaining Power is responsible for the treatment given'.

[18] This also has an added legal problem of identifying who was the capturing nation and therefore what legal standards are applied to a given prisoner.

[19] 'Relief in place' is the process whereby one unit relieves another and takes charge of their location (including prisoners) thereby freeing up forces to continue an assault/advance.

[20] See Article 18 GC III 1949. A number of prisoners were found with large sums of money that may have been evidence of financial inducement by the regime to take part in the fighting.

[21] The author personally inspected the ISO containers where the property of prisoners had been deposited on arrival at the facility.

facility was also used by both UK and US forces who had received different training and had no comprehensive instructions for keeping prisoners and their possessions together. Personal possessions suffered from the same systemic failings as capture tags and bracelets. What possessions were recovered by capturing units were generally placed in unmarked bin bags that were then deposited in an ISO container at the POW camp. Indeed, such was the chaotic state of prisoner property that, at the time of release, prisoners were compensated with $100 for the assumed loss of their property. In any event, without such evidence at the outset the task of beginning an investigation into the status of a prisoner was severely impaired and made the task of even starting to investigate extremely difficult.

As well as details of capture and prisoner property there was the even more basic problem of establishing exactly who had been captured. One of the first problems on arrival at the POW facility was establishing the identity of a prisoner. Prisoners in Iraq could give up to four different names. Some gave nicknames, some gave family names, some were known by their second or third names and a sizeable number were illiterate, making identification almost impossible. If the name of the prisoner cannot be identified, then the task of investigating a claim over status is almost impossible from the start as one simply does not know who one is dealing with. Many prisoners claimed to be farmers or innocent bystanders caught up in the confusion. However, without a proper name, or any other evidence relating to capture or equipment, it was impossible to verify if the individual was entitled to combatant status or was indeed simply an innocent victim, as alleged.

As well as these preliminary problems, and even if a prisoner could be identified, there were secondary issues. After the first week of investigations, the SNCO heading the investigation team was questioned as to why no cases had been properly investigated. It was explained that, even where the identity of a prisoner had been established, this was only the start of the problems. Depending on the account given, in order to investigate the claim the investigators would normally be required to travel to interview witnesses or organisations (such as an employer or records office). There was the primary problem of language and the lack of translators. Each investigator required not only an interpreter but an interpreter who could be trusted. Secondly, any investigation was potentially hazardous. It could take the Military Police to a remote location where there might be a danger of ambush or kidnap and they would therefore need force security in order to carry out the investigation.[22] Those who have visited Basra know that there are parts of Basra you should not visit for long, and certainly not without proper security. Alternatively, it might be the wrong or a false address, or indeed the witness might not agree to speak for fear of reprisal. There was also the possibility of revenge against a family given the ignominy of capture.[23] Added to this was the geographical spread of Iraqi forces, and those captured reflected this trend. Many of Saddam's forces in the south of Iraq were drawn from the north of Iraq. The Shia uprising of 1991[24] had made Saddam Hussein very cautious about locating locally recruited troops in their home town and (admittedly with some authenticity) prisoners often claimed to come from the north of Iraq. Whilst this might give credence to their claim, such claims still needed investigation where status was challenged. Iraq is larger than France and, given the distances involved and the security problems, it was almost impossible to travel from the south to the north of Iraq.[25] In such circumstances, it is hard to envisage how any such claims might be properly investigated at all.

The United Kingdom had a sizeable problem on its hands. It was legally bound to hold a tribunal[26] and, at the same time, there was considerable pressure to reduce the number of POWs in the facility, given the immense pressure on manning, support and materiel. The tension between the Commandant of the POW facility[27] and HQ 1st (UK) Armoured Division became intense[28] and a solution had to be found. The proposed solution was what came to be termed 'initial assessments', which, as the title suggests, was a determination at the outset to determine whether or not the individual was a combatant. This question was considered by an assessment panel that consisted of a legal

22 As well as the Military Police ('Red caps') killed in Majar-al-Kabir in 2003, over 200 foreign hostages were seized in Iraq and many were executed.

23 This also raises the difficult issue of the duty of care owed to a prisoner by UK forces and the right to life under Article 2 of the European Convention on Human Rights and Fundamental Freedoms (ECHR).

24 There was a Shia uprising in the aftermath of the first Iraq War, which was ruthlessly crushed by Saddam Hussein and the Republican Guard.

25 For instance, it is 300 miles to Baghdad from Basra and 500 miles to Kirkuk in the north of Iraq.

26 Article 5 GC III 1949.

27 Lieutenant Colonel G. Baldwin QDG.

28 See Baha Mousa report (n. 12, above), vol. 3. There was an attempt to hold Boards of Inquiry with 250 names annexed to each inquiry so that a large number of prisoners could be released after each one. This was stopped after intervention from the SO2 Legal Officer (Major David Christie) in the POW facility.

officer, an intelligence officer and another regular officer or warrant officer (or SNCO). In the absence of any real evidence, this was done entirely through questioning the individual prisoner. The intelligence officer was on the panel to use his expertise in intelligence to assess the veracity of the account and the legal officer was employed similarly to assess the facts and also to ensure that the provisions of the law of armed conflict were complied with. The third officer was also required to assess the veracity of the account given and all three officers acted, collectively, to judge whether the prisoner was telling the truth or not. Given the fact that this was an *ad hoc* arrangement, there were no rules of procedure or evidence, nor was there a convening order with terms of reference attached, as required for a BOI. It was designed simply for speed and simplicity. The words of Article 5 GC III state: 'Should any doubt arise as to whether persons, having committed a belligerent act and having fallen into the hands of the enemy, belong to any of the categories enumerated in Article 4, such persons shall enjoy the protection of the present Convention until such time as their status has been determined by a competent tribunal.' In accordance with the wording of Article 5, if the panel had *any doubt* as to the status of the individual, they retained him as a POW. The status of POW, and the privileges it conferred, could only be relinquished if there was *no* doubt that the individual was a civilian. The rationale was that POW status was protected under international law and could not be lightly relinquished.[29] The initial assessments were considered the only expedient way of carrying out a review of prisoner status, given the constraints of obtaining evidence in belligerent occupation and with very limited military assets.

It was realised, however, that there was a legal risk involved in adopting such a system. The problem (and the proposed solution) was discussed with the International Committee of the Red Cross (ICRC)[30] representative in Basra. The presence of the ICRC was both welcome and of enormous assistance to military lawyers. They were immensely helpful and were not only engaged with the issues but also understood the constraints of military operations. As a result of our discussions with the ICRC, the problem, and the proposed solution, was staffed to the ICRC Headquarters in Geneva. The ICRC, understanding the limitations involved in such situations and also understanding that we were trying our very best under international law, were content to approve the system we had devised for prisoner review. This was immensely

[29] Article 7 GC III 1949. [30] See www.icrc.org/eng/.

reassuring and also provided a foil to possible criticism and legal challenge at a later date. To date, no criticisms have been raised about the initial assessments. However, this was not a wholly satisfactory state of affairs and the 'solution' was only a temporary measure to deal with the immediate crisis in prisoner numbers at the POW Camp in the immediate aftermath of a conflict. The description of the problems experienced clearly demonstrates that such tribunals are not fit for purpose. Furthermore, if a prisoner had been released incorrectly, and therefore denied the privileges afforded to a POW or came to harm, there was the potential for future legal challenge. At the same time, if a prisoner was held unlawfully then this too might be subject to legal challenge and possibly damages for false imprisonment. The question therefore remains as to how such tribunals might be designed and conducted in any future international armed conflicts, particularly in situations of belligerent occupation.

Finding a solution to this problem is not easy either. There has been relatively little state practice in the operation of Article 5 tribunals since 1949 and, even where states have conducted such tribunals, there is little or no common ground. In addition, there is no guidance on the matter in either the Conventions or the Commentary.[31] The USA and Canada, for instance, use military tribunals, whereas Israel uses civilian courts. However, there is another very important factor that has arisen since the Iraq War in 2003, which is the applicability of the European Convention on Human Rights (ECHR). In 2011, the European Court of Human Rights in Strasbourg delivered its judgment in the case of *Al Skeini*[32] and determined that the ECHR applied during the belligerent occupation in Iraq. One of the key factors to take into account therefore, when designing an Article 5 tribunal that is 'fit for purpose in the twenty-first century', is not only to address the practical requirements mentioned above but also to ensure that any tribunal also meets its legal obligations. This inevitably raises the (still) vexed question of the ECHR and its extraterritorial applicability.

Having taught the laws of war for many years,[33] it is often the case that, at the end of each period of conflict, there is generally a further international treaty or treaties designed to address some of the

[31] See Pictet's commentary: www.icrc.org/eng/resources/documents/publication/p0203.htm.

[32] *Al-Skeini and Others* v. *United Kingdom*, 55721/07 (2011) ECHR 1093 (7 July 2011).

[33] The author has been on the teaching staff of the International Institute of Humanitarian Law in San Remo, Italy since 2000.

problems and shortfalls that have arisen in the previous conflict.[34] The remarkable development after the Iraq War 2003 was the decision in the case of *Al Skeini* regarding the applicability of the ECHR in situations of belligerent occupation. The question over applicability of the ECHR in situations of international armed conflict proved very controversial in the Iraq War in 2003; indeed, the debate was already underway in advance of the conflict itself, having been raised by lawyers from Army Legal Services with the Ministry of Defence (MOD) lawyers at Permanent Joint Headquarters (PJHQ) in January 2003.[35] As a result of the disclosure of documents in the Baha Mousa trial, and subsequent public inquiry,[36] it became clear that there was a marked difference of opinion between military lawyers and MOD lawyers on the issue during the war. Whereas the Command Legal Adviser for HQ 1st (UK) Armoured Division in 2003 argued that the ECHR would apply during the occupation of southern Iraq, this was resolutely rejected by the MOD lawyers at PJHQ. In a memorandum to PJHQ dated 23 March 2003 from the Command Legal Adviser at HQ 1st (UK) Armoured Division (three days after the war had begun and whilst under intermittent missile attack), the following advice was proffered in theatre on the extraterritorial application of the ECHR in occupation:

> In my opinion it is an all or nothing situation, as we either exercise jurisdiction over the territory or not. Presumably, if we are in occupation we have jurisdiction. I have always been of the view that the ECHR would apply.[37]

This opinion was resisted by the MOD who responded:

> During Phase III (b)/Phase IV *lex specialis* operates to oust the ECHR. This means there is no requirement for you to provide guidance on the application of the ECHR/HRA. I hope this is clear.[38]

Despite the clear direction from the MOD that the ECHR did not apply in belligerent occupation and that there was 'no requirement to provide guidance' on the matter, three years later the MOD conceded that the ECHR did apply when a person was held in the custody of the United

[34] For instance, the 1925 Geneva Protocol for the Prohibition of the Use in War of Asphyxiating, Poisonous or Other Gases after the First World War and the 1997 Ottawa Convention on the Prohibition of Anti-Personnel Mines at the end of the Balkans War in 1992–6.

[35] *Al-Skeini and Others* v. *United Kingdom* (n. 32, above). [36] *Ibid.* [37] *Ibid.* [38] *Ibid.*

Kingdom.[39] In the case of Baha Mousa in the House of Lords in 2006 the UK government conceded the judgment of the Divisional Court whereby:

> The Secretary of State originally contended in these proceedings that none of the claimants' complaints fell within the limited extraterritorial exceptions recognised by the Strasbourg court. But the Queen's Bench Divisional Court (Rix LJ and Forbes J, [2004] EWHC 2911 (Admin), [2007] QB 140) held that although the first five of the present claims fell outside the scope of the Convention the sixth, that of Colonel Mousa, did not. That is a ruling which the Secretary of State now accepts.

The Divisional Court held that Baha Mousa's case fell within Article 1 ECHR because:

> a British military prison, operating in Iraq with the consent of the Iraqi sovereign authorities, and containing arrested suspects, falls within even a narrowly limited exception exemplified by embassies, consulates, vessels and aircraft, and in Hess v. UK 2 DR 72, a prison.[40]

The Court of Appeal upheld this decision, but on the basis that 'Mr Mousa came within the control and authority of the UK from the time he was arrested at the hotel and thereby lost his freedom at the hands of British troops.'[41]

Although the United Kingdom did not concede that the other five cases heard at the same time came within the jurisdiction of the ECHR it is very notable that they reversed the legal direction they had given so emphatically in 2003.

With regard to the other five cases, which concerned the death of Iraqi nationals during belligerent occupation in 2003–4, the European Court of Human Rights held that the Convention did apply during a belligerent occupation by a signatory state. The European Court of Human Rights stated:

> Another exception to the principle that jurisdiction under Article 1 is limited to a State's own territory occurs when, as a consequence of lawful or unlawful military action, a Contracting State exercises effective control of an area outside that national territory. The obligation to secure, in such an area, the rights and freedoms set out in the Convention, derives from the fact of such control, whether it be exercised directly, through the

[39] The UK conceded before the House of Lords that the Human Rights Act 1997 applied where the prisoner (Baha Mousa) was held in UK custody.

[40] *Al Skeini* v. *Secretary of State for Defence*, [2004] EWHC 2911 (Admin), para. 287.

[41] For the full judgment, see www.redress.org/downloads/casework/SkeiniHouseofLordsJudgement.pdf.

> Contracting State's own armed forces, or through a subordinate local administration [. . .] the controlling State has the responsibility under Article 1 to secure, within the area under its control, the entire range of substantive rights set out in the Convention and those additional Protocols which it has ratified. It will be liable for any violations of those rights.[42]

The decision of the European Court is of immense legal importance but, for the purposes of this chapter, the pertinent question is the potential impact on Article 5 tribunals in the future. The second issue is deciding on how to design any future tribunal when the law is still not clear and on what is the best approach to take in such circumstances. Indeed, the culture of uncertainty over the ECHR, which gave rise to so much disagreement in the Iraq War, in 2003, might similarly affect the design of any future Article 5 tribunal.

If it is acknowledged that the ECHR applies in such circumstances, then this could have a considerable impact on any future Article 5 tribunals and the procedures adopted. Under Article 5, although it is clear that the detention is, on the face of it, lawful under the law of armed conflict,[43] where there is doubt this may have to be reviewed by a judicial authority. Under Article 5(2) of the Convention reasons for the arrest have to be given and under Article 5(3) there is a requirement for pre-trial detention and trial within a reasonable time. Taking Article 5(2) in the first instance, this would be difficult. For a combatant to become a POW he simply has to 'fall into the power of the enemy'.[44] However, there is no requirement for the POW to be given reasons as to why he has been detained. However, Article 5(2) requires 'the elementary safeguard' to inform a prisoner 'as to why he has been deprived of his liberty'.[45] This is not insurmountable, but, at the very least, this would require notice to be given to those prisoners who were challenging their detention once their intent to challenge their detention was known. It could even be argued that the right to challenge their detention should be given at the point of detention itself. This could be done on registration of the prisoner or at a later date, but this is an important element in the

[42] *Al-Skeini and Others* v. *United Kingdom* (n. 32, above), para. 138.

[43] Under Article 5 GC III 1949, they become prisoners at such time as they 'fall into the power of the enemy'.

[44] *Ibid.*

[45] *Fox, Campbell and Hartley* v. *United Kingdom*, 12244/86, 12245/86,12383/86, ECHR 182 (30 August 1990), para. 40.

detention process and could become grounds for potential challenge if omitted.

The most difficult problem, however, is Article 5(3) and the requirement for the individual to be 'brought promptly before a judge or other officer authorised by law [. . .] and trial within a reasonable time'. During the Iraq War 2003, the challenges to detention were considerable and were dealt with in a largely haphazard fashion. No more than half a dozen cases were ever investigated and no investigation was ever completed. The provisions of Article 5(3) might now require every prisoner challenging their detention to be brought before a judge (say), within twenty-eight days, so that their case could be reviewed in the first instance. This would be an enormous administrative burden and would require a sophisticated case management system to operate at the POW facility, particularly if a sizeable number of prisoners were challenging their detention. As for the provision of a judge or other officer authorised by law, this could be satisfied by the provision of a legal officer from any of the three legal services in the Armed Forces,[46] as long as this was deemed to be suitably 'independent and impartial' under Article 6.[47]

During the Iraq War 2003, HQ 1st (UK) Armoured Division requested that a judge should be sent into theatre generally to oversee detention.[48] This proposal was blocked by the MOD. However, a Judge Advocate (JA) could indeed be provided by the Ministry of Justice for such an eventuality. Many of the JAs, for instance, have prior military experience and also satisfy the strict criteria for independence and impartiality.[49] The reason for the decision by the MOD is not clear, but it is not beyond the realms of probability that the MOD resisted such a request because their own direction over prisoners may have come under greater scrutiny and possibly faced challenge from within. At the same time, there are allegations that UK Armed Forces, under the direction of the MOD, were operating so-called 'black sites' for prisoners within the Western Desert, which would almost certainly have been challenged if an independent judge had come into theatre to oversee

[46] Naval Legal Services, Army Legal Services and RAF Legal Services. It should be noted that military operations in the UK are generally tri-service.

[47] Article 6(1) ECHR. See *Grieves* v. *UK* (2004) 39 EHRR 2.

[48] A Judge Advocate with prior military experience was available to come into theatre. See Baha Mousa report (n. 12, above).

[49] Judge Advocates are appointed independently by the Ministry of Justice and therefore are neither appointed nor controlled by the Ministry of Defence.

detention.[50] The provision of a judge is not insurmountable, but at the heart of the problem, and linked to the practical difficulties set out earlier in this chapter, is the provision regarding 'trial within a reasonable time'.[51]

The practical difficulties involved in obtaining the relevant evidence have been described, in detail, earlier in this chapter and there is no easy solution. Indeed, if one were to change the theatre of war to Afghanistan the problem would be the same and the difficulties in obtaining evidence probably even more hazardous. Even if the support of the local police was employed, the vastly different standards in evidence and legal systems could also render the task nearly impossible. This problem would be further compounded by Articles 5(4) and 5(5), which require a remedy to challenge the legality of detention and the right to compensation for illegal detention. Again, the administrative and judicial apparatus for such provisions are extensive, not to mention the added problem of providing legal advice and assistance for the prisoner.[52] The burdensome and extensive problems of investigating any claim would inevitably find their way into challenges relating to detention and the compensation claims that would inevitably follow.

The obvious way to mitigate the obligations under Articles 5 and 6 ECHR is to derogate under Article 15 of the ECHR, but this too might be problematic. Article 15 provides that:

> In time of war or other public emergency threatening the life of the nation any High Contracting Party may take measures derogating from its obligations under this Convention to the extent strictly required by the exigencies of the situation, provided that such measures are not inconsistent with its other obligations under international law.

Although this seems to be an obvious legal solution, the opportunity to derogate might also create its own legal problems. In the first instance, the UK government might still be unwilling to derogate 'in time of war', or at all. The judgment in *Al Skeini* held that 'the deceased relatives fell within the jurisdiction of the respondent State',[53] thereby clearly

[50] See, e.g., www.guardian.co.uk/world/2013/apr/01/camp-nama-iraq-human-rights-abuses and www.dailymail.co.uk/news/article-2163799/UK-soldiers-beat-innocent-Iraqi-men-black-ops-jails-new-secret-justice-law-means-torture-hidden-forever.html.

[51] See also Article 6 ECHR.

[52] During the Iraq War each detainee was given legal advice and assistance by a legal officer at the POW Camp, although this was, understandably, very superficial.

[53] *Al-Skeini and Others* v. *United Kingdom* (n. 32, above).

establishing that the ECHR applies in belligerent occupation. The Court of Appeal, however, said that 'Mr Mousa came within the control and authority (of) the UK from the time he was arrested'.[54] This still leaves the vexed question as to whether the ECHR would apply to POWs held during the war fighting phase, or only during a belligerent occupation. However, if the position was taken that the ECHR only applied to its prisoners once they were in belligerent occupation, this could lead to the unsatisfactory position whereby the UK only applied the ECHR to its prisoners once they were in belligerent occupation and not before. This would be a very difficult position to take, and probably also unworkable. It would also mean that POWs acquired greater rights as the conflict continued. There is also the added problem of defining when an occupation comes into existence and over what territory.[55] Occupation can extend to a limited amount of territory and, indeed, it was conceded in Iraq that Coalition forces were in occupation of some Iraqi territory on the first day of the ground war.[56] Furthermore, the provisions of Article 19 GC III make it a legal obligation for prisoners to be held 'far enough away from the combat zone for them to be out of danger'. Such areas are likely to be in occupied territory in any event.[57] This provision regarding the protection of prisoners has also meant that prisoners have, in the past, been held on-board ship.[58] This could possibly give some prisoners greater rights than others as the ECHR would clearly apply on the UK ship but might not similarly apply in a POW facility in recently captured enemy territory. This too would be unsatisfactory.

Part of the reluctance to concede that the ECHR applied at all in Iraq 2003 was, no doubt, the concern that if military lawyers said that the ECHR applied, either as a matter of law or of policy, then this might place the UK in an awkward position if legal proceedings were brought in the aftermath of the conflict as a claimant might seek to bring a claim under the Convention. The UK government might still be reluctant to derogate for the same reason. If they do, however, they will find

[54] *Al Skeini* v. *Secretary of State for Defence* [2005] EWCA Civ 1609 (21 December 2005).

[55] See Article 42 Hague Convention IV 1907.

[56] Known as 'G+1'. G+1 means 'Ground +1', in other words, the first day of the ground war. In the Iraq War 2003, Um Qsar fell to Coalition forces on the first day of the ground war and it was acknowledged that the UK was in occupation from that moment. However, it was not until early May that 'active hostilities' came to an end.

[57] Article 19 GC III 1949.

[58] Falklands War 1982. A similar suggestion was made in the Iraq War 2003 but never had to be implemented.

themselves with the same legal dilemma that they had to face in Iraq. If they concede in advance that the ECHR applies by derogating, then they, no doubt, fear future action against them. However, if they fail to concede that the ECHR applies in advance, they will inevitably face protracted legal action regarding the applicability of the ECHR and the possible payment of damages for any breach. They also face the possibility of being held to account against a higher legal standard than might otherwise have applied if they had derogated. Derogation can, of course, legalise what would normally be illegal under a human rights treaty. This dilemma remains for the next time the United Kingdom finds itself in such a predicament, but it would indeed be sensible to reach a decision on this point well in advance of any conflict.

This issue, however, leads on to a bigger question regarding the general treatment of prisoners in an armed conflict and may have a bearing on how to approach such a dilemma.

Without any doubt, the mistreatment of prisoners has inflicted enormous damage on the British Army. At the time of writing, the MOD has settled 162 cases of prisoner mistreatment at a cost of £8.2 million and another 700 claims are waiting to be heard.[59] At the same time, there are legal proceedings currently in session which have decided that there should be independent inquiries into all the allegations of mistreatment of prisoners by UK forces for the entire period that the British Army was involved in Iraq.[60] The legal ramifications are immense and, whereas the outstanding claims concern allegations of mistreatment, they also raise a very interesting point about how to approach a legal dilemma, such as those mentioned above in relation to Article 5 tribunals. Where there is a moot point of law – in this case the extraterritorial application of the ECHR – what approach should be adopted? In the Iraq War 2003, the problem was approached differently by the MOD and the military lawyers. On the one hand, the MOD lawyers did not wish to make any concessions as to the extraterritorial applicability of the ECHR for fear of future claims against the government. On the other, the military lawyers were keen to ensure that the commanders and theatre troops remained on the right side of the law and that there was no potential for future claims against them or anyone else. In the view of the military lawyers, where there was a moot point of law, keeping theatre troops on the right side of the law with any degree of certainty could only be achieved by

[59] See www.thetimes.co.uk/tto/news/uk/defence/article3672367.ece.

[60] *Ali Zaki Mousa* v. *Secretary of State for Defence* [2011] EWCA Civ. 1334.

applying the higher of the two legal standards. If this approach was adopted, then the command and theatre troops could probably not be challenged in law, or would certainly avoid criticism for trying to apply the highest legal standards under international and domestic law. Furthermore, as matters transpired, it became clear that when a lesser standard was applied, or there was room for legal debate, then there was the potential for abuse – with tragic consequences in the case of Baha Mousa. As one US Commander remarked, 'complex situational ethics cannot be applied during the stress of combat. The rules must be firm and absolute'.[61] It is worthy of note that Sir William Gage stated that 'the MOD did not have a grasp on, or adequate understanding of its own interrogation policy'.[62] Furthermore, the political intransigence in the United Kingdom to do anything more than the legal minimum required has caused endless litigation and immense damage to our national reputation – and it could so easily have been avoided.

In retrospect, the approach by the United Kingdom seems politically naive and the policy adopted by the MOD clearly failed to work in Iraq and is unlikely to succeed elsewhere. As the Australian Armed Forces realised in East Timor,[63] 'there are considerable political and diplomatic risks with not dealing with prisoners appropriately'[64] and the failure to look after detainees properly can have 'national, international, host nation and military implications'.[65] Indeed, it is now obvious that the treatment of prisoners is not just a legal issue but also carries immense political and strategic importance at the same time – as well as considerable risk. The power of the media is now far better understood and it is now stating the obvious that winning the war is achieved not just through combat power but by shaping public perception at the same time. In the matter of prisoners, 'the public perception of the treatment [. . .] alters the strategic threshold of what is considered a successful military operation'.[66] One US Commander described the failure of the US forces with regard to prisoners as having 'disastrous

[61] General Charles Krulac USMC and General Joseph Hoar CinC CENTCOM, 'It's Our Cage Too', *Washington Post*, 17 May 2007.

[62] See n. 12, above.

[63] The International Force for East Timor (INTERFET) was a multinational peacekeeping taskforce, mandated by the United Nations to address the humanitarian and security crisis that took place in East Timor from 1999 to 2000.

[64] B. Oswald, 'Detention in Military Operations: Some Military, Political and Legal Aspects', 46 *Military Law and the Laws of War Review* (2007) 341, 343.

[65] *Ibid.*, 347. [66] *Ibid.*

consequences' and, at its worse, it can assist what General David Petraeus described as the 'recuperative power' of the 'terrorist enemy'.[67]

However, there are other factors which should persuade the military and politicians to adopt the highest possible standards when dealing with prisoners. The first of these is what has been termed 'lawfare'.[68] This has traditionally been viewed as obliging armies to fight with 'one hand tied behind their back'.[69] However, this is the wrong way to approach the issue. The application of the law in the conduct of military operations is no surprise to the generation of UK military lawyers who served in Northern Ireland before the Belfast Agreement in 1998.[70] Every time a suspected terrorist was captured by UK forces operating in Northern Ireland there was an inevitable legal challenge, both to the arrest and the subsequent process of detention and questioning. Such challenges were anticipated as a matter of course and indeed the only way to protect UK forces and the security services against legal challenge (and to secure a conviction) was to ensure that their treatment was of the 'highest legal standards' at all times. By adopting such standards, the UK military was in a position where a suspected terrorist could be tried successfully and the armed forces were confident that they were operating in accordance with the law at all times and that public opinion would remain on the side of the security forces, or, at the very least, it would ensure that they did not assist the terrorist and their constituents. This is the only effective way to deal with prisoners.

However, this brings me on to the final point with regards to detainees and that is the moral component of the fighting force. This expression may seem old fashioned, but it is still considered to be a vital component of a fighting force and one of the qualities required for leadership at all levels.[71] All those serving in the Armed Forces are in the 'profession of arms' and must adopt the highest professional standards at all times. As Napoleon pointed out, 'the moral is as three to one with the physical'.[72] This means that the Armed Forces must 'fight justly and being seen to fight justly'.[73] It was perfectly possible for the United Kingdom in Iraq to have achieved the 'exemplary' standards set by the Australian Army three years earlier in East Timor and it is a matter of profound regret

[67] See n. 61, above. [68] See n. 64, above. [69] *Ibid.*

[70] See http://cain.ulst.ac.uk/events/peace/docs/agreement.htm.

[71] 'Fit and Proper Persons' Officership Revisited by Dr Patrick Mileham, Sandhurst Occasional Papers No. 10, Central Library, Royal Military Academy, Sandhurst (2012).

[72] See G. F. H. Henderson, *The Science of War* (London: Longmans, 1906), 173.

[73] See n. 71, above.

that all efforts to achieve these standards were so vehemently resisted by the MOD.

The question remains as to whether the law of armed conflict is 'fit for purpose in the twenty-first century' and, as the Iraq conflict illustrates, there are immense challenges in conducting Article 5 tribunals, particularly in asymmetric warfare. It is now highly unlikely that the initial assessments that were introduced, *in extremis*, in the Iraq War 2003 would be sufficient or would satisfy the requirements under the ECHR. The practical difficulties encountered in 2003 can be overcome, to a degree, by better training, the preservation and recording of evidence from the battlefield and the continuity and preservation of that evidence in the POW facility. This will go some way to providing the real and circumstantial evidence required for a tribunal to begin to consider a case. However, the chaos and exigencies of combat will always make this problematic and the circumstances will also, obviously, differ from one conflict to another. Secondary issues, such as resources in manpower and materiel, are also relevant and the need for a dedicated team of lawyers and investigators, together with translators and administrative facilities, are also going to be paramount in any future conflict. Lack of resources will not be a defence to a legal challenge where liberty and the right to fair trial are concerned and signatory states are going to have to ensure that they are properly resourced in any future conflict. This can be achieved by a dedicated legal and provost team, which is part of the establishment of any future POW facility.

The pivotal question as to whether the ECHR will apply to Article 5 tribunals is going to have to be resolved before any future conflict, but the decision in *Al Skeini* strongly suggests that it will apply. Indeed, other judgments[74] also suggest that the MOD is going to lose this struggle against the ECHR, which is, in any event, counter-productive. If this is the case, then the UK should concede this point whilst drafting the regulations for a new Article 5 tribunal and then seek to derogate at the outset of hostilities. Given the practical and other difficulties which can arise, then this would be a very sensible course of conduct and show proper regard for the rule of law. It will also assist in the drafting of any new rules as well as protecting the United Kingdom against any future legal challenge. The appointment of a judge should also be included in the provisions of any new tribunal. Not only would the judge sit on any

[74] *Al Jedda* v. *The United Kingdom*, Application no. 27021/08, dated 7 July 2011 and *Smith, Ellis and Allbutt* v. *MOD*, 2013 UKSC, dated 19 June 2013.

tribunal, but would be able generally to oversee the treatment of prisoners in any future conflict. It would also help prevent further abuse and ensure proper regard for the GC and ECHR by the MOD, who are unfit to police themselves. The problems are sizeable but if Article 5 of the ECHR is not going to break Article 5 of the Third Geneva Convention, then significant changes and legal creativity lie ahead. As matters stand at the time of writing, no further progress has been made towards designing a modern tribunal that might be appropriate for future conflicts, despite over a decade elapsing since the United Kingdom last attempted to conduct Article 5 tribunals. Although the legal framework is in place,[75] no new Royal Warrant has been issued. Article 5 tribunals are not yet fit for purpose.

[75] S.23 of the Armed Forces Act 2011 provides for a new s.371(a) to the 2006 Act to make provision in relation to protected prisoners of war and (1) Her Majesty may by warrant make provision with respect to protected prisoners of war.

8

Direct participation and the principle of distinction: squaring the circle

CHARLES GARRAWAY

Introduction

Peter Rowe was studying the laws of war long before it became fashionable. He befriended and taught, both formally and informally, several generations of service lawyers and, as a result, has had a vast influence on their development and, through them, on state practice. He was also one of the first to acknowledge the growing influence of human rights law on the conduct of the military both in war and in peacetime. It is, therefore, highly appropriate that he should continue to be influential and involved in the ongoing debates.

War is hell. Few would disagree with that statement, least of all those who have experienced it. I listened once in horror at the wedding dinner of the daughter of two concentration camp survivors when an elderly guest described how the Second World War had not been 'that bad'. We can all, whether we agree or not, have great sympathy with the principled view of pacifists that war is always evil and can never be justified, even if it means that tyrants, such as Hitler, Saddam Hussein and Colonel Gaddafi, must be allowed to wreak their havoc. Others of us take a more pragmatic approach and, whilst accepting that war is evil, argue that, on occasions, it is the lesser of two evils. It is from this latter strand that the great theologians and philosophers developed 'just war' theory.

However, whilst just war theory concentrates principally on the right to use force, the *jus ad bellum*, equally important, and recognised as such, are the methods by which such force is used, the *jus in bello*, also known as international humanitarian law (IHL) or the law of armed conflict. Certain principles developed over the centuries have now been codified into international law and now appear both as custom and in treaty form. These principles – humanity, military necessity, proportionality and distinction – lie at the basis of the law of armed conflict and all black-letter treaty law needs to be checked against them for validity. They are universal in application and can be applied in all the changing scenes of warfare. Perhaps the most critical of these is the principle of distinction, which is what I wish to concentrate on here.

The principle of distinction

It has been accepted for centuries that, if war is necessary, its effects must be limited. To achieve this a line is drawn between those entitled to take part in combat – and therefore liable in return to be engaged or targeted – and those who are not so entitled and so are to be protected. A similar distinction is drawn between those objects that contribute towards the war effort, and so can be attacked, and those that do not, and should also be protected. In both human and inanimate categories, certain groups are given special protection as it is recognised that they are more vulnerable than others or, as in the case of medical personnel and hospitals, are at particular risk due to the activity that they pursue.

After the Treaty of Westphalia, war became the prerogative of states. Prior to that, it had often been difficult to distinguish between the various factions involved in war, many of whom would change sides depending on the success or failure of operations or the money offered. Now states controlled the use of force. If one fought on behalf of a state, one was entitled to the privileges that went with that status; if one was fighting without the authority of a state, one was not. For ease of recognition, not least by one's own forces, soldiers began to wear distinctive uniforms. The problem of distinction was not so significant on ships as it was the ship itself that needed to be distinguished and all those on-board ran the same risks, at least until capture.

The height of this era of distinction was probably the nineteenth century, with armies vying with each other over the colours of their uniforms. The Boer War began the change as the British soon discovered that bright red tunics were not the best thing to wear in the South African bush. In part, this lesson had begun to be learned in the various Afghan wars and the colours of uniforms began to change from red to the more mundane 'khaki', itself a word derived from Hindustani and Urdu.

The Boer War also began to challenge another item of conventional wisdom: the separation of fighting forces from the civilian population. In the nineteenth century, the range of weaponry was short and there was no such thing as 'air power'. Battles were fought, for the most part, between regular formations outside urban areas. Indeed, for some, such battles were a spectator sport. It is reported that, at the First Battle of the Bull Run in 1861 during the American Civil War, civilians with picnics gathered on the surrounding high ground to watch the armies fighting. This turned into chaos with the unexpected rout of the Union forces.[1] However, the Boer War was almost a case of 'war amongst the people' as there was little distinction between the Boer forces and the civilian population.

As weaponry improved and air power began to take effect, the principle of distinction came under severe pressure. Nevertheless, war was still principally conducted by regular armed forces. However, the Boer War proved to be ahead of its time. As international armed conflict became increasingly overtaken by internal violence and non-international armed conflict, the role of the non-state actor rose to prominence. If the 'combatant privilege' applied only to regular forces in international armed conflict, what was the position of the guerrilla force in such conflict, the non-state actor in a civil war, or even state forces outside international armed conflict?

Traditionally, as we have seen, certain people – members of the state's armed forces – were authorised to take part in hostilities and, in turn, could be targeted. But the battlefields of the world – now more accurately referred to as 'battle spaces' – were no longer solely populated by state armed forces. Growing numbers of people could be found there, ranging from militia forces linked to a state, to individuals who had taken it upon themselves to join in the fight for personal reasons.

Modern developments

In 1977, a revision of the law sought to deal with this issue by dividing people in international armed conflict into two types: the armed forces of a party to the conflict (i.e., a state), which were defined as 'all organized armed forces, groups and units which are under a command responsible to that Party for the conduct of its subordinates',[2] and

[1] See, e.g., J. MacPherson, *Battle Cry of Freedom: The Civil War Era* (Oxford: Oxford University Press, 1988).

[2] Article 43(1) Protocol Additional to the Geneva Conventions of 12 August 1949, and Relating to the Protection of Victims of International Armed Conflicts, 8 June 1977 (hereinafter AP I), reprinted in A. Roberts and R. Guelff (eds), *Documents on the Laws of War* (Oxford: Oxford University Press, 2000), 444.

'civilians' – everybody else.[3] Civilians were entitled to protection from direct attack 'unless and for such time as they take a direct part in hostilities'.[4]

It had been anticipated that somewhat similar principles would apply to non-international armed conflict, but at the last minute Additional Protocol II, dealing with such conflicts, was substantially reduced in content. No such division of parties is made in Additional Protocol II, although a similar provision is to be found on the protection of 'civilians' from attack.[5] The difficulty of course is that 'civilians' are now undefined and the negative definition in Additional Protocol I can only apply by analogy.

A further complication has developed over the last twenty years with the growing overlap between human rights law and the law of armed conflict. For decades, states showed a marked reluctance to acknowledge the existence of a non-international armed conflict on their territory. As a result, states treated insurgencies as 'internal disturbances and tensions' not amounting to armed conflict. Thus, the application of the laws of armed conflict did not arise. Northern Ireland is such an example, as it is at least arguable that, at the height of the 'Troubles', the factual requirements for an armed conflict were met. However, at no time did the British government acknowledge the existence of an armed conflict. The deployment of thousands of military personnel was 'military aid to the civil power'[6] and the paramilitary groups, on all sides, were viewed as criminals and were dealt with as such.

One of the results of the end of the cold war was the release of ethnic tensions across large swathes of the world. The break-up of Yugoslavia into its component parts led to the formation of new armed groupings out of the Yugoslav army. Some of these looked like regular forces, wearing uniforms and under a command structure. Others operated more loosely, with some units operating outside any form of command chain. The wars in Africa, such as Sierra Leone and the Democratic Republic of Congo, showed a similar trend. Wars were no longer only fought by regular armed forces, but increasingly by armed groups who

[3] Article 50(1) AP I, 448. [4] Article 51(3) AP I, 448.

[5] Article 13 Protocol Additional to the Geneva Conventions of 12 August 1949, and Relating to the Protection of Victims of Non-International Armed Conflicts, 8 June 1977 (hereinafter AP II), reprinted in Roberts and Guelff, *Documents on the Laws of War*, 490.

[6] See, e.g., House of Commons Defence Committee, *Statement on the Defence Estimates 1996*, 7th Report (London: HMSO, 1996), paras 205–13.

did not respect – or even know of – the principle of distinction. How was the principle to operate in these new anarchic situations? If all these new groups outside the regular structure of armed forces were, by definition, 'civilians', what rules of targeting applied to them? If they could only be targeted when, and for such time as, they took a direct part in hostilities, then it could be argued that they were in a better position than regular armed forces who were targetable at all times, even when off duty.

International Committee of the Red Cross initiative

The International Committee of the Red Cross (ICRC) realised that this new phenomenon – or rather throwback to a pre-Westphalian form of conflict – put a severe strain not only on the principle of distinction but also on the complete structure of the law of armed conflict. If one of the foundational pillars was no longer holding, for how long could the structure itself remain standing? As a result, in conjunction with the Asser Institute in the Netherlands, the ICRC brought together a group of experts to discuss the whole concept of direct participation in hostilities. These experts came from across the globe and from many different backgrounds. There were military practitioners and government lawyers, as well as academics and representatives from human rights organisations, all participating in their private capacities. The group met on some five occasions between 2003 and 2008 and the debate was intense. Each meeting was preceded by a paper prepared by the ICRC on a particular aspect of the subject and was followed up by a detailed report of the meeting.

The experts began by looking at two key issues: the definition of 'civilian' and the meaning of 'taking a direct part in hostilities', both in terms of the required conduct itself and also the temporal scope. A third issue arose during the negotiations and was to prove perhaps the most controversial of all: the consequences of the loss of protection. The conclusion of the meetings was somewhat unsatisfactory, as far as many of the experts were concerned. Unsurprisingly, perhaps, agreement was hard to find, although there was probably more than many expected. Consequently, the ICRC decided to publish their own Interpretive Guidance on the Notion of Direct Participation in Hostilities.[7] Very fairly, the President of the ICRC, Dr Jakob Kellenberger, said the following in his foreword to the pamphlet version:

[7] 'Interpretive Guidance on the Notion of Direct Participation in Hostilities under International Humanitarian Law', 90 IRRC (2008) 991.

> [T]he Interpretive Guidance is an expression solely of the ICRC's views. While international humanitarian law relating to the notion of direct participation in hostilities was examined over several years with a group of eminent legal experts, to whom the ICRC owes a huge debt of gratitude, the positions enunciated are the ICRC's alone.[8]

He continued:

> [W]hile reflecting the ICRC's views, the Interpretive Guidance is not and cannot be a text of a legally binding nature. Only State agreements (treaties) or State practice followed out of a sense of legal obligation on a certain issue (custom) can produce binding law.[9]

These statements are important in considering the effect of the Interpretive Guidance.

The timings of these meetings were also significant. They took place at a time when there was intensive debate on combatant status arising out of the hostilities in Iraq and Afghanistan and the highly polarised arguments, particularly in the USA, as to the relevance, or otherwise, of the law of armed conflict to modern-day conflicts. Were the Geneva Conventions 'quaint' and 'obsolete', as described by one leading US official?[10]

Definition of 'civilian'

The first issue, that of the definition of 'civilian', was, to some extent, seeking to fill the vacuum created in 1977 by the failure of states to agree a definition of 'civilian' in non-international armed conflict, whilst retaining some of the same language in relation to the protection of civilians in international armed conflict. There were two conflicting philosophies. The first was exemplified by those who argued that the term 'civilian' should be defined as widely as possible, so as to provide the maximum level of protection. On the other hand, there were those who took a more pragmatic approach and reasoned that a member of an armed group, falling outside the definition of regular armed forces of a state, is at least as dangerous, if not more so, than a member of the regular armed forces, who, in theory at least, are subject to a command and disciplinary chain that can enforce the law of armed conflict. How could it be explained

[8] See N. Melzer, *Direct Participation in Hostilities* (Geneva: ICRC, 2009), 6. [9] *Ibid.*

[10] See A Gonzales, 'Memorandum for the President, "Decision re Application of the Geneva Convention on Prisoners of War to the Conflict with Al Qaeda and the Taliban"', 25 January 2002, reprinted in K. Greenberg and J. Dratel (eds), *The Torture Papers – The Road to Abu Ghraib* (Cambridge: Cambridge University Press, 2005), 118.

to a regular soldier that the person in civilian clothes trying to kill him actually had more legal protection from attack than he did?

It was agreed that the problem was principally, but not entirely, applicable to non-international armed conflict. The existing definitions were workable in international armed conflict, even if a little frayed at the edges at times. Therefore, it was quickly decided that in international armed conflict the current definitions should be retained, though it may be necessary to expand somewhat on those definitions by way of commentary. A side issue was the meaning of the words 'belonging to' a party to the conflict. However, there was a reasonable degree of consensus amongst the experts on this issue.[11]

The problem, as had been anticipated, came in relation to non-international armed conflict. Here there is no combatant status. The provision, in relation to international armed conflict, that defined who are '[t]he armed forces of a Party to the conflict' and who, thus, as combatants, 'have the right to participate directly in hostilities',[12] does not appear in the Second Protocol applying to non-international armed conflict. Thus, the negative definition of 'civilian' – anyone who is not a combatant[13] – cannot apply directly. No alternative definition is provided.

The two extreme positions are simply expressed, but each has serious difficulties. In the first position, if there are no 'combatants', then everyone is a 'civilian' and can only be targeted when taking a direct part in hostilities. This would apply to regular forces, members of armed groups and individuals alike. The effect would be to operate something akin to a law enforcement paradigm where targeting would be based entirely on the threat posed by the individual at the particular moment. Whilst this could work in low-intensity armed conflicts where violence is comparatively limited, it would be unworkable in those conflicts that equate to international armed conflict in terms of intensity and violence, such as the civil war in Sri Lanka or Helmand in 2011.

The other extreme would be to state that all members of regular armed forces and armed groups do not qualify as civilians and are, therefore, targetable at all times. This would lead to an enormous loss of protection. Even amongst regular armed forces, religious and medical personnel are excluded from the definition of 'combatant' in international armed conflict.[14] The matter is compounded in the case of non-state actors by

[11] 'Interpretive Guidance', 999–1001.
[12] Article 43 AP I (n. 2, above).
[13] Article 50(1) AP I (n. 3, above).
[14] Article 43(2) AP I (n. 2, above).

the amorphous nature of the organisations themselves. Just as states are made up of far more than armed forces, so are non-state actors. Many of these actors who are parties to conflicts almost equate to states in terms of their control of territory. They have political wings and also social wings, responsible for matters like education and welfare. Therefore, one cannot simply equate regular armed forces and armed groups without narrowing down the definition of who in the armed group is targetable. People carrying out teaching duties in schools run by Hezbollah or Hamas are no more legitimate targets than Israeli teachers.

Thus, the issue became where to draw the dividing line. There was substantial agreement that members of regular armed forces should be excluded from the definition of 'civilian', even in non-international armed conflict. But how should armed groups be dealt with? For some, the answer was for all members of armed groups to be categorised as civilians, with only regular armed forces targetable at all times. But this would run against the principle of equality between parties in the law of armed conflict and encourage even states to rely on irregular militias, 'death squads', for whom they could have plausible deniability. Another approach was to consider members of armed groups as civilians, but deem that those who equated to members of the regular armed forces in their function should be regarded as continuously taking a direct part in hostilities. This would mean that, like their regular counterparts, they would be targetable at all times. This could not carry a majority as there were fears that it would prove too difficult to decide on who equated to a member of the regular armed forces. Was a cook for an armed group equivalent to a member of the regular armed forces, or did it depend on whether the cooking function of the state armed forces had been contracted out and was no longer filled by members of the regular armed forces? The proposal seemed to founder upon an evidential burden, despite general acceptance that 'in case of doubt whether a person is civilian, that person shall be considered to be a civilian'.[15]

The course chosen by the ICRC was both complex and, to some extent, novel. They defined 'organized armed group' as consisting 'only of individuals whose continuous function it is to take a direct part in hostilities ("continuous combat function")'.[16] Such persons did not count as civilians and, therefore, did not have civilian protection. This was seen by many as having two main flaws. First, it created a new category of persons who were neither members of the regular armed

[15] Article 50(1) AP I (n. 3, above). [16] 'Interpretive Guidance', 995.

forces nor civilians. This ran counter to what had been achieved in international armed conflict where the two categories were mutually exclusive. Secondly, it raised a further difficult question of what was meant by 'continuous combat function'.

The ICRC sought to define 'continuous combat function' as follows:

> Continuous combat function requires lasting integration into an organized armed group acting as the armed forces of a non-State party to an armed conflict. Thus, individuals whose continuous function involves the preparation, execution or command of acts or operations amounting to direct participation in hostilities are assuming a continuous combat function. An individual recruited, trained and equipped by such a group to continuously and directly participate in hostilities on its behalf can be considered to assume a continuous combat function even before he or she carries out a hostile act.[17]

Many state representatives amongst the group of experts considered that this definition infringed the principle of equality between parties and was an unworkable test. Of course, it also raised the next question that the group had to consider – what conduct amounted to taking a direct part in hostilities?

The required conduct

Here there was much agreement on the principles, but not so much on the application of those principles. The group identified three key elements: threshold of harm, direct causation and belligerent nexus. In so far as the threshold of harm was concerned, the ICRC defined this in the following terms:

> In order to reach the required threshold of harm, a specific act must be likely to adversely affect the military operations or military capacity of a party to an armed conflict, or, alternatively, to inflict death, injury or destruction on persons or objects protected against direct attack.[18]

For the most part, this is uncontroversial, although it has been argued that it is 'under-inclusive'.[19] Schmitt argues that the definition is restricted to acts causing negative consequences to the enemy when there may be acts of a beneficial nature, such as repairing a battle-damaged runway,

[17] *Ibid.*, 1007. [18] *Ibid.*, 1016.

[19] See M. Schmitt, 'Deconstructing Direct Participation in Hostilities: The Constitutive Elements', 42 *New York University Journal of International Law and Politics* (2010) 697, 714.

which also would affect military operations.[20] Of course, there is also a risk of being over-inclusive and a line has to be drawn somewhere. Whilst it may be argued that the line has been drawn slightly too tightly, this reflects the humanitarian concerns implicit in the concept of civilian protection and so should not necessarily be criticised as a rule of thumb.

The second principle is direct causation and is defined as follows:

> In order for the requirement of direct causation to be satisfied, there must be a direct causal link between a specific act and the harm likely to result either from that act, or from a coordinated military operation of which that act constitutes an integral part.[21]

Again, this sought to reflect the consensus amongst the experts that there should be a relatively close relationship between the act and its consequences. The difficulty, however, lies in the detail. The ICRC commentary seeks to put flesh on these bare bones and, in particular, to give examples illustrating the application of the principle. It is on these examples that much of the debate focuses.

One of the major disagreements amongst the experts was over the position of 'human shields'. It was accepted, almost without dissent, that involuntary human shields, such as the hostages taken by Saddam Hussein in the Kuwait war of 1990, were not taking a direct part in hostilities. Clearly, they had no wish to be in the unfortunate position in which they found themselves and were entitled to be considered as protected civilians. The use of such hostages to 'shield' military objectives was equally clearly illegal, but it did not change the status of the individuals themselves. Voluntary human shields, however, proved more contentious. The ICRC drew a distinction between situations where human shields gave physical cover to enemy forces, as in the example given of a woman who shielded two fighters with her billowing robes,[22] and cases where the use of human shields did not affect the physical operation, but merely the proportionality calculation, as in an air attack on a military objective. Many of the experts, particularly those with military experience, found this an unrealistic difference and disagreed fundamentally with the line taken by the ICRC.

In some ways the problem lies in the absolute positions taken by both sides. To the ICRC, a person is either a civilian (and so fully protected) or

[20] *Ibid.*, 720. [21] 'Interpretive Guidance', 1019. [22] *Ibid.*, 1024.

is not. Thus, 'voluntary human shields' retain their full protection and weight in the proportionality balance. On the other hand, the proponents of the argument that voluntary human shields have lost their civilian protection also have to take the line that they cease to count in the proportionality balance for that reason. This seems to be the effect of the black-letter treaty law. However, in reality, as George Orwell put it, 'all animals are equal but some animals are more equal than others'.[23] Under the Orwell principle, it could be argued that voluntary human shields remain civilians, but carry less weight in the proportionality balance owing to their chosen course of action, falling short of direct participation. This is challenged on the basis that it introduces a further degree of relativity into an area that is already too 'weak'. On the other hand, this represents reality. An example might make the point.

An air attack is planned on an ammunition factory, a clear military objective. The planners decide to attack at night when the civilian workforce are not present, thus reducing the risk of civilian casualties. However, they also have to consider the angle of attack. There are two possible angles, north–south, or east–west. A north–south attack would mean that if there was a weapons malfunction causing an overshoot, the barracks housing the 200 civilian workers would be at risk. On the other hand, an east–west axis would put at risk a home for unmarried mothers with twenty occupants, including children. If 'all animals are equal', then the planners would be forced to use the east–west axis to minimise civilian casualties. I suspect that most military planners would give a higher priority to protecting the mothers and children. In reality, not all animals are equal. It is the failure to appreciate this point that leads to much of the dispute in this area. The law and morality seem to be in opposition.

The third principle in this section is belligerent nexus. This is described as follows:

> In order to meet the requirement of belligerent nexus, an act must be specifically designed to directly cause the required threshold of harm in support of a party to the conflict and to the detriment of another.[24]

This is the area of least dissent, even when it comes to detail. It distinguishes between the act and the intent of the actor. Thus a civilian, or even a child, forced into carrying out an act will be judged by the act

[23] George Orwell, *Animal Farm* (Harmondsworth: Penguin, 1951), 114.
[24] 'Interpretive Guidance', 1025.

itself, not by his or her subjective intent. This is the only realistic approach. A child soldier armed with an AK-47 and attacking your position is just as dangerous whether s/he is a volunteer or a conscript. The criticism here is limited to the last part of the principles. It will not always be the case that acts may be 'in support of a party to the conflict and to the detriment of another'. In modern conflict it is possible to have situations where acts may be carried out to the detriment of one party, without being intended in any way to support another.[25] Modern warfare is not as clear-cut as the principle would have us believe.

Another area that proved controversial related to presumptions in case of doubt. All accepted that, in relation to status, where there is doubt as to whether a person is a civilian, that person is entitled to the benefit of the doubt and should be considered a civilian.[26] But does that presumption extend to the question of whether a person is taking a direct part in hostilities? The military and government experts all held that it could not. The ICRC differed.[27] The experts agreed that an attacker must do everything feasible to verify that the objective of attack is indeed a military objective and not a civilian or a civilian object,[28] but that is different from a presumption. Civilians have a responsibility to 'remain as distant from the conflict as possible'.[29] As Schmitt points out, this supposed presumption would only arise at the borders between indirect and direct participation where the person is already acting on his or her own volition.[30]

Consequences

The final issue before the group related to the consequences of direct participation. This was initially seen as relating to the temporal issue of when, and for how long, protection ceased. However, during the discussions a further, and highly controversial, matter was introduced – the level of response that could be made to direct participation.

On the temporal issue, concern had been expressed at an early stage as to the concept of the 'revolving door' – farmer by day, fighter by night. The ICRC, correctly, argued that this was an inherent part of the law that

[25] See Schmitt, 'Deconstructing Direct Participation in Hostilities', 736.
[26] Article 50(1) AP I (n. 3, above). [27] 'Interpretive Guidance', 1037.
[28] Article 57(2)(a)(i), AP I, 452 (n. 2, above).
[29] See Schmitt, 'Deconstructing Direct Participation in Hostilities', 738. [30] *Ibid.*

provided that civilians would not lose protection 'unless and for such time as they take a direct part in hostilities'.[31] The problem was reduced, to some extent, by the concession that members of armed groups, as defined by their 'continuous combat function' were to be excluded from the definition of 'civilian' and, as a result, would be targetable at all times. However, the occasional 'direct participator' would continue to be governed by Article 51(3) of Additional Protocol I[32] and so there would inevitably be a degree of the 'revolving door'. Nevertheless, where somebody was regularly taking a direct part in hostilities s/he would, probably, also fall into the 'continuous combat function' mode and so be excluded from the definition of civilian.

There was also discussion on when 'direct participation' started – 'preparatory acts' – and when it ended – 'deployment and return'. Whilst there was some disagreement on the margins here, the basic premise that preparatory acts, deployment and return could be included was agreed.[33]

Of much greater controversy were the consequences of direct participation. As stated, discussion on this was a late issue and arose largely out of the decision to exclude members of armed groups from the definition of civilians. It also relates to a direct conflict between the law of armed conflict and human rights law.

Under the law of armed conflict, arising out of international armed conflict, the traditional rule has been that lethal force can be used against combatants purely on the basis of status. There has never been a requirement for a graduated use of force, subject only to the ancient principle of preventing unnecessary suffering.[34] Human rights law approaches matters from entirely the opposite view. The default position is that there is a fundamental right to life.[35] That right can only be sacrificed in very clearly defined circumstances, largely based on the threat posed by the individual concerned. This conflict is recognised in the European Convention on Human Rights, which allows for derogation from the provision on the right to life in relation to 'deaths resulting from

[31] 'Interpretive Guidance', 1035. [32] Article 51(3) AP I (n. 4, above).

[33] 'Interpretive Guidance', 1031.

[34] See W. H. Parks, 'Part IX of the ICRC "Direct Participation in Hostilities" Study: No Mandate, No Expertise, and Legally Incorrect', 42 *New York University Journal of International Law and Politics* (2010) 769, 778.

[35] See Article 3, Universal Declaration of Human Rights, reprinted in I. Brownlie (ed.), *Basic Documents in International Law* (Oxford: Oxford University Press, 2002), 193.

lawful acts of war'.[36] But what does that mean? In 1950, 'war' referred to international armed conflict. What is the position in relation to non-international armed conflict? This issue has never really been resolved as, even in relation to international armed conflict, states have chosen not to derogate, relying instead on the *lex specialis* rule.

Jean Pictet, who wrote the Commentaries to the 1949 Geneva Conventions, argued that:

> [i]f we can put a soldier out of action by capturing him, we should not wound him; if we can obtain the same result by wounding him, we must not kill him. If there are two means to achieve the same military advantage, we must choose the one which causes the lesser evil.[37]

However, this has never gained traction, and at the expert meetings 'it was generally recognized that the approach proposed by Pictet is unlikely to be operable in classic battlefield situations involving large-scale confrontations'.[38] For this reason, it was argued that this could not be a general rule of law. However, the ICRC, over the objections of many of the experts, pressed for it to be included. Indeed, it was this issue that was principally responsible for the failure of the expert group to reach general agreement.

The ICRC Guidelines duly incorporated the principle in the following manner:

> In addition to the restraints imposed by international humanitarian law on specific means and methods of warfare, and without prejudice to further restrictions that may arise under other applicable branches of international law, the kind and degree of force which is permissible against persons not entitled to protection against direct attack must not exceed what is actually necessary to accomplish a legitimate military purpose in the prevailing circumstances.[39]

Whilst the Commentary argued that this was based on existing law, and so should not pose any difficulties, it was seen as a reversal of the traditional position and a preference for the human rights approach.

Whilst others have written on this at great length,[40] a few points should be made here. First, this principle is not limited to those civilians

[36] Article 15 European Convention for the Protection of Human Rights, 4 November 1950, reprinted *ibid.*, 249.

[37] J. S. Pictet, *Development and Principles of International Humanitarian Law* (Dordrecht: Martinus Nijhoff, 1985), 75.

[38] 'Interpretive Guidance', 1044. [39] *Ibid.*, 1040.

[40] See, e.g., Parks, 'Part IX of the ICRC "Direct Participation in Hostilities"' (n. 34, above).

who directly participate in hostilities. It applies to all who are 'not entitled to protection against direct attack', which includes combatants in international armed conflict. Therefore, it goes far beyond the remit of the expert group or that of the Interpretive Guidance itself.[41] Whilst the ICRC argues strongly that it does not introduce a responsibility to capture rather than kill,[42] it certainly puts the onus on the attacker to justify the level of force used.

Secondly, the use of the word 'actually' is problematic as it seems to narrow the options even further. If somebody approaches me with a gun raised, I may decide to shoot him before he shoots me. If it turns out that the gun had no ammunition, was it 'actually' necessary for me to shoot him? It may have been reasonable but, as an objective matter, it would not appear to have been 'actually' necessary. This may be a linguistic issue and the ICRC may not have realised the distinction – indeed the commentary does not seek to make this point. However, it is illustrative of the danger of seeking to simplify legal principles in this way. As written, it goes far beyond even the domestic rules on self-defence found in most countries.

The underlying problem

It is unfortunate that the ICRC's Interpretive Guidance has raised as many questions as it has answered. It was a sincere effort to solve one of the most difficult issues in modern day conflict. But why is it so difficult? Surely, with the principle of distinction being so fundamental to the law of armed conflict, there should be no difficulty in reaching agreement on how it should be implemented. But therein lies the rub! One can approach the principle of distinction from two different perspectives and, whilst in the vast majority of cases, the result will be the same, in the most difficult cases – those that are most likely to arise in the cauldron of conflict – there will be no agreement.

The reason for this lies partly in the confused attitude that civilians currently have towards members of the armed forces. In the time of Wellington, the army was described as made up of 'the scum of the

[41] *Ibid.*, 794.

[42] See N. Melzer, 'Keeping the Balance between Military Necessity and Humanity: A Response to Four Critiques of the ICRC's Interpretive Guidance on the Notion of Direct Participation in Hostilities', 42 *New York Journal of International Law and Politics* (2010) 831, 899–90.

earth'[43] and, to a large extent, that was true. Officers were gentlemen, but in the ranks were to be found the dregs of society. Soldiers were looked upon as cannon fodder and, in the words of Alfred, Lord Tennyson, 'Theirs not to reason why, theirs but to do and die!'[44]

Soldiers were not looked upon as sentient beings, but as cogs in a machine. It was for this reason that the great international lawyer Oppenheim, writing at the start of the twentieth century, put the doctrine of superior orders in the following terms:

> In case members of forces commit violations ordered by their commanders, the members may not be punished, for the commanders are alone responsible and the latter may therefore be punished as war criminals on their capture by the enemy.[45]

Remnants of this view of soldiers can be seen today in the opinion, seemingly held by many, that a soldier's life on the battlefield is of less value than that of a civilian. This is often argued on the basis that soldiers are volunteers and choose to take part in armed conflict, whereas civilians do not. But how true is this? First, many soldiers are conscripts, not volunteers, and have no wish to fight. Child soldiers are rightly looked upon as 'victims', but, in modern-day conflicts, many of the adults involved in fighting are 'pressed men'. Secondly, even in those countries where the armed forces are made up of volunteers, it is rarely the armed forces themselves who embark upon military adventures. Such countries are mainly liberal democracies where one of the key principles is civilian control of the military. There is, therefore, to some extent, a modern version of Tennyson's famous verse. This was seen during the 2003 Gulf War, where, whilst many in the military, including some military lawyers, were far from convinced with the legal justification provided by the British government's civilian lawyers, it was not for them to challenge openly the decision of a democratically elected government. The only option open to a dissenter is personal resignation. In those few cases where individual servicemen have sought to challenge the legality of the

[43] See E. Longford, *Wellington – The Years of the Sword* (London: Weidenfeld & Nicolson, 1969), 321.

[44] Alfred, Lord Tennyson, 'The Charge of the Light Brigade', in *The Works of Alfred Lord Tennyson* (London: Macmillan, 1915), 222.

[45] L. Oppenheim, *International Law: A Treatise* (London: Longmans, Green & Co., 1906), vol. 2, 264.

campaigns in both Iraq and Afghanistan they have been unsuccessful. 'Theirs not to reason why, theirs but to do and die!'[46]

On the other hand, there has been an increasing tendency to recognise the individual personality of servicemen and their individual rights. This has also caused some difficulty. There have been a number of civil cases in the United Kingdom where the Ministry of Defence has been held to have a duty of care towards service personnel in armed conflict, not just in peacetime. The Ministry has been criticised for failures of equipment, inadequate equipment and even tactical decisions.[47] However, this raises a conflict of principles. Under the law of armed conflict, states have an obligation to ensure that '[t]he civilian population and individual civilians shall enjoy general protection against dangers arising from military operations'.[48] But, under human rights law, states also have a duty of care towards their service personnel. Indeed, Peter Rowe, in his book on the impact of human rights law on armed forces, posed the question, 'could the soldier, himself, be a victim of a breach of his right to life by his own State?'[49] How are these two conflicting principles to be reconciled? Is it permissible for a state, under human rights law, to conduct an operation that will inevitably involve higher military casualties in an attempt to reduce the risk to civilians or civilian objects? Again, are all animals equal?

One of the reasons why UK military forces were deployed to Afghanistan was to conduct 'stability operations', operations to assist the Afghan government to improve security and governance in Afghanistan. However, those forces were allegedly deployed with inadequate equipment in the form of Snatch Land Rovers, which were found to be inadequate against the threat of improvised explosive devices (IEDs). It has been argued that the United Kingdom was at fault for continuing to use these vehicles as the IED threat increased.[50] However, the alternative might have been to withdraw troops to barracks, which would have increased the risks to the civilian population that the troops were there to protect. Faced with this sort of 'no-win' situation, is it any surprise that

[46] Tennyson, 'The Charge of the Light Brigade' (n. 44, above).

[47] For a summary of the position under UK law, as at June 2011, see *R. (on the application of Smith) (FC) (Respondent)* v. *Secretary of State for Defence (Appellant) and Another* [2010] UKSC 29.

[48] Article 51(1) AP I, 448 (n. 2, above).

[49] Peter Rowe, *The Impact of Human Rights Law on Armed Forces* (Cambridge: Cambridge University Press, 2006), 137.

[50] See *Smith and others (FC)* v. *The Ministry of Defence* [2013] UKSC 41.

states are increasingly reluctant to involve their service personnel in 'expeditionary' operations?

It would seem that we are now reaching a crossroads. The law of armed conflict, *jus in bello*, grew out of the recognition that war was part of human nature and, whilst undesirable, could not be eliminated. Therefore, regulation was the least worst option. It developed separately from the law to restrict or eliminate war, *jus ad bellum*. The UN Charter has sought to strengthen the *jus ad bellum* to the extent that the use of force between states is now prohibited, except in self-defence or when authorised by the UN Security Council under Chapter VII of the Charter. This purist position has been tested in recent years on occasions where the veto power of particular countries has prevented the Security Council from acting where it perhaps should. As a result, the doctrine of self-defence has been stretched and 'humanitarian intervention' suggested as a possible additional justification for the use of force.

However, as war is increasingly viewed as 'illegal', the relevance of seeking to regulate an 'illegal' activity has also been questioned. The law of armed conflict has always been blind to the cause of a conflict, being applicable across the board to all parties to the conflict. There is now a body of opinion that argues that this should not be so.[51] Why should the 'aggressor' be entitled to the benefits of the law of armed conflict? Surely 'justice' requires that there be a distinction between the 'good' and the 'bad'. However, the difficulty is that there is no 'referee' who can immediately adjudicate on who is 'good' and who is 'bad'. Both sides seek to claim the moral high ground and so the effect of such a distinction would be to destroy the law of armed conflict completely. Each side would claim that the other was not entitled to its privileges. There was an element of this to be found in some of the arguments put forward within the Bush Administration when debating the fate of prisoners captured in Afghanistan.[52] It was years before even the United States Supreme Court was able to rule on Guantanamo.[53] In due course, there may be a ruling from the International Court of Justice, or some other judicial body, on

[51] For an assessment of the arguments, see A. Roberts, 'The Equal Application of the Laws of War: A Principle under Pressure', 90 *IRRC* (2008) 931.

[52] See, e.g., J. Yoo and R. Delahunty, 'Memorandum for William J Haynes II, General Counsel, Department of Defense, "Re. Application of Treaties and Laws to al Qaeda and Taliban Detainees"', dated 9 January 2002, reprinted in Greenberg and Dratel, *The Torture Papers*, 50.

[53] *Rasul* v. *Bush* 542 US 466 was decided by the United States Supreme Court in 2004.

the legality of a particular conflict, but this would inevitably be too late to influence the action on the ground.

The growth of human rights law, and its increasing application in conflict situations, has also led to complications. Whilst it is now generally accepted that human rights law applies, to some degree, in armed conflict,[54] what happens when the two legal systems appear to conflict? In the case of *Al-Jeddah* v. *United Kingdom*, the ECtHR seemed to imply that the right to detention, given to an occupying power under the Fourth Geneva Convention of 1949, could not override the limitations on detention imposed by human rights law as it was not an 'obligation' to detain.[55] The law of armed conflict never imposes an 'obligation' to detain, any more than it imposes an 'obligation' to kill or wound. If the Court were to follow that argument consistently, all use of force cases would have to be decided under the human rights paradigm, rather than under the law of armed conflict.

The rise in international criminal justice has also played a part. The horrors of the Balkans and Rwanda led to a ready belief that anyone who took part in those conflicts was guilty of something, a belief strengthened as the stories unfolded before the relevant international tribunals. Fuelled by the human rights position that the right to life is the most fundamental right, there is a growing reversal of the 'burden of proof'. Any death must be accounted for, even in the heat of battle. 'Collateral damage' is unacceptable.

There is a serious danger here. First, the law of armed conflict has always been based on an understanding of the reality of conflict. If the law becomes detached from that reality, it will be the law that suffers. There are signs that this is already beginning to happen. An example is the case of expanding bullets, the infamous dumdums.

In 1899, the use of expanding bullets was prohibited in international armed conflict.[56] In the first case decided before the International Criminal Tribunal for the former Yugoslavia, the *Tadić* decision, the Tribunal stated:

> Indeed, elementary considerations of humanity and common sense make it preposterous that the use by States of weapons prohibited in armed

[54] *Legality of the Threat or Use of Nuclear Weapons* (Advisory Opinion), ICJ Reports 1996, 226, 240.

[55] *Al-Jedda* v. *United Kingdom* [2011] ECtHR 1092 (7 July 2011), para. 107.

[56] See Hague Declaration 3 Concerning Expanding Bullets, 29 July 1899, reprinted in Roberts and Guelff, *Documents on the Laws of War*, 64.

> conflicts between themselves be allowed when States try to put down rebellion by their own nationals on their own territory. What is inhumane, and consequently proscribed, in international wars, cannot but be inhumane and inadmissible in civil strife.[57]

In 2010, the Review Conference for the Rome Statute of the International Criminal Court, meeting in Kampala, extended the prohibition on the use of expanding bullets to non-international armed conflict, at least so far as international criminal law was concerned.[58]

Logically, this argument sounds eminently correct – but logic and reality do not necessarily go together. Let us examine the reality of conflict, then and now. In 1899, weapons had limited range and war was still mainly fought between regular armies, away from the civilian population. The advantage of an expanding bullet was that it was more likely to cause a quick death; the disadvantage was that, in doing so, it would cause additional pain and suffering. An expanding bullet is not a pleasant means of death. The alternative was a regular bullet. This might not have the same instant effect and was more likely to ricochet. The test applied was the ancient principle of avoiding unnecessary suffering. If a regular bullet was used, the only people, in 1899, who would be at risk if death was not almost instantaneous, or if the bullet was subject to ricochet, were fellow combatants. It was felt, therefore, that the additional suffering caused by the use of an expanding bullet could not be justified.

Now let us fast forward 100 years. The principle of avoiding unnecessary suffering recognises that, in war, there is such a thing as necessary suffering. In war people do get killed and things do get broken. In the last 100 years, the character of warfare has altered. We now have a preponderance of civil wars, marked by what General Rupert Smith calls 'war amongst the people'.[59] Terrorism has increased, both within and without conflict. In the last quarter of the twentieth century, aircraft hijacking was a common form of terrorism and principally considered as requiring a law enforcement response.[60] However, these responses often involved

[57] *Prosecutor* v. *Tadic*, Decision on the Defence Motion for Interlocutory Appeal on Jurisdiction (Appeals Chamber), Case No. IT-94-1, 2 October 1995, para. 119.

[58] See ICC Review Conference of the Rome Statute, Resolution RC/Res.5, adopted at the 12th Plenary Meeting, on 10 June 2010, by consensus.

[59] See R. Smith, *The Utility of Force: The Art of War in the Modern World* (London: Penguin, 2005).

[60] See, e.g., the focus of the United Nations Convention for the Suppression of Unlawful Seizure of Aircraft (16 December 1970) 860 UNTS 105.

elite anti-terrorist units, sometimes made up of members of the armed forces. The storming of an aircraft and the release of hostages required the use of special techniques. In particular, it was essential that the terrorist(s) were incapacitated as quickly as possible in order to prevent them from detonating explosives, or discharging weapons in a confined space. It was also necessary to reduce the risk of ricochet in order to minimise any risk to the hostages themselves. The ammunition of choice, for many such units, was the expanding bullet. The balance between necessary and unnecessary suffering had changed. The need here was to ensure that any attack was as discriminatory as possible and that the risk to the hostages was minimised.

Today's conflicts are much closer to the terrorist incidents of the late twentieth century. The rise in irregular armed forces, as we have seen in the earlier part of this chapter, makes it much harder to distinguish between those entitled to take a direct part in hostilities and those who are (and do) not. Civilians and fighters are intermingled, particularly in non-international armed conflict. It is in exactly this sort of situation where the use of expanding bullets may be necessary to reduce civilian casualties. Consequently, one has to ask whether the inclusion of such a prohibition under international criminal law is in accord with reality in conflict and whether compliance with it may actually result in more 'collateral damage', rather than less. It is true that the Resolution passed at Kampala states:

> and understanding that the crime is committed only if the perpetrator employs the bullets to uselessly aggravate suffering or the wounding effect upon the targets of such bullets, as reflected in customary international law.[61]

However, this provision is not reflected in the text of the Statute itself, and the Elements of Crimes, in which it is reflected, are advisory only.[62] For a lawyer advising Special Forces in such a situation the choice is difficult, as failure to use expanding bullets may lead to a human rights claim by the families of the hostages, if casualties occur as a result.

This leads to the second danger – that all those who take part in conflict are looked upon as embryonic war criminals. Already, the demands for enquiries into even combat deaths mean that service

[61] Preambular Para. 9, Resolution RC/Res. 5 (n. 58, above).

[62] See K. Dörmann, *Elements of War Crimes under the Rome Statute of the International Criminal Court* (Cambridge: Cambridge University Press, 2003), 8.

personnel are being challenged at every stage. War is not something that allows for mature reflection. Decisions are made at short notice by people who are tired and under stress, usually with incomplete information. A delay in taking a decision is in itself a decision and may cost lives. Asking for further information may not be an option: the decision has to be taken on what is 'reasonably available to [the decision maker] at the relevant time'.[63] War is not a computer game, but a very human activity where mistakes will be made in good faith. It is that human element that often leads to the greatest acts of humanity in times of war, acts that no computer would ever accept. We lose that element at our peril.

Conclusion

Thus, we return to the principle of distinction and direct participation in hostilities. The principle of distinction is fundamental to the law of armed conflict. It guides us between the Scylla of all-out war, where all the adversary population contribute to the war effort and are, therefore, legitimate targets, and the Charybdis of pacifism, where nothing can be targeted at all. Between these two positions are many shoals and whirlpools to trap the unwary sailor and on each position there are siren voices seeking to draw the mariner towards that shore. The need is to ensure a balance: one that reflects the reality of war, but at the same time seeks to protect the innocent. This involves compromise. In war, innocent lives will inevitably be lost – that is embedded in the principle of proportionality. Not every civilian death is a war crime. Not to accept that is not to accept the reality of war. That way lies the divorce of war and law, a divorce where there will be no winners.

[63] See UK Statement (c) made on ratification of AP I, reprinted in Roberts and Guelff, *Documents on the Laws of War*, 510.

9

Droning on: some international humanitarian law aspects of the use of unmanned aerial vehicles in contemporary armed conflicts

DAVID TURNS

Introduction

If anyone doubted the technological future of the means of warfare in the early twenty-first century, such doubts will have been dispelled by the Pentagon's announcement, in February 2013, of the creation of a new medal for US troops for 'extraordinary achievement' in combat operations. The putative recipients of this award, directors of cyber-attacks and the operators of unmanned aerial vehicles (UAVs, often referred to as 'drones'), do not physically participate in ground operations or directly risk their own lives.[1] It is the first new US military combat award to be created since the Bronze Star Medal during the Second World War.[2] The journey from recognising the meritorious service of those who 'lead miserable lives of extreme discomfort and [...] who must close in personal combat with the enemy'[3] to a non-combat 'accomplishment so exceptional and outstanding as to clearly set the individual apart from comrades or from other persons in similar situations'[4] speaks volumes for the direction in which the

Opinions stated herein are those of the author and do not necessarily reflect the views or policies of Her Majesty's government, the Ministry of Defence or the British Armed Forces. By the same token, the author retains full responsibility for any errors or omissions.

[1] 'Pentagon Creating New Medal For Drones, Cyberattacks', *Huffington Post*, 13 February 2013: www.huffingtonpost.com/2013/02/13/pentagon-drone-medal_n_2678810.html.

[2] Executive Order 9419 – Bronze Star Medal, 4 February 1944, 9 Fed. Reg. 1495.

[3] General George C. Marshall's memorable characterisation of the soldiers for whom the institution of the Bronze Star was primarily intended: see his Memorandum for the President (through the Secretaries of War and the Navy), 3 February 1944, in L. I. Bland and S. Ritenor (eds), *The Papers of George Catlett Marshall* (Lexington, VA: The George C. Marshall Foundation, 1981), 4–225.

[4] 'Pentagon Creating New Medal For Drones, Cyberattacks'.

nature of warfare has evolved over the last seven decades. Although a certain element of physical bravery undoubtedly retains its place on contemporary battlefields, and will no doubt continue to do so in the future, the need to bash an enemy's brains out with a club – or at least to have visual contact in order to shoot him with a rifle – has been replaced by the firing of a missile at a target on a computer screen, with the push of a button, in an air-conditioned office up to thousands of kilometres away from the scene of the engagement.

More than twelve years after the advent of the so-called 'global war on terror', heralded by the terrorist attacks on the World Trade Center in New York and the Pentagon on 11 September 2001, references to drones – some cautiously enthusiastic, a great many more anguished, those from officialdom often merely opaque – are ubiquitous in the contemporary literature for any student of the laws of war. While not all of these references specifically relate to the focus of this volume – the international law of armed conflict – they do all concern, in one way or another, aspects of the deployment of drones by armed forces in military operations.[5] They range from criticisms of the policy of targeted killings of hostile leaders or operatives by UAVs,[6] denunciations of 'excessive collateral damage' to civilians or civilian objects,[7] allegations of violations of the territorial integrity and sovereignty of states on whose territory such operations are executed, freedom of information lawsuits aimed at obtaining disclosure of official information about drone strikes, through to guarded expressions of approbation for the military utility and reliability of UAVs[8] and muted announcements that their use will be

[5] As much of the debate about UAVs centres on ethics and morality as on law. For a flavour of the opposing views, see R. C. Arkin, 'The Case for Ethical Autonomy in Unmanned Systems', 9 *Journal of Military Ethics* (2010) 332; B. J. Strawser, 'Moral Predators: The Duty to Employ Uninhabited Aerial Vehicles', 9 *Journal of Military Ethics* (2010) 342; N. Sharkey, 'Saying "No!" to Lethal Autonomous Targeting', 9 *Journal of Military Ethics* (2010) 369.

[6] For example, United Nations Human Rights Council, Report of the Special Rapporteur on Extrajudicial, Summary or Arbitrary Executions, Philip Alston – Addendum – Study on Targeted Killings, 28 May 2010 (UN Doc. A/HRC/14/24/Add.6) (hereinafter Alston Report); the use of UAVs for targeted killings is specifically addressed at paras 79–86.

[7] For example, N. Sharkey, *Weapons of Indiscriminate Lethality* (2009) FIfF-Kommunikation 1/2009, 26: http://fiff.de/publikationen/fiff-kommunikation/fk-2009/fiff-ko-1-2009/fiko_1_2009_sharkey.pdf.

[8] For example, Sqn Ldr C. Wills, 'The Potential for Unmanned Combat Air Systems to Gain Control of the Air in Future Warfare', 15 *Air Power Review* (2012) 33; Flt Lt K. Fuchter, 'The First Drone War: Air Power for Strategic Effect', 15 *Air Power Review* (2012) 17.

expanded. The use, or proposed use, of drones in military operations is, in fact, regularly in the news nowadays and has generated what one commentator has called 'an acrimonious legal debate [. . .] that has too often proven vacuous and emotive'.[9] That this is so should not prove too surprising when statistics are so freely bandied around (such as the high number of civilian casualties, or 'collateral damage', allegedly incidental to drone strikes, or the exponential expansion of their use by President Barack Obama's administration since 2009)[10] and such heavy emphasis (often using hyperbolic language) is placed by media coverage of the use of such strikes deliberately to eliminate named individuals[11] – despite the fact that this is only one use to which UAVs are put. The consequence of adopting these parameters by which to frame the debate in terms of international humanitarian law (IHL) is that several distinct legal issues are conflated: the legality of UAVs as a weapon system *per se*, the legality of targeted killings as lethal uses of force against designated individuals (sometimes in zones far removed from any recognisable 'battlefield'), the consequences of 'direct participation in hostilities' (DPH) by either the UAV operators or the targets, the legality of collateral damage and the question – sitting partly in IHL and partly in international criminal law – of where legal responsibility for the use of UAVs lies.[12]

The sudden rush of publicity and debate has fuelled a perception that UAVs are a 'new' type of weapon, but this is correct only in the sense that they can remain aloft for extended periods of time and provide intelligence. Although the specific technology used to operate them is very contemporary, remotely controlled unmanned weapons have been in the skies for nearly a century. Even before the First World War, an inventor named Elmer Sperry had attracted the US Navy

[9] M. N. Schmitt, 'Unmanned Combat Aircraft Systems and International Humanitarian Law: Simplifying the Oft Benighted Debate', 30 *Boston University International Law Journal* (2012) 595, 595–6.

[10] For example, see the Bureau of Investigative Journalism, 'Obama 2013 Pakistan Drone Strikes', 3 January 2013: www.thebureauinvestigates.com/2013/01/03/obama-2013-pakistan-drone-strikes/; New America Foundation, 'The National Security Studies Program': http://natsec.newamerica.net/.

[11] For example, 'Drone Strikes Threaten 50 Years of International Law, Says UN Rapporteur', *Guardian*, 21 June 2012: www.guardian.co.uk/world/2012/jun/21/drone-strikes-international-law-un.

[12] There are other dimensions to the use of UAVs concerning, most notably, the legality of their use in possible violation of another state's territorial sovereignty (which is a matter of the *jus ad bellum*, not IHL) and questions of ethics and morality surrounding their use. This chapter does not seek to address those discrete issues.

Bureau of Ordnance's interest with an early prototype radio-controlled aircraft, the abortive Curtiss-Sperry Flying Bomb. Although a plan was proposed to use it to attack U-boat bases on Germany's North Sea coast after America's entry into the war in 1917, tests were only partially successful and the end of the war in 1918 meant that the weapon was never used.[13] In the Second World War it was the Germans who were at the forefront of developing technology in unmanned flight. Although the *Vergeltungswaffen* (literally: retaliation, retribution or vengeance weapons) were the most infamous products of this work, these were flying bombs and missiles[14] rather than UAVs as the term is understood today. More premonitory of later technology was the Ruhrstahl SD 1400 X glider bomb (more commonly known to the Allies as the 'Fritz X'), which was released from a medium-range bomber and guided to its target by a radio-control transmitter operated manually from the deploying aircraft. It was used by the *Luftwaffe* on a number of occasions during the Italian Campaign and scored its most spectacular success on 9 September 1943 when two Fritz X bombs hit the battleship *Roma*, the flagship of the Italian Fleet, while she was underway in the Strait of Bonifacio to surrender to the British at Malta following the Italian Armistice. The *Roma*'s number two forward gun turret magazines detonated and the ship capsized and broke in two, with the loss of 1,253 men (including Admiral Carlo Bergamini, the Fleet Commander).[15] The Fritz X, however, was a weapon *per se*, unlike current unmanned air systems which are merely *platforms* for weapons. In later decades, the first recognisably modern UAVs were deployed by the Americans (for observation in Vietnam) and the Israelis (against the Syrian Air Force over Lebanon in 1982).[16]

A snapshot of current publicly available information, news and recent developments in relation to drones, at the time of writing, includes the following:

- The American Civil Liberties Union (ACLU) and the Center for Constitutional Rights (CCR) filed a lawsuit against the US Department

[13] See L. Pearson, 'Developing the Flying Bomb', in A. O. Van Wyen et al., *Naval Aviation in World War I* (Washington, DC: US Government Printing Office, 1969), 70–2.

[14] Respectively, the V-1 and the V-2. Neither could be guided or controlled in any way once launched.

[15] See C. Kopp, 'The Dawn of the Smart Bomb', Air Power Australia Technical Report APA-TR-2011-0302, 26 March 2011: www.ausairpower.net/WW2-PGMs.html#mozTocId46276.

[16] See Defense Update, 'Israel – An Unmanned Air Systems (UAS) Super Power', 3 May 2013: http://defense-update.com/20130503_israel-as-unmanned-air-systems-super-power.html.

of Defense, challenging as unconstitutional the 2011 targeted killing of three US citizens in drone strikes in Yemen, outside any apparent zone of armed hostilities.[17] The Administration responded with a motion to dismiss the lawsuit[18] and an internal legal opinion on the lawfulness of targeted killings in such circumstances was famously leaked to the press.[19] A letter from the US Attorney General to the Chairman of the Senate Committee on the Judiciary dated 22 May 2013 has since disclosed classified information about the killings and set out a formal legal justification for them.[20] Specific standards and procedures for such operations were announced by President Obama in a Presidential Policy Guidance document (PPG) signed on the same date.[21]

- The ACLU also has two other lawsuits running concurrently against the US Administration, under the Freedom of Information Act (FOIA), seeking disclosure of a large amount of official information regarding the government's targeted killings programme, covering its basis in domestic law, the oversight of drone operators, through to statistical data concerning combatant and civilian casualties resulting from drone strikes.[22] A further FOIA request has since been submitted by the ACLU concerning a strike in Yemen in April 2012.[23]

17 *Al-Aulaqi* v. *Panetta*, Complaint, United States District Court for the District of Columbia, 18 July 2012: www.aclu.org/files/assets/tk_complaint_to_file.pdf.

18 *Al-Aulaqi* v. *Panetta*, Defendant's Motion to Dismiss, United States District Court for the District of Columbia, 14 December 2012: www.aclu.org/files/assets/tk_govt_motion_to_dismiss.pdf.

19 United States Department of Justice White Paper, *Lawfulness of a Lethal Operation Directed against a US Citizen Who is a Senior Operational Leader of Al-Qa'ida or an Associated Force* (undated): http://msnbcmedia.msn.com/i/msnbc/sections/news/020413_DOJ_White_Paper.pdf.

20 See www.justice.gov/slideshow/AG-letter-5-22-13.pdf.

21 The White House, 'US Policy Standards and Procedures for the Use of Force in Counterterrorism Operations Outside the United States and Areas of Active Hostilities', 22 May 2013: www.whitehouse.gov/sites/default/files/uploads/2013.05.23_fact_sheet_on_ppg.pdf.

22 The lawsuit was filed in June 2010 and dismissed at first instance, but is under appeal at the time of writing. For the initial decision, see *American Civil Liberties Union et al.* v. *Department of Justice et al.*, Memorandum Opinion, United States District Court for the District of Columbia, 9 September 2011: www.aclu.org/files/assets/34_-_opinion_09_09_2011.pdf. For the appeal, see *American Civil Liberties Union and American Civil Liberties Union Foundation* v. *Central Intelligence Agency*, Brief for Plaintiffs-Appellants, United States Court of Appeals for the District of Columbia Circuit, 15 March 2012: www.aclu.org/files/assets/drone_foia_aclu_appeal_brief.pdf. Oral arguments were heard in the appeal in September 2012, but as of February 2013 no date had been announced for the appellate court's decision.

23 See www.aclu.org/files/assets/al-majalah_missile_foia.pdf.

- Noor Khan, a Pakistani British citizen, filed a case against the Foreign and Commonwealth Office in the High Court, in which he is seeking disclosure of the extent of the United Kingdom's cooperation with US drone strikes. It has been argued that the passing of intelligence by the United Kingdom to the United States to facilitate the latter's drone strikes could amount to the war crime of complicity in murder.[24] Arguments were heard in October 2012 but no date has yet been set for judgment.
- The United Nations Secretary-General and Under-Secretary-General for Peacekeeping Operations requested,[25] and the Security Council authorised, the 'trial use' of UAVs for surveillance purposes by the United Nations Organisation Stabilisation Mission in the Democratic Republic of the Congo (MONUSCO).[26] Although the Security Council meeting at which the request was discussed was closed, so no *procès-verbal* has been published,[27] the request was strongly supported by France, the United Kingdom and the USA, although Rwanda and Pakistan voiced strong concerns.[28] At a press conference the following month, Under-Secretary-General Hervé Ladsous responded agitatedly to a question about 'the possibility of the use of drones going beyond mere surveillance': 'Let me say first that maybe the word should not be "drones" because these days you know people associate drones with the image of missiles being launched. No, no, no. This clearly is UAVs for surveillance purposes only, basically a flying camera. [...] Clearly, this is a situation of its own [...] and we shall see how this experiment goes on. Of course there are a number of other operations where this could be considered as a useful tool.'[29]

[24] 'UK Support for US Drones in Pakistan May Be War Crime, Court is Told', *Guardian*, 23 October 2012: www.guardian.co.uk/world/2012/oct/23/uk-support-us-drones-pakistan-war-crime.

[25] Letter dated 27 December 2012 from the Secretary-General Addressed to the President of the Security Council (UN Doc. S/2013/43), 2.

[26] Letter dated 22 January 2013 from the President of the Security Council Addressed to the Secretary-General (UN Doc. S/2013/44).

[27] See La France à l'ONU, *République démocratique du Congo, Derniers développements à New York, Chronologie*, 8 January 2013: www.franceonu.org/la-france-a-l-onu/dossiers-geographiques/afrique/republique-democratique-du-congo/article/chronologie-6886.

[28] 'UN Wants to Use Surveillance Drones in Congo', *Associated Press*, 9 January 2013.

[29] UN Department of Peacekeeping Operations, Hervé Ladsous press conference, 6 February 2013, near-verbatim transcript, 7–8: www.un.org/en/peacekeeping/articles/USG%20Ladsous.PC.transcript.060213.final.rtf.pdf.

- Following the announcement that British MQ-9 Reaper drones deployed in Afghanistan are since April 2013 being operated from the territory of the United Kingdom[30] by the Royal Air Force's XIII Squadron, six 'Disarm the Drones' activists broke into the squadron's base at RAF Waddington in Lincolnshire in protest against the alleged violations of international law that British use of the UAVs entails. At their trial before Lincoln Magistrates on charges of causing criminal damage (ongoing at the time of writing), a legal opinion[31] has been put forward to the effect that the 1950 European Convention for the Protection of Human Rights and Fundamental Freedoms (ECHR)[32] applies to the use of UAVs in Afghanistan.[33]
- Responding to a formal request by Pakistan and a group of other concerned states at the 2012 session of the UN Human Rights Council, the Special Rapporteur on the promotion and protection of human rights and fundamental freedoms while countering terrorism announced in January 2013 the launch of an official inquiry into 'the evidence that drone strikes and other forms of targeted killing have caused disproportionate civilian casualties in some instances, and to make recommendations concerning the duty of States to conduct thorough independent and impartial investigations into such allegations'.[34] The inquiry is expected to focus on twenty-five examples of drone strikes that have occurred in Pakistan, Afghanistan, Yemen, Somalia and 'the State of Palestine'; a report is expected to be presented to the UN General Assembly in October 2013.[35]

[30] 'Afghan Drones Controlled by Pilots in UK', *British Forces News*, 25 April 2013: http://bfbs.com/news/afghanistan/afghan-drones-controlled-pilots-uk-63402.html.

[31] Public Interest Lawyers, 'The Legality of the UK's Use of Armed Unmanned Aerial Vehicles (Drones) – Opinion', 3 June 2013: www.publicinterestlawyers.co.uk/go_files/files/ME1IAPC380F3.pdf.

[32] 213 UNTS 221 (1953).

[33] 'UK's Use of Drones in Afghanistan "May be in Breach of International Law"', *Guardian*, 8 June 2013: www.guardian.co.uk/world/2013/jun/08/uk-drones-afghanistan-legal-challenge.

[34] UN Human Rights, Office of the High Commissioner, Statement by Ben Emmerson, UN Special Rapporteur on Counter-Terrorism and Human Rights concerning the launch of an inquiry into the civilian impact and human rights implications of the use of drones and other forms of targeted killing for the purpose of counter-terrorism and counter-insurgency, 24 January 2013: www.ohchr.org/Documents/Issues/Terrorism/SRCTBenEmmersonQC.24January12.pdf, 5.

[35] *Ibid.*, 6–7.

- Another UN Special Rapporteur, Christof Heyns, recently issued a report[36] on the 'next generation' of drones: lethal autonomous robots (LARs),[37] machines that can select and engage targets without human intervention once programmed and activated, in true 'Terminator' style.[38] He has since called for a global moratorium on the development and deployment of LARs to allow for 'serious and meaningful international engagement on this issue before we proceed to a world where machines are given the power to kill humans'.[39]

This chapter will consider the legality of UAVs and their use in armed conflict from the standpoint of current IHL,[40] both in general (legality *per se*) and specific (legality of use) terms, in light of the many criticisms that have been levelled at these systems. The analysis will focus initially on whether UAVs comply with the regulation of weaponry in IHL generally, before concentrating particularly on the use of UAVs for the kinetic application of (potentially) lethal force. The latter will entail consideration of their compliance with the law of targeting operations, as well as the question of the legal status of their operators and the consequences of that status. Finally, the question of legal responsibility for the use of drones in armed conflicts will be addressed. The chapter will conclude that no new regulatory legal framework is necessary for drones, but that while they are not inherently unlawful under IHL, their actual use in armed conflict must be compliant with that body of law.

36 UN Human Rights Council, Report of the Special Rapporteur on extrajudicial, summary or arbitrary executions, Christof Heyns, 9 April 2013 (UN Doc. A/HRC/23/47).

37 The UAVs that have been at the centre of the 'drone debate' so far all require human direction and control to track their targets and release their payloads. Human operators make all the crucial decisions regarding actual strikes, hence the term 'human-in-the-loop systems'. LARs, on the other hand, are 'human-out-of-the-loop systems' that operate with complete (albeit pre-programmed) autonomy. Currently, no state is reported as envisaging the deployment of such systems in theatres of conflict.

38 The reference is to the famous series of Hollywood films, the *Terminator* series (1984–2009), starring Arnold Schwarzenegger; but see the qualifications elaborated in Sharkey, 'Saying "No!" to Lethal Autonomous Targeting', 376–7.

39 Office of the High Commissioner for Human Rights, 'UN Human Rights Expert Calls for a Moratorium on Lethal Autonomous Robots', 30 May 2013: www.ohchr.org/EN/NewsEvents/Pages/DisplayNews.aspx?NewsID=13380&LangID=E.

40 The legality of the use of UAVs under other relevant legal regimes, namely, the *jus ad bellum* and international human rights law, falls outside the scope of this chapter.

Drones, weaponry and means of warfare in international humanitarian law

It should be remembered at the outset that drones can be (and are) used for a wide variety of tasks other than combat, including those that overtly assist military operations, such as observation and reconnaissance, intelligence collection, target acquisition, but also search and rescue, delivery of humanitarian aid and transport of equipment (both civilian and military).[41] Since none of those tasks is in any way illegal under IHL, it follows that drones *per se* cannot be unlawful. What is pertinent is the legality of their use to deliver kinetic, lethal force.[42] In this context it is often assumed that the first aspect to be considered is whether they are lawful weapons *ab initio*. In fact, this question is misplaced. Properly speaking, drones are not an actual weapon at all, but only a *platform* for the delivery of a weapon.[43] Thus, in the case of the MQ-9 Reaper, it is the Hellfire missiles and laser-guided bombs with which the drones are armed that constitute the actual weapons, not the drones themselves. A mere platform for a weapon system or for the delivery of a weapon cannot, in and of itself, be prohibited under IHL. However, it is appropriate to consider UAVs (being a weapons platform that can be 'used directly to deliver force during hostilities')[44] as a means of warfare and therefore subject to the general rule that 'The right of belligerents to adopt means of injuring the enemy is not unlimited.'[45] This means that UAVs can and should be regulated by the strictures of IHL regarding

[41] For an example of the use of drones in humanitarian missions, see 'Why Drones Deserve a Second Look', *The Hindu*, 29 July 2013: www.thehindu.com/opinion/op-ed/why-drones-deserve-a-second-look/article4963947.ece. It is these types of drone that are properly referred to as UAVs; those that carry weapons and can deliver them to a target are more correctly described as unmanned combat aerial vehicles (UCAVs). Popular and media usage, however, somewhat inevitably conflates the two under the single tag of UAVs or, even more commonly, drones. This does not accord with military usage of the terminology.

[42] See W. H. Boothby, *Weapons and the Law of Armed Conflict* (Oxford: Oxford University Press, 2009), 229–31.

[43] *Ibid.* See also the historical part of the Introduction to this chapter, above. If UAVs cannot properly be said to be a weapon at all, they certainly cannot constitute a 'new' weapon. However, if they did, they would be subject to the requirement, in Article 36 AP I, that states undertake a legal review of new weapons before their introduction in order to ascertain their compliance with IHL and any other applicable rules of international law. See *ibid.*, 342–52.

[44] *Ibid.*, 4.

[45] Regulations Respecting the Laws and Customs of War on Land, Annexed to The Hague Convention IV, 18 October 1907, 2 *AJIL* Supp. 90, Article 22.

means and methods of warfare, a body of law of great antiquity which determines, *inter alia*, *what* ways of injuring the enemy may be used and *how* they may be used. The rules in question originated in customary international law and have, in modern times, been updated in treaty form, namely, in the Hague Regulations of 1899 and 1907, and Additional Protocol I of 1977, supplemented by a long list of treaties that outlaw or restrict the use of specific types of weaponry. Many of those latter treaties are now themselves arguably part of customary international law.[46]

As the terms of the popular debate make clear, the answer to the '*what*' question is that there is currently no provision in the law of armed conflict that actually outlaws UAVs as such, nor places any explicit restrictions on their use to deliver lethal force. No specific treaty has yet been concluded with respect to drone technology or its use in armed conflicts; however, there are generalised treaty-based rules prohibiting the use of weapons that cause superfluous injury or unnecessary suffering,[47] or that are indiscriminate.[48] Both of these general rules are said to be part of customary international law,[49] although in practice it is thought unlikely that either could be the sole basis for declaring any given weapon or weapons system illegal.[50] The first of these general rules on weaponry operates to prohibit weapons that cause unnecessary or inhumane injuries (irrespective of whether or not they are actually lethal) to combatants. The only way that this could apply to a drone would be if the weapon system mounted on it contained components, the effect of which would be to cause such injuries.[51] The example has been suggested of a warhead on a drone-mounted missile that is packed with glass, the broken shards of which in the human body would doubtless

[46] But see, for criticism, S. Haines, 'Weapons, Means and Methods of Warfare', in E. Wilmshurst and S. Breau (eds), *Perspectives on the ICRC Study on Customary International Humanitarian Law* (Cambridge: Cambridge University Press, 2007), 262.

[47] Protocol I Additional to the Geneva Conventions of 12 August 1949, and Relating to the Protection of Victims of International Armed Conflicts (hereinafter AP I), 8 June 1977, 16 ILM 1391, Article 35(2).

[48] Article 51(4) AP I.

[49] See J.-M. Henckaerts and L. Doswald-Beck (eds), *Customary International Humanitarian Law*, vol. 1, *Rules* (Cambridge: Cambridge University Press, 2005), Rules 70 and 71, 237–50 (hereinafter CIHL Study).

[50] See D. Turns, 'Weapons in the ICRC Study on Customary International Humanitarian Law', 11 *JCSL* (2006) 201, 214.

[51] *A fortiori*, the drone would fall afoul of the law if the warhead were packed with a weapon or component that is itself prohibited, for example, chemical gas; this would be a violation of the Chemical Weapons Convention, 32 ILM (1993) 804.

render medical treatment much more complicated whilst increasing the agony of the victim.[52] The second general rule prohibits weapons that are incapable of discriminating between lawful targets (i.e., combatants or military objectives) and persons or objects protected from attack (i.e., civilians or civilian objects). An example might be a warhead containing flechettes – steel darts that scatter on impact over an area of several hundred metres.[53] It should be noted in this context, however, that whilst any weapon is capable of *being used* in an indiscriminate manner[54] – as in cases captured on film of irregular fighters in Freetown, Sierra Leone, during that country's civil war in the 1990s, waving their Kalashnikov AK-47 automatic rifles wildly above their heads and firing without taking aim at any particular target – what the law actually prohibits is weapons whose very *nature or design* precludes their being directed against a particular target.[55] A drone is no different in this respect.

It is clear, therefore, that in respect of the legality of using UAVs under IHL it is the '*how*' question that is relevant. This is confirmed by the only current restatement of IHL to refer specifically to UAVs, which expressly includes them within its purview.[56] Furthermore, two of the very few countries to have published official doctrines on the use of drones in military operations – the USA[57] and the United Kingdom[58] – are in agreement, as are relevant international organisations[59] and principal

[52] J. S. Thurnher, 'The Law that Applies to Autonomous Weapon Systems', 17(4) *ASIL Insights* (2013) 2: www.asil.org/insights130118.cfm.

[53] But see the decision of the Supreme Court of Israel, sitting as a High Court of Justice, in *Physicians for Human Rights* v. *Doron Almog, OC Southern Command*, 42 ILM (2003) 882.

[54] See Boothby, *Weapons and the Law of Armed Conflict*, 82–3.

[55] See Haines, 'Weapons, Means and Methods of Warfare', 266; cf. F. Kalshoven, cited by Boothby, *Weapons and the Law of Armed Conflict*, 76 n. 23.

[56] See Program on Humanitarian Policy and Conflict Research at Harvard University, Manual on International Law Applicable to Air and Missile Warfare, Berne, 15 May 2009 (Cambridge, MA: Program on Humanitarian Policy and Conflict Research) (hereinafter Harvard Manual). Note that the Manual correctly distinguishes between UAVs and UCAVs: Harvard Manual, Rule 1(dd)–(ee).

[57] US Department of Defense, Directive Number 3000.09 (21 November 2012), Autonomy in Weapon Systems, § 4(b).

[58] UK Ministry of Defence, Joint Doctrine Note 2/11 (30 March 2011), The UK Approach to Unmanned Aircraft Systems, para. 502 (UK JDN).

[59] For example, see 31st International Conference of the Red Cross and Red Crescent, International Humanitarian Law and the Challenges of Contemporary Armed Conflicts – Report (October 2011), 38–40.

legal academic commentators on the subject,[60] that the use of drones must be in accordance with the general rules and principles of IHL. In practice, particularly in the context of the lethal strikes or targeted killings that have been the focus of so much of the debate, the relevant IHL rules are those governing the selection of targets and precautions in attack – in other words, the law of targeting operations – and it is to those rules that this discussion must now turn.

Generalities of targeting under international humanitarian law

The rules of targeting are generally quite well known in the modern world, albeit not always very well understood. The widespread awareness and misunderstanding alike are thanks largely to constant media reporting of contemporary armed conflicts (sometimes called the 'CNN effect'), a phenomenon that has been prevalent since the First Gulf War (1991).[61] These rules are contained in Additional Protocol I and may for present purposes be summarised fairly briefly. The Protocol is now very widely ratified – 173 states out of 195 are parties[62] and a further three have signed but not ratified[63] – and many states accept that the targeting rules in particular constitute customary international law[64] while some even apply them, as a matter of policy if not of legal obligation, in non-international (as well as international) armed conflicts.[65]

60 For example, Schmitt, 'Unmanned Combat Aircraft Systems and International Humanitarian Law'; Boothby, *Weapons and the Law of Armed Conflict*, 230–3; M. N. Schmitt, 'Drone Attacks under the *Jus ad Bellum* and *Jus in Bello*: Clearing the "Fog of Law"', 13 *YIHL* (2010) 311; M. E. O'Connell, 'The International Law of Drones', 14(37) *ASIL Insights* (2010): www.asil.org/insights/volume/14/issue/37/international-law-drones.

61 For a discussion of its effect in contemporary armed conflicts, see R. Smith, *The Utility of Force: The Art of War in the Modern World* (London: Penguin, 2006), 284–9.

62 International Committee of the Red Cross, Treaties and States Parties to Such Treaties: www.icrc.org/applic/ihl/ihl.nsf/States.xsp?xp_viewStates=XPages_NORMStatesParties&xp_treatySelected=470.

63 Namely, Iran, Pakistan and the United States: International Committee of the Red Cross, Treaties and States Parties to Such Treaties: www.icrc.org/applic/ihl/ihl.nsf/States.xsp?xp_viewStates=XPages_NORMStatesSign&xp_treatySelected=470.

64 Thus, US and Coalition/NATO forces applied them during the 1st Gulf (1991) and Kosovo (1999) wars; see M. N. Schmitt, 'The Law of Targeting', in Wilmshurst and Breau, *Perspectives on the ICRC Study*, 131–2 and 134.

65 For example, UK Ministry of Defence (2010), *Joint Doctrine Publication 3-46: Legal Support to Joint Operations*, 2nd edn, para. 130: www.mod.uk/DefenceInternet/MicroSite/DCDC/OurPublications/JDWP/Jdp346LegalSupportToJointOperations2ndEdition.htm.

Moreover, the same rules are also generally considered to apply, *mutatis mutandis*, to targeting in both the maritime[66] and aerial[67] warfare operational environments.[68]

First comes the 'basic rule' of distinction: 'In order to ensure respect for and protection of the civilian population and civilian objects, the Parties to the conflict shall at all times distinguish between the civilian population and combatants and between civilian objects and military objectives and accordingly shall direct their operations only against military objectives.'[69] Next, specific protections are provided for the civilian population, which may not be attacked or terrorised as such.[70] Civilians (that is, persons who are not combatants) are protected 'unless and for such time as they take a direct part in hostilities'.[71] Indiscriminate attacks – that is, those that are not directed at a specific military objective[72] or which employ a method or means of warfare which cannot be so directed[73] or whose effects cannot be limited as required by the Protocol,[74] and which consequently fail to observe the basic rule of distinction – are prohibited. Belligerent reprisals against civilians are prohibited,[75] as is the use of the latter, by a party to an armed conflict, as human shields in order 'to render certain points or areas immune from military operations'.[76]

Similar general protection is provided for civilian objects. Like civilians, these benefit only from a negative definition – a civilian object is anything which is not a military objective.[77] Therefore, the definition of such objectives becomes absolutely crucial to the interpretation and application of the law, just as the definition of combatant status has been essential in determining civilian (that is, protected) status. Certain types of objects additionally benefit from specific protection from attack under the terms of the Protocol – cultural property,[78] objects indispensable to the survival of the civilian population (such as foodstuffs, crops, livestock and drinking water installations)[79] and works and installations containing dangerous forces ('namely dams, dykes and nuclear electrical

[66] See L. Doswald-Beck (ed.), *San Remo Manual on International Law Applicable to Armed Conflicts at Sea* (Cambridge: Cambridge University Press, 1995), part III.

[67] See Harvard Manual, sections D–H.

[68] The Protocol itself also provides for the application of its rules on protection of the civilian population in respect of 'any land, air or sea warfare' and 'all attacks from the sea or from the air against objectives on land': Article 49(3) AP I.

[69] Article 48 AP I. [70] Article 51(2) AP I. [71] Article 51(3) AP I.

[72] Article 51(4)(a) AP I. [73] Article 51(4)(b) AP I. [74] Article 51(4)(c) AP I.

[75] Article 51(6) AP I. [76] Article 51(7) AP I. [77] Article 52(1) AP I.

[78] Article 53 AP I. [79] Article 54(2) AP I.

generating stations').[80] Finally, the parts of the Protocol specifically concerned with targeting operations place extensive obligations on an attacking force to take stringent precautions in both the selection of targets and the prosecution of attacks thereon,[81] whilst also requiring a defending force to take rather minimalist and generic precautions against the effects of attacks.[82]

These rules, and particularly the basic rule of distinction from which the others all flow, apply to persons and objects alike and, since civilians and civilian objects are not defined in the treaty texts of IHL (other than in negative terms), it is essential to understand the definitions of permissible targets in respect of both persons (combatants) and objects (military objectives). Both have been analysed in great detail elsewhere.[83] For present purposes, the definitions may be briefly summarised as follows: combatants are members of regular state armed forces and associated militias, or members of other militias who satisfy the requirements enumerated in Article 1 of the 1907 Hague Regulations and Article 4 of 1949 Geneva Convention III.[84] Everyone else in an international armed conflict[85] is a civilian and *ipso facto* protected from direct attack, save for the proviso (as mentioned above) that civilians who 'take a direct part in hostilities' forfeit their right to such protection.[86]

Military objectives are defined as 'those objects which by their nature, location, purpose or use make an effective contribution to military action

[80] Article 56(1) AP I. [81] Article 57 AP I. [82] Article 58 AP I.

[83] For example (as to combatants), A. P. V. Rogers, 'Combatant Status', in Wilmshurst and Breau, *Perspectives on the ICRC Study*, 101; (as to objects), C. Byron, 'International Humanitarian Law and Bombing Campaigns: Military Objectives and Excessive Collateral Damage', 13 *YIHL* (2010) 175.

[84] Note also the controversial modern extension of combatant and prisoner of war status in Articles 43–4 AP I. For discussion, see Y. Dinstein, *The Conduct of Hostilities under the Law of International Armed Conflict*, 2nd edn (Cambridge: Cambridge University Press, 2010); D. Turns, 'The Law of Armed Conflict (International Humanitarian Law)', in M. D. Evans (ed.), *International Law*, 3rd edn (Oxford: Oxford University Press, 2010), 825–8.

[85] In non-international armed conflict there is no legal concept of personal status, hence the question of combatant status does not formally arise as such. However, for targeting purposes, it is suggested that in such conflicts the terms 'combatant' and 'civilian' may be understood on a functional basis, dependent on conduct: see Rogers, 'Combatant Status', 109–10.

[86] Article 51(3) AP I; International Committee of the Red Cross (ICRC), 'Interpretive Guidance on the Notion of Direct Participation in Hostilities', 90 *IRRC* (2008) 991; for criticism, see 'Forum: Direct Participation in Hostilities: Perspectives on the ICRC Interpretive Guidance', 42 *New York University Journal of International Law and Politics* (2010) 637.

and whose total or partial destruction, capture or neutralization, in the circumstances ruling at the time, offers a definite military advantage'.[87] Thus, the test for determining whether a given object is in fact a military objective has two cumulative elements: (1) if, for one of the specific reasons listed, it makes an effective contribution to military action, and (2) targeting it would offer the attacker a definite military advantage. Prominent by its absence from the treaty regime, but nevertheless often present in contemporary armed conflicts, is the dual-use object: that is, an object that is primarily civilian in character but has some military uses in armed conflict, such as to convert it into a military objective. Examples include broadcasting facilities and national electricity grids – the latter may power military communications and other facilities whilst also supporting many of the most basic necessities of daily civilian existence, such as water purification or sewage treatment plants. In a sense, *prima facie*, this should be a non-issue in IHL. The term 'dual-use object' as such is nowhere to be found in Additional Protocol I and the rare mentions of it in the context of customary law only serve to emphasise its ambiguity and subjectivity.[88]

One of the most consistently misrepresented of the law's strictures is the recognition, in the doctrine of collateral damage, that civilian casualties may in any event occur as a result of the targeting process and will not necessarily be unlawful, provided that they are judged not to be disproportionate to the corresponding military advantage. Collateral damage is defined in law as 'incidental loss of civilian life, injury to civilians, damage to civilian objects, or a combination thereof'[89] – the word 'incidental' clearly indicating that it is an undesired (but inevitable or accidental) corollary of an attack on a *legitimate military objective*. The concept of collateral damage is not relevant if an attack is deliberately directed against civilians or is indiscriminate. Such attacks, as violations of Articles 51(2) and 51(4) respectively, automatically qualify as war crimes and the damage resulting therefrom would not be in any sense 'collateral'. Collateral damage will only be unlawful if it 'may be expected' to cause death or injury to civilians or damage to civilian objects, 'which would be excessive *in relation to the concrete and direct*

[87] Article 52(2) AP I.

[88] International Criminal Tribunal for the former Yugoslavia, 'Final Report to the Prosecutor by the Committee Established to Review the NATO Bombing Campaign against the Federal Republic of Yugoslavia', 39 *ILM* (2000) 1257, 1266–7; CIHL Study, 32.

[89] Article 51(5)(b) AP I.

military advantage anticipated [from the attack]'.[90] Thus, as part of the targeting process, commanders are expected to engage in a calculation of a difficult balancing act. They must weigh up the expected collateral damage incidental to an otherwise lawful attack and decide (on the basis of all the available intelligence and with the benefit of legal advice) whether it would be disproportionate to the anticipated military advantage that would accrue from the attack; if it would, the law expects them to decide not to launch the attack,[91] or to cancel or suspend it if it is already in progress.[92] There are other precautions to be taken, both in attack and defence, in order to spare the civilian population. Those who plan or decide upon an attack must do everything feasible to verify that the objectives to be attacked are in fact military objectives,[93] must 'take all feasible precautions in the choice of means and methods of attack with a view to avoiding, and in any event to minimizing' collateral damage[94] and must give 'effective advance warning' of attacks which may affect the civilian population, 'unless circumstances do not permit'.[95] Where there is a choice between different targets that may be attacked to obtain a similar military advantage, the one expected to cause the least collateral damage should be selected.[96] Defenders must take specific precautions to remove the civilian population under their control from the vicinity of military objectives and avoid locating such objectives within or adjacent to densely populated areas, along with other general necessary precautions.[97]

Targeting and drones: specific aspects and issues

The application of the targeting rules, thus briefly summarised, does not differ according to the precise means used. Hence, attacks executed by UCAVs are treated no differently by the law than attacks conducted by manned aircraft, artillery batteries on land or submarines.[98] The paramount issue is always going to be whether unmanned systems can

[90] *Ibid.* (emphasis added). [91] Article 57(2)(a)(iii) AP I. [92] Article 57(2)(b) AP I.
[93] Article 57(2)(a)(i) AP I.
[94] Article 57(2)(a)(ii) AP I. This means that an attacking commander with a choice of weaponry at his disposal should choose the weapon(s) least likely to cause collateral damage.
[95] Article 57(2)(c) AP I. [96] Article 57(3) AP I. [97] Article 58 AP I.
[98] The only specific mention of drones in any IHL text so far asserts that the normal rules of IHL regarding precautions in attack apply to UCAVs as they do to any other weapon system: Harvard Manual, Rule 39.

comply with the detailed rules of IHL, especially those that relate to the application of lethal force in targeting operations. In essence, as long as the target of a UCAV strike is either (a) a military objective, (b) a combatant, or (c) a civilian who is directly participating in hostilities, *and* (d) the anticipated collateral damage is not excessive in relation to expected military advantage, such a strike will *prima facie* be lawful. Up until the present time, the only UCAVs that have been deployed for the application of lethal force have been operated by humans. Thus, the final decision in all reported cases (to strike or not to strike) has been made by a human, to whom the IHL requirements in targeting are as applicable in respect of a UCAV as they are in respect of tanks, field artillery or submarines. The oft-used language of 'assassinations', with its inexorable connotations of presumed illegality, is neither helpful nor indeed particularly relevant for the IHL-centred debate on the use of UCAVs. 'Assassinations' are only unlawful in armed conflict if they are committed by means of perfidy,[99] that is, '[a]cts inviting the confidence of an adversary to lead him to believe that he is entitled to, or is obliged to accord, protection under the rules of international law applicable in armed conflict, with intent to betray that confidence'.[100] But targeting a specified individual in the hostile force during an armed conflict, absent perfidy, is not unlawful as long as the target is in fact a combatant or a civilian who is directly participating in hostilities.[101] A UCAV might be used in a way that constitutes perfidy; for example, if it carries out targeted killings while painted with one of the protected emblems of the Geneva Conventions and Additional Protocols – the Red Cross, Red Crescent or Red Crystal.[102]

What *would* eventually be very problematic for the law, however, would be the deployment of LARs – fully autonomous weapon systems that would operate entirely independently of any human control or oversight, apart from initial programming and activation. Schmitt avers that 'It is only a matter of time before UAVs and other unmanned

[99] Article 23(b) Hague Regulations. This forbids killing or wounding the enemy 'treacherously', which in the modern law is interpreted as 'perfidiously'.

[100] Article 37(1) AP I.

[101] See *Public Committee against Torture in Israel* v. *Government of Israel*, 46 ILM (2006) 375.

[102] Perfidious use of the Red Lion and Sun would doubtless be too easy to see through, unless, perhaps, it were to be used by Iranian armed forces (since the Islamic Republic has expressly reserved the right to make use of this emblem in the future, should it wish to do so).

systems conduct attacks without the involvement of a human decision-maker.'[103] The central issues here are twofold: (1) how to ensure that the targeting process required by IHL can be complied with, particularly as regards the selection of targets and the taking of precautions in attack, and (2) how to ensure legal responsibility – whether at the individual or command level – for any use of LARs that might violate IHL. It might be notionally possible to envisage LARs with programmes sufficiently advanced that they enable accurate autonomous distinction between combatants and civilians or between military objectives and civilian objects, as required by the law, but such an outcome is so fraught with ethical and technical difficulties that it is surely not to be attempted lightly. Advanced sensors could no doubt identify and compute likely collateral damage but how, for instance, would LARs balance such collateral damage against the expected military advantage of attacking a given target? How would a LAR be able to distinguish a person who is trying to effect a surrender from one who is simply waving his or her arms around in fear or panic? Or whether a person who is lying on the ground is hors de combat from wounds or sickness, and therefore protected from attack, or simply trying to avoid being shot at? It is also not clear how LARs might safely take prisoners. As for the question of legal responsibility, absent sentient drones, it is difficult to see where precisely human accountability for LAR violations of IHL might lie. The chain of command may be dispersed, often to a very senior political (i.e., civilian) level, so would it be necessary to resort to putting computer program designers or installers on trial? If the intelligence that enables a particular LAR operation to go ahead is provided by a human source and turns out to be inaccurate, with the result that the law is violated, would the source be prosecuted? Or if the LAR itself interprets information received in accordance with a programmed algorithm and gets its analysis wrong ... what then? Come to that, how would the law provide for responsibility in the event of any technical malfunction? The UK MoD notes that:

> In practice, such operations would present a considerable technological challenge and the software testing and certification for such a system would be extremely expensive as well as time consuming. Meeting the

[103] M. N. Schmitt, *War, Technology and International Humanitarian Law*, Harvard University Program on Humanitarian Policy and Conflict Research, Occasional Paper Series, 4 (2005), 27: www.hpcrresearch.org/sites/default/files/publications/OccasionalPaper4.pdf.

> requirement for proportionality and distinction would be particularly problematic, as both of these areas are likely to contain elements of ambiguity requiring sophisticated judgement. Such problems are particularly difficult for a machine to solve and would likely require some form of artificial intelligence to be successful. [. . .] *It should be noted that the MOD currently has no intention to develop systems that operate without human intervention in the weapon command and control chain.*[104]

Although it might be thought that the unmanned nature of the drones, with the lack of human 'eyes on target', is already somehow inherently problematic, there is no reason why this should be so. The human operators of the drones presently deployed actually do see the target, albeit on a high-resolution video screen thousands of kilometres from the battlefield. By contrast, in 1918, the Germans used a Krupp long-range railway-mounted giant gun (officially known as the *Kaiser-Wilhelm-Geschütz*, although the Allies mistakenly called it 'Big Bertha', a name actually applied to the Krupp L/12 *M-Gerät* 14 Howitzers used to destroy the Belgian forts around Liège, Namur and Antwerp in 1914) to bombard Paris from a distance of 120 kilometres, without the benefit of any sight of the target at all – by definition, such a weapon could only be aimed at a target the size of a large city and was intended exclusively to damage the morale of the French civilian population.[105] Despite this, there was never any suggestion of any illegality in the Germans' use of such an imprecise means of warfare. The history of warfare shows that the use of indirect fire (that is, artillery bombardment, attack or targeting without the benefit of a direct line of sight to the target)[106] has not been considered a legal issue in and of itself[107] and the same may confidently be asserted in respect of UAVs.[108] Indeed, the point has been made that

[104] UK JDN, para. 508 (emphasis added).

[105] See US Ordnance Department Document No. 2034, *A Report on the Characteristics, Scope of Utility, etc. of Railway Artillery*, Appendix I, 'The German Long-Range Gun and the Bombardment of Paris' (Washington, DC: Government Printing Office, 1921), 726–8.

[106] See generally, F. W. Sweet, *The Evolution of Indirect Fire* (Palm Coast, FL: Backintyme, 2000).

[107] See G. S. Corn and Lt Col. G. P. Corn, 'The Law of Operational Targeting: Viewing the LOAC through an Operational Lens' (2012) 47 *Texas International Law Journal* 337, 366–70. For recent judicial consideration of an operation involving the shelling of targets by artillery without a direct line of sight, see *Prosecutor* v. *Ante Gotovina, Ivan Čermak & Mladen Markač* (ICTY Trial Chamber I, Case No. IT-06-90-T), Judgment, 15 April 2011; *Prosecutor* v. *Ante Gotovina & Mladen Markač* (ICTY Appeals Chamber, Case No. IT-06-90-A), Judgment, 16 November 2012.

[108] See Schmitt, 'Unmanned Combat Aircraft Systems and International Humanitarian Law', 599–600.

the operators of drones do in fact have sight of their targets, albeit at a remove of (often) thousands of kilometres, as in the case of targets in Afghanistan being attacked by drones piloted by operators sitting in control rooms in Creech Air Force base in Nevada. The operators see their targets in real time on computer screens and are in fact able to observe them more closely and for longer periods of time, in incomparably greater comfort and safety, than soldiers located on the physical battlefield.[109]

A popular suggestion is that this physical remove from the battlefield inevitably leads to operators developing an emotional and mental disconnect (what one commentator has termed 'moral disengagement')[110] with the conduct of hostilities, or even the 'risk of developing a "Playstation" mentality to killing'[111] whereby enemy personnel are somehow divorced from reality and are perceived by drone operators as though they were dehumanised characters to be eliminated in a video game.[112] In a similar vein, some have suggested that the 'information overload' that operators suffer from could compromise their ability to comply with the relevant rules of IHL,[113] although military or former military personnel typically dismiss such claims as 'speculative at best, and in the vast majority of situations [. . .] counter-factual'.[114] No doubt this is an area in which further psychological research and substantially more experience is required before the effects of this method of warfare will become fully clear, but in the meantime it may just be that the Pentagon's institution of the new medal mentioned at the beginning of this chapter is justified by the stress under which UAV operators work. As one commentator suggests:

> while there is no danger of [a small-arms] round or [rocket-propelled] grenade hitting the Reaper pilot or sensor operator thousands of miles away, the individuals cannot fully be said to be without a physical response. Adrenaline, the body's fuel for 'fight or flight', still surges

[109] *Ibid.*, 599. [110] Sharkey, 'Saying "No!" to Lethal Autonomous Targeting', 371.

[111] Alston Report, para. 84. For a fascinating comparative-empirical discussion of these, and similar, claims, see P. Lee, 'Remoteness, Risk and Aircrew Ethos' (2012) 15 *Air Power Review* 1, especially 11–16.

[112] A trend that is arguably reflected in some of the language used, at least by American UCAV operators, to refer to 'drone kills': see Lt Col. Andrew Roe, '"Bugsplat" and Fallible Humans: The Hi-Tech US Drone Campaign over North-West Pakistan' (2012) 15 *Air Power Review* 65.

[113] 31st International Conference of the Red Cross and Red Crescent – Report, 39.

[114] Schmitt, 'Unmanned Combat Aircraft Systems and International Humanitarian Law', 615.

> when a Reaper crew is tasked to provide close air support to allied soldiers or marines on the ground. An overabundance of adrenaline experienced over an extended period can have a debilitating physical effect on the human body – including the brain – regardless of its proximity to war.[115]

The other side of this coin is the argument that the very remoteness and disconnectedness of drone warfare paradoxically makes it easier to go to war and to authorise the application of deadly force, thereby lowering the threshold for the use of such force and risking an ever-greater escalation of violence.[116] Quite apart from the consequent alleged likelihood of routinely increased collateral damage, this also has implications for those who would use UCAVs to carry out targeted killings: greater involvement by non-military personnel generally and easier involvement by the top level of government officials. It is well known that President Obama personally signs off on 'kill lists' presented to him by the Central Intelligence Agency (CIA), which is responsible for carrying out targeted killings by UCAVs in Pakistan.[117] Contrast this increasing personal engagement by the US President in the specific authorisation of detailed military operations with the situation which obtained during the Falklands War (1982), in which Prime Minister Margaret Thatcher's personal approval of the sinking of the Argentine cruiser *ARA General Belgrano* was a comparatively rare example of a tactical operational decision being made at the very highest level of government.[118] While the debates at the time of the Falklands War make it clear that decisions involving the application of lethal force were of the utmost gravity and only to be taken sparingly and reluctantly,[119] the impression now, in relation to UCAV targeted killings, is that authorisation of such operations is almost routine. The other aspect of this trend is the increasing civilianisation of armed conflict. Although the drones used

[115] Lee, 'Remoteness, Risk and Aircrew Ethos', 13.

[116] Alston Report, para. 80. To some extent this is an argument that derives from the *jus ad bellum*. Once an armed conflict is already underway, the use of deadly force is governed by IHL and its legality in each individual case will essentially rest on (a) whether the target is a lawful military objective, and (b) whether the anticipated collateral damage (if any) is proportionate to the expected military advantage to be gained from the operation.

[117] 'Secret "Kill List" Proves a Test of Obama's Principles and Will', *New York Times*, 29 May 2012: www.nytimes.com/2012/05/29/world/obamas-leadership-in-war-on-al-qaeda.html?pagewanted=all&_r=0.

[118] See Hansard, HC, vol. 23, col. 16 (4 May 1982).

[119] Hansard, HC, vol. 23, cols 29–37 (4 May 1982).

in Afghanistan are operated by uniformed USAF personnel (and British drones by their RAF equivalents),[120] those that are deployed in Pakistan and Yemen are operated by the CIA, a civilian intelligence organisation. CIA operatives, as much as the President himself, could therefore be said to be directly participating in hostilities within the meaning of Article 51(3) of Additional Protocol I and – in the event that America's enemies would pay any attention to the international law of armed conflict – would lose their entitlement to protection from attack. Assassination of the President by a Taliban agent on US soil, for example, would then present no *prima facie* evidence of a violation of IHL. The application of the IHL notion of direct participation in hostilities in the case of CIA-operated drones – rather ironically, in light of Western states' refusal to regard Taliban, Al-Qaeda and other such enemies in Afghanistan, Pakistan, Yemen and elsewhere as lawful combatants – has the inevitable effect of placing US operatives on the same legal footing as their enemies, which virtually amounts to inverting the notion of reciprocity.[121] By the same token, CIA installations from which UCAVs are operated could be viewed as becoming military objectives by their use, as stipulated in Article 52(2) of Additional Protocol I. It would therefore be lawful, for example, for the Taliban to mount an attack on CIA Headquarters in Langley, Virginia – a development that would have profound and negative consequences for escalation of the conflict.

Notwithstanding the above points, drones perfectly suit the increasing unwillingness of professional military commanders to risk their troops' lives unnecessarily (the 'body bag effect'). This tendency, coupled with the public's aversion, in liberal democratic societies, to casualties if vital national interests (e.g., territory) are not immediately and directly at stake, represents a form of 'war on the cheap', which, in an age of sustained economic crisis, austerity and defence budget cuts, is additionally attractive to political and military decision-makers alike.[122] Moreover, in terms of specific compliance with IHL, commentators such as Schmitt argue that UAVs are both more reliable and more accurate than manned weapon systems, enhance military forces' ability to verify the nature of the target, provide high-quality information about the target area in real

[120] Although note that the UK MoD appears concerned about the legal status and susceptibility to attack of UAV operators: see UK JDN, para. 515. To the extent that British drones are operated by uniformed RAF personnel, such concerns are misplaced.

[121] In the sense that the principle of reciprocity, being one of the foundations of IHL, normally operates to encourage mutual respect for the law.

[122] See Smith, *The Utility of Force*, 292–7.

time and for extended periods of time without ever getting tired or exposing human life (of the forces using them) to risk and, therefore, permit more refined and accurate assessments of likely collateral damage when authorising strikes.[123] The concept of fighting a war without incurring any casualties has been prevalent in Western states' political approaches to armed conflict since at least the Kosovo War (1999) and although it is not *per se* inconsistent with IHL[124] it does lead to an uncomfortable feeling regarding the asymmetry of contemporary armed conflicts, which makes one wonder about the moral implications of our increasingly technological warfare. To date, UCAVs have only been deployed in armed conflict by highly advanced Western states and are viewed as a 'weapon of choice' within that paradigm. However, what would the reaction be if they were used against UK forces by, for example, Iran (which is known to possess them), in the event of British participation in an international armed conflict against that country? Conversely, would the United Kingdom be prepared to use them against, for example, Argentine forces in the event of a renewed armed conflict over the Falkland Islands?[125]

Schmitt has posited a concept of 'normative relativism' in IHL, whereby the technologically advanced party to an armed conflict is held to a higher legal standard than its opponent, particularly in terms of the precautions expected in attack, and notes the problems caused by lack of reciprocity in such asymmetric conflicts.[126] The corollary of this, however, is that the technologically disadvantaged party will sooner or later strike back by any means he possesses. In the context of the present 'drone war' in Afghanistan and Pakistan, that will probably include terrorist attacks launched or directed from the apparent theatre of conflict and can only lead to more attacks on civilians – a risk enhanced by the increasing civilian direct participation in hostilities noted above.

[123] Schmitt, 'Unmanned Combat Aircraft Systems and International Humanitarian Law', 314, 320. A similar argument is couched in moral (rather than legal) terms by both Arkin, 'The Case for Ethical Autonomy in Unmanned Systems' and Strawser, 'Moral Predators'.

[124] See A. P. V. Rogers, 'Zero-Casualty Warfare', 837 *IRRC* (2000) 165.

[125] Admittedly, this is a question of ethics rather than law. At present its parameters are mainly defined through the America-centric debate about the use of US drones to target US citizens. See D. Byman, 'Why Drones Work: The Case for Washington's Weapon of Choice', 92 *Foreign Affairs* (2013) 32; A. K. Cronin, 'Why Drones Fail: When Tactics Drive Strategy', 92 *Foreign Affairs* (2013) 44.

[126] Schmitt, 'Unmanned Combat Aircraft Systems and International Humanitarian Law', 57–8.

This, in turn, will probably lead to more extensive use by Western states of ever more sophisticated weaponry,[127] which will, in turn, encourage more attacks on civilians and lead to a vicious circle of timeless conflict in which outright victory will elude either side.[128] If this indeed becomes the pattern of our contemporary armed conflicts, it will be a striking vindication of Smith's view that Western states have since the end of the cold war completely failed to comprehend the utility of force.

Conclusion

Reference has already been made in this chapter, by way of historical analogy to certain aspects of the use of drones, to the German bombardment of Paris by long-range artillery in 1918. While the Great War was still raging a British Royal Artillery officer delivered a lecture about the subject at the Royal Artillery Institute, which he concluded with the following remarks:

> I want particularly to emphasize the fact that there is nothing abnormal about this gun the Hun is using, because all the points I have drawn your attention to in connection with it are points that have been known to us for many years. 'Punch' has said, 'The gunnery experts of the Allies say that we could have built guns of this nature, if only we had thought of it[']. Well, we did not think of it, but we must now take the Long Range Gun seriously. It has come to take its place amongst all the other weapons that are being used in the Great War. I do not say for a moment that the employment of such a gun would win the war; far from it, but it fulfils a mission, as does each engine of war devised. [. . .] It will probably have a rapid development in the future – say in the next 20 years: Peace or War, it must be considered. [. . .] As regards the question – 'What useful purpose will such a gun serve?' my reply is – Quite apart from any policy that may dictate its employment as a weapon of war, we should be able to add quite a lot of valuable information to our scientific knowledge of artillery [. . .] Progress demands that we must always be marching towards a further goal or higher limit.[129]

Since the 1860s, the development of modern IHL has often been shaped by advances in weapon technology, which is as true in respect of UAVs as it was in respect of the Russian invention of a type of bullet that exploded

[127] Rogers, 'Zero-Casualty Warfare', 168–9.
[128] See Smith, *The Utility of Force*, 289–92.
[129] Maj. J. Maitland-Addison, RA, 'The Long Range Guns', *Field Artillery Journal* 8 (1918), 321, 337–8.

on contact with a hard surface.[130] Although states might seek to adopt a new general treaty to regulate the use of drones in armed conflict, an outright ban would appear unlikely given the interest that so many states are showing in possessing such systems. In addition, there seems to be little appetite for even a lighter regulatory touch in the form of non-binding guidelines or some similar soft law instrument. This chapter has shown that twenty-first-century IHL is 'fit for purpose' in that its existing provisions can and do already apply to the use of unmanned weapon systems. The challenge is to ensure that they are *actually* applied.

[130] See A. Roberts and R. Guelff, *Documents on the Laws of War*, 3rd edn (Oxford: Oxford University Press, 2000), 53–4.

10

Does the law of targeting meet twenty-first-century needs?

WILLIAM BOOTHBY

Introduction

There is something inherently backward-looking about the law, and perhaps about lawyers. So far as public perceptions are concerned, perhaps it is the sight of distinguished members of the profession clad in somewhat dated garb and sporting head-dresses fashioned from horses' hair that generates this general impression. Perhaps where the domestic law is concerned it is the reliance on legislation passed in a bygone age and interpretations of long-dead but highly eminent judges that, to a degree, reinforces this assumption.

But is international, as opposed to domestic, law in fact rooted in the past and if so is that a bad thing and, more specifically, does it mean that the law is somehow of reduced relevance when confronted by modern challenges? In seeking to answer these questions by reference to the law of targeting, we should start by considering what, in summarised form, the relevant law consists of. We should then reflect on the ways in which targeting activities have developed in recent decades and should then consider whether those developments call into question the suitability of the established legal principles and rules. While such an analytical process may appear to address the topic fully, a more complete answer will, it is suggested, only emerge if we also consider the 'soft law' approaches that we have seen in recent years and we should then go on to consider how those processes might interact with the development of substantive law.

The law of targeting: early beginnings

There was in truth little or no conventional targeting law until the last year of the nineteenth century. The Hague Regulations of that year, superseded by the 1907 text to which we will refer, drew attention to the fact that there are legal limits to the means of injuring the enemy.[1] Specific rules prohibit the employment of poison, the treacherous killing or wounding of members of the hostile army, the killing or wounding of enemy personnel who have surrendered, declarations of no quarter, improper use of certain flags, insignia and uniforms and destruction or seizure of enemy property that is not 'imperatively demanded by the necessities of war'.[2] Ruses of war and the gathering of information about the enemy are specifically stated to be lawful,[3] while the bombardment by whatever means 'of towns, villages, dwellings, or buildings which are undefended is prohibited'.[4] Everything possible must be done by an attacking commander to warn before commencing a bombardment, other than in the case of an assault,[5] and in bombardments all necessary steps must be taken 'to spare, as far as possible, buildings dedicated to religion, art, science or charitable purposes, historic monuments, hospitals, and places where the sick and wounded are collected, provided they are not being used at the time for military purposes'.[6] Pillage, even of towns taken by assault, is prohibited.[7]

In 1907, a regime to regulate naval bombardment was also agreed.[8] This was significant because land and sea represented the then principal

[1] Regulations Respecting the Laws and Customs of War on Land, Annexed to Hague Convention IV, 18 October 1907 (hereinafter Hague Regulations), Article 22.

[2] Article 23 Hague Regulations. [3] Article 24 Hague Regulations.

[4] Article 25 Hague Regulations. [5] Article 26 Hague Regulations.

[6] Article 27 Hague Regulations, which also in the case of siege requires that the besieged use signs to indicate the presence of such buildings.

[7] Article 28 Hague Regulations.

[8] Convention IX Concerning Bombardment by Naval Forces in Time of War, 18 October 1907. The Convention prohibited 'the bombardment by naval forces of undefended ports, towns, villages, dwellings, or buildings' (Article 1) unless the local authorities, after due notice and a formal summons, decline to comply with requisitions that are proportionate for the place and that are for provisions or supplies needed by the naval forces (Article 3). If, however, no other means are possible, naval artillery may be used to destroy military works, military or naval establishments, depots of arms or war *materiel*, workshops or plant which could be utilised for the hostile fleet or army or warships in harbour if, after an appropriate warning and reasonable waiting time, the local authorities have not themselves destroyed them within the time fixed (Article 2). Article 5(1) required the taking of all necessary measures in naval bombardment to 'spare as far as possible sacred edifices, buildings used for artistic, scientific, or charitable purposes, historic monuments, hospitals, and places where the sick or wounded are collected, on the understanding that they are not used at the time for military purposes'. Article 5(2), on the other hand, required the inhabitants to indicate such monuments, edifices or buildings using visible signs. If the military situation permits, the commander of the attacking naval force is required to do his utmost to warn the authorities before the bombardment commences (Article 6).

media of warfare. But another environment for warfare was being developed and in the earliest stages of that process international law was formulated, in the form of Hague Declaration I of 1899 prohibiting the launching of projectiles and explosives from balloons and other methods of a similar nature.[9] Its replacement of 1907 prohibited the discharge of explosives and projectiles from balloons.[10] It is a moot issue whether discussion should focus on the fact that a very early but in retrospect imperfect attempt was being made to address emerging technical developments regarded at the time with increasing concern, or whether our attention should instead centre on the failure of those measures to halt the tide of scientific advance in the matter of aerial warfare. Irrespective of whether in that sense this cup is viewed as half full or half empty, the 1907 Declaration was soon ignored as the capabilities of, and opportunities offered by, military aviation became manifest with the consequence that the First World War and later conflicts saw extensive military operations from and in the air.

While the First World War experience may have inspired the work of the Hague jurists and technical advisers in 1922 and 1923, we must again reflect on the failure to adopt the rules they drafted[11] in legally binding form. While legal thinking on the issues raised by this new environment of war may have been taking place, clearly states were reluctant to bind themselves to particular rules. The unstable security situation in Europe at the time may well have been a factor underlying that reluctance. The legal effect of it was that in 1947 the former Commander in Chief of RAF Bomber Command, Air Chief Marshal Sir Arthur Harris, was able to comment: 'International law can always be argued pro and con, but in this matter of the use of aircraft in war, there is it so happens no international law at all.'[12]

Indeed, arguably, it was not until 1977 with the adoption of Additional Protocol I[13] that formal international agreement was achieved on a set of

[9] Declaration IV, I to Prohibit, for the Term of Five Years, the Launching of Projectiles and Explosives from Balloons, and other Methods of Similar Nature, The Hague, 29 July 1899.

[10] Declaration Prohibiting the Discharge of Projectiles and Explosives from Balloons (Hague Declaration XIV), 18 October 1907.

[11] General Report on the Revision of the Rules of Warfare, Part II, The Rules of Aerial Warfare, The Hague, 19 February 1923, generally and accurately referred to as the Hague Draft Rules of Aerial Warfare.

[12] A. Harris, *Bomber Offensive* (London: Collins, 1947), 177.

[13] Protocol Additional to the Geneva Conventions of 12 August 1949 and Relating to the Protection of Victims of International Armed Conflicts, Geneva, 8 June 1977 (Additional Protocol I).

rules that would regulate the engagement from the air of targets on land. That this legal provision was adopted as many as seventy years after the adoption of the last, inadequate and ignored legal text on the subject would cause most people to question whether international law is at all responsive to the needs triggered by advances in weapons technology. But before reaching such a conclusion we should perhaps consider the topic in greater detail.

Before doing so, however, we should acknowledge one piece of legal responsiveness that did take place. There is little doubt that it was the horrific experience of gas attacks in the trenches of the First World War and the demonstrated inadequacies of Hague Declaration 2 of 1899[14] to control gas warfare that precipitated the negotiation of the Geneva Gas Protocol of 1925. However, that topic lies more in the field of weapons law than targeting law and will not therefore be considered further here.

Using the environment as a weapon

More closely connected to the law of targeting is the notion of using the environment as a weapon in warfare. Arguably, military operations to influence climate during the Vietnam War, for example, with the particular aim of impeding Viet Cong resupply operations on the Ho Chi Minh and associated trails, inspired the adoption of the Environmental Modification Convention.[15] This treaty prohibits 'military or any other hostile use of environmental modification techniques having widespread, long-lasting or severe effects as the means of destruction, damage or injury to any other State Party'.[16]

It will immediately be appreciated that the treaty only applies in international armed conflicts and that the treaty is only breached if the techniques have either widespread or long-lasting or severe effects. These terms are, by virtue of an understanding issued by the Consultative Committee of Experts established under the Convention, to be understood

[14] Declaration IV, 2 Concerning Asphyxiating Gases, The Hague, 29 July 1899.

[15] Convention on the Prohibition of Military or Any Other Hostile Use of Environmental Modification Techniques, Geneva, 2 September 1976.

[16] Article I ENMOD. The term 'environmental modification technique' is defined to mean 'any technique for changing, through the deliberate manipulation of natural processes, the dynamics, composition, or structure of the Earth, including its biota, lithosphere, hydrosphere and atmosphere, or of outer space' (Article II). States parties are also prohibited to assist, encourage or induce any state, group of states or international organisation to engage in the prohibited activities (Article I(2)).

as having the following meanings: 'widespread; encompassing an area on the scale of several hundred square kilometres; long-lasting; lasting for a period of months, or approximately a season; severe; involving serious or significant disruption or harm to human life, natural and economic resources or other assets'.[17]

The significance of Additional Protocol I

In 1977, the law of targeting made a very considerable leap forward with the adoption of Additional Protocol I and its targeting rules in Articles 48 to 67. Its legal arrangements are comprehensive and have been ratified now by 172 states.[18] Many of the detailed rules in these articles are recognised to have customary status. The treaty incorporates the by 1977 well-established principles of distinction[19] and discrimination,[20] and spells out these rules by way of examples of the latter[21] and detailed expressions of the former which serve to give appropriate protection to civilians[22] and to civilian objects.[23] Cultural objects,[24] objects indispensable to the survival of the civilian population,[25] the natural environment,[26] works and installations containing dangerous forces,[27] non-defended localities,[28] demilitarised zones[29] and civil defence[30] are all the subject of specific provision affording particular protections drafted to take account of the needs of each. In recognition of how targeting is in fact undertaken in the modern age, Articles 57 and 58 prescribe precautions that must be taken respectively by those planning, deciding upon or undertaking attacks[31]

[17] Understanding submitted in a report with the text of the draft Convention by the Conference of the Committee on Disarmament to the General Assembly at its Thirty-First Session.

[18] Source: www.icrc.org (accessed 18 August 2012). [19] Article 48 AP I.

[20] Article 51(4) and (5) AP I. [21] Article 51(5) AP I. [22] Article 51 AP I.

[23] Article 52 AP I. [24] Article 53 AP I. [25] Article 54 AP I.

[26] Articles 35(3) and 55 AP I. [27] Article 56 AP I. [28] Article 59 AP I.

[29] Article 60 AP I. [30] Articles 61–7 AP I.

[31] Article 57 AP I is a provision of vital importance to the practical implementation of the protections listed earlier and, in somewhat paraphrased form, some of its provisions are summarised here. In its first paragraph, it requires that in the conduct of military operations constant care must be taken to spare civilians and civilian objects. Planners and those who decide upon attacks must then do everything feasible to verify that the objectives to be attacked are neither civilians nor civilian objects and are not subject to special protection, but that they are military objectives as defined in Article 52(2) of the treaty. They must take all feasible precautions in the choice of means and methods of

and by those in a position to take precautions against the effects of attacks.[32]

Other articles address the basic rules as to methods and means of warfare, provisions on perfidy, the misuse of recognised emblems, the denial of quarter and the safeguarding of persons who are *hors de combat*.[33]

Additional Protocol I's targeting rules: scope, content and applicability

So if the package of provision is as a whole fairly comprehensive, attention must now focus on the scope of its application. At the risk of stating the obvious, the treaty rules only apply as a matter of treaty law to states that are party to the Protocol. States not party such as the USA and Israel[34] are bound by customary law rules, which are unlikely to include all of the targeting rules in Additional Protocol I[35] and which, in some respects, may not be expressed in identical terms.

Be that as it may, the basic rule of distinction in Article 48 refers to how parties to the conflict may direct 'their operations', a notion which is clearly very broad, and which does not imply any restriction by reference to the technological medium whereby a particular 'operation' is undertaken. The general protection of civilians is expressed in article 51(1) in terms of enjoying 'general protection against dangers arising from military operations', another broad expression that does not presuppose

attack in order to avoid and in any event to minimise incidental loss of civilian life, injury to civilians and damage to civilian objects and they must refrain from deciding to launch an attack which may be expected to cause disproportionate collateral damage. There is a general requirement to cancel or suspend attacks if it becomes clear that the target is no longer a military objective or is subject to special protection or that the attack may be expected to occasion excessive collateral damage. Warnings must be given of attacks that may affect the civilian population unless circumstances do not permit, and, where there is a choice available between objectives of attack for achieving a similar military advantage, the objective to be chosen must be that the attack may be expected to cause least danger to civilian lives and to civilian objects.

32 Article 58 AP I prescribes precautions against the effects of attacks. Its broad requirements are that, subject to Article 49 GC IV, the parties to the conflict remove civilians and civilian objects from the vicinity of military objectives, that they avoid locating military objectives in or near densely populated areas and that they take other measures to protect civilians and civilian objects under their control from military operations.

33 See respectively Articles 35 and 37–41 AP I.

34 www.icrc.org (accessed 19 August 2012).

35 For example, it is well known that the USA rejects any suggestion that Articles 35(3), 55 or 56 as expressed are customary.

any particular nature of operations other than that they must be military in nature. Article 53 most relevantly prohibits committing 'any acts of hostility' against cultural objects and using them in support of the military effort. Whether the use of a particular technology against such objects will amount to an act of hostility will depend on the nature of the act involved. It would seem likely, however, that any use of technology that has the effect of damaging or destroying the cultural property in whole or in part will be regarded for these purposes as a hostile act.

Objects indispensable to the survival of the civilian population are protected against attack, destruction, removal or rendering useless. The first of these terms will be discussed shortly. In the absence of a treaty definition, it is suggested that the remaining terms must be given their ordinary meaning, such that if the use of a new kind of weapon against, say, crops being grown for the sustenance of the local population has the effect of rendering the crops inedible, this would amount to rendering them useless and thus be prohibited by Article 54. In short, whether use of a new method of targeting, and thus of attack, is engaged by the rule will depend on whether its use has the consequences prohibited by the article.

Articles 35(3) and 55 have the combined effect that care must be taken to protect the natural environment from widespread, long-term and severe damage, there being no specification of the kinds of agency that are contemplated as producing such damage. Again, this rule will be capable of application to new technologies and methods of attack. States that are party to Additional Protocol I will therefore be obliged to consider whether a new means or method of warfare is intended or may be expected to have the prohibited environmental consequences and, if so, to refrain from developing or procuring it. Finally, among the precautionary rules to which reference was made earlier, Article 57(1) contains the general principle that 'in the conduct of military operations, constant care shall be taken to spare the civilian population, civilians and civilian objects'. We discussed the notion of 'military operations' earlier, and concluded that this rule also is capable of application to novel technologies if the operation in which they are employed can properly be described as military in nature.

The significance of the notion of 'attack'

Other key targeting rules specifically apply in the case of attacks – for example, the detailed precautionary rules in Article 57, the Article 56 rules relating to works and installations containing dangerous forces, the reference in Article 54(2) to attacks on objects indispensable to the survival of the civilian population, the protection in Article 52 of civilian objects and particular protections for civilians in Article 51. This of course begs the question, of particular relevance to the present discussion, of what attacks comprise. Article 49 of Additional Protocol I defines them as 'acts of violence against the adversary, whether in offence or defence'.[36] While there can be little doubt that the use of bullets, bombs, missiles, rockets, mortars and other kinetic munitions against the enemy constitute attacks, the employment of some other technologies may appear to be of more doubtful status. How, the rhetorical question might go, can the depressing of an 'Enter' key to send a damaging computer worm on its way to a targeted computer system truly be equated with an 'act of violence' for the purposes of Article 49? Professor Michael Schmitt has wrestled with this vexed question, and has sensibly concluded that the focus should properly be on the effects of the act, with the result that military activity that has violent effects is capable of being an attack for these purposes.[37] This, in the view of the present author, most respectable approach to the problem, has the consequence that the whole of targeting law can be directly applied in relation to cyber operations that are designed or intended to have violent effects, that is of causing death or injury to persons or destruction or damage of property.

In the specific cyber context, that then raises the issue of whether destruction of computer data alone can be regarded as damage for these purposes. The better view seems to be that it can if the effect of the data destruction is that a repair in the ordinary sense of the targeted computer system is required before it can resume operation. These are, however, most complex issues which were considered by a Group of Experts convened by the Tallinn-based NATO Cooperative Cyber Defence Centre of Excellence. The Experts started their work in 2009 and in 2013 the Tallinn Manual on the International Law Applicable to Cyber Warfare was published, a document which constitutes the most authoritative statement of international law on these issues.

[36] Article 49(1) AP I.

[37] It is the violent consequences that are critical: M. N. Schmitt, 'Cyber Operations and the *jus in bello:* Key Issues', International Law Studies, vol. 87 (Newport, RI: US Naval War College, 2011), 93–4.

Article 49: limitations of scope

Returning to our consideration of Article 49, while arguably cyber warfare operations will not have been in the forefront of the negotiators' minds, they must have been at least aware of the prospect of military operations in outer space[38] and yet there is no reference to the use of that environment in the treaty's scope provisions. Legal provisions in relation to military activities in outer space therefore consist of the Outer Space Treaty[39] and customary rules of the sort we have already mentioned, such as the principles of distinction and discrimination. Indeed, Article 49(3) makes it clear that while air warfare that may affect the civilian population, individual civilians or civilian objects on land and air attack of ground objectives are covered by the Additional Protocol I targeting rules, they have no application to air-to-air combat. So, given that the texts of 1899 and 1907 had no application to air-to-air combat, it is at least arguable that no conventional international law regulates such activities, and that customary principles and rules apply. For this reason, the work in recent years by an International Group of Experts under the auspices of Harvard University to write the HPCR Manual on International Law Applicable to Air and Missile Warfare[40] is to be warmly welcomed. That Manual and its associated commentary distil the whole of the contemporary law applicable to all forms of air and missile warfare.

We should close our consideration of Additional Protocol I targeting law, and in particular of Article 49, with a brief summation of the conclusions that seem to emerge. We have already noted that some of the targeting rules will apply to future technologies because of the broad terms in which the activities to which they relate are expressed. The applicability of other rules will largely depend on whether the application of the novel means or method of warfare can properly be described as an 'attack'. Customary principles and rules of law are likely to apply to future military operations employing novel technologies. However, where the language of the twentieth century is not apposite to the techniques of the twenty-first, gaps in legal coverage may surface and the question is then whether international law can demonstrate sufficient flexibility to cover the gap.

38 Note, for example, the explicit reference to outer space in Article II ENMOD, which was, of course, adopted the previous year.

39 Outer Space Treaty, New York, 10 October 1967.

40 Program on Humanitarian Policy and Conflict Research, Harvard University, Manual on International Law Applicable to Air and Missile Warfare, published with a commentary in March 2010.

Unmanned operations

The last ten years have seen a development in air-to-ground operations of major importance, namely, the use of unmanned remotely piloted air vehicles (or drones as they are sometimes inaccurately called) to attack ground targets. One of the early operations of this type was undertaken in the Yemen by the USA in 2002.[41] Such unmanned aerial vehicles are controlled by an operator who may be located at a considerable distance from the scene of military operations – for example, at a control centre in the USA. The operator will be fed data including imagery of the relevant geographical area and will decide when and where any attack is to be undertaken. He will in practice have information available to him that is similar, though not necessarily identical, to that which would be available to a pilot of a manned aircraft undertaking a similar operation. The important differences of course are that there is no pilot to place himself at material risk in order to undertake the attack and there is no possibility of a direct, as opposed to a sensor-based, viewing of the target area before the attack proceeds, absent friendly forces personnel in the area.

This is not the place for a protracted debate as to the ethical acceptability of such an apparent disparity of risk between the attacking operator, located far away from the targeted area, and those in danger of injury or death at the scene of the proposed attack. From a strictly legal perspective, and viewed in somewhat clinical terms, there is no doubt that the targeting rules that we have discussed, including crucially the rules as to precautions, will apply equally to such unmanned attack operations. The responsibility to ensure that those rules are complied with will rest on the shoulders of those planning the mission, those setting up the sensors, guidance systems and platforms that will be used to undertake it and the operators whose decisions will directly determine who or what is to be attacked.

Legal issues raised by autonomous attack

If unmanned 'man in the loop' operations of the sort we have so far considered raise ethical issues, the next likely technical development towards fully autonomous unmanned operations take us into an entirely different league of likely ethical and perhaps legal controversy.

[41] See BBC News Report, CIA 'killed al-Qaeda suspects' in Yemen, 5 November 2002, available at http://news.bbc.co.uk/1/hi/2402479.stm.

Contemporary research is seeking to develop technology that will enable a machine to differentiate with ever greater fidelity between objects which do, and respectively do not, constitute military objectives. Algorithm-based technology enables the machine to compare the observed image with pre-programmed criteria in order to determine whether sufficient points of similarity exist to constitute an acceptable recognition of the observed object as a military objective. The present author has in the past concluded that such technology is capable of satisfying the Article 57 requirement to verify that an object of attack is a military objective.[42] The same article of Additional Protocol I requires, however, that precautions be taken to ensure compliance with the discrimination principle as reflected in Article 51(4) and (5). This, as we have seen, requires consideration of the proportionality of a planned attack, consideration whether the chosen target minimises civilian dangers and consideration whether any individuals who are the object of the attack are *hors de combat*. These judgments are inherently qualitative and, in some cases, relative in nature and there is no known technology in existence at the time of writing that will fulfil all of these requirements.[43] The author has therefore in the past concluded that autonomous attack will only be feasible, using currently available technology, in relatively limited circumstances where the planned target is remote from civilians or civilian objects.[44] Thus, if, for example, a high-value military objective is located in a desert area or a location where for whatever reason civilian persons are absent, if the areas of search for the unmanned autonomous platform can be suitably restricted and if the time period for such search can also be appropriately limited, then it may be possible at the sortie planning stage to make the proportionality and other qualitative and relative judgements in advance of commencement of the sortie with a

[42] W. H. Boothby, *Weapons and the Law of Armed Conflict* (Oxford: Oxford University Press, 2009), 230–3.

[43] Consider, however, the work currently being undertaken by Arkin and others in these complex fields of scientific research; for example, note R. Arkin, *Governing Lethal Behavior in Autonomous Robots* (Boca Raton, FL: Chapman & Hall/CRC, 2009) and R. Arkin, 'Governing Lethal Behavior: Embedding Ethics in a Hybrid Deliberative/ Reactive Robot Architecture', available at www.cc.gatech.edu/ai/robot-lab/online-publi cations/formalizationv35.pdf (accessed 19 August 2012).

[44] W. H. Boothby, 'Autonomous Systems: Precautions in Attack', in International Institute of Humanitarian Law, *International Humanitarian Law and New Weapon Technologies*, ed. W. Heintschel von Heinegg (Report of the 34th Round Table on Current Issues) (Milan: FrancoAngeli, 2012), 123–4.

sufficient confidence that the assessments will remain valid for the duration of the sortie.

If these restrictive criteria do not apply, the opinion of the author is that autonomous attack operations cannot be undertaken consistently with currently applicable targeting law. Autonomous attack will only become a legally viable option in a broader range of circumstances if technology demonstrates that the qualitative and relative determinations to which we have referred can properly be made by machines. We are not there yet.

For completeness, it should be made clear that the comments in the preceding paragraphs apply particularly in the case of autonomous attacks on objects. While, as any recent visitor to airport immigration desks is aware, technology in the field of mechanical recognition of humans is advancing, it is not, however, clear that it has reached the point at which the sensors aboard an unmanned aircraft can with acceptable reliability autonomously recognise an individual on the ground. Until adequately reliable performance by technology of such a sort has been demonstrated, and that may well be many years into the future, it would seem unlikely that such a planned attack would satisfy the verification obligation in Article 57(2)(a)(i).

If, as is assumed, autonomous attack technology is only fielded if it can be shown to comply with the existing targeting law requirements, this will go a long way toward showing us where the balance lies in the contest between technological advance and existing international law norms. Proper application by states of Article 36 will require review of such technologies by reference to those existing norms, with the obvious inference that those found not to comply will not be further developed or fielded. This ought therefore to be the mechanism whereby the primacy of the existing law in this potential contest is assured.

Nanotechnology

K. Eric Drexler's early-1990s doctoral thesis explored the substance and potential of nanotechnology.[45] Dr Drexler contemplated nano-construction machines being instructed to build a structure using atomic-level ingredients. He envisaged this as the focus for advances in

[45] K. E. Drexler, 'Molecular Machinery and Manufacturing with Applications to Computation', PhD thesis, Massachusetts Institute of Technology (1991): http://e-drexler.com/d/09/00/Drexler_MIT_dissertation.pdf.

the technology associated with warfare and its use for more peaceful purposes.[46] While it appears that industrial undertakings and some states are now actively engaged in nanotechnology research that may have applications across a range of activities, including weapons research, there are also concerns about the possible implications.

Nanotechnology, as a term, is derived from the nanometre, a unit of measurement amounting to one billionth of a metre. This technology is all about the manipulation of matter at the atomic and molecular level. Potential applications of the technology include medical diagnosis and therapy[47] and improvement of production processes. Production of materials that achieve given properties at reduced weight but with improved strength and durability may have military implications for protective and offensive equipment production. Enhanced heat resistance in materials, lighter yet more durable vehicles, faster but lighter missiles, weapons made of non-metal nanofibre composites and improved projectile penetration all become possibilities as a result of the application of the new technology.[48] The literature also contemplates micro-robots to be used in combat, micro-nuclear weapons, new chemical-based and biological-based agents and even improving the performance of personnel.[49]

Some nanotechnologies are already likely to have transitioned from the scientist's laboratory to the armoury shelf. Considerable secrecy surrounds current development plans, and where secrecy persists, suspicion and misunderstanding, even fear, may be generated. While it will be for states to apply existing law through the prism of Article 36 legal reviews[50] or their customary law equivalents, in deciding whether to

[46] For a wider discussion of these possibilities, see K. E. Drexler, *Engines of Creation: The Coming Era of Nanotechnology* (New York: Anchor Books, 1986).

[47] For potential medical applications, see, e.g.: www.nanotechproject.org/inventories/medicine/.

[48] For further information as to potential applications, see, e.g., H. Nasu and T. Faunce, 'Nanotechnology and the International Law of Weaponry: Towards International Regulation of Nano-Weaponry: Towards International Regulation of Nano-Weapons', 20 *Journal of Law Information and Science* (2009–10) 23: www.austlii.edu.au/au/journals/JlLawInfoSci/2010/3.html.

[49] Ministry of Defence, Development, Concepts and Doctrine Centre, Global Strategic Trends – Out to 2040, 4th edn, 12 January 2010, 141.

[50] This is a reference to Article 36 AP I, which requires as follows: 'In the study, development, acquisition or adoption of a new weapon, means or method of warfare, a High Contracting Party is under an obligation to determine whether its employment would, in some or all circumstances, be prohibited by this Protocol or by any other rule of international law applicable to the High Contracting Party.'

develop and field any particular nanotechnology-based capability, the following thoughts may be of assistance:

- Current law should be applied to a nanotechnology weapon, means or method of warfare in the same way as it is applied to any other weapon, method or means.
- It is unlikely to prove useful to seek to assess nanotechnology in the abstract – it is the particular application of the technology in respect of a given weapons programme that will be the subject of review and that must therefore be assessed according to customary principles, rules and applicable treaty provisions.
- Some applications of the technology may pose special difficulties.

Thus it may be hard to determine whether some substances have the character of, for example, biological toxins or chemical agents. Indeed, some emerging substances may combine characteristics of both, such that it becomes difficult to know whether the Biological Weapons Convention applies, or the Chemical Weapons Convention applies, or both apply, or neither applies. If that situation arises, it would seem to the present author that tests will be required to determine what dangers if any the new substances pose for combatants, populations in general, civilian objects and indeed the environment. The threshold for the application of Articles 35(3) and 55 of Additional Protocol I is very high. It is, however, entirely possible that an effect to be expected from an individual use of such a new substance would fall below this high threshold but would nevertheless occasion humanitarian concern about the possibility of more extensive employment of such technologies. That is, it is suggested, the sort of situation in which new treaty law may be called for to address the novel substances and their associated threat.

Targeting using new technology and new law

Whether in relation to autonomous attack, nanotechnology or for that matter any other new development in the field of methods of attack, any initiative for new law is likely to have to wait until the nature of the emerging capability, its opportunities, limitations and risks have become clear. States seem to be reluctant to legislate in a vacuum. Indeed, as the author has observed in the past,[51] it is for the proponents of legal change to make their case, and this is a case that can only be expressed with suitable

[51] Boothby, *Weapons and the Law of Armed Conflict* (n. 42, above), 353–70.

clarity when the relationship between the generic military advantage to be anticipated from the weapon under development and the humanitarian risks it poses can be evaluated, measured and then compared. Accordingly there is an inevitability about a process in which technical change precedes any alteration of the law, frequently with a considerable interval between the two. If such alterations are deemed appropriate, treaty negotiators will wrestle with the details and, as we have seen, the agreed arrangements, if any, will reflect what the states are prepared to accept.

Soft law and the prospects for development of targeting law

Since 1977, there has been little or no development in the law of targeting. Much of the diplomatic and negotiating horsepower has been directed at developing the law of weaponry. Some targeting law rules have been included as part of that process, such as the limitations on the use of incendiaries in Protocol III to the Conventional Weapons Convention. And yet there have been significant developments in targeting activities, not least the opening up of whole new environments for targeting such as outer space and cyberspace. Soft law, in the form, for example, of the HPCR and Tallinn Manuals referred to earlier, has been employed in an attempt to address this legal gap. It is, however, important to understand the status of such documents, their legal value and their legal limitations. The first and most important point is that such documents usually constitute restatements of the law but do not have the status of sources of the law. The most authoritative list of acknowledged sources of international law is to be found in Article 38 of the Statute of the International Court of Justice.[52] While judicial decisions and writings of publicists of suitable eminence are listed in paragraph (d), they are only subsidiary means for identifying rules of law. Accordingly, the Manuals to which we have referred and the ICRC Customary International Humanitarian Law Study report[53] do not have the status

[52] The Article lists the following as the sources of international law which the Court will apply, namely: 'a. international conventions, whether general or particular, establishing rules expressly recognized by the contesting states; b. international custom, as evidence of a general practice accepted as law; c. the general principles of law recognized by civilized nations; d. subject to the provisions of Article 59, judicial decisions and the teachings of the most highly qualified publicists of the various nations, as subsidiary means for the determination of rules of law'.

[53] J.-M. Henckaerts and L. Doswald-Beck, *Customary International Humanitarian Law*, 3 vols (Cambridge: Cambridge University Press, 2005).

of sources of the law as such but, rather, are secondary sources from which an understanding can be derived as to the law contained in customary principles, customary rules and treaty law.

The gaps

So we come back to the apparent inactivity of states where development of the law of targeting is concerned and ask whether there are gaps in legal provision that ought to be, but which in fact are not being, filled. Clearly, the Additional Protocol I targeting rules apply to the conflicts listed in Article 1 of that treaty. Specifically, they do not apply to non-international armed conflicts for which Additional Protocol II makes rudimentary targeting provision. In its Customary Law Study, the ICRC identifies a number of rules of customary law[54] that would apply to targeting in non-international armed conflicts. However, it will be for states to decide whether they accept each statement in the Study as constituting customary law binding on that state. Given that many of the most bloody conflicts in the world these days are non-international in character, the time is now surely right for more comprehensive treaty provisions as to targeting in non-international armed conflicts to be agreed between states, recognising as one must that this would require states to grapple at some point with the implications of the lack of combatant status in non-international armed conflicts.

Recent anti-satellite operations in space[55] suggest that outer space will certainly be a sphere of military operations in a future major conflict, particularly given the degree of reliance that many states place on satellites for communication, navigation, observation and other military and infrastructural purposes. The present limited provision in the Outer Space Treaty, combined with customary legal principles and rules whose basis of application in space may be a matter for dispute, suggests that some form of treaty provision covering targeting activities in this medium is already long overdue.

[54] The principle of distinction and the core rules associated with it are found by the ICRC to apply similarly in international and non-international armed conflicts; see ICRC, *Customary International Humanitarian Law Study*, vol. 1, *Rules*, Rules 1, 2, 6–20, 22 and 23. Note that Rules 21 and 24 are considered arguably to apply in non-international armed conflicts and that Rules 3, 4 and 5 are stated to apply subject to certain modifications.

[55] For example, the 2007 Chinese operation to target one of its own satellites in orbit.

Cyberspace raises many legal issues that lie outside the scope of the present chapter. The Tallinn Manual does much to clarify these issues and the approaches to at least some of them may prove acceptable to states. It would seem to the author, however, that states, commentators and others would do well to take time to consider the contents of the Manual thoroughly first, using its contents to inform decisions as to where the gaps in legal provision lie and what action to address them, if any, is appropriate.

But there is a more fundamental question that we should, for completeness, consider, namely, whether the law of targeting as written in Articles 48–67 of Additional Protocol I will itself stand the test of time. In the view of the present author, it will, partly at least because of the relative terms in which it is written. Notions of distinction, discrimination, proportionality and separation are inherently relative in nature. What is proportionate in future years will be informed by future appreciations as to the acceptable relationship between anticipated military advantage and given levels of collateral damage. Perhaps technological advance will itself influence those perceptions. It is not inconceivable that technology may become the victim of its own success hitherto in improving accuracy and reliability in aerial bombardment, for example.

Whether military objectives are 'separated and distinct' for the purposes of Article 51(5)(a) will be a function of the technical ability of then available weapons technology to treat them as separate and distinct. For the purposes of Article 57, that which is feasible by way of attackers' precautions will be a function of what technology, organisation and the military art in general render, in the words of the UK interpretive statement, 'practicable or practically possible'.[56] There is therefore an inherent timelessness about the core principles and rules of the law of targeting. The notion of excessive collateral damage is just as capable of application in the context of an attack on a ground target during a conventional armed conflict as it is to an outer space anti-satellite operation in which the consequences of the kinetic impact will be to terminate important civilian communication services and to place a large and damaging cloud of space debris into potential collision with third-party space vehicles. The legal notions continue to make sense. It is their practical application in the new environments that may prove

[56] Statements made by the United Kingdom on ratification of AP I, on 28 January 1998, para. (b).

challenging. Perhaps that is the value of the soft law Manuals in showing how the existing rules can be sensibly applied in the new context.

Depersonalised warfare

There is, however, a more complex and intractable issue that lies ahead of us. While, as noted earlier, the development of autonomous attack can be regarded on one plane as merely the most recent development of a notion of remote attack which has its origins in the early cannon and crossbows of the ancient Greeks, for many observers the creation and refinement of drone technology marks a process of depersonalisation in warfare. This raises the question, noted earlier, of whether autonomy challenges the law or whether the law will challenge autonomy. We answered that question by observing that if Article 36 is properly applied, it is the law that will challenge technology to come up with legally compliant solutions. But there is a deeper question to consider here, namely, whether remote attack (perhaps dissociated attack would be a better description) is getting to the point at which the very concepts of armed conflict and its conduct and purpose are called into question. When the armed contest ceases to be between combatants representing parties thereto and becomes an activity undertaken by machines, what is it that we are about, and what does the outcome of such an activity demonstrate, apart that is from the technical superiority of one side over the other? Such a situation lies perhaps long in the future. For the time being we have conflicts where one party may undertake remote targeting, but in which persons or military objectives of the opposing party are the target and clearly the established targeting rules, as we have demonstrated, continue to apply.

Other aspects of technical advance will continue to improve accuracy and reliability in attack, thus making it on balance easier to comply with targeting law norms. Perhaps in future man will increasingly be seen as the weakest link, the point of foreseeable error, which might also imply a shift towards even more mechanistic methods of warfare, but these developments would be a far cry from the hoplite, the phalanx and the heroic Homeric tradition on which, arguably, many of our contemporary notions of chivalry are grounded.

Conclusion

So will law meet the future challenges in the targeting sphere? At one level, of course, the question cannot be answered. We have no way of knowing the precise nature of future conflict, the events that will trigger it, the nature of the parties to it, the methods of warfare they will employ, and thus whether the law that we know will be relevant to those methods. Inevitably, much of the above discussion has been by reference to technologies or methods that are either already known or at least that are in some sort of development. For the more distant future, we can only point to the inherent flexibility of much of current targeting law and note that any gaps will only be addressed by law if states feel the collective need to agree ad hoc treaty provision. That, in the present author's view, is only likely to happen if the dangers posed by a particular technology or method of warfare are shown, to the satisfaction of the international community, to justify treaty provision. The humanitarian initiatives that led to the Ottawa Convention and to the Cluster Munitions Convention, and the failure of the CCW delegates to agree treaty provision in respect of mines other than anti-personnel mines in 2006 and in respect of cluster munitions in 2011,[57] illustrate the sort of case that will need to be made before such a diplomatic initiative is likely to be undertaken, let alone to succeed.

Absent such a case, we must continue with what we have, however imperfect it may appear to be. At least the writings of Groups of Experts in the Manuals that we have mentioned make it clear to all how existing law constrains the new methods covered by the Manual in question, what the limits therefore are for the application of existing law, and thus provide a sure foundation for any evaluation of the gaps that exist and whether, and if so how, they should be filled.

[57] In 2006, an initiative of the USA and Denmark that had achieved significant support among other states proposing practical measures on detectability and fencing and marking of mines other than anti-personnel mines failed to achieve consensus among Conventional Weapons Convention states parties. The proposed Protocol to the Convention was not therefore adopted; Report of the Work in 2006 on Mines other than Anti-Personnel Mines, Annex II, 10 October 2006, CCW/CONF.111/7/Add.2. The Fourth Review Conference of the Conventional Weapons Convention again failed to reach consensus on the draft Protocol VI concerning cluster munitions, although this failure may in part be attributable to the adoption in 2008 of the Cluster Munitions Convention.

11

International humanitarian law and the protection of civilians from the effects of explosive weapons

MAYA BREHM

> Once the bombs started we ran [. . .] I couldn't take my son's wheelchair, so I had to carry him, and run. We thought it is better for us to die in the street than under the rubble of our house. [. . .] In the morning we came back to our home, but it was ruined. There's no place for us to go to, no safe space to go to at all. I think there is no safe space in Syria. It is beyond imagining.[1]

Introduction

Explosive violence (the use of explosive weapons) has a devastating humanitarian impact. Harrowing testimonies, like the one above from 'Hiba' who fled Syria with her daughter and disabled son, describe the immense suffering caused by the use of explosive weapons in Syria over the last years: family members and friends killed or gravely wounded, homes, schools and hospitals destroyed, and entire neighbourhoods levelled to the ground by artillery shelling, bombardment and powerful improvised explosive devices (IEDs). In 2012–13, Syria was the country most affected by explosive violence, with much of it taking place in populated areas, such as villages or residential neighbourhoods.[2] However, harm from explosive weapons is geographically widespread. Iraq, Pakistan, Afghanistan and Nigeria, the Gaza Strip and Sri Lanka's

[1] Testimony of 'Hiba', in N. Martlew, *Childhood Under Fire: The Impact of Two Years of Conflict in Syria* (London: Save the Children, 2013), 6.

[2] The Independent International Commission of Inquiry on Syria established by the Human Rights Council noted that 'Most deaths in Bab Amr during the military operation that began in February 2012 were caused by extensive and indiscriminate shelling by Government forces of primarily civilian infrastructure and residential areas'. United Nations Human Rights Council, Updated Report on the Work of the Commission of Inquiry on the Situation in the Syrian Arab Republic, 16 August 2012 (UN Doc. A/HRC/21/50), para. 91.

Vanni region have also experienced high levels of explosive violence over recent years.[3]

Explosive weapons, such as grenades, rockets, mortar rounds, artillery shells, air-dropped bombs or IEDs share the common characteristic that they affect an area around the point of detonation with blast and fragmentation (fragments from the weapon and debris from the surroundings). Due to these effects, the use of explosive weapons in a populated area 'exposes the civilian population and infrastructure to heightened – and even extreme – risks of incidental or indiscriminate death, injury or destruction'.[4] Data indicates that the overwhelming majority of casualties directly resulting from the use of explosive weapons in populated areas are civilians – people who enjoy 'general protection against dangers arising from military operations' under international humanitarian law (IHL).[5]

Because of its distinct humanitarian impact, the use of explosive weapons in populated areas is increasingly recognised as a core challenge to the protection of civilians and, more specifically, to the protection of children in armed conflict. Non-governmental organisations (NGOs) affiliated with the International Network on Explosive Weapons (INEW), the International Committee of the Red Cross (ICRC), United Nations (UN) actors and a growing number of states are supporting efforts to reduce and prevent harm from explosive violence through focused international policy discussions and greater normative constraints on the use of explosive weapons in populated areas.[6]

[3] H. Dodd and R. Perkins, *An Explosive Situation: Monitoring Explosive Violence in 2012* (London: Action on Armed Violence, 2013), 9.

[4] International Committee of the Red Cross (ICRC), 'International Humanitarian Law and the Challenges of Contemporary Armed Conflicts', 31st International Conference of the Red Cross and Red Crescent, International Humanitarian Law and the Challenges of Contemporary Armed Conflicts – Report (October 2011), 41.

[5] Protocol Additional to the Geneva Conventions of 12 August 1949, and relating to the Protection of Victims of International Armed Conflicts (AP I), 8 June 1977, Article 51(1).

[6] International Network on Explosive Weapons (INEW), 'Preventing Human Suffering from the Use of Explosive Weapons in Populated Areas – The INEW Call': www.inew.org/about-inew/inew-call-commentary (accessed 6 June 2013). ICRC President Maurer questioned whether 'applicable IHL rules [are] sufficient to identify under which circumstances explosive force delivered by heavy weapons might be used in densely populated areas' (P. Maurer, 'ICRC President on the Challenges of the Evolving Battlefield', Intercross, 4 April 2013: http://intercrossblog.icrc.org/blog/icrc-president-challenges-evolving-battlefield (accessed 7 June 2013)). For a compilation of policy statements by states and UN actors recognising the harm caused by explosive weapons and supporting

This chapter begins by presenting data on the pattern of harm associated with the use of explosive weapons in populated areas. Against this background, an overview of how explosive weapons are regulated under international law is provided. The chapter analyses a number of explosive weapon-specific treaties and evaluates the contribution of expert discussions on 'blast and fragmentation weapons' in the 1970s to the regulation of explosive weapons. The chapter then examines constraints that IHL rules governing the conduct of hostilities place on the use of explosive weapons in populated areas, with a focus on the prohibition of indiscriminate attacks.[7] The final part identifies some challenges that the use of explosive weapons in populated areas poses for IHL. As the protection of civilians against the effects of hostilities is a cornerstone of IHL, the documented pattern of civilian harm from the use of explosive weapons in populated areas puts the adequacy and effectiveness of IHL into question. The chapter concludes by presenting measures that could help to prevent and reduce harm from explosive violence, thereby effectively strengthening the relevance of IHL as an important legal framework for protecting civilians in situations of armed conflict.

The humanitarian impact of explosive violence

The use of explosive weapons, particularly in populated areas, is associated with a specific pattern of harm. People in the vicinity of an explosion are at grave risk of suffering mutilating ballistic, blast and burn injury, and incidents of explosive violence generally produce multiple casualties.[8] Explosive weapons produce a wide range of injuries to

measures to address the problem, see INEW, 'Acknowledging the Harm': www.inew.org/acknowledgements (accessed 6 June 2013).

[7] The use of explosive weapons is closely associated with the conduct of hostilities. It is widely accepted today that international human rights law also applies to such use of force, but this chapter focuses on the regulation of explosive weapons as a means or method of warfare under IHL and weapon-specific treaties. For a brief discussion of the use of explosive weapons under international human rights law, in times of armed conflict and in other situations, see M. Brehm, 'The Use of Explosive Weapons in Populated Areas in 2012', in S. Casey Maslen (ed.), *The War Report: 2012* (Oxford: Oxford University Press, 2013).

[8] According to data collected by the civil society organisation Action on Armed Violence (AOAV), on average, sixteen people were killed or injured in explosive weapon incidents in a populated area in 2012. Certain explosive weapon types are associated with even higher numbers of victims per incident. Dodd and Perkins, *An Explosive Situation*, 15; H. Dodd and R. Perkins, *Monitoring Explosive Violence: The EVMP Dataset 2011* (London: Action on Armed Violence, 2012), 9; R. Moyes, *Explosive Violence, The Problem of Explosive Weapons* (London: Landmine Action, 2009), 23.

many areas of the body. The combination of different injury mechanisms produces a complex array of combined injuries that victims may not survive, or that can result in lifelong mental and physical disability.[9] The blast can cause the traumatic amputation of limbs, the rupture of internal organs and blunt trauma. Fragment projection can lead to deep penetration wounds.

Explosive violence can also affect populations indirectly and over a prolonged period of time. Damage to, or the destruction of, homes, productive assets and public infrastructure can have serious knock-on effects on communities. Explosive weapons have, notably, been identified as a key threat to the provision of health care during armed conflict.[10] Use of explosive weapons in populated areas has also been shown to be a major driver of population displacement[11] and to impede the delivery of humanitarian aid.[12] In addition, unexploded remnants pose a continued threat of death and injury, constitute an obstacle to the safe return of displaced persons and can impede socio-economic development for years, even decades, after explosive weapons were used.[13]

Tragically, the use of explosive weapons in populated areas kills and injures significant numbers of civilians – people who must be respected and protected under IHL.[14] According to the British civil society organisation, Action on Armed Violence (AOAV), civilians made up 78 per cent

[9] S. B. Brevard, H. Champion and D. Katz, 'Weapons Effects', in E. Savitsky and B. Eastridge (eds), *Combat Casualty Care: Lessons Learned from OEF and OIF* (Washington, DC: Office of the Surgeon General, 2012), 54–73. For more information on the medical impacts of explosive weapons, see R. F. Bellamy and R. Zajtchuk (eds), *Conventional Warfare: Ballistic, Blast, and Burn Injuries*, Textbook of Military Medicine, 4 parts (Washington, DC: Office of the Surgeon General, 1991), part 1, vol. 5.

[10] *Health Care in Danger: A Sixteen-Country Study* (Geneva: ICRC, 2011), 2.

[11] S. Bagshaw, 'Driving Displacement: Explosive Weapons in Populated Areas', *Forced Migration Review*, 41 (December 2012): www.fmreview.org/sites/fmr/files/FMRdownloads/en/preventing/bagshaw.pdf (accessed 7 June 2013).

[12] C. Wille and L. Fast, 'Humanitarian Staff Security in Armed Conflict: Policy Implications Resulting from Changes in the Operating Environment for Humanitarian Agencies', *Insecurity Insight* (2013): www.insecurityinsight.org/files/Policy_Brief_1_Humanitarian_Staff_and_Armed_Conflict.pdf (accessed 25 July 2013).

[13] For an introduction to the humanitarian and development challenges posed by explosive remnants of war, see *A Guide to Mine Action*, 4th edn (Geneva: International Centre for Humanitarian Demining, 2010). Explosive materials can also have toxic properties that can raise environmental and health concerns. M. Ghalaieny, 'Toxic Harm: Humanitarian and Environmental Concerns from Military-Origin Contamination', The Toxic Remnants of War Project (2013): www.toxicremnantsofwar.info/wp-content/uploads/2013/03/Toxic_Harm_TRWProject.pdf (accessed 6 June 2013).

[14] Article 48 1977 AP I.

of all recorded casualties from explosive violence in 2012.[15] Of all recorded incidents in 2012, 61 per cent took place in what AOAV described as a 'populated area'.[16] In these incidents, 91 per cent of casualties were civilians. When explosive weapons were used in other locations, civilians made up 32 per cent of casualties. These figures are consistent with the results of earlier studies.[17] That civilians make up a bigger proportion of casualties in populated areas compared to other places is not surprising in view of the likelihood of civilians being present in these locations, the higher population density, the projection of blast and fragmentation over an area and the capacity of explosive weapons to cause entire buildings to collapse. Even so, the proportion of civilian casualties from explosive violence in populated areas is extremely high. Whilst some civilian harm results from attacks targeting civilians in violation of IHL,[18] it is alarming that 80 per cent of casualties were still civilians, even in explosive weapon incidents in populated areas reportedly targeting armed actors or military objectives.[19] There is also

[15] In 2012, AOAV recorded 2,742 explosive violence incidents in which 34,758 people were killed or injured (Dodd and Perkins, *Monitoring Explosive Violence*, 3). AOAV records casualties as 'civilians' unless otherwise stated. Casualties are recorded as 'armed actors' if they are reported as being members of the military, members of non-state armed groups, or security personnel who are likely to be armed. The notion of 'civilian' used by AOAV for data collection purposes therefore broadly accords with the definition of civilians protected from attack under IHL, albeit with some exceptions. 'Casualties' means 'people who were killed or physically injured' by an incident involving the use of (an) explosive weapon(s). AOAV makes no claim to capture every casualty from explosive violence. The data is gathered from English-language media sources across the world, and captures death and injury *directly* resulting from incidents involving explosive weapons. This method allows the identification of significant patterns of harm and provides a measure of the scope and scale of explosive violence. However, the method under-represents harm from large-scale explosive violence, such as continuous shelling over several days, and it does not capture harm in the form of mental trauma, direct material damage or destruction, and indirect or long-term impacts. Dodd and Perkins, *Monitoring Explosive Violence*, 38–9.

[16] The notion of 'populated area' used by AOAV is based on the Protocol on Prohibitions or Restrictions on the Use of Incendiary Weapons (Protocol III to the CCW), 10 October 1980, 1342 UNTS 171 (Dodd and Perkins, *An Explosive Situation*, 38).

[17] In 2011, overall, 71 per cent of all recorded casualties of explosive weapons were civilians. Of all the casualties that were recorded in populated areas, 84 per cent were civilians. Dodd and Perkins, *Monitoring Explosive Violence*, 5. See also Moyes, *Explosive Violence*, 24–5.

[18] As a rule of customary IHL, parties to an armed conflict must at all times distinguish between civilians and combatants, and attacks must not be directed against civilians. Article 51(2) 1977 AP I; J.-M. Henckaerts and L. Doswald-Beck, *Customary International Humanitarian Law*, 3 vols (Cambridge: Cambridge University Press, 2005), vol. 1, *Rules*, Rule 1.

[19] Dodd and Perkins, *Monitoring Explosive Violence*, 15.

concern that particularly vulnerable population groups may be disproportionately affected by explosive violence.[20]

Certain types of explosive weapons tend to cause especially high levels of civilian harm. According to data collected by AOAV in 2012, 'when air-delivered explosive weapons were used in populated areas, four out of every five casualties were civilians'.[21] In one incident on 18 November 2012, Israeli forces dropped a large bomb on a three-storey home in Gaza city, one of the world's most densely populated areas. This attack killed ten members of the same family household – one man, five women, and four children, as well as a young man and an elderly woman living next door.[22]

Used more frequently in populated areas than air-delivered explosive weapons are ground-launched explosive weapons. Ground-launched explosive weapons are often used in large numbers, such as during the shelling of Homs, one of the most populated cities in Syria, by the Syrian armed forces between February and April 2012.[23] Among ground-launched weapons, mortars emerge as particularly problematic

[20] M. H.-R. Hicks et al., 'The Weapons that Kill Civilians: Deaths of Children and Noncombatants in Iraq, 2003–2008', 16 *New England Journal of Medicine* (2009) 360: http://content.nejm.org/cgi/content/full/360/16/1585 (accessed 19 June 2013), 1585–8 and R. Moyes, 'Impact of Explosive Weapons by Gender and Age – Iraq 2003–2011', AOAV (June 2012): www.richardmoyes.com (accessed 19 June 2013) find women (and children) to be at a particular risk of harm from explosive violence in Iraq. On the impact of explosive weapons on children, see K. Brown, *Explosive Weapons and Grave Violations against Children* (London: Save the Children, 2013) and Martlew, *Childhood Under Fire*. Men make up the majority of victims from certain IEDs in Nepal according to O. O. Bilukha et al., 'Fatal and Non-Fatal Injuries due to Intentional Explosions in Nepal, 2008–2011: Analysis of Surveillance Data', *Conflict and Health*, 7(5) (2013): www.conflictandhealth.com/content/7/1/5 (accessed 19 June 2013). H. Guerra, 'The Use of Hand Grenades in Mexico: A Problem of Explosive Violence in Populated Areas? A Media Review, 2011–2012', SEHLAC (2013): www.sehlac.org/wp-content/uploads/2013/02/Explosive-violence-in-Mexico-Hector-Guerra.pdf (accessed 25 July 2013) reaches a similar finding regarding victims of grenades in Mexico. Reports by the United Nations Assistance Mission in Afghanistan (UNAMA) on the protection of civilians in armed conflict contain some data disaggregated by age and gender from some attacks involving explosive weapons (such as air strikes or IED attacks) available at http://unama.unmissions.org (accessed 6 June 2013).

[21] Dodd and Perkins, *Monitoring Explosive Violence*, 21.

[22] According to 'Israel/Gaza: Israeli Airstrike on Home Unlawful', Human Rights Watch (December 2012): www.hrw.org/news/2012/12/07/israelgaza-israeli-airstrike-home-unlawful (accessed 6 June 2013), this attack amounted to a 'clear violation of the laws of war'. A different conclusion is reached in 'The Examination of Alleged Misconduct during Operation "Pillar of Defence" – An Update', Israel Defense Forces, Military Advocate General, 11 April 2013 [incorrectly dated April 11, 2012]: www.law.idf.il/SIP_STORAGE/files/4/1364.pdf (accessed 6 June 2013).

[23] 'Syrian Army "Steps up Homs Offensive"', *Aljazeera*, 6 February 2012: www.aljazeera.com/news/middleeast/2012/02/20122614732355122.html (accessed 6 June 2013).

in populated areas. According to AOAV, 90 per cent of mortar casualties in 2012 were civilians. The great majority of recorded mortar incidents (137 of the 161 incidents) took place in a populated area. When mortars were used in populated areas, a shocking 98 per cent of casualties were civilians.[24]

Various types of IEDs are also causing high levels of civilian casualties. According to AOAV, 80 per cent of casualties from IEDs in 2012 were civilians. Car bomb explosions in populated areas caused an average of thirty-two civilian casualties per incident.[25] IEDs tend to be used by non-state actors and the prevention of 'bombings' has long been a particular focus of counter-terrorism efforts.[26] IEDs have also been the subject of expert discussions in the framework of the 1980 Convention on Certain Conventional Weapons (CCW).[27] Irrespective of whether the user is a state or a non-state actor, however, the data presented here shows that explosive weapons that affect a wide area with blast and fragmentation pose a particular risk of harm to civilians in populated areas.

Wide area effects can be due to several factors: an individual explosive weapon having a large blast or fragmentation radius, multiple explosive weapons being launched at an area, insufficient precision in the delivery of explosive weapons, or a combination of these factors.[28] In international policy forums, humanitarian concern around wide area effects is sometimes expressed in terms of the use of 'heavy weapons' in population centres.[29] UN Security Council resolution 2042 (2012) and the

[24] Dodd and Perkins, *Monitoring Explosive Violence*, 23–4; email exchange between the author and R. Perkins (4 June 2013), on file with the author. On 27 August 2012, for instance, a volley of mortar rounds hit a residential area in Sheikh Mero Baba, Pakistan. Nine people were killed on the spot; one person later died in the hospital; several houses were destroyed. 'Khyber Agency: Mortar Shell Death Toll Reaches 10', *Express Tribune*, 27 August 2012: http://tribune.com.pk/story/426630/khyber-agency-mortar-shell-death-toll-reaches-10/ (accessed 6 June 2013).

[25] Dodd and Perkins, *Monitoring Explosive Violence*, 25.

[26] For example, International Convention for the Suppression of Terrorist Bombings, 15 December 1997, 2149 UNTS 256.

[27] Final Document, Tenth Annual Conference of the High Contracting Parties to Amended Protocol II to the CCW, 23 January 2009 (UN Doc. CCW/AP.II/CONF.10/2), para. 23.

[28] B. Clarke, 'Proportionality in Armed Conflicts: A Principle in Need of Clarification?', 3 *International Humanitarian Legal Studies* (2012) 113. For illustrations, see 'Wide of the Mark', Action on Armed Violence (December 2012): www.inew.org/site/wp-content/uploads/2013/01/AOAV_Wide_of_the_Mark1.pdf (accessed 6 June 2013).

[29] In connection with arms control, the term 'heavy weapons' evokes the divide between 'small arms and light weapons' (SALW) and 'major conventional weapons', a distinction oriented towards different-sized calibres and the portability of weapons. 'Heavy weapons' are not formally recognised in international human rights law or IHL

annexed Six-Point Proposal of the Joint Special Envoy of the UN and the League of Arab States, for instance, called on the Syrian government to 'cease all use of heavy weapons in such centres'.[30] In light of the grave harm caused by explosive weapons with wide area effects, the UN Secretary-General, in his 2012 report on the protection of civilians, urged all parties to conflict 'to refrain from using explosive weapons with a wide area impact in densely populated areas'.[31] Several states, high-level UN representatives, the ICRC and civil society actors have since lent support to this policy orientation.[32] However, as the UN Secretary-General has also observed, while the humanitarian impact, in both the short run and the long run, can be disastrous for civilians, 'the use of certain explosive weapons in populated areas may, in some circumstances, fall within the confines of the law'.[33] The remainder of this chapter aims to provide an idea of what the confines of the law are.

Explosive weapons and 'the necessities of war'

The St Petersburg Declaration 1868, the first formal agreement of modern international law to ban a specific type of weapon, concerns a weapon with explosive effects. The Declaration prohibits the employment 'of any projectile of a weight below 400 grammes, which is either explosive or

instruments, but the primary issue of humanitarian concern in relation to these weapons is death and injury to civilians, and damage to civilian objects, from the use of heavy *explosive* weapons in populated areas. For more information on the link between heavy weapons and explosive weapons, see R. Moyes, M. Brehm and T. Nash, 'Heavy Weapons and Civilian Protection', Article 36 (9 August 2012): www.article36.org/wp-content/uploads/2012/08/Heavy-weapons-and-civilian-protection.pdf (accessed 19 June 2013).

30 UN Security Council Resolution 2042 [On authorisation of the deployment of an advance team of up to thirty unarmed military observers to the Syrian Arab Republic], 14 April 2012 (UN Doc. S/RES/2042 (2012)).

31 Report of the Secretary-General on the Protection of Civilians in Armed Conflict, 22 May 2012 (UN Doc. S/2012/376), para. 75.

32 Report of the Special Representative of the Secretary-General for Children and Armed Conflict (6 August 2012) (UN Doc. A/67/256), para. 69; ICRC, 'Challenges of Contemporary Armed Conflicts', 4, 42; Co-chairs' summary, Oslo Global Conference: Reclaiming the Protection of Civilians under International Humanitarian Law (May 2013): www.regjeringen.no/upload/UD/Vedlegg/Hum/recommendations_final.pdf (accessed 19 June 2013), Recommendation 1(6). Statements to this effect were also made by Austria, Belgium, Germany, Sweden, and the European Union: available at www.inew.org/acknowledgements (accessed 6 June 2013).

33 Report of the Secretary-General on the Protection of Civilians in Armed Conflict (UN Doc. S/2012/376), para. 75; Similarly, ICRC, 'Challenges of Contemporary Armed Conflicts', 41.

charged with fulminating or inflammable substances'.[34] This prohibition has since evolved into a ban on 'exploding bullets' under customary IHL.[35] The impetus for the convocation of the St Petersburg Conference was a Russian rifle projectile with explosive and incendiary effects, whose modification in the 1860s led it to detonate in contact with soft substances, including human flesh. The projectile had first been developed in the 1850s, primarily to blow up enemy ammunition crates. The detonation of the projectile upon impact with the human body caused injuries that were far more severe than those associated with non-explosive rifle projectiles in use at the time. The nations subscribing to the St Petersburg Declaration felt that projectiles of this type would 'uselessly aggravate the sufferings of disabled men, or render their death inevitable'. Hence, their use would go beyond what states 'should endeavour to accomplish during war', namely, 'to weaken the military forces of the enemy', for which it was 'sufficient to disable the greatest possible number of men'. Thus, the ban on explosive projectiles was the first concrete application of a more general rule, also enshrined in the St Petersburg Declaration, against the 'employment of weapons, projectiles and material and methods of warfare of a nature to cause superfluous injury or unnecessary suffering' (the so-called 'SIrUS rule').[36]

The 400 grammes limit introduced by the St Petersburg Declaration to distinguish between permissible and impermissible explosive weapons was, in effect, a dividing line between artillery and rifle projectiles.[37] That explosive projectiles of 400 grammes and above were excluded from the ban was largely a matter of military expedience. According to the diplomatic records, the British delegate voiced the concern that if cannons were also covered by the ban, 'cela pourrait avoir des inconvénients'

[34] Declaration Renouncing the Use, in Time of War, of Certain Explosive Projectiles Under 400 Grammes Weight, 29 November/11 December 1868.

[35] Henckaerts and Doswald-Beck, *Customary International Humanitarian Law*, vol. 1, Rule 78.

[36] In its contemporary formulation, the rule is reflected in Article 35(2) 1977 AP I. The prohibition on 'The use of means and methods of warfare which are of a nature to cause superfluous injury or unnecessary suffering' is part of customary IHL, applicable in non-international and international armed conflict. Henckaerts and Doswald- Beck, *Customary International Humanitarian Law*, vol. 1, Rule 70. The ICJ referred to it as a 'cardinal principle' (International Court of Justice, *The Legality of the Threat or Use of Nuclear Weapons* (Advisory Opinion of 8 July 1996), ICJ Reports 1996, 226, para. 78).

[37] F. Kalshoven, 'Wartime Use of Weapons: Legal History, 1868 to 1934', 191 *Arms, Armaments and International Law*, Collected Courses of the Hague Academy of International Law (1985) 207.

(this could have some drawbacks). He was immediately assured by the Russian representative that the ban did not apply to cannonballs and shells.[38] This position was not uncontested at the time. In particular, military experts opposed to a ban argued that the effects of 'rifle-shells' were not more inhumane than those of other explosive weapons, such as rockets, fougasses and the 'angular fragments of segment shells'.[39]

In this sense, the St Petersburg Declaration can be seen as formal recognition of the grave medical effects of blast and fragmentation. However, by 'fix[ing] the technical limits at which the necessities of war ought to yield to the requirements of humanity' at 400 grammes, the effects of explosive artillery shells, rockets and bombs became formally part of 'the necessities of war'. These effects were not deemed contrary to 'the laws of humanity'. It has since proven difficult, under IHL, to articulate concerns relating to the degree of suffering, severity of injury or likelihood of death resulting from explosive weapon use.[40] The dominant view is that the SIrUS rule only finds application in relation to combatants (and, possibly, civilians directly participating in hostilities). IHL rules protecting civilians from harm do not provide an opportunity to link patterns of injury to specific weapon technologies.[41] Thus, concern about the humanitarian impact of explosive weapons on civilians tends to be framed, under IHL, in terms of indiscriminate or disproportionate effects.

[38] C. Samwer and J. Hopf, *Nouveau recueil général de traités, conventions et autres transactions remarquables, servant à la connaissance des relations étrangères des puissances et états dans leurs rapports mutuels* (Göttingen: Librarie de Dieterich, 1873), vol. 18, 455.

[39] See the extracts of Major Fosbery's discourse in F. Kalshoven, 'Wartime Use of Weapons', 209. In the same vein, A. Cassese, 'Means of Warfare: The Present and the Emerging Law', 1 *Belgian Review of International Law* (1976) 149–50: 'The same projectiles were instead allowed if fired by artillery'.

[40] The treatment of explosive weapons as 'conventional' and, by implication, unproblematic weapons, is deeply engrained in IHL discourse. The ICRC's SIrUS project in the late 1990s proposed to use data relating to the effects of 'conventional weapons', those that cause physical trauma by explosions and projectiles, as a baseline for determining what constitutes superfluous injury or unnecessary suffering. R. M. Coupland (ed.), *The SIrUS Project: Towards a Determination of which Weapons Cause 'Superfluous Injury or Unnecessary Suffering'* (Geneva: ICRC, 1997), 22. For a practical example, see 'Memorandum for AAC/JAQ (Mr Luthy) regarding Requested Legal Review of the Massive Ordnance Air Blast (MOAB) Weapon', Department of the Air Force, The Judge Advocate General, 21 March 2003: 'Blast and fragmentation are historic and common anti-personnel effects in lawful military weapons. There are no components that would cause unnecessary suffering.'

[41] Under IHL, civilians must not be the object of attack, and must be generally protected against the effects of hostilities.

Blast and fragmentation weapons: still waiting for that protocol

Protecting civilians from the effects of certain explosive weapons is the stated objective of a number of weapon treaties. Protocol II (1980) and Amended Protocol II (1996) to the CCW,[42] for instance, impose restrictions on the use of certain landmines, booby-traps and other devices in order to 'protect the civilian population from unintended exposure to dangerous explosives'.[43] Amended Protocol II establishes a presumption against the use of booby traps and other devices, including IEDs, 'in any city, town, village or other area containing a similar concentration of civilians', reflecting recognition of the particular risks that these weapons pose to civilians in populated areas.[44]

To put an end to the unacceptable harm to civilians caused by anti-personnel landmines and cluster munitions, the 1997 Mine Ban Convention completely bans anti-personnel landmines as defined under that treaty, and the 2008 Convention on Cluster Munitions imposes a similar ban on cluster munitions.[45] Evidence of the short- and the long-term humanitarian impact on civilians of landmines and cluster

[42] Protocol on Prohibitions or Restrictions on the Use of Mines, Booby-Traps and Other Devices (Protocol II to the CCW), 10 October 1980, 1342 UNTS 168; Protocol on Prohibitions or Restrictions on the Use of Mines, Booby-Traps and Other Devices as amended on 3 May 1996 (Amended Protocol II to the CCW) 3 May 1996, 2048 UNTS 133. The protection of civilians plays a role to varying degrees in other instruments and treaty provisions on explosive weapons, e.g., Convention Relative to the Laying of Automatic Submarine Contact Mines (Hague Convention VIII), 18 October 1907; Declaration Prohibiting the Discharge of Projectiles and Explosives from Balloons (Hague Declaration XIV), 18 October 1907. Participants at the first Hague Peace Conference of 1899 also discussed more general restrictions on explosive weapons. A proposition was, for example, put forward 'not to make use of mining shells (*obus brisants ou à fougasses*) for field artillery', and another 'not to make use of any new explosives, or of any of the class known as high explosives for the bursting charges of projectiles'. Both proposals were ultimately rejected. 'Report of Captain Crozier to the Commission of the United States of America to the International Conference at the Hague Regarding the Work of the First Committee of the Conference and its Sub-committee', in J. B. Scott, *The Hague Peace Conferences of 1899 and 1907*, 2 vols (Baltimore, MD: The Johns Hopkins Press, 1909), vol. 2, p. 30.

[43] M. N. Schmitt, 'Military Necessity and Humanity in International Humanitarian Law: Preserving the Delicate Balance', 50 *VJIL* (2010) 814.

[44] Articles 2(5) and 7(3), 1996 CCW AP II.

[45] Preamble and Article 1, Convention on the Prohibition of the Use, Stockpiling, Production and Transfer of Anti-Personnel Mines and on their Destruction (Mine Ban Convention), 18 September 1997, 2056 UNTS 241; Article 1, Convention on Cluster Munitions, 30 May 2008.

munitions was an important driver in the development of these treaties.[46] In terms of the effects at the time of use, the Convention on Cluster Munitions places particular emphasis on the prevention of 'indiscriminate area effects'.[47] This generated interest in reassessing explosive weapons more widely in order to find ways of reducing the suffering they cause.[48] After all, it can be argued 'that cluster munitions are very similar to other explosive weapons' and that 'all explosive weapons have some tendency to strike without distinction in the area that they affect'.[49]

Weapons that affect an area with blast and fragmentation were already identified as raising distinct humanitarian concerns in the 1970s. The question of 'blast and fragmentation weapons' was considered in detail in governmental expert discussions and at sessions of the Diplomatic Conference on the Reaffirmation and Development of International Humanitarian Law Applicable in Armed Conflicts – the processes that eventually led to the adoption of Additional Protocol I 1977 to the Geneva Conventions and of the CCW. An expert report of 1973 identifies 'explosive and penetrating weapons' as one of the principal categories of weapons of humanitarian concern.[50] The 'wide area coverage' of certain blast and fragmentation weapons was seen to make them especially prone to 'affect combatants and civilians without

[46] J. Borrie et al., 'Learn, Adapt, Succeed: Potential Lessons from the Ottawa and Oslo Processes for other Disarmament and Arms Control Challenges', 1 *Disarmament Forum* (2009), 20. The Convention on Cluster Munitions' preamble reflects states parties' determination 'to put an end for all time to the suffering and casualties caused by cluster munitions at the time of their use, when they fail to function as intended or when they are abandoned'. Similarly, the Mine Ban Convention's preamble provides: 'Determined to put an end to the suffering and casualties caused by anti-personnel mines, that kill or maim hundreds of people every week, mostly innocent and defenceless civilians and especially children, obstruct economic development and reconstruction, inhibit the repatriation of refugees and internally displaced persons, and have other severe consequences for years after emplacement.'

[47] Article 2(2)(c) 2008 Convention on Cluster Munitions. A commentary notes that 'The distribution of explosive force and fragmentation over a wide area was one of the technical characteristics of cluster munitions first identified as problematic' (G. Nystuen and S. Casey-Maslen (eds), *The Convention on Cluster Munitions: A Commentary* (Oxford: Oxford University Press, 2010), paras 0.93 and 2.122).

[48] J. Borrie, *Unacceptable Harm: A History of How the Treaty to Ban Cluster Munitions Was Won* (Geneva: United Nations, 2009), 335.

[49] R. Moyes and B. Rappert, 'Looking Inwards and Looking Outwards – Specific Challenges and Strategic Directions from the Prohibition of Cluster Munitions', 15 *Austrian Review of International and European Law* (2010) 89–108.

[50] *Weapons that may Cause Unnecessary Suffering or have Indiscriminate Effects*, Report on the Work of Experts (Geneva: ICRC, 1973), 19.

discrimination',[51] and several proposals aiming at the prohibition of certain blast and fragmentation weapons, or at restrictions on their area of effectiveness, were discussed.[52] In a resolution calling for follow-up regarding the prohibition or restriction of use of certain conventional weapons, the Diplomatic Conference of 1974–7 specifically referred to the effects of 'blast and fragmentation weapons'.[53]

However, as '[n]o general ban on blast and fragmentation weapons as a class' had been proposed, experts soon 'concentrated their attention on specific weapons falling within this category',[54] with focus on regulating the use of certain blast and fragmentation weapons against persons (as opposed to materiel). The only immediate result of these deliberations was a protocol prohibiting the use of weapons 'the primary effect of which is to injure by fragments which in the human body escape detection by X-rays'.[55] At the time, this prohibition was already considered to be of little consequence.[56] It certainly did not address the humanitarian concerns discussed in relation to blast and fragmentation weapons. This caused some consternation among commentators, not least because the regulation of blast and fragmentation weapons did not appear to present any significant legal obstacles. One scholar interpreted the absence of legal difficulties as an encouraging

[51] Conference of Government Experts on the Use of Certain Conventional Weapons (2nd session, Lugano, 28 January–26 February 1967), Report (Geneva: ICRC, 1976) (hereinafter Lugano Report), 17.

[52] One proposal sought to prohibit the use of anti-personnel cluster warheads and similar devices that have 'a wide area coverage and, hence, could easily affect combatants and civilians without discrimination': Lugano Report, 17. See the 'Explanatory Memorandum to the Working Paper Submitted to by Algeria, Austria, Egypt, Lebanon, Mali, Mauritania, Mexico, Norway, Sudan, Sweden, Switzerland, Venezuela, Yugoslavia' (Doc. CDDH/IV/201, Lugano Report, 199, 204). 'Working Paper Submitted by the Experts of Sweden' (Doc. COLU/202) proposes a prohibition on the 'anti-personnel use of weapons which for their effects rely exclusively on shock waves in the air' (Lugano Report, 167). See also *Official Records, Diplomatic Conference on the Reaffirmation and Development of International Humanitarian Law Applicable in Armed Conflicts, 1974–1977*, 16 vols (Bern: Swiss Federal Political Department, 1978), vol. 16, pp. 613–26.

[53] Resolution 22(IV): Follow-up Regarding Prohibition or Restriction of Use of Certain Conventional Weapons, 9 June 1977, *Official Records*, vol. 1, p. 215.

[54] Lugano Report, 17.

[55] Protocol on Non-Detectable Fragments (Protocol I to the CCW), 10 October 1980, 1342 UNTS 168.

[56] J. Goldblat, 'The Convention on Inhumane Weapons', 38 *Bulletin of the Atomic Scientists* (1983) 24.

sign that these weapons would be regulated by a CCW protocol in the near future.[57]

As is well known, no protocol on blast and fragmentation weapons has since been adopted. A categorical orientation to these weapons is, however, implicit in Protocol V (2003) to the CCW that deals with explosive remnants of war (ERW) – the remnants of explosive weapons. Protocol V places no restrictions on the use of explosive weapons, but it establishes a responsibility on users of explosive weapons to minimise the post-conflict risks and effects of explosive weapons.[58] Protocol III (1980) to the CCW, which deals with incendiary weapons, also treats explosive weapons as a category. Article 1(1)(ii) excludes from the definition of an 'incendiary weapon', and, hence, from the scope of the Protocol, 'Munitions designed to combine penetration, blast or fragmentation effects with an additional incendiary effect, such as armour-piercing projectiles, fragmentation shells, explosive bombs and similar combined-effects munitions.'[59] In spite of the categorical management of explosive weapons in the practice of states (as reflected in these instruments, national laws and policies, military practice and medical literature),[60] explosive weapons are not subject to comprehensive restraints under international treaty law. Their use as a means and method of warfare remains subject to the general rules of IHL governing the conduct of hostilities.

[57] M. Arrassen, *Conduite des hostilités, droit des conflits armés et désarmement* (Brussels: Bruylant, 1986), 433: 'Les armes à fragmentation et à effet de souffle dont la réglementation ne soulève pourtant aucun problème juridique insurmontable n'ont guère retenu l'attention de la CNUAC'; *ibid.*, 442: 'les armes à fragmentation et à effet de souffle ne soulèvent pas de difficultés majeures lorsqu'on les examine à la lumière des trois critères juridiques et humanitaires fondamentaux. C'est en prévision de leur réglementation prochaine, un signe encourageant'.

[58] Article 5, Title 3 of the Technical Annex to the Protocol on Explosive Remnants of War (Protocol V to the CCW), 28 November 2003, 2399 UNTS 100. For a discussion, see Moyes, *Explosive Violence*, 61.

[59] Article 1(1)(ii) 1980 CCW Protocol III.

[60] B. Rappert, R. Moyes and I. Lang, 'The Case for Addressing Explosive Weapons: Conflict, Violence and Health', 75.11 *Social Science & Medicine* (2012) 2048: www.sciencedirect.com/science/article/pii/S0277953612005977 (accessed 19 June 2013); W. H. Boothby, *Weapons and the Law of Armed Conflict* (Oxford: Oxford University Press, 2009), 224: 'Long-range artillery, air delivered bombs, ground- and air-launched missiles, and all analogous weapons systems' can be considered as a group for the purposes of discussing application of weapons law to particular weapon systems.

Explosive weapons and the prohibition on indiscriminate attacks

Under IHL, the civilian population and individual civilians 'enjoy general protection against dangers arising from military operations'.[61] To this end, parties to an armed conflict are obliged to distinguish, at all times, between the civilian population and combatants and between civilian objects and military objectives.[62] They must not make civilians the object of attack and they must refrain from launching indiscriminate and disproportionate attacks. Article 51(4) of Additional Protocol I 1977 to the 1949 Geneva Conventions defines indiscriminate attacks as:

> (a) those which are not directed at a specific military objective;
> (b) those which employ a method or means of combat which cannot be directed at a specific military objective; or
> (c) those which employ a method or means of combat the effects of which cannot be limited as required by this Protocol; and consequently, in each such case, are of a nature to strike military objectives and civilians or civilian objects without distinction.

The Protocol provides two examples of such indiscriminate attacks: area bombardment and disproportionate attacks. Area bombardment is described as:

> an attack by bombardment by any methods or means which treats as a single military objective a number of clearly separated and distinct military objectives located in a city, town, village or other area containing a similar concentration of civilians or civilian objects.[63]

This provision was adopted in response to the devastating effects of 'saturation' or 'carpet' bombing of population centres and vast stretches of land practised during and after the Second World War. Although the scope of the prohibition is not limited to air-launched explosive weapons,[64] the special mention of 'bombardment' demonstrates that

61 Article 51(1) AP I 1977. This rule is also contained in preambular para. 2 of the CCW.

62 Article 48 AP I 1977.

63 Article 51(5)(a) AP I 1977. The term 'area bombardment' is not used in the Protocol, but, under customary IHL, the norm is generally referred to as the prohibition on 'area bombardment'. See Henckaerts and Doswald-Beck, *Customary International Humanitarian Law*, vol. 1, Rule 13.

64 The prohibition does not apply to 'direct fire by small arms', according to C. Pilloud et al. (eds), *Commentary on the Additional Protocols of 8 June 1977 to the Geneva Conventions of 12 August 1949* (Geneva: ICRC/Martinus Nijhoff, 1987), para. 1968. Note that the rule on area bombardment is also reflected in Article 3(9) 1996 CCW Amended Protocol II,

the prohibition on indiscriminate attacks itself evolved with particular reference to the use of multiple explosive weapons in populated areas.[65] Some provisions in the statutes of the International Criminal Tribunal for the former Yugoslavia (ICTY) and the International Criminal Court retain the differentiation between 'bombardment' and attacks. It is doubtful, though, that the specific mention of bombardment retains legal significance for the regulation of the conduct of hostilities today. At least since the adoption of Additional Protocol I 1977, bombardment has been subsumed under the broader notion of 'attack'.[66]

The application of the prohibition on indiscriminate attacks to means and methods of warfare is not entirely settled. As a matter of customary international law, 'the use of weapons which are by nature indiscriminate is prohibited'.[67] In the absence of a treaty prohibition, which weapons are illegal under this rule is, however, contested. V1 and V2 rockets, Scud missiles, and Katyusha rockets are often cited as examples of indiscriminate weapons.[68] Their use is said to result in an indiscriminate attack in all circumstances, on the grounds that they cannot be directed at a specific military objective. Reference is to the rule codified in Article 51(4)(b) of Additional Protocol I. From this perspective, the

For a detailed discussion, see H. Blix, 'Area Bombardment: Rules and Reasons', *British Yearbook of International Law*, 49(1) (1978) 31–69.

[65] Consider Article 10 on 'Target-area bombing', *Draft Rules for the Limitation of the Dangers Incurred by the Civilian Population in Time of War*, International Committee of the Red Cross, September 1956. See also International Committee of the Red Cross, *Protection of the Civilian Population against Dangers of Hostilities*, Conference of Government Experts on the Reaffirmation and Development of International Humanitarian Law Applicable in Armed Conflicts, Geneva, 24 May–12 June 1971, 8 vols (Geneva: ICRC, 1971), vol. 3, pp. 103–9. For an overview of legal rules specifically addressing bombardment, see A. McDonald and T. Bruha, 'Bombardment', in *Max Planck Encyclopedia of Public International Law*, Max Planck Institute for Comparative Public Law and International Law: www.mpepil.com (accessed 19 June 2013). 'Concentration of civilians', 'populated area' and 'densely populated area' are well-established, largely equivalent legal notions used in various instruments in relation to the protection of civilians from the effects of hostilities. These locations can be of a permanent nature (cities, towns or villages) or of a temporary one, such as camps or columns of displaced people. Article 7(3) 1996 CCW Amended Protocol II; Article 4(2) 1980 CCW Protocol II; Articles 1(2) and 2(2) 1980 CCW Protocol III.

[66] For more detail, see M. Brehm, *Protecting Civilians from the Effects of Explosive Weapons: An Analysis of International Legal and Policy Standards* (Geneva: United Nations, 2012), 30–3.

[67] Henckaerts and Doswald-Beck, *Customary International Humanitarian Law*, vol. 1, Rule 71; *Legality of the Threat or Use of Nuclear Weapons*, ICJ Reports 1996, para. 78.

[68] Henckaerts and Doswald-Beck, *Customary International Humanitarian Law*, vol. 2, *Practice Relating to Rule 71.*

source of harm to civilians is inherent in the weapon's delivery mechanism and, thus, amenable to a technical solution. Hence, the focus on laser-guidance and other systems that allow for greater accuracy of delivery.

Factors other than accuracy, which influence the propensity of an explosive weapon to have indiscriminate effects, receive far less attention in scholarly literature.[69] The effect of the other prongs of Article 51(4) on the legality of explosive weapons, and of their use in a particular setting, remains contested.[70] Although the argument has been made that within their area of blast and fragmentation explosive weapons strike without distinction,[71] most legal doctrine does not support the view that explosive weapons are 'indiscriminate by nature'.[72]

However, can the effects of an attack with long-range artillery or unguided mortars, a 500 kg air-dropped bomb, a multiple-barrel rocket

[69] Note the distinction between inaccuracy and other causes of indiscriminate effects in ICRC, *Protection of the Civilian Population against Dangers of Hostilities*, 112 (emphasis added): 'principles relating to weapons which, by virtue of their effects *or* their imprecision risk reaching the civilian population in an indiscriminate manner'. See also Institute of International Law, *The Distinction between Military Objectives and Non-Military Objectives in General and Particularly the Problems Associated with Weapons of Mass Destruction*, 9 September 1969, para.7: 'Existing international law [. . .] prohibits the use of weapons the destructive effect of which is so great that it cannot be limited to specific military objectives or is otherwise uncontrollable (self-generating weapons), *as well as* of "blind" weapons' (emphasis added).

[70] Pilloud et al., *Commentary*, para. 1424: 'Certain [. . .] weapons that may have an indiscriminate effect continue to be the object of controversy [. . .] These include, for example, certain blast and fragmentation weapons.' K. Watkin, '21st Century Conflict and International Humanitarian Law: Status Quo or Change?', in M. N. Schmitt and J. Pejic (eds), *International Law and Armed Conflict: Exploring the Faultlines* (Leiden: Martinus Nijhoff, 2007), 276: 'the use of airpower and long range artillery continue to challenge the principle of distinction'.

[71] Report of the Secretary-General on the Protection of Civilians in Armed Conflict (UN Doc. S/2012/376), para. 35; Moyes and Rappert, 'Looking Inwards and Looking Outwards'; 'Use of Explosive Weapons in Populated Areas: Some Questions and Answers', Background Paper No. 2 of the Discourse on Explosive Weapons (DEW) project, United Nations Institute for Disarmament Research, July 2010: www.unidir.org/programmes/weapons-of-societal-disruption/discourse-on-explosive-weapons-dew (accessed 28 May 2014).

[72] Arrassen, *Conduite des hostilités*, 443; G. S. Corn and G. P. Corn, 'The Law of Operational Targeting: Viewing the LOAC Through an Operational Lens', 47 *Texas International Law Journal* (2012) 372–4. Vallentgoed, on the contrary, describes cluster bombs and 'dumb bombs' as weapons that are 'indiscriminate by their nature', and notes at n. 102 that 'in many circumstances the nature of artillery can place it in this category' (D. Vallentgoed, 'The Last Round? A Post-Gotovina Reassessment of the Legality of Using Artillery against Built-up Areas', 18 *JCSL* (2013) 41).

launcher or a cluster munition on military objects in a populated area really be 'limited as required' under IHL? It is routinely argued that this question calls for an assessment on a case-by-case basis where the answer depends on the particular circumstances of the attack. As long as there are conceivable circumstances (however hypothetical) in which the weapon could be used in compliance with IHL, the weapon is not seen to be indiscriminate 'by nature'. This approach shifts attention away from the weapon technology and locates the source of civilian harm in the modality of the weapon's use, the intention of its user and contextual factors.[73]

It is submitted that the tendency to treat explosive weapons as indiscriminate weapons only when they cannot be accurately delivered, and the prevailing practice to assess methods of combat on a case-by-case basis, unduly limit the potential of the prohibition on indiscriminate attacks to protect civilians from the effects of explosive weapons.[74] For, even if the prohibition of indiscriminate attacks is seen to relate 'more often to [. . .] methods of using weapons than to specific weapons per se', the fact that 'weapons are capable of being used indiscriminately' is 'a ground for prohibiting such types of use'. In some cases, it is even 'the normal or typical use' of a weapon that has indiscriminate effects.[75]

[73] Department of the Air Force, 'Memorandum for AAC/JAQ (Mr Luthy)' illustrates this approach. The memorandum concerns the review of a GPS-guided munition that uses 18,000 lbs of H6 high-explosive material to produce a 'tremendous explosion', and causes injury or death to persons primarily by blast or fragmentation. The relevant standard of review with respect to distinction is stated as 'whether the weapon is capable of being controlled so as to be directed against a lawful target, i.e. it is not indiscriminate in its effect'. Applying this standard, the review finds that 'Although the MOAB weapon leaves a large footprint, it is discriminate [. . .] The guidance system ensures that the weapon will hit (within acceptable variables) the target that it is intended to hit.' Consideration of issues relating to the presence of 'non-combatants' in the area affected by the weapon is deferred to the time of use. The review notes that 'the commander authorizing the weapon's use must consider its characteristics' in order to ensure consistency with rules of engagement and IHL, but the review does not provide any guidance or specify limitations for the use of a MOAB in, say, a populated area.

[74] Cassese considered that 'the prohibitory intent' of the general rules banning indiscriminate weapons has proved 'scarcely effective' and that the majority's position on this question is 'tantamount to saying that States consider the general principle on indiscriminate weapons to have become valueless' (A. Cassese, 'The Prohibition of Indiscriminate Means of Warfare', in A. Cassese, P. Gaeta and S. Zappalà (eds), *The Human Dimension of International Law: Selected Papers of Antonio Cassese* (Oxford: Oxford University Press, 2008), 183–5).

[75] ICRC, '1973 Experts Report', para. 27 (emphasis added). Baxter notes in this regard: 'The idea of indiscriminacy comes from the law with respect to the manner of employment of weapons rather than the law of illegality of use *per se*. [. . .] because there is no possibility of confining its effects to the military target, the weapon might be stigmatized as unlawful on that account.

The ICRC Commentary to Additional Protocol I underlines that 'The nature of the means used is not the only criterion: the power of the weapons used can have the same consequences.'[76] The Commentary recalls that many of the drafters of the Protocol were of the view that:

> the definition [of the term 'indiscriminate attacks'] was not intended to mean that there are means or methods of combat whose use would involve an indiscriminate attack in all circumstances. Rather it was intended to take account of the fact that means or methods of combat which can be used perfectly legitimately in some situations could, in other circumstances, have effects that would be contrary to some limitations contained in the Protocol, in which event their use in those circumstances would involve an indiscriminate attack.[77]

The ICRC recently pointed out in respect of explosive weapons that 'A circumstance that could make the use of a certain weapon indiscriminate is certainly its use in a densely populated area'.[78]

The second example of an indiscriminate attack listed in Additional Protocol I is:

> an attack which may be expected to cause incidental loss of civilian life, injury to civilians, damage to civilian objects, or a combination thereof, which would be excessive in relation to the concrete and direct military advantage anticipated.[79]

Even conventional bombardment may fall afoul of this restriction, and various new forms of weapons, such as fragmentation bombs, have on occasion been characterized as unlawful because of their incidental effects on civilians' (R. R. Baxter, 'Conventional Weapons under Legal Prohibitions', 1 *International Security* (1977) 48).

76 Pilloud et al., *Commentary*, para. 1963 gives the use of an explosive weapon in a populated area as an example: 'if a 10 ton bomb is used to destroy a single building, it is inevitable that the effects will be very extensive and will annihilate or damage neighboring buildings, while a less powerful missile would suffice to destroy the building'. Consider that, according to the United States Department of the Army, *The US Army/Marine Corps Counterinsurgency Field Manual* (Chicago: University of Chicago Press, 2007), 365, para. E-6, airstrikes in counterinsurgency operations should not only be carried out with 'precisely delivered weapons with a demonstrated low failure rate', but also employing weapons with 'appropriate yield, and proper fuse'.

77 Pilloud et al., *Commentary*, para. 1962. Arrassen notes in this regard: 'La cause principale du caractère indiscriminé des effets des armes à fragmentation et à effet de soufflé se situerait plutôt au niveau des méthodes de leur emploi par les parties au conflit. [...] Naturellement, cela n'interdit pas de soumettre leur utilisation à des limitations contraignantes pour mieux assurer la protection de la population et des biens à caractère civil' (Arrassen, *Conduite des hostilités*, 443).

78 ICRC, 'Challenges of Contemporary Armed Conflicts', 41.

79 Article 51(5)(b) 1977 AP I. Launching a disproportionate attack is prohibited under customary IHL applicable in both international and non-international armed conflicts. Henckaerts and Doswald-Beck, *Customary International Humanitarian Law*, vol. 1, Rule 14.

Although it has been noted that 'the use of heavy or explosive weapons in urban areas raise[s] proportionality concerns because they put civilians and civilian objects at particular risk of harm',[80] the rule on disproportionate attacks is generally considered unsuited as a 'criterion against which the legitimacy of a weapon can sensibly be considered'.[81] Given the difficulties, uncertainties and considerable disagreement surrounding the prohibition on disproportionate attacks, and owing to the prevailing view that determinations about proportionality can only be made on a case-by-case basis, no generic pronouncement on the proportionality of particular weapons or their use in particular settings (such as populated areas) is likely to emerge under IHL.[82]

Area bombardment, area targeting and area weapons

Although one method of combat that involves the use of multiple explosive weapons in a populated area – area bombardment – is already prohibited as a matter of customary IHL, the ongoing pattern of harm caused by the bombing and shelling of cities, towns and villages attests to the limits of this prohibition effectively to protect civilians from the effects of explosive weapons.[83] The prohibition on area bombardment

[80] Clarke, 'Proportionality in Armed Conflicts', 99.

[81] Boothby, *Weapons and the Law of Armed Conflict*, 79.

[82] The potentially wide-ranging and prolonged knock-on effects on the civilian population from an attack with explosive weapons in a populated area raise difficult questions under the rule on proportionality. There has been intense debate about the extent to which 'reverberating' and 'cumulative' effects should be factored into the proportionality assessment. It is widely accepted today that foreseeable long-term effects have to be taken into consideration when determining what civilian harm may be expected from an attack. However, there does not seem to be agreement about which effects are to be deemed 'foreseeable'. For recent discussions, see R. J. Barber, 'The Proportionality Equation: Balancing Military Objectives with Civilian Lives in the Armed Conflict in Afghanistan', 15 *Journal of Conflict & Security Law* (2010) 480–1; Clarke, 'Proportionality in Armed Conflicts, 73–123.

[83] Examples from recent years are documented in 'Death from the Skies: Deliberate and Indiscriminate Air Strikes on Civilians', Human Rights Watch (2013): www.hrw.org/reports/2013/04/10/death-skies; 'Under Siege: Indiscriminate Bombing and Abuses in Sudan's Southern Kordofan and Blue Nile States', Human Rights Watch (2012): www.hrw.org/reports/2012/12/12/under-siege; 'Somalia: No End in Sight: The Ongoing Suffering of Somalia's Civilians', Amnesty International (6 March 2010): www.amnesty.org/en/library/info/AFR52/003/2010; 'Sri Lanka: Desperate and Unacceptable Situation for Trapped Population', Doctors without Borders (26 February 2009): www.doctorswithoutborders.org/article/sri-lanka-desperate-and-unacceptable-situation-trapped-population (all accessed 19 June 2013).

only prevents the bombardment of a populated area if clearly separated and distinct military objects within that area can be targeted separately. Not only does this formulation leave some degree of latitude for determining when military objectives should be considered to be 'clearly separated and distinct', but, according to the dominant doctrinal view, the very determination whether separate targeting is feasible is to be taken with a view to 'the means available' to the attacker.[84] It is readily apparent that this interpretation has great potential to strip the prohibition of much of its normative content.

Neither the prohibition on area bombardment nor the general rule on indiscriminate attacks has proven a strong barrier to the military practice of 'area targeting', even in the vicinity of civilians.[85] Typically, area targeting involves the use of explosive area weapons, such as mortars, artillery or cluster munitions.[86] It has been noted that area weapons 'have an obvious and uncontrollable tendency towards indiscriminateness'.[87] As was mentioned above, cluster munitions are subject to a treaty ban, due, in part, to their indiscriminate area effects, and were already widely considered inappropriate for use in populated

[84] Pilloud et al., *Commentary*, paras 1972 and 1975; Blix, 'Area Bombardment: Rules and Reasons', 66.

[85] 'Barrage fire', for instance, is 'designed to fill a volume of space or area rather than aimed specifically at a given target', and 'distributed fire' aims at dispersing fire 'to engage most effectively an area target'. *NATO Glossary of Terms and Definitions (English and French)*, North Atlantic Treaty Organization Standardization Agency, NATO Doc. AAP-6 (2013), 2013, sections 2-B-1, 2-D-8. According to Pilloud et al., *Commentary*, barrage fire could 'of course [. . .] only concern limited areas and not vast stretches of territory', applying 'primarily to narrow passages, bridgeheads or strategic points such as hills or mountain passes'. The Commentary also states that, in contrast to 'sparsely populated areas', military objectives located in populated areas, 'may only be attacked separately *without* leading to civilian losses outside the military objectives themselves' (para. 1973, emphasis added). This does, however, not prevent the use of an 'area weapon' against an area target constituting a military objective, in a populated area.

[86] *NATO Glossary*, sect. 2-A-18 defines an 'area target' as 'a target consisting of an area rather than a single point'. Mortars and artillery are typically considered area weapons, e.g., in UN Human Rights Council, Human Rights in Palestine and Other Occupied Arab Territories, Report of the United Nations Fact-Finding Mission on the Gaza Conflict, 15 September 2009 (UN Doc. A/HRC/12/48), para. 699. Cluster munitions are described as 'area weapons' in International Committee of the Red Cross, *Humanitarian, Military, Technical and Legal Challenges of Cluster Munitions*, Expert Meeting, 18–20 April, Montreux, Switzerland, 2007, 17: www.icrc.org/eng/assets/files/other/icrc_002_0915.pdf (accessed 19 June 2013).

[87] ICRC, '1973 Experts Report', 48.

areas prior to that ban.[88] Moyes and Rappert observe that none of the weapon characteristics specified under the Convention on Cluster Munitions to avoid indiscriminate area effects relates to the accuracy of the container munition. Thus, indiscriminate area effects of cluster munitions are wholly considered to result from the use of multiple explosive items to distribute blast and fragmentation randomly across a predefined area.[89] The ban on cluster munitions could, therefore, become an important precedent for placing limits on the distribution of explosive force over an area by firing salvos of explosive shells or rockets at it.

Although 'no court or authoritative treatise has ever held that artillery cannot be used against lawful military targets situated in populated areas',[90] it is clear from the heated debates surrounding the *Gotovina* case before the ICTY that the use of explosive weapons with wide area effects in populated areas is highly controversial.[91] Leaving aside issues of international criminal law, a core point of contention in that case was the acceptability and permissibility of the shelling of populated areas

[88] Article 2(2)(c) 2008 Convention on Cluster Munitions; 'Declaration on Cluster Munitions', Third Review Conference of the States Parties to the Convention on Certain Conventional Weapons, 20 November 2006 (UN Doc. CCW/CONF.III/WP.18); International Criminal Tribunal for the former Yugoslavia, *Prosecutor* v. *Milan Martić*, IT-95-11-A, 2008, para. 251; UN Human Rights Council, Report of the Special Rapporteur on extrajudicial, summary or arbitrary executions, Philip Alston; the Special Rapporteur on the right of everyone to the enjoyment of the highest attainable standard of physical and mental health, Paul Hunt; the Representative of the Secretary-General on human rights of internally displaced persons, Walter Kälin; and the Special Rapporteur on adequate housing as a component of the right to an adequate standard of living, Miloon Kothari, Mission to Lebanon and Israel (7–14 September 2006), 2 October 2006 (UN Doc. A/HRC/2/7), para. 56.

[89] Moyes and Rappert, 'Looking Inwards and Looking Outwards'.

[90] W. B. Huffman, 'Margin of Error: Potential Pitfalls of the Ruling in the Prosecutor v. Ante Gotovina', 211 *Military Law Review* (2012) 21.

[91] International Criminal Tribunal for the former Yugoslavia, *Prosecutor* v. *Ante Gotovina, Ivan Čermak, Mladen Markač*, IT-06-90-T, Judgment, 15 April 2011; International Criminal Tribunal for the former Yugoslavia, *Prosecutor* v. *Ante Gotovina, Mladen Markač*, IT-06-90-A, Judgment, 16 November 2012. A detailed analysis of this case is beyond the scope of this chapter. For a discussion with focus on international criminal law aspects, see J. N. Clark, 'Courting Controversy: The ICTY's Acquittal of Croatian Generals Gotovina and Markac', 11 *Journal of International Criminal Justice* (2013) 399–423; D. Vallentgoed, 'The Last Round?'; W. B. Huffman, 'Margin of Error'; International Humanitarian Law Clinic at Emory University School of Law, Operational Law Experts Roundtable on the Gotovina Judgment: Military Operations, Battlefield Reality and the Judgment's Impact on Effective Implementation and Enforcement of International Humanitarian Law, Expert Meeting Report, 2012.

with long-range, unobserved fire from 130 mm tube artillery and 122 mm BM-21 multiple-barrel rocket launchers. Military experts notably questioned the appropriateness of using the latter weapon for attacks on towns. Several experts considered that '122-mm rockets [...] are not suited for attacks against point targets' and that the use of 122-mm multiple rocket launchers is 'inappropriate and disproportionate [...] against targets within a town'.[92]

The *Gotovina* case also illustrates that there are widely divergent opinions on how compliance of explosive weapon use in a populated area is to be assessed in light of the relevant IHL rules. The Trial Chamber held that the use of multiple-barrel rocket launchers, though 'generally less accurate than Howitzers or mortars', 'was not inherently indiscriminate'.[93] But it also considered that 'even a small number of artillery projectiles can have great effects on nearby civilians' and evaluated a range of factors to assess the permissibility of the shelling, including the accuracy of artillery, the blast and fragmentation effects of artillery shells, the time of shelling and the likelihood and number of civilians present in the target area, the number and calibre of shells fired and the distance they were fired from.[94] The Majority of the Appeals Chamber, in contrast, focused almost entirely on a standard of accuracy proposed by the Trial Chamber in relation to some artillery strikes (the contested '200 metres standard'). The Appeals Chamber rejected that standard, but failed to present an alternative means of assessing the permissibility of the shelling. Unfortunately, therefore, the judgment falls far short of 'adding significant definition to the legal paradigm that governs' complex operational targeting considerations as some had hoped it would do.[95]

[92] Lt Gen. Applegate concurring with Lt Gen. Shoffner in *Prosecutor* v. *Ante Gotovina, Mladen Markač*, Notice of Filing of Public Redacted Version of Prosecution Response to Gotovina's Second Rule 115 Motion, and Request for Change in Status of Corrigendum, 6 August 2012, A5668; Maj. Gen. Ashmore concurring with Lt Gen. Brown (*ibid.*, A5586): 'I would agree with General Brown that the use of MRL in populated areas could be regarded as reckless and indiscriminate.' Lt Gen. Applegate recalls with respect to a superior multiple-barrel rocket launcher, the MLRS rockets system, that it 'was not deployed to support UN forces in Bosnia because of its inherently larger spread of fire and lack of discrimination when engaging targets in built-up areas occupied by non-combatants' (*ibid.*, A5678). An MLRS M270 can fire up to twelve rockets in less than one minute. 'Multiple Launch Rocket System M270', Lockheed Martin: www.lockheedmartin.com/us/products/MLRSM270.html (accessed 12 June 2013).

[93] *Prosecutor* v. *Ante Gotovina et al.*, Judgment, 15 April 2011, para. 1897.

[94] *Ibid.*, para. 1910.

[95] International Humanitarian Law Clinic at Emory University School of Law, *Operational Law Experts Roundtable*, 2.

Particularly worrisome is that neither the Trial, nor the Appeals judgment, discusses precautionary measures in any detail.[96] This is surprising, as attacks with explosive weapons in a populated area raise important questions in this respect.[97] Under IHL, parties to an armed conflict have to take constant care 'to spare the civilian population, civilians and civilian objects' in the conduct of military operations.[98] To further this goal, parties must, to the maximum extent feasible, avoid locating military objectives within or near densely populated areas. They must also choose the means and methods of attack 'with a view to avoiding, and in any event to minimizing' incidental civilian harm.[99] These measures are critical for preventing indiscriminate or disproportionate attacks, but it should be stressed that the obligation to take measures to spare the civilian population has independent legal effect and is of broader application than the prevention of these extreme forms of illegal attacks.[100]

Increasing urbanisation, the challenging situation of 'co-location' and 'intermingling' brought about by the tendency of states and non-state actors alike, to fight in populated areas, and decreasing tolerance for civilian casualties, must affect what means and methods of combat are considered appropriate and permissible for use in populated areas.[101]

[96] The two strongly worded dissenting opinions of Judge Carmel Agius and of Judge Fausto Pocar discuss some of the shortcomings of this judgment. Judge Pocar criticises that the Majority of the Appeals Chamber was silent on the legal principles of IHL that the Trial Chamber should have applied to assess whether the artillery attacks were lawful. *Prosecutor* v. *Ante Gotovina, Mladen Markač*, Judgment, 16 November 2012, Dissenting Opinion of Judge Fausto Pocar, para. 13.

[97] Pilloud et al., *Commentary*, paras 2185 and 2190 notes in respect of Article 57, 1977 AP I: 'the precautions prescribed here will be of greatest importance in urban areas because such areas are most densely populated', noting that some of the drafters feared the 'general rule of bombardments of reducing incidental loss to a minimum was insufficient for the particular situation of bombardments on towns and cities behind the lines'.

[98] This rule is codified in Article 57(1) AP I 1977; Henckaerts and Doswald-Beck, *Customary International Humanitarian Law*, vol. 1, Rule 15.

[99] Articles 57(1), 57(2)(a)(ii) and 58(b) AP I 1977.

[100] J.-F. Quéguiner, 'Precautions under the Law Governing the Conduct of Hostilities', 88(864) *International Review of the Red Cross* (2006) 796–7. 'After all, the purposes of Articles 51 and 57 are not to provide a factual description of the military decision-making process; rather, they set out an objective standard for the judgment of military behaviour of carrying out attacks on military objectives involving the risk of excessive injury to the civilian population.' F. Kalshoven, *Reflections on the Law of War: Collected Essays* (Leiden: Martinus Nijhoff, 2007), 221.

[101] Quéguiner, 'Precautions', 800 argues that the obligation under Article 57(2)(a)(ii) is not to be reduced 'to the mere duty to promote, as far as possible, the accuracy of bombing raids conducted against military objectives situated in densely populated areas'. Rather, it 'can also serve to impose restrictions on the location of an attack by requiring, where

Rowe points out that 'In practical terms the aerial (or artillery) bombing of objects in heavily populated cities carries with it much greater responsibility to avoid civilian casualties than does a similar discharge of high explosives in a battle area, given that in such an area civilians are unlikely to be present.'[102] A variety of operational policies and practices already constrain the use, in populated areas, of explosive weapons with wide area effects. Restrictions on indirect fire (particularly unobserved indirect fire), the designation of restricted-fire or no-fire zones and the imposition of large safety distances are common measures taken by states to avoid civilian harm in and near populated areas.[103] For example, a stricter policy on the use of indirect fire by the African Union Mission in Somalia (AMISOM) reportedly reduced instances of indiscriminate shelling in Mogadishu.[104] Among other measures, the policy entailed the establishment of 'no-fire zones' in 'public places' where civilians are known to be present.[105] Over the last few years, NATO's International Security Assistance Force (ISAF) in Afghanistan has placed increasing restrictions on 'air-to-ground munitions and indirect fires' against residential compounds and other locations likely to produce civilian casualties.[106] Recent reports indicate that policies curtailing such strikes

circumstances permit, that parties avoid attacking a densely populated area if the attack is likely to cause heavy civilian losses'.

[102] P. Rowe, 'Kosovo 1999: The Air Campaign: Have the Provisions of Additional Protocol I withstood the Test?', *International Review of the Red Cross* (2000): www.icrc.org/eng/resources/documents/misc/57jqct.htm (accessed 17 June 2013).

[103] For example, Rule 27(A), *Rules of Engagement Handbook*, International Institute of Humanitarian Law (November 2009), reflects a presumption against the use of unobserved, observed or all indirect fire, or at least in specific situations, such as populated areas. The 'safety zone' policy of the Israeli Defence Forces for artillery strikes near populated areas is discussed in 'Indiscriminate Fire: Palestinian Rocket Attacks on Israel and Israeli Artillery Shelling in the Gaza Strip', Human Rights Watch (July 2007), 55–8: www.hrw.org/sites/default/files/reports/iopt0707web.pdf (accessed 19 June 2013). See also Inter-American Court of Human Rights, *Santo Domingo* v. *The Republic of Colombia*, Case No. 12.416, 2012, para. 220, which refers to Colombian military regulations on strikes with different explosive weapon types near populated areas. Arrassen, *Conduite des hostilités*, 443–4 discusses safety distances in relation to American 'Rules of Engagement for the Employment of Firepower in the Republic of Viet Nam'.

[104] W. Lotze and Y. Kasumba, 'AMISOM and the Protection of Civilians in Somalia', *Conflict Trends*, 2 (2012), 23.

[105] *Ibid.*, 22; 'For the Record: Maj. Gen. Nathan Mugisha Discusses Civilian Casualties', *AMISOM News Bulletin*, 17 (2010), 2.

[106] E. Schmitt, 'Allies Restrict Airstrikes on Taliban in Civilian Homes', *New York Times*, 10 June 2012: www.nytimes.com/2012/06/11/world/asia/allies-restrict-airstrikes-against-taliban-in-homes.html?_r=2 (accessed 19 June 2013); International Security Assistance Force (ISAF), *Tactical Directive* [referring to General Stanley McChrystal's Tactical Directive of

may have a positive effect in terms of reducing civilian casualties from aerial operations.[107] A US field manual establishing doctrine for military operations in a counterinsurgency environment notes with respect to combat in an urban area that 'direct-fire weapons may be more appropriate' than 'bombs delivered by fixed-wing close air support' owing to the risk of collateral damage to nearby buildings and non-combatants located nearby, and that choosing weapons appropriate to the situation in some cases means 'avoiding the use of area munitions'.[108]

Scholars have also made suggestions for placing greater formal constraints on the use of explosive weapons in populated areas better to protect civilians. For instance, a doctoral thesis, published in 1986, proposes a protocol to the CCW on 'blast and fragmentation weapons', based on two basic principles: a strong presumption against the use of explosive weapons within concentrations of civilians, unless they are delivered by direct fire; and a requirement that use of explosive weapons near a populated area is permitted only beyond a specified safety distance from that area.[109] Equally of note is Rowe's suggestion for a protocol to the CCW, according to which it would be:

> prohibited to make any military objective located within a concentration of civilians the object of attack, except when such military objective is clearly separated from the concentration of civilians, and all feasible

2 July 2009], 6 July 2009; International Security Assistance Force (ISAF), 'General Petraeus Issues Updated Tactical Directive: Emphasizes "Disciplined Use of Force"', 4 August 2010; International Security Assistance Force (ISAF), COMISAF's Tactical Directive [referring to General John R. Allen's Tactical Directive], 30 November 2011. In August 2012, ISAF reportedly published 'COMISAF Tactical Directive, Rev. 5.1', which incorporates restrictions on using indirect fire and air delivered munitions on civilian dwellings and other structures that may contain civilians, except in cases of self-defence when other options are not available. UNAMA and UN Office of the High Commissioner for Human Rights, Afghanistan Annual Report on Protection of Civilians in Armed Conflict 2012, February 2013, available at http://unama.unmissions.org.

107 UNAMA and UN Office of the High Commissioner for Human Rights, Afghanistan Annual Report on Protection of Civilians in Armed Conflict 2012, 31.

108 United States Department of the Army, *The US Army/Marine Corps Counterinsurgency Field Manual*, 248, para. 7–36.

109 Arrassen, *Conduite des hostilités*, 444. The safety distance would be between 500 and 3,000 metres, depending on the nature and calibre of the munition. The proposed basic principles are: '(1) les attaques lancées contre les objectifs militaires situés à l'intérieur d'une concentration civile au moyen d'armes à fragmentation et à effet de souffle doivent être interdites à moins qu'elles soient menées exclusivement au moyen de systèmes d'armes à tir direct; (2) les attaques lancées contre les autres objectifs militaires au moyen d'armes à fragmentation et à effet de souffle doivent être interdites dans le cas où la distance séparant ledit objectif d'une zone d'habitation ou sur laquelle se trouvent des biens culturels est inférieure aux distances de sécurité fixées par ledit Protocole.'

> precautions are taken with a view to limiting the effects of the attack to the military objective and to avoiding, and in any event to minimizing, incidental loss of civilian life, injury to civilians and damage to civilian objects.[110]

Such a rule would create a presumption against strikes within concentrations of civilians and would, in effect, require that the target be at a certain distance ('clearly separated') from the concentration of civilians. Stringent precautionary obligations would apply to attacks near a concentration of civilians, including that the effects of the attack be limited to the military objective itself. Importantly, the proposal does away with the balancing act required under the rule of proportionality. Rowe's proposition was formulated with a view to the use of 'smart' weapons in populated areas. As concerns about accuracy do not occupy centre-stage in relation to 'smart' weapons, the proposition is of relevance to explosive weapons in populated areas more widely.

Such scholarly writings and certain existing operational practices could be drawn upon to develop stronger, internationally agreed standards on the use of explosive weapons with wide area effects in populated areas.

Harm from explosive weapons: a challenge to the effectiveness of international humanitarian law

The central theme of this book is the question of whether IHL is still 'fit for purpose' in regulating 'modern' warfare. Practices characterising 'modern' warfare are often described as 'radically different' from those prevailing in 1949 or 1977. However, the humanitarian concerns raised by the use of explosive weapons in populated areas are not new. The challenge that such use poses for IHL lies not in its exceptionality or novelty (in contrast to new forms of delivering explosive weapons, such as by drones), but lies in its commonness, familiarity and the 'conventional' nature of the weapons involved. Civilian harm from unconventional, relatively novel weapons, such as dense inert metal explosives (DIMEs) or depleted uranium (DU) projectiles, is often the focus of great public concern and attention, as media coverage of the 2009 conflict in Gaza demonstrated.[111] In contrast, the risks that

110 Rowe, 'Kosovo 1999: The Air Campaign'.

111 'Explosive Violence: Israel and Gaza', Landmine Action Policy Brief, 30 January 2009: www.landmineaction.org/resources/Explosive%20violence%20-%20Israel%20and%20Gaza.pdf (accessed 19 June 2013).

explosive weapons pose to civilians in populated areas seem to have become acceptable.[112] Today, 'the idea of a weapon that kills or injures by blasting pieces of flesh off the victim is generally not considered problematic, because blasting pieces of flesh off people is seen as common in armed conflict'. In spite of an extensive pattern of death and injury to civilians and damage to buildings associated with the use of explosive weapons (particularly those with wide area effects) in populated areas, the technology is considered 'normal' in armed conflict and its use is seen as 'inevitable'.[113]

This 'moral outrage gap'[114] is also reflected in the dominant legal discourse. The serious medical effects caused by blast and fragmentation cannot be easily articulated under IHL since the St Petersburg Declaration formally made them part of 'the necessities of war'. The regulation of explosive weapons under weapon-specific treaty law is fragmentary. Explosive weapons were a central theme of governmental expert discussions in the 1970s, but they are not explicitly recognised as a coherent category in formal legal standards. These discussions informed the elaboration of international legal standards on the use of certain explosive weapons, but only two types of explosive weapons, anti-personnel landmines and cluster munitions, are banned under international treaty law. Whether other treaty-based restrictions on certain explosive weapon types place constraints on their use that go beyond what is mandated by general rules of IHL is an open question. General rules of

[112] Use of 'unconventional' weapons, such as chemical weapons, is often used to draw a political 'red line' and as an indicator that urgent political action is required. As the Syrian situation tragically illustrates, this orientation risks sanctioning other forms of violence that are perceived as 'conventional', and around which a threshold for decisive political action becomes difficult to articulate. In relation to the situation in Syria, see D. MacKenzie, 'Syria has Crossed Chemical Red Line, Says Obama', *New Scientist*, 14 June 2013: www.newscientist.com/article/dn23704-syria-has-crossed-chemical-red-line-says-obama.html#.UcF7QueLDTo (accessed 19 June 2013); R. Perkins, '"New Levels of Brutality" in Syria says New UN Report', AOAV (June 2013): www.aoav.org.uk/2013/new-levels-of-brutality-in-syria-says-new-un-report/ (accessed 17 June 2013). For a general discussion, see R. Moyes, 'State Use of Explosive Weapons: An Indicator of Crisis', Article 36, January 2012: www.article36.org/wp-content/uploads/2012/02/Explosive-weapon-use-as-an-indicator.pdf#www.article36.org/wp-content/uploads/2012/02/Explosive-weapon-use-as-an-indicator.pdf (accessed 17 June 2013).

[113] B. Rappert et al., 'The Roles of Civil Society in the Development of Standards around New Weapons and other Technologies of Warfare', 94 (886) *IRRC* (2012) 773.

[114] R. Boer, B. Schuurman and M. Struyk, *Protecting Civilians from Explosive Violence: Defining the Humanitarian Problem* (Utrecht: IKV Pax Christi, 2011), 6: www.ikvpaxchristi.nl/media/files/protecting-civilians-from-explosive-violence.pdf (accessed 19 June 2013).

IHL do not adequately acknowledge the specific risk that the projection of blast and fragmentation poses to civilians and civilian objects in the particular context of a populated area. Although the notion of 'bombardment' is still present in some legal texts, it has lost legal significance and the same rules on attacks apply to all means and methods of warfare, regardless of the weapon involved and the context of use. The customary prohibition on area bombardment is a formal recognition of the particular humanitarian concerns raised by the use of multiple explosive weapons in populated areas, but the use of 'area weapons' and 'area targeting' in and near populated areas is not subject to special restrictions under IHL.

The pattern of harm associated with the use of explosive weapons in populated areas is a direct challenge to the effectiveness of IHL.[115] Legal scholars and operational law experts frequently state that IHL rules (or 'the laws of war'), are 'informed by the realities of armed conflict', are 'conceptually rooted in operational reality', reflect 'the core logic of military operations' and 'facilitate the ability of belligerents to accomplish military objectives'.[116] These characteristics are believed to be key factors for compliance with the law. Calls for greater constraints on means and methods of combat are often portrayed as upsetting the 'carefully evolved balance' between military necessity and humanitarian restraint. Law which fails to respect this 'delicate balance', the argument goes, 'distorts the prescriptive process' and 'is likely to be, and remain, ineffective'.[117] However, the continuing level of casualties inflicted on civilians raises serious doubts about how humanity and military necessity are being balanced in practice.[118] It is submitted that if IHL is to 'humanise' war and 'impose effective humanitarian limits on the conduct of war', rather than lending 'unwarranted legitimacy to customary

[115] J. Borrie and M. Brehm, 'Enhancing Civilian Protection from Use of Explosive Weapons in Populated Areas: Building a Policy and Research Agenda', 93(883) *International Review of the Red Cross* (2011) 12.

[116] For an example, see Corn and Corn, 'The Law of Operational Targeting', 358; Huffman, 'Margin of Error', 15.

[117] Schmitt, 'Military Necessity', 838; W. H. Boothby, 'The Law of Weaponry – Is It Adequate?', in M. N. Schmitt and J. Pejic (eds), *International Law and Armed Conflict: Exploring the Faultlines* (Leiden: Martinus Nijhoff, 2007), 315.

[118] Rappert et al., 'The Roles of Civil Society', 767; B. Rappert, 'Out of Balance, the UK Government's Efforts to Understand Cluster Munitions and International Humanitarian Law', Landmine Action, 2008: www.landmineaction.org/resources/Out%20of%20Balance.pdf (accessed 19 June 2013).

military practices',[119] its effectiveness depends, above all, on its capacity to protect the victims of war. In the light of evidence showing that the use, in populated areas, of explosive weapons with wide area effects causes extremely high levels of civilian casualties, assertions that the rules on the conduct of hostilities are sufficient risk undermining IHL.

The debate about explosive weapons also points to fundamental questions about the role of IHL in disarmament initiatives driven by humanitarian concerns ('humanitarian disarmament').[120] The international body mandated to 'prohibit or restrict further the use of certain conventional weapons' for humanitarian reasons and in order to promote disarmament is the CCW. States parties to the CCW tend to portray such prohibitions or restrictions as resulting from the application of general rules of IHL to particular types of weapons, whilst striking a balance between humanitarian and military considerations. But IHL rules leave ample room for divergent interpretations. They do not indicate where and how the line of unacceptable harm should be drawn and what exactly, if anything, should be done about it.[121] The inclination towards case-by-case assessments under IHL is perceived by some as being consistently used to argue against the establishment of categorical boundaries.[122] This is one of the reasons why the Convention on Cluster Munitions, like the Mine Ban Treaty before it, were negotiated outside of

[119] C. af Jochnick and R. Normand, 'The Legitimation of Violence: A Critical History of the Laws of War', 35 *Harvard International Law Journal* (1994) 56.

[120] 'Working Together to Advance Humanitarian Disarmament', Humanitarian Disarmament Campaigns Summit, 20–21 October 2012: www.4disarmament.org/2012/10/23/humanitarian-disarmament-campaigns-summit/ (accessed 19 June 2013); A. Moodie and M. Moodie, 'Alternative Narratives for Arms Control Bringing Together Old and New', 17(2) *Nonproliferation Review* (2010); Det Kongelige Utenriksdepartement [Norwegian Ministry of Foreign Affairs], *Norsk Humanitaer Politikk* (2009) 33–4; J. Borrie and V. Martin Randin (eds), *Alternative Approaches in Multilateral Decision Making: Disarmament as Humanitarian Action* (Geneva: United Nations, 2005): www.unidir.org.

[121] For a detailed discussion in relation to cluster munitions, see R. Moyes and B. Rappert, 'Failure to Protect: A Case for the Prohibition of Cluster Munitions', Landmine Action, 2006: www.stopclustermunitions.org/wp/wp-content/uploads/2008/07/failuretoprotect-lma.pdf (accessed 19 June 2013).

[122] Rappert describes how attaching a general pattern of harm to an overarching category of weapons can reframe the debate by directing attention to what is normally deemed conventional and moving away from attending to individual instances of attack, where civilian harm is easily portrayed as the result of isolated instances of misconduct or the unfortunate and unforeseeable consequence of 'the fog of war'. He notes that by recognising explosive weapons as a coherent category 'attention is on *what* is used rather than on *who* acts or necessarily *how*'. B. Rappert, *How to Look Good in a War, Justifying and Challenging State Violence* (London: Pluto Press, 2012), 113–14.

the CCW.[123] Likewise, efforts to mobilise attention to the harm caused by explosive weapons rejected the CCW and IHL as a starting point for discussions. The manner in which most states discharge their obligation under Article 36 of Additional Protocol I adds to the sense of disappointment over IHL's capacity to regulate the technologies of violence. As alternative approaches are being pursued to constrain armed violence, critical evaluation of the role of IHL in weapons regulation seems to be called for.[124]

Conclusion

Data presented in the first section of this chapter demonstrates that the use of explosive weapons in populated areas has a devastating humanitarian impact, with civilians, tragically, making up the overwhelming majority of victims. Explosive weapons that affect a wide area with blast and fragmentation are a particular concern for the protection of civilians in populated areas. Given the extraordinary capacity of explosive weapons to damage public infrastructure and private property, explosive violence also tends to have far-reaching and long-term impacts on communities.

This chapter has argued that IHL fails adequately to articulate the serious risk of harm inherent in the use of explosive weapons in populated areas. Since the St Petersburg Declaration, suffering from explosive weapons, other than exploding bullets, is formally considered part of 'the necessities of war'. Civilian harm from the use of explosive weapons

[123] States parties to the CCW pursued parallel and ultimately unsuccessful negotiations on a protocol that would have placed much more limited restrictions on cluster munitions than the ban imposed by the Convention on Cluster Munitions. Fourth Review Conference of the States Parties, Revised Draft Protocol on Cluster Munitions, 24 November 2011 (UN Doc. CCW/CONF.IV/9/Rev.1).

[124] For a recent articulation of these questions, see Rappert et al., 'The Roles of Civil Society'. Rappert and Moyes point out that recent humanitarian disarmament treaties (like the Convention on Cluster Munitions or the Mine Ban Treaty) prohibit particular explosive weapons 'in all circumstances', which challenges the partitioning of armed violence into 'armed conflict' and other situations upon which the application of IHL is premised (Moyes and Rappert, 'Looking Inwards and Looking Outwards'). It is noteworthy that the first international body formally to raise concerns around autonomous weapon systems ('killer robots') is the UN Human Rights Council and not one of the traditional disarmament or arms control forums. 'UN Human Rights Expert Urges Global Pause in Creation of Robots with "Power to Kill"', UN News Centre, 30 May 2013: www.un.org/apps/news/story.asp?NewsID=45042#.Ub-BfvYY25J (accessed 17 June 2013).

tends to be perceived as common and 'normal' in war. Although 'blast and fragmentation weapons' were identified as one of the principal weapon categories of humanitarian concern in deliberations preceding the adoption of Additional Protocol I and of the CCW, and although a categorical approach to explosive weapons is reflected in the common practice of states, explosive weapons are not formally recognised as a coherent category under international law. Whilst it is increasingly acknowledged that the use, in populated areas, of explosive weapons with wide area effects is highly problematic from a humanitarian standpoint, general rules of IHL governing the conduct of hostilities provide little specific guidance regarding the prevention of civilian harm, aside from the prohibition on 'area bombardment' and the recognition that certain unguided rockets are 'inherently indiscriminate'. IHL rules, as applied in practice, have not proven a strong barrier against the bombing and shelling of cities, towns, villages and other locations containing concentrations of civilians.

In view of its devastating humanitarian impact there is urgent need critically to question the acceptability of the use of explosive weapons in populated areas, and reframe conventional attitudes towards this practice. Stronger international standards, including certain prohibitions and restrictions, could help reduce the humanitarian impact of explosive weapons.[125] Whilst other framings have been proposed,[126] international policymakers have brought up the possibility of further normative development.[127] IHL can play an important role in this regard. Scholarly writings and certain operational practices can serve as a point of reference for the elaboration of stronger international standards on the use of explosive weapons. Movement towards a formal prohibition on the use, in populated areas, of explosive weapons with wide area effects is one possibility.[128] A practical first step in the near term could be a political

[125] 'Preventing Human Suffering from the Use of Explosive Weapons in Populated Areas – The INEW Call', INEW: www.inew.org/about-inew/inew-call-commentary (accessed 19 June 2013).

[126] B. Rappert, *How to Look Good in a War*, 120–1; C. Buhmann, 'The Direct and Indirect Costs of Explosive Violence: Recognition and Documentation Need to Translate into Policy Action and Political Support', 339 *British Medical Journal* (2009) 761; B. Rappert, R. Moyes and I. Lang, 'The Case for Addressing Explosive Weapons: Conflict, Violence and Health', 75 *Social Science & Medicine* (2012) 2047–54.

[127] ICRC, 'Challenges of Contemporary Armed Conflicts', 41; Statement by Ms Juen (Austria) in UN Security Council, 67th year, 6790th meeting, Monday, 25 June 2012, 3 p.m., New York (UN Doc. S/PV.6790) (Resumption 1), 2012, 16.

[128] Brehm, *Protecting Civilians from the Effects of Explosive Weapons*, 159; Clarke, 'Proportionality in Armed Conflicts', 113: 'use of explosive weapons with wide area

declaration by states that recognises the grave humanitarian impact of explosive weapons. The declaration could identify practical measures to prevent and reduce harm to civilians, including efforts by states to review and strengthen national policies and practices and establish a strong presumption against the use of explosive weapons with wide area effects in populated areas.[129]

Over time, as other arms-related contexts indicate, evidence of the grave humanitarian harm caused by the use of explosive weapons in populated areas, and critical questions asked about a practice that appears increasingly incompatible with the humanitarian imperative to protect civilians from the effects of hostilities, will raise doubts in the minds of policymakers and publics about its acceptability.[130] In the future, as one scholar recently put it, 'there may well be no place for artillery in cities'.[131]

effects in populated areas should be avoided – even if the attack is expected to be proportionate'.

129 K. Brown proposes a number of concrete measures that states and other actors can take to improve the protection of children from explosive weapons and prevent grave violations against children: *Explosive Weapons and Grave Violations against Children.*

130 J. Borrie and T. Caughley, 'After Oslo: Humanitarian Perspectives and the Changing Nuclear Weapons Discourse', United Nations Institute for Disarmament Research, 18 June 2013: www.unidir.org/files/publications/pdfs/after-oslo-en-469.pdf (accessed 18 June 2013) with respect to nuclear weapons.

131 Vallentgoed, 'The Last Round?', 39.

12

The International Committee of the Red Cross and the initiative to strengthen legal protection for victims of armed conflicts

MICHAEL MEYER

Introduction

International humanitarian law (IHL), in its current state, continues to provide an appropriate framework for regulating the conduct of parties engaged in armed conflicts.[1] This was the conclusion reached by the

The views expressed in this chapter are those of the author alone and do not necessarily reflect those of the British Red Cross. Special thanks are due to Claire Clement, International Law Adviser, British Red Cross, for her substantive contribution to this article.

I first met Peter Rowe in 1985. The British Red Cross organised a weekend conference at our then training centre, Barnett Hill, near Guildford in Surrey. The aim of the meeting was to raise awareness of the then little known subject of international humanitarian law (IHL) among academics at universities in the UK. This was with a view to encourage teaching in the subject and, if possible, engagement in research. Peter kindly attended and his keen interest in the topic was clear. At the end of the event, he generously offered to help the British Red Cross in its efforts to promote IHL. Since then he has done so on many occasions, not only by supporting activities of the British Red Cross but also those of the International Committee of the Red Cross (ICRC). He has done so as a speaker (including at meetings overseas), as a writer and, on occasions, as an adviser.

Peter has never been content merely to consider the theory of law. He is practical by nature and he has always had a particular interest in the effective implementation of international humanitarian law. In his research, Peter has explored ways in which the law might be developed to improve its implementation, at both the international and the domestic levels. For such reasons, it seemed appropriate, as my contribution to this collection of essays in honour of Peter Rowe, to consider the current efforts being made by the ICRC to strengthen legal protection for the victims of armed conflicts.

[1] 'Strengthening Legal Protection for Victims of Armed Conflicts', 31st International Conference of the Red Cross and Red Crescent, International Humanitarian Law and the Challenges of Contemporary Armed Conflicts – Report (October 2011), 4: www.icrc.org/eng/assets/files/red-cross-crescent-movement/31st-international-conference/31-int-conference-5-1-1-report-strength-ihl-en.pdf.

ICRC following a two-year internal study, initiated in 2008, to assess the ongoing relevance of IHL. An extensive consultation with states on the outcomes of this study largely confirmed the ICRC's conclusions: in particular that, in most cases, the best means of meeting the victims' needs, rather than seeking to create new rules, is to ensure respect for the many that already exist.[2]

Notwithstanding this general positive affirmation, the ICRC study also identified four areas in which further development of the rules of IHL would be warranted.[3] While many of those states consulted recognised that each of these areas gives rise to practical concerns, it was felt that working on all four topics at once was unrealistic. Two areas in particular were highlighted for future focus: (1) strengthening legal protection for persons deprived of their liberty, particularly in situations of non-international armed conflict; and (2) strengthening mechanisms for monitoring compliance with IHL. A resolution adopted at the 31st International Conference of the Red Cross and Red Crescent in late 2011 endorsed a programme of work on these two subjects.[4]

The work to strengthen legal protection for victims of armed conflicts in each of the above-mentioned areas is at a relatively early stage. At this juncture, while specific outcomes are unclear, all options remain open for consideration, including the preparation of soft-law instruments, the identification of best practices and the facilitation of expert processes aimed at clarifying existing rules.[5] This chapter explains the key bodies involved in the initiative, the steps already taken, as well as those planned. It also offers initial comments on the possible outcomes and prospects for success.

[2] *Ibid.*, 5

[3] The four areas identified by the ICRC are as follows: (1) protection for persons deprived of their liberty, especially in situations of non-international armed conflict; (2) international mechanisms for monitoring compliance with IHL and reparation for victims of violations; (3) protection of the natural environment; and (4) protection of internally displaced persons.

[4] Resolution 1 of the 31st International Conference of the Red Cross and Red Crescent, 28 November–1 December 2011, Geneva: www.icrc.org/eng/resources/documents/resolution/31-international-conference-resolution-1-2011.htm.

[5] K. Dörmann, 'Detention in Non-International Armed Conflicts', in K. Watkin and A. J. Norris (eds), *Non-International Armed Conflict in the Twenty-first Century*, International Law Studies, vol. 88 (Newport, RI: US Naval War College, 2012), 359.

Key bodies involved in the initiative: the ICRC, the International Conference of the Red Cross and Red Crescent and the Swiss government

The initiative to strengthen legal protection for victims of armed conflicts has been instigated and led by the ICRC, with cooperation and support from various other bodies. While it is obvious that the responsibility for creating new rules of international law lies with states, the ICRC has a recognised role in supporting any development of IHL (also called the law of armed conflict).[6]

The International Conference of the Red Cross and Red Crescent also has a recognised role in matters of IHL. Meeting every four years, the International Conference is a special forum consisting of delegations from the states parties to the 1949 Geneva Conventions and from Red Cross and Red Crescent organisations (the latter are collectively known as the International Red Cross and Red Crescent Movement).[7] One of its stated functions is to 'contribute to the respect for and development of international humanitarian law and other international conventions of particular interest to the Movement'.[8] In line with this function, the 31st International Conference of the Red Cross and Red Crescent invited the ICRC to pursue further research and discussion aimed at exploring ways to strengthen the application of IHL, in cooperation with states and recognising their primary role in developing IHL.[9]

While all states, by virtue of their membership of the International Conference of the Red Cross and Red Crescent and, perhaps additionally, their involvement in consultations with the ICRC, have had some

[6] The ICRC's special responsibilities in IHL and in situations of armed conflict are enshrined in the 1949 Geneva Conventions and their Additional Protocols. Its role in the development of IHL is recognised in the Statutes of the International Red Cross and Red Crescent Movement (Article 5(2)(g)), as well as in its own Statutes (Article 4(1)(g)). The ICRC contributes to the development of IHL by 'organising, or participating, in consultations on the possibility of adopting new rules; and preparing, or contributing to, draft texts for submission to diplomatic conferences. The ICRC may also organise consultations with a view to clarifying existing rules'. 'Development of International Humanitarian Law', ICRC website: www.icrc.org/eng/what-we-do/other-activities/development-ihl/overview-development-ihl.htm.

[7] The member organisations (called 'components') of the International Red Cross and Red Crescent Movement are the 189 recognised National Red Cross and National Red Crescent Societies and the two Geneva-based bodies: the International Federation of Red Cross and Red Crescent Societies (International Federation) and the ICRC.

[8] Article 10(2), Statutes of the International Red Cross and Red Crescent Movement.

[9] The work on compliance mechanisms is being taken forward as a joint initiative of the Swiss government and the ICRC.

measure of engagement in this initiative, the government of Switzerland has assumed a leading role, in cooperation with the ICRC, in relation to the work on strengthening IHL compliance mechanisms.[10] As the birthplace of modern IHL and the depositary of the Geneva Conventions, Switzerland has a particular interest in IHL matters. Following the adoption of Resolution 1 of the 31st International Conference of the Red Cross and Red Crescent, in early 2012 the Swiss government and the ICRC jointly launched an initiative aimed at facilitating regular engagement between states on the issue of strengthening IHL compliance mechanisms.

Finally, National Red Cross and National Red Crescent Societies, as members of the International Conference and as humanitarian auxiliaries to their respective governments,[11] are encouraged to participate in the work on strengthening legal protection for the victims of armed conflicts. Such participation may include, for example, ensuring that their public authorities and other relevant national stakeholders are well-informed on the progress being made in relation to this initiative and encouraging state engagement on this issue.[12]

Track one: strengthening legal protection for persons deprived of their liberty, particularly in situations of non-international armed conflict

It is generally acknowledged that, while there are a great number of IHL treaty rules applicable to persons deprived of their liberty in international armed

[10] Resolution 1 of the 31st International Conference of the Red Cross and Red Crescent expresses its appreciation to the Swiss government for 'its commitment to explore and identify concrete ways and means to strengthen the application of international humanitarian law and reinforce dialogue on international humanitarian law issues among States and other interested actors, in cooperation with the ICRC'. A joint pledge along these lines, and highlighting compliance mechanisms in particular, was also agreed between the Swiss government and the ICRC at the International Conference.

[11] Each National Red Cross or National Red Crescent Society must be formally recognised by its government as an auxiliary to the public authorities in the humanitarian field. Among other tasks, National Societies support their governments in disseminating and implementing IHL (Article 3, para. 2 of the Statutes of the International Red Cross and Red Crescent Movement).

[12] For example, the British Red Cross promoted work in the area of persons deprived of their liberty in non-international armed conflicts through a seminar run jointly with the Commonwealth Secretariat in February 2013 and aimed at government officials and other relevant national stakeholders. In addition, the British Red Cross has been involved in UK-based efforts to advance work on strengthening IHL compliance mechanisms, including with other organisations such as Chatham House.

conflicts, the number of provisions relevant to such persons in situations of non-international armed conflict are, in contrast, few.[13] This relative paucity of IHL has caused uncertainty over the source and content of the rules governing detention in situations of non-international armed conflict and there is continuing debate regarding the applicability and substance of both customary IHL rules and IHRL.[14] The members of the 31st International Conference of the Red Cross and Red Crescent agreed that a number of humanitarian issues related to persons detained, interned or transferred in non-international armed conflicts require serious attention and highlighted the need for further research, analysis and consultation.[15] Such issues include the need to ensure humane treatment and adequate conditions of detention in such contexts, as well as to implement the requisite procedural and legal safeguards.

During the consultations on the initial, two-year internal study undertaken by the ICRC, states recognised the need to ensure, in particular, better legal protection for persons detained for security reasons during non-international armed conflicts and to have clear guidance to prevent arbitrary detention.[16] Some states also raised matters related to the transfer of detainees between authorities, as well as the specific protection needs of certain categories of persons in detention, such as women, children, the elderly and the disabled.[17]

[13] This is notwithstanding customary rules of IHL relevant to such circumstances, the application of which is not uniformly agreed by all states. The ICRC, in its 2005 Study on Customary International Humanitarian Law, identified a large number of customary rules applicable to persons deprived of their liberty in non-international armed conflicts. See Rules 118–28, in J.-M. Henckaerts and L. Doswald-Beck, *Customary International Humanitarian Law*, vol. 1, *Rules* (Cambridge: Cambridge University Press, 2005). In addition, while the primary focus of the current initiative is on strengthening rules of IHL, it should be mentioned that there is uncertainty as to the applicability of specific rules of international human rights law (IHRL) in such contexts. For further discussion of these issues, see J. Pejic, 'Procedural Principles and Safeguards for Internment/Administrative Detention in Armed Conflict and Other Situations of Violence', 87(858) *International Review of the Red Cross* (2005) 375–91 and Dörmann, 'Detention in Non-International Armed Conflicts'.

[14] 'Update on the ICRC's Work on Strengthening Legal Protection for Victims of Armed Conflicts', ICRC Briefing Note for National Societies, 15 May 2013, 2.

[15] 'Strengthening Legal Protection for Persons deprived of their Liberty in Relation to Non-International Armed Conflict: Regional Consultations 2012–13', Background Paper prepared by the ICRC, 2.

[16] 'Strengthening Legal Protection for Victims of Armed Conflicts – States' Consultations and Way Forward', Statement addressed to the permanent missions in Geneva by Dr J. Kellenberger, President of the ICRC, 12 May 2011: www.icrc.org/eng/resources/documents/statement/ihl-development-statement-2011-05-12.htm.

[17] *Ibid.*

The 31st International Conference of the Red Cross and Red Crescent invited the ICRC to pursue further research, consultation and discussion on this area. Shortly thereafter, the ICRC announced its intention to conduct four regional consultations with governmental experts in late 2012 and 2013 in Africa, Latin America, Europe and Asia, all of which have now taken place.[18] The regional consultations aimed to facilitate discussion on three issues: humanitarian problems related to detention in non-international armed conflicts; the adequacy of the existing international legal framework to address those humanitarian concerns; and the desired outcomes of the process and how it may be achieved.[19] While the consultations were not intended to deliver any final outcomes, they were able to continue the discussions on these matters that had begun at the 31st International Conference.[20] Following their completion, the ICRC reported that states participating in the regional consultations had generally agreed with the topics it had identified as requiring further attention: conditions of detention, vulnerable categories of detainees, transfers of detainees and grounds and procedures for internment.[21] At the time of writing, public reports of each of the consultations are being prepared,[22] as well as a synthesis report and proposed strategy, to be presented to Permanent Missions in Geneva towards the end of 2013.[23]

In order to ensure complementarity, work on this issue is being undertaken with full consideration of other processes on the protection of persons deprived of their liberty.[24] One such recently concluded process, which was raised by states during the initial consultations on this topic, is the Copenhagen Process on the Handling of Detainees in

[18] Representatives from ninety-three states took part in the four regional consultations. The first was held in Pretoria, South Africa, the second in San José, Costa Rica (bringing together experts from Latin America and the Caribbean), the third took place in Montreux, Switzerland (bringing together experts from Europe, the USA, Canada and Israel) and the fourth was held in Kuala Lumpur, Malaysia (bringing together representatives from Asia-Pacific and the Middle East).

[19] 'Strengthening Legal Protection for Persons deprived of their Liberty in Relation to Non-International Armed Conflict: Regional Consultations 2012–13', Background Paper prepared by the ICRC, 2.

[20] *Ibid.*, 3.

[21] 'Update on the ICRC's Work on Strengthening Legal Protection for Victims of Armed Conflicts', ICRC Briefing Note for National Societies, 15 May 2013, 2–3.

[22] The reports of the four public consultations will be made available on the ICRC's website in due course.

[23] 'Update on the ICRC's Work on Strengthening Legal Protection for Victims of Armed Conflicts', ICRC Briefing Note for National Societies, 15 May 2013, 3.

[24] *Ibid.*

International Military Operations.[25] The ICRC, which participated as an observer in the Copenhagen Process meetings, has explained that the present initiative is broader than the Copenhagen Process in that it covers all forms of non-international armed conflict, not only those involving the participation of multinational forces.[26] Furthermore, while the Copenhagen Process involved clarification of existing law in the form of operational guidance, in the ICRC's view the present initiative should also consider whether some of the gaps in the law applicable to persons deprived of their liberty may require, among other solutions, the development of new legally binding rules.[27] A discussion of possible outcomes and prospects for success is included below.

A further separate and ongoing initiative, led by the UN Commission on Crime Prevention and Criminal Justice, aims to review the Standard Minimum Rules for the Treatment of Prisoners, approved in 1957. This text, although not legally binding, sets out good principles and practice for the treatment of 'criminal, civil, untried or convicted' prisoners, including 'persons arrested or imprisoned without charge'.[28] The Standard Minimum Rules, although in need of updating in some areas, are generally regarded as having worked well over time and continue to represent minimum standards applicable to the detention and treatment of prisoners.[29] Unlike the ICRC-led process on strengthening legal protection for persons deprived of their liberty, which is focused specifically upon situations of non-international armed conflict, this initiative is not limited to a particular context.

[25] Launched in 2007, and led by the Danish government, the Copenhagen Process brought together a number of states and interested organisations to examine operational issues in the handling and transfer of detainees in multinational operations. The Process concluded in October 2012 with the adoption of the Copenhagen Process: Principles and Guidelines. The Principles and Guidelines do not seek to create new law, but rather to clarify existing rules. Specifically, they are a set of non-legally binding principles and guidelines on the handling of detainees in internationalised internal armed conflict and in peace operations. For further information about the Copenhagen Process and its outcomes, see B. Oswald and T. Winkler, 'Copenhagen Process Principles and Guidelines on the Handling of Detainees in International Military Operations', 16(39) *ASIL Insights* (2012).

[26] 'Strengthening Legal Protection for Victims of Armed Conflicts', 24.

[27] *Ibid.*

[28] 'Protecting Detainees', ICRC website: www.icrc.org/eng/resources/documents/feature/2012/12-07-detention-law.htm.

[29] Report on the meeting of the Expert Group on the Standard Minimum Rules for the Treatment of Prisoners held in Vienna from 31 January to 2 February 2012, UNODC/CCPCJ/EG.6/2012/1, 16 February 2012, 2: www.unodc.org/documents/justice-and-prison-reform/AGMs/Meetings_Report-E-.pdf.

Track two: strengthening mechanisms for monitoring compliance with international humanitarian law

The second area agreed by states as warranting further discussion and consultation is that of strengthening mechanisms for monitoring compliance with IHL. In its original internal two-year study, the ICRC coupled this topic with an additional area concerning reparations for victims.[30] However, states were generally not supportive of the proposal to examine the matter of reparations further; subsequently, it was not included in Resolution 1 of the 31st International Conference of the Red Cross and Red Crescent.

It has been identified that a central weakness of IHL is its absence of effective means for halting violations of the rules when they occur.[31] It is generally acknowledged that IHL compliance mechanisms are few,[32] limited in scope[33] and have been severely under-used. In contrast, monitoring of, and compliance with, IHRL is overseen by a complex structure of intergovernmental bodies, expert committees, special rapporteurs and specific human rights courts (the last primarily at the regional level).[34] In the absence of effective IHL compliance mechanisms, these human rights bodies appear to be increasingly driven to examine matters of IHL, in addition to their established remits. Such a development carries considerable risks, in terms both of potentially

30 For further discussion as to the ICRC's rationale for inclusion of the topic of reparations for victims, see 'Strengthening Legal Protection for Victims of Armed Conflicts', 13. The legal basis for reparations under IHL is general and confined to international armed conflicts. It gives rise to many issues, including whether reparations may be awarded directly to individual victims or whether it is limited to inter-state relations. Reparations may take different forms, such as financial compensation, restitution and rehabilitation. It is perhaps unsurprising therefore that the topic – although significant – was not considered to be a priority in developing the law.

31 'Strengthening Legal Protection for Victims of Armed Conflicts', 11.

32 Existing compliance mechanisms under IHL include an Enquiry Procedure, a Protecting Power System and an International Humanitarian Fact-Finding Commission.

33 While most modern armed conflicts are non-international in nature, the existing IHL compliance mechanisms apply to international armed conflicts only.

34 Specific international human rights mechanisms include, for example, UN Charter bodies and special procedures, such as the Human Rights Council and the various Special Rapporteurs, and UN treaty bodies, such as the Human Rights Committee and the Committee against Torture, among others. Regional human rights courts and other mechanisms exist in Africa, the Americas, Europe and, most recently, in South East Asia.

reducing the credibility of IHL as a neutral and separate body of law and possibly undermining or weakening both bodies of law.[35]

As mentioned previously, the initiative on strengthening IHL mechanisms of compliance is being led jointly by the Swiss government and the ICRC. In 2012 and 2013, two Meetings of States on Strengthening Compliance with International Humanitarian Law were held in order to take forward work on this issue.[36] In the interim period between these two meetings, Switzerland and the ICRC conducted bilateral and multilateral discussions with a broad range of states in order to gather additional perspectives. The initial Meeting of States and other early discussions focused on, amongst other things, a review of existing IHL compliance mechanisms, the reasons why they did not work and whether some of these are able to be 'resuscitated'.[37] In addition, lessons that may be able to be learned from other bodies of law have been considered. The second Meeting of States examined the possible functions of an IHL compliance system in more depth, including, for example, periodic reporting, fact-finding, early warnings, urgent appeals, non-binding legal opinions and, importantly, a possible format for a regular dialogue on IHL compliance among states.[38]

The potential development of new international law compliance mechanisms carries with it a considerable risk of politicisation, as is apparent from an examination of the international human rights system. Mindful of the need to avoid such an outcome, as well as the desire to

[35] Such human rights bodies, in particular the Human Rights Council, have been criticised for their inherent politicisation as well as their lack of expertise in applying IHL principles and rules (whether such application is explicit or implicit). It has further been argued that, by distorting human rights principles through the use of humanitarian law language (yet not distinguishing between the two), there is a risk of weakening both bodies of law. See C. Droege, 'The Interplay between International Humanitarian Law and International Human Rights Law in Situations of Armed Conflict', 40(2) *Israel Law Review* (2007) 310, 349.

[36] Further information about the work being undertaken on strengthening IHL compliance mechanisms, including relevant documents relating to each of the Meetings of States, may be found at www.eda.admin.ch/IHL2013.

[37] In particular, many states expressed the view that it was worth examining how the International Humanitarian Fact-Finding Commission, established under Article 90 of Additional Protocol I 1977 to the 1949 Geneva Conventions, could be put to better use. In contrast, doubts were raised about the continuing relevance of, and ability to reform, both the Protecting Power System and the Enquiry Procedure. Chair's Conclusions, Second Meeting of States on Strengthening Compliance with International Humanitarian Law, Geneva 17–18 June 2013, 3: www.eda.admin.ch/etc/medialib/downloads/event/ihl136.Par.0008.File.tmp/Chairs'%20Conclusions%20-%20Meeting%2017.-18.06.2013.pdf.

[38] *Ibid.* For a state perspective, see the opening statement of the United Kingdom.

encourage transparency, inclusivity and openness, a framework of principles has been developed to guide the overall process of development. These principles are as follows:

- the need for an IHL compliance system to be effective;
- the importance of avoiding politicisation;
- the state-driven character of the process;
- the avoidance of unnecessary duplication with other compliance systems;
- the requirement to take resource considerations into account.[39]

A further consideration that has been identified in the process is the need for any future IHL compliance mechanisms to be able to address matters relating to situations of non-international armed conflict (and, consequently, the need for such mechanisms to apply to non-state actors, as well as to states themselves). The existing IHL compliance mechanisms apply to international armed conflicts only; this belies the reality that the majority of modern armed conflicts are non-international in nature and, perhaps, provides some explanation as to their non-use. The need to provide appropriate ways to enhance compliance with IHL in non-international armed conflicts by all parties was acknowledged by many states during consultations on this area.[40]

Concerning the next steps planned for the process, a further Meeting of States will be held from 30 June to 1 July 2014. This meeting was preceded by two preparatory meetings held in December 2013 and April 2014, each of which was open to all interested governments.[41] In the interim, the Swiss government and the ICRC plan to develop concrete proposals based upon the results of the consultations already undertaken. In particular, the proposals will focus on the following elements: the form and content of a periodic reporting system on national compliance; the form, content and possible outcome of thematic discussions on IHL issues; the modalities for fact-finding, including possible ways to make use of the International Humanitarian Fact-Finding Commission; and the tasks and features of a regular 'Meeting of States' on IHL compliance matters.[42]

[39] *Ibid.*, 1. [40] *Ibid.*

[41] The background documents and Chairs' Conclusions for each of the preparatory meetings are available at www.icrc.org/eng/what-we-do/other-activities/development-ihl/strengthening-legal-protection-compliance.htm.

[42] In addition, in order to ensure as broad a consultation as possible, interested states have been encouraged to share any proposals, views or comments directly with the Swiss government and/or the ICRC. *Ibid.*, 5.

Possible outcomes and prospects for success

The 31st International Conference of the Red Cross and Red Crescent requested that, after having consulted with states and other relevant actors on the above-mentioned issues, the ICRC identify a range of options and propose recommendations for consideration at the 32nd International Conference, to be held in 2015.[43] As mentioned above, the importance of examining all options, including those of a legally binding and non-binding nature, has been emphasised throughout the process. This being said, at this juncture it would appear that, while the ICRC continues to emphasise the need to consider seriously the development of new laws, where these are appropriate to fill perceived normative gaps, states are somewhat more reticent to pursue potential outcomes of a binding nature (such as new treaty provisions).[44] This would seem to be true of the process on persons deprived of their liberty in non-international armed conflicts, where, although it is perhaps too early to determine a specific outcome, states have generally expressed a preference for an instrument of a non-binding nature.[45]

Regarding the work being undertaken on strengthening IHL compliance mechanisms, general support has been expressed for the creation of a platform for regular exchanges among states on matters of IHL compliance (a 'Meeting of States').[46] Unlike many other international treaties,[47] the 1949 Geneva Conventions and their Additional Protocols do not provide for such a mechanism.[48] Aside from facilitating an

[43] Resolution 1 of the 31st International Conference of the Red Cross and Red Crescent, operative paras 6 and 8.

[44] Dörmann, 'Detention in Non-International Armed Conflicts', 358.

[45] 'Update on the ICRC's Work on Strengthening Legal Protection for Victims of Armed Conflicts', ICRC Briefing Note for National Societies, 15 May 2013, 3.

[46] Chair's Conclusions, Second Meeting of States on Strengthening Compliance with International Humanitarian Law, Geneva, 17–18 June 2013, 11.

[47] Other international treaties often provide for an intergovernmental platform to discuss issues of common concern and to perform tasks related to treaty implementation. These normally take the form of a Conference of States Parties, a Meeting of States Parties, a Meeting or a Conference of High Contracting Parties or an Assembly of States Parties. Additional intergovernmental bodies, such as the Human Rights Council, may be established by a resolution of a relevant body. Chair's Conclusions, Second Meeting of States on Strengthening Compliance with International Humanitarian Law, Geneva, 17–18 June 2013, 11.

[48] 1977 AP I to the 1949 Geneva Conventions does contain a provision permitting the depositary (the Swiss Federal Council) to convene a meeting of the High Contracting Parties to consider general problems relating to the application of the Conventions and the Protocol (Article 7). However, such a meeting must be requested by one or more of

exchange of views on IHL-related matters, the possibility of attaching a reporting mechanism to such a platform has been raised.[49]

Discussions on a potential Meeting of States have also brought up the issue of the relationship of such a mechanism to other IHL-related forums, including the quadrennial International Conference of the Red Cross and Red Crescent, which, as set out above, has a formal role in contributing to respect for and the development of IHL. While it is true that the membership and mandate of the International Conference are broader than those currently envisaged for a Meeting of States, in order to preserve the special function and status of the International Conference it would seem imperative to establish a suitable association or complementarity between the two bodies. For example, it has been suggested that a Meeting of States, if held every one or two years, could submit activity reports to the International Conference.[50]

At a general level, it is perhaps obvious that the prospects for achieving success in this initiative are dependent upon the proper engagement of those who will be primarily responsible for the implementation of any outcomes. This necessitates a full and widespread dialogue with states and, importantly, the encouragement of a sense of ownership by governments in the work being undertaken. In order to be effective, it is vital that any measures proposed are practical in nature and are not viewed by states as overly arduous, thereby lessening their likelihood of being utilised. At this juncture, the ICRC would appear to be making every

the Parties to the Protocol and have the approval of the majority of the High Contracting Parties. The deficiencies are clear, including the fact that some significant states, such as the USA, India, Israel and Pakistan, are not yet Parties to Protocol I. That being said, it does not necessarily follow that the creation of a suitable intergovernmental forum to address matters of IHL compliance would necessitate an addition or amendment to existing treaty law.

49 Chair's Conclusions, Second Meeting of States on Strengthening Compliance with International Humanitarian Law, Geneva, 17–18 June 2013, 11.

50 *Ibid.*, 12. The same concern was raised, and a similar recommendation made, when the 26th International Conference of the Red Cross and Red Crescent (held in Geneva in 1995) endorsed the recommendation that the Depositary of the 1949 Geneva Conventions (Switzerland) organise periodical Meetings of the States Parties to consider general problems regarding the application of IHL. The 26th International Conference recommended that the outcome of these meetings be transmitted to the next International Conference of the Red Cross and Red Crescent, as well as to states party to those Conventions (Resolution 1, operative para. 7). One Periodical Meeting was held 19–23 January 1998. It addressed two topics: respect for, and security of, the personnel of humanitarian organisations and armed conflicts linked to the disintegration of state structures. The Chairman's Report of the First Periodical Meeting is available at www.icrc.org/eng/resources/documents/misc/57jpcn.htm.

effort to encourage the interest of, and engagement by, a broad range of states in the two areas of work. As set out above, multiple consultations and discussions involving governmental experts from all regions have already been held and more such meetings and dialogue are planned in the coming two years.

Conclusion

The continuing relevance of IHL, as the specialised body of international law applicable in situations of armed conflict, has been confirmed both by the ICRC and by a majority of states. However, there is little doubt that, in certain areas, further strengthening of the rules is warranted. The 31st International Conference of the Red Cross and Red Crescent invited the ICRC to pursue research and discussion aimed at exploring ways to strengthen the application of IHL in two such areas: legal protection for persons deprived of their liberty, especially in situations of non-international armed conflict, and mechanisms of IHL compliance. The ICRC has been tasked with carrying out this body of work in cooperation with states in recognition of the Committee's primary role in developing IHL. One state, Switzerland, has taken a particular interest in the work on strengthening IHL compliance mechanisms and is jointly leading on this area with the ICRC.

To date, the initiative has focused on widespread consultations, primarily with governmental experts, in order to understand better the perspective of states on the perceived normative gaps, as well as to discuss and examine possible ways forward. This approach, while time-consuming, is imperative in order to secure ongoing interest and engagement in the process by governments, who will bear the overall responsibility for the implementation of any measures proposed.

While specific outcomes at this early juncture are somewhat unclear, it would seem that, in the area of detention in non-international armed conflict, states are generally in favour of an instrument or document of a non-binding nature. While the reticence to create new rules of IHL is perhaps understandable,[51] it is clear that the ICRC would prefer to leave

[51] In addition to the sensitivity regarding the adoption of treaty rules applicable in non-international armed conflicts, there has been a general trend for states to eschew treaty-making in the area of IHL. It is beyond the scope of this chapter to consider the possible reasons for this, such as the difference in perspectives between Western states and others. It may be that the content of any soft law instrument on persons deprived of their liberty in non-international armed conflicts will ultimately be reflected in states'

open the possibility of developing further such rules, should it prove to be appropriate.

In the area of IHL compliance mechanisms, further discussions will, in part, focus on the feasibility of creating a regular platform for states to discuss matters of IHL compliance. While such a body would, in principle, seem to be a useful means of encouraging greater compliance with IHL, it is important that it operates in a complementary manner to existing forums with a formal role in promoting respect for IHL, in particular the International Conference of the Red Cross and Red Crescent. It is also vital that any proposed new body is, as far as possible, free of politicisation and that it seeks to address issues arising from non-international armed conflicts, in addition to those of an international nature.

States may be more willing to agree to the attachment of a reporting mechanism to this platform if they were convinced that the reporting obligation would not be too onerous.[52] In this regard, it might prove helpful to note that bodies already exist at the national level that could be used to assist governments in the preparation of periodic reports. Such bodies include the National Committees for the Implementation of International Humanitarian Law, established in over 100 countries,[53] and the National Red Cross and Red Crescent Societies, present in 189 states. As detailed above, the latter have an officially recognised role to support the governments of their respective countries in ensuring respect for IHL.[54]

Military Manuals and this will be a way to ensure the development of new customary rules and their implementation.

52 The proposal of a reporting mechanism was also raised at the 26th International Conference of the Red Cross and Red Crescent in 1995 (see n. 50, above) and earlier that same year at the meeting of the Intergovernmental Group of Experts for the Protection of War Victims. On the first occasion, the Dutch government proposed the establishment of a worldwide mandatory reporting system on national implementation of IHL, which did not receive sufficient support among states. Following the 26th International Conference, a small group of European National Red Cross Society legal advisers then produced a report setting out the parameters of a voluntary review procedure (Voluntary Review Procedure on National Implementation of International Humanitarian Law, International Law Committee of the Danish Red Cross, 1998). The proposal was noted by a Movement statutory body, the Council of Delegates, and National Societies were invited to examine the proposal with their respective governments (Council of Delegates 1997, Resolution 4, operative paras 7 and 8: www.icrc.org/eng/resources/documents/resolution/council-delegates-resolution-4-1997.htm). It is interesting to note that the concept of a reporting mechanism, like regular Meetings of States, is now receiving serious attention.

53 Details are available at www.icrc.org/eng/war-and-law/ihl-domestic-law/national-committees/index.jsp.

54 See n. 11, above.

PART III

Responsibility and accountability

13

Corporate criminal responsibility for war crimes and other violations of international humanitarian law: the impact of the business and human rights movement

ALEX BATESMITH

Introduction

Ever since the International Military Tribunal established the principle of individual criminal responsibility for violations of international humanitarian law (IHL), war crimes prosecutors have predominantly targeted senior-ranking individuals within military and government structures. With the notable exception of the post-Second World War trials of German industrialists, prosecutions of corporate officials or employees have been limited. Cases brought against corporations as legal entities have been virtually non-existent.

However, times are changing. The way in which war is fought, furnished and financed is more complicated than ever. The prevalence of so-called 'asymmetrical' warfare and the proliferation of non-state actors are well documented,[1] as is the concomitant need for IHL to adapt to these modern realities. One such development is the increasing focus on business enterprises, particularly those operating in regions affected by armed conflict and instability, and their potential involvement in, or contribution to, human rights abuses and violations of IHL.

As has been acknowledged elsewhere, criminal law has traditionally focused on individual, rather than collective, guilt.[2] Not only has it been difficult for some to conceptualise the moral culpability of companies

[1] See generally, M. Cherif Bassiouni, 'The New Wars and the Crisis of Compliance with the Law of Armed Conflict by Non-State Actors', 98 *Journal of Criminal Law and Criminology* (2008) 711–810.

[2] M. Pieth and R. Ivory, *Corporate Criminal Liability: Emergence, Convergence and Risk, Ius Gentium: Comparative Perspectives on Law and Justice* (Dordrecht: Springer, 2011), 4.

and the nature of any punishment they may receive,[3] there has also been an understandable reluctance to impose on a group what might be seen as collective punishment for the wrongdoing of an individual.[4] However, developments in how and where large corporations do business call for these old attitudes to be revised.

Multinational and transnational corporations (MNCs and TNCs) wield tremendous economic, social and political power.[5] The products they manufacture, the services they provide and the suppliers they use have a direct impact on the regions in which they operate. The potential for businesses to harm, as well as help, has long been highlighted, particularly when companies trade or operate within conflict zones or other challenging environments.[6]

IHL and its younger sibling, international criminal law (ICL), have developed at a dramatic pace over the last seventy years. The negative impact of business involvement in areas of conflict is under the microscope – and victims of such abuses are being emboldened to seek justice, not only against individual businessmen, but also against the corporations as entities in their own right.

There is an increasingly coordinated crescendo of voices demanding greater corporate accountability. Quite apart from the monographs of academics and practitioners,[7] there are now official calls to action. On 15 June 2011, the United Nations Human Rights Council (HRC) took the unprecedented[8] step of unanimously endorsing Special Representative

[3] See, e.g., A. W. Altschuller, 'Two Ways to Think about the Punishment of Corporations,' 46 *American Criminal Law Review* (2009) 1359.

[4] J. Hasnas, 'The Centenary of a Mistake: One Hundred Years of Corporate Criminal Liability,' 46 *American Criminal Law Review* (2009) 1329.

[5] In a recent World Bank report, Shell, Exxon/Mobil and Wal-Mart were listed as the 32nd, 35th and 37th largest economies in the world (significantly bigger than many sovereign countries): Cities and Climate Change: An Urgent Agenda (December 2010), 10.

[6] See, e.g., I. Bannon and P. Collier, *Natural Resources and Violent Conflict: Options and Actions* (Washington, DC: World Bank, 2003); M. Pieth and R. Ivory, *Corporate Criminal Liability*, 4–5.

[7] For example, A. Clapham, 'Extending International Criminal Law beyond the Individual to Corporations and Armed Opposition Groups', 6 *JICJ* (2008) 899–926; E. Duruigbo, 'Corporate Accountability and Liability for International Human Rights Abuses: Recent Changes and Recurring Challenges', 6 *Northwestern Journal of International Human Rights* (2008) 222–61; S. S. Beale, 'A Response to the Critics of Corporate Criminal Liability', 46 *American Criminal Law Review* (2009) 1481; D. Stoitchkova, *Towards Corporate Liability in International Criminal Law*, Intersentia, School of Human Rights Research Series, vol. 38 (2010).

[8] Unprecedented because it was the first time the HRC had endorsed normative guidance on any subject that governments had not put forward: speech of Professor John Ruggie at

John Ruggie's 'Guiding Principles on Business and Human Rights'.[9] The Guiding Principles were designed 'to provide for the first time a global standard for preventing and addressing the risk of adverse impacts on human rights linked to business activity'.[10] Eighteen months later, the HRC organised the first world Forum on Business and Human Rights, held in Geneva. It was feted as the largest-ever global dialogue on the impact of businesses on human rights.[11] These (and other) initiatives have sufficiently coalesced to be a real force in modern global human rights discourse, a force that is only set to grow stronger over the coming decade and one that will certainly influence the thinking of courts dealing with corporate violations of human rights abuses.

The object of this chapter is to analyse the extent to which what might be described as the business and human rights 'movement' is having an impact upon the prosecution of corporations, or their executives and employees, for violations of international law, chiefly IHL or ICL, at both the international and domestic levels. The historical and current legal context will be examined and the revision of attitudes towards corporate prosecutions discussed. It will be demonstrated that the new approach, advocated by proponents of the business and human rights movement, will lead to changes in practice and to the increased likelihood of business actors being held accountable for involvement in international crimes. It is argued that this would better reflect the true culpability for mass crimes committed in modern-day armed conflicts.

A brief history of corporate criminal responsibility for international humanitarian law violations at the international level

The first time in which corporate criminality was addressed in court was directly after the Second World War. Evidence of the central role of business in the Nazi war effort revealed the extent of corporate crimes committed by enterprises, both large and small, through the forcible

the Forum on Business and Human Rights, Geneva, 3 December 2012 (Geneva Forum) (author's own notes).

9 United Nations Doc. A/HRC/17/L.17/Rev.1. The Guiding Principles are available at www.ohchr.org/Documents/Publications/GuidingPrinciplesBusinessHR_EN.pdf.

10 See www.ohchr.org/en/NewsEvents/Pages/DisplayNews.aspx?NewsID=11164 (accessed 16 January 2013).

11 See www.ohchr.org/EN/Issues/Business/Pages/ForumonBusinessandHR2012.aspx (accessed 16 January 2013).

transfer and enslavement of millions of people, the production of arms used to wage aggressive war and the supply of poisonous chemicals for the destruction of civilians in concentration camps.[12] It was unsurprising that the prosecuting Allies were keen to address this dimension of the crimes of the Third Reich. As Robert Jackson wrote in relation to the indictment of the International Military Tribunal (IMT):

> It has at all times been the position of the United States that the great industrialists of Germany were guilty of the crimes charged in this Indictment quite as much as politicians, diplomats, and soldiers.[13]

However, Jackson and his fellow prosecutors were deprived of the prominent focus they had sought to place on business enterprises at the IMT. Judges ruled that Gustav Krupp, head of the giant Krupp arms manufacturing company, would not face trial with the other senior Nazis as his senility rendered him medically unfit.[14]

Subsequent prosecutions, under Control Council Law Number 10,[15] of executives and employees of major German enterprises went some way to reflecting Jackson's views. Whilst not as prominent as the trial of the remaining twenty-two senior Nazis, the cases against executives and employees of I. G. Farben,[16] Flick,[17] Krupp,[18] Roechling[19] and the three defendants accused of knowingly supplying Zyklon B gas for the

[12] J. A. Bush, 'The Prehistory of Corporations and Conspiracy in International Criminal Law: What Nuremberg Really Said', 109 *Colombia Law Review* (2009) 1094, 1105.

[13] Answer of the United States Prosecution to the Motion on Behalf of the Defendant Gustav Krupp von Bohlen, International Military Tribunal Document, 12 November 1945, document available at http://avalon.law.yale.edu/imt/v1-11.asp (accessed 16 January 2013).

[14] For a detailed examination of the history of the trials of German industrialists, see J. A. Bush (n. 12, above); also K. R. Jacobson, 'Doing Business with the Devil: The Challenges of Prosecuting Corporate Officials Whose Business Transactions Facilitate War Crimes and Crimes against Humanity', 56 *Air Force Law Review* (2005) 167.

[15] *Trials of War Criminals before the Nuernberg Military Tribunals under Control Council Law No. 10*, 15 vols (Washington, DC: US GPO, 1949–53) www.loc.gov/rr/frd/Military_Law/NTs_war-criminals.html (accessed 16 January 2013) (*Trials of War Criminals*).

[16] *The United States of America* v. *Carl Krauch et al.*, Military Tribunal VI, 7–8 *Trials of War Criminals* (1948).

[17] *The United States of America* v. *Friedrich Flick et al.*, Military Tribunal IV, 6 *Trials of War Criminals* (1947).

[18] *The United States of America* v. *Alfred Krupp et al.*, Military Tribunal IIIA, 9 *Trials of War Criminals* (1948).

[19] *Commissioner* v. *Hermann Roechling* (Military Tribunal in the French Zone), 14, *Trials of War Criminals* (1948). See also the Ministries Case, *The United States of America* v. *Von Weizsaecker*, XIV, *Trials of War Criminals* (1952), 621–2.

extermination of prisoners in the concentration camps,[20] nevertheless remain relevant as the starting point for any discussion of corporate criminal responsibility.

Although companies were not prosecuted as legal entities *per se* by the Allies after the Second World War, there is evidence that criminal charges against corporations were considered entirely permissible, even if not ultimately used. As has been noted, concepts of corporate and associational criminal liability were seriously explored, but were rejected for political, rather than legal, reasons.[21] Throughout the prosecutions there were significant references to the prominent criminal role that businesses had played, revealing an 'underlying implication' that the corporations, for which the industrialists worked, had also committed violations of IHL.[22]

One scholar has remarked that the significance of these industrialist trials has been somewhat exaggerated, pointing to the fact that many of the defendants were acquitted and initial plans to charge broad conspiracy liability against individual corporate defendants were abandoned after the main judgment of the IMT.[23] But, if nothing else, this initial impetus to prosecute corporate actors still powerfully resonates with those who seek to prevent impunity for business involvement in international crimes.

There was a hiatus of nearly forty-five years before the next international criminal tribunals could revisit the question of corporate criminal responsibility. Even then, the issue was virtually ignored. Discussions on the establishment of the International Criminal Tribunals for the former Yugoslavia and Rwanda rejected the notion of corporate criminal responsibility and the crimes in these regions did not involve businesses

[20] Trial of Bruno Tesch, Karl Weinbacher and Joachim Drosihn, British Military Court, Hamburg 1946 in United Nations War Crimes Commission, *Trials of War Criminals* (1947), 1.

[21] Bush, 'The Prehistory of Corporations and Conspiracy in International Criminal Law', 1239.

[22] A. Ramasastry, 'Corporate Complicity: From Nuremberg to Rangoon – An Examination of Forced Labor Cases and their Impact on the Liability of Multinational Corporations', 20 *Berkeley Journal of International Law* (2002) 105; E. Engle, 'Extraterritorial Corporate Criminal Liability: A Remedy for Human Rights Violations?', 20 *St John's Journal of Legal Commentary* (2006) 291–2; *Business and International Crimes: Assessing the Liability of Business Entities for Grave Violations of International Law*, a project of the International Peace Academy and Fafo, Fafo Report 467 (Oslo: Fafo, 2004), 20 (hereinafter Fafo Assessing Liability).

[23] Bush, 'The Prehistory of Corporations and Conspiracy in International Criminal Law', 1237.

to any great extent.[24] Coincidentally, it was around this time that the United Nations Sub-Commission on the Promotion and Protection of Human Rights published the Draft Norms on business responsibilities towards human rights.[25] However, such ideas were not sufficiently powerful or pervasive enough to have any determining impact upon the question of including corporate entity jurisdiction within the statute of the new permanent International Criminal Court (ICC).

Corporate criminal liability was just one of many difficult issues being debated at the month-long Rome Conference in the summer of 1998. As has been well documented,[26] the French delegation proposed a restricted form of corporate criminal liability, limited to private (rather than public or state) corporations and requiring corporate criminal responsibility to be linked to the individual criminal responsibility of a leading member of a corporation.[27]

[24] United Nations Secretary-General Boutros-Ghali made passing reference to the desirability of criminalising certain juridical persons 'such as an association or organisation' under the Statute of the ICTY, but ultimately rejected this idea in favour of focusing on natural persons; such persons would be subject to the jurisdiction of the International Tribunal irrespective of membership in groups: see Report of the Secretary-General Pursuant to Paragraph 2 of Security Council Resolution 808, para. 51, 3 May 1993 (UN Doc. S/25704). Though note the case of *Prosecutor* v. *Alfred Musema* (International Criminal Tribunal for Rwanda, case number ICTR-96-13), a civilian tea factory manager who exercised legal and financial control over his employees, including the power to appoint or remove them and to prevent or to punish their use of factory equipment that was in fact used in the crimes. He was held responsible for the actions of his employees who participated in the killing of Tutsis, and convicted of genocide.

[25] Draft Norms on the Responsibilities of Transnational Corporations and Other Business Enterprises with Regard to Human Rights, E/CN.4/Sub.2/2003/12 (2003).

[26] See, e.g., K. Haigh, 'Extending the International Criminal Court's Jurisdiction to Corporations: Overcoming Complementarity Concerns', 14 *Australian Journal of Human Rights* (2008) 199–219; J. Kyriakakis 'Corporate Criminal Liability and the ICC Statute: A Comparative Challenge', Monash University Research Paper No. 2009/45; L. Van den Herik, 'Subjecting Corporations to the ICC Regime: Analysing the Legal Counterarguments', in C. Burchard, O. Triffterer and J. Vogel (eds), *The Review Conference and the Future of the International Criminal Court* (Neuwied: Kluwer, 2010), 155–74.

[27] The linked guilty corporate representative must have been in a position of control within the company and must have committed the crimes acting on behalf of, and with the explicit consent of, the corporation in the course of its activities: *Corporate Complicity and Legal Accountability; Report of the International Commission of Jurists Expert Legal Panel on Corporate Complicity in International Crimes,* vol. 2, *Criminal Law and International Crimes* (Geneva: ICJ, 2008) (ICJ Report), 56: www.icj.org/report-of-the-international-commission-of-jurists-expert-legal-panel-on-corporate-complicity-in-international-crimes/.

The French proposal failed, although there are differing opinions as to why. According to one delegate present in Rome,[28] the proposition was rejected for essentially three reasons: first, that it would detract from the focus on individual criminal accountability; second, that it would pose insurmountable evidentiary problems; and third, that, as there was no recognised global standard of corporate responsibility, the concept of complementarity would be unworkable. Others have stated that the negotiators simply ran out of time and, despite having made 'considerable progress'[29] on the concept of corporate criminal responsibility, the focus had to be on concluding the negotiations.

One US court has recently suggested that the failure to agree any form of corporate entity liability is indicative of the absence of a rule of customary international law on the point.[30] This is firmly refuted by Ambassador David Scheffer, who was part of the US delegation at the Rome Conference.[31] Ambassador Scheffer also referred to the more widespread acceptance of corporate criminal liability twelve years on from the Rome Conference, illustrating a trend towards more, rather than less, corporate criminal liability, as shall be discussed below.[32]

In any event, at present the only business actors capable of being prosecuted before the ICC, or other international tribunals, are individual businessmen and women. The ICC's complementarity principle ensures that the primary obligation to investigate and prosecute individuals for international crimes rests upon the domestic authorities with jurisdiction over the alleged offences.[33] Complementarity ensures that states parties to the ICC have an obligation to enact legislation to

[28] See K. Ambos in O. Triffterer (ed.), *Commentary on the Rome Statute* (Baden-Baden: Nomos Verlagsgesellschaft, 1999), Article 25, margin no. 4 discussing the Rome negotiations on corporate liability.

[29] According to W. Schabas: *An Introduction to the International Criminal Court* (Cambridge: Cambridge University Press, 2011), 224–5.

[30] *Kiobel* v. *Royal Dutch Petroleum*, United States Court of Appeals for the Second Circuit, 06-4800-cv, 06-4876-cv, 17 September 2010.

[31] *Kiobel*, On Writ of Certiorari to the United States Court of Appeals for the Second Circuit: Brief of Ambassador David J. Scheffer, Northwestern University School of Law as amicus curiae in support of the petitioners No. 10-1491, 20 December 2011, 5–7 (hereinafter Scheffer amicus).

[32] Scheffer amicus, 16.

[33] See generally, Haigh, 'Extending the International Criminal Court's Jurisdiction to Corporations'.

ensure that the international crimes listed in the Rome Statute can be prosecuted in their domestic criminal justice system.[34] Soon after his inauguration, ICC Prosecutor Luis Moreno Ocampo stated that corporate officials who participate in activities falling under the court's jurisdiction would be subject to prosecution.[35] Ocampo was discussing the conflict in the Democratic Republic of Congo and the part played by companies engaged in the trade of natural resources, the money from which financed rebel or government forces thereby enabling them to continue the fighting. Ocampo's successor, Fatou Bensouda, has also very recently reaffirmed the commitment of the Office of the Prosecutor (OTP) to investigate business institutions responsible for contributing to international crimes. As she put it, conflicts are driven either by financial enrichment or ideology; therefore, a thorough investigation of the finances behind a conflict helps to identify suspects and develop a more complete picture of responsibility.[36]

Although no individual business executives have yet been investigated by the court, such public statements on the connections between business and conflict are another step towards the international criminal liability for corporate actors becoming a reality.[37] For now, however, domestic jurisdictions afford the most likely prospect for corporate accountability, whether against an individual businessman or a business entity in its own right.

[34] In the United Kingdom, the International Criminal Court Act 2001 gives effect to the ICC's statute in UK law; see J Kyriakakis, 'Australian Prosecution of Corporations for International Crimes', 5 *JICJ* (2007) 809–26 for a description of the Australian position.

[35] Reported in J. Podgers, 'Corporations in the Line of Fire', 90 *American Bar Association Journal* (2004) 13.

[36] Fatou Bensouda, giving the keynote address at the Paris Conference on International Corporate Responsibility in Conflict Zones, 21 March 2013, French Ministry of Foreign Affairs (from the author's own notes).

[37] Ocampo cited recent United Nations reports that companies based in twenty-five countries had connections with illegal exports of natural resources, and thus may have funded groups suspected of committing war crimes. See J. Graff, 'Corporate War Criminals and the International Criminal Court: Blood and Profits in the Democratic Republic of Congo', 11 *American University Washington College of Law Human Rights Brief* (2004) 23–6; and the American Non-Governmental Organizations Coalition for the International Criminal Court, *Information Regarding the Potential Liability of Businesspersons for Atrocity Crimes under the Rome Statute*: www.amicc.org/docs/ICCandBusTrans.pdf (accessed 16 January 2013).

Corporate criminal responsibility at the domestic level: jurisdictional issues

There are essentially three potential venues at the domestic level for prosecuting companies or executives alleged to have committed, or been complicit in, international crimes: the 'host' state on whose territory the crimes were committed; the 'home' state in whose territory the executive lives or where the corporation is legally domiciled; or any state exercising universal jurisdiction over the crimes considered to be of concern to the entire international community.

There are some obvious challenges for domestic authorities in 'host' states conducting criminal investigations against foreign businesses or executives. The worst human rights violations are, by definition, committed during armed conflict where the rule of law is severely compromised, if not totally absent. Many wars are fought in countries with a weak police and judicial infrastructure where there is limited physical capacity to undertake even the most basic prosecutions. 'Host' authorities may themselves be involved in the abuses. They may have a vested interest in not investigating or prosecuting foreign companies for fear of jeopardising overseas investment and development.

It can be equally problematic for the 'home' state to investigate and prosecute alleged crimes committed by an executive or a company abroad. Practically speaking, extraterritorial international investigations can be a real headache, even for well-established national authorities. Taking statements from witnesses on the other side of the world, in a challenging environment, an alien culture and using an unfamiliar language is difficult enough. Ensuring adequate protection and support for such witnesses may prove particularly troublesome, particularly where the 'home' authorities are uncooperative or do not have control over certain territory.[38]

However, as various recent studies have shown, it is becoming easier to investigate corporate human rights abuses.[39] With more informed and organised victim groups, the practical difficulties are being overcome

[38] As was discovered in the aborted criminal investigation in Australia against Anvil Mining and the so-called 'Kilwa massacre' in the Democratic Republic of Congo: *Pierre* v. *Anvil Mining Management NL* [2008] SCWA 30.

[39] See, e.g., M. B. Taylor, R. C. Thompson and A. Ramasastry, *Overcoming Obstacles to Justice: Improving Access to Judicial Remedies for Business Involvement in Grave Human Rights Abuses* (Oslo: Fafo, 2010), 21 (hereinafter Fafo Report 2010).

and businesses can no longer be complacent.[40] Equally of importance, jurisdictional difficulties are being sidestepped. States have international treaty obligations to bring those alleged to have committed such crimes to justice within their domestic criminal justice systems[41] and international criminal law is now widely incorporated into domestic penal codes.[42] Even where a country has not ratified the major conventions, the prevailing view is that all states, under the doctrine of universal jurisdiction,[43] are obliged effectively to investigate and prosecute international crimes, regardless of where the crimes took place and irrespective of the nationality of the victim or the accused.[44] In the absence of any connection to the prosecuting state, universal jurisdiction is asserted over 'the most serious crimes of concern to the international community',[45] a contentious, but necessary, weapon in the fight against impunity for such crimes.[46]

The Criminal Justice Act 1988 of England and Wales is a prime example of a specific enactment of universal jurisdiction. Section 134 criminalises the offence of torture, whether committed in the United Kingdom or elsewhere, and has been well used by the prosecuting authorities.[47] Although this provision is often unpopular with the home state of the accused, the Foreign and Commonwealth Office

[40] *Ibid.*

[41] For example, under the Convention on the Punishment and Prevention of Genocide, the Geneva Conventions and their Additional Protocols and the Convention against Torture.

[42] A. Ramasastry and R. S. Thompson, *Commerce, Crime and Conflict: Legal Remedies for Private Sector Liability for Grave Breaches of International Law – A Survey of Sixteen Countries* (Oslo: Fafo, 2006) (hereinafter Fafo Survey 2006).

[43] For a discussion on the merits and drawbacks to universal jurisdiction, see A. Addis, 'Imagining the International Community: The Constitutive Dimension of Universal Jurisdiction', 31 *Human Rights Quarterly* (2009) 129–62.

[44] J. Zerk, 'Extraterritorial Jurisdiction: Lessons for the Business and Human Rights Sphere From Six Regulatory Areas', Working Paper of the Corporate Social Responsibility Initiative, June 2010, Working Paper 59; see also Arrest Warrant Case (*Congo* v. *Belgium*), International Court of Justice, Case No. 121, 14 February 2002.

[45] Preamble, Rome Statute of the International Criminal Court.

[46] For a list of examples of domestic prosecutions using universal jurisdiction, see J. Rikhof, 'Fewer Places to Hide? The Impact of Domestic War Crimes Prosecutions on International Impunity', 20 *Criminal Law Forum* (2009) 1–51.

[47] Most recently in the case against Colonel Kumar Lama on 3 January 2013, who, whilst visiting the UK, was arrested on two counts of torture allegedly committed in Nepal in 2005. See International Justice Resource Centre website: www.ijrcenter.org/2013/01/09/uk-exercises-universal-jurisdiction-to-prosecute-nepalese-colonel-for-torture/ (accessed 15 January 2013).

explains that arrests of foreign nationals on allegations of torture are consistent with UK law 'and the UK's international obligation to uphold human rights as a party to the UN convention against torture'.[48]

In today's modern world of transnational business entities, globalised trade and commercial activity in conflict zones, it is certainly foreseeable that corporate defendants, alleged to be complicit in torture or other international crimes, may find themselves being arrested and investigated under the doctrine of universal jurisdiction. As one commentator puts it:

> [G]lobalisation has posed challenges to the effectiveness of [the] territorially-based system. Increasingly, governments recognise that, in some areas, effective regulation of activities within their territories demands some degree of control over private activities beyond their borders. Moreover, globalising factors – such as international trade and travel, foreign investment, and modern communications technologies – have all greatly increased the potential for overlapping jurisdictional claims.[49]

It cannot yet be said that universal jurisdiction is uniformly applied or accepted, but, given the difficulties in bringing criminal cases against foreign companies in 'host' states, the doctrine will certainly play a part in shaping how they will be held elsewhere.

Domestic recognition and modes of corporate criminal liability

Individual criminal responsibility is one of the most fundamental principles of almost all legal systems.[50] The basis of most corporate criminal liability will therefore be the individual liability of company directors and other staff. As to corporate entity liability, different countries, and different legal systems, deal with the issue of corporate criminal responsibility in different ways. Theoretical arguments on the merits of corporate guilt are outside the remit of this analysis,[51] as is any comparative

[48] *Ibid.* [49] Zerk, 'Extraterritorial Jurisdiction', 5.

[50] 'Rule 102: No one may be convicted of an offence except on the basis of individual criminal responsibility' – International Committee of the Red Cross, Customary International Law Database: www.icrc.org/customary-ihl/eng/docs/home (accessed 17 January 2013).

[51] Pieth and Ivory, *Corporate Criminal Liability*, ch. 1; Hasnas, 'The Centenary of a Mistake'; Albert W. Alschuler, 'Two Ways to Think about the Punishment of Corporations', 46 *American Criminal Law* Review (2009) 1359.

assessment of how the concept of corporate criminality is realised (or not) in different jurisdictions.[52] However, recent studies have found that most countries now permit corporations to be prosecuted for criminal offences.[53] State practice has clearly expanded towards greater, not lesser, corporate accountability.

Similarly, an increasing number of states have incorporated international criminal law into their domestic criminal legislation.[54] Consequently, there is a basis for finding companies liable for international crimes within most domestic legal systems. Whether states choose to act on this legal possibility is another matter entirely. This may depend on political will, but also on other legal issues, such as ensuring that the correct mode of liability can be proved.

The scope of corporate criminal involvement is potentially very broad. The *Red Flags* initiative lists nine principal corporate activities that may attract international criminal liability, including expelling people from their communities, slavery, handling questionable assets, making illicit payments, engaging abusive security forces and allowing the use of company assets for abuses.[55]

Accusations of *direct* commission of international crimes against companies or their executives as principal perpetrators have been rare, but not unheard of. According to a recent study, the four most common forms of direct violations are the use of forced labour (a crime against humanity when part of a widespread or systematic abuse of a civilian population), pillage and plunder, use of child soldiers and use of land-mines (all war crimes).[56]

Over the last twenty years, international courts have developed flexible theories of group liability for holding joint perpetrators criminally responsible as principals. The International Criminal Tribunals for the former

[52] For a discussion of this, see Fafo Assessing Liability; Pieth and Ivory, Corporate Criminal Liability, ch. 1; Kyriakakis, 'Corporate Criminal Liability and the ICC Statute', 340 and n. 36.

[53] Fafo Survey 2006. There are still a number of prominent countries who do not accept corporate criminal responsibility, including Brazil, Bulgaria, Greece, Hungary, Luxemburg, the Slovak Republic, Mexico, Sweden and Ukraine; Germany and Italy have adopted administrative schemes in lieu of criminal liability: Kyriakakis 'Corporate Criminal Liability and the ICC Statute', 342.

[54] See National Prosecution of International Crimes, a comparative initiative of the Max Planck Institute: www.mpicc.de/ww/en/pub/forschung/forschungsarbeit/strafrecht/nationale_strafverfolgung.htm (accessed 15 January 2013).

[55] For the full list, see the Red Flags website: www.redflags.info/ (accessed 15 January 2013).

[56] Fafo Assessing Liability, 18. To this list might also be added direct acts of employees of private military and security companies (PMSCs) that amount to unlawful killing or injuring of civilians or protestors.

Yugoslavia and for Rwanda (ICTY and ICTR respectively) championed three forms of joint criminal enterprise (JCE)[57] and the ICC has developed the notion of co-perpetration under Article 25 of the Rome Statute.[58]

Whilst it is beyond the scope of this chapter to discuss JCE or co-perpetratorship in any detail, the importance of theories of collective liability for corporate accountability for international crimes is clear. As underlined by the International Commission of Jurists in their study 'Corporate Complicity and Legal Accountability', citing the ICTY's Appeals Chamber, crimes under international law are often 'manifestations of collective criminality carried out by individuals pursuing a common criminal design'.[59] Parallels between the complexities of corporate entities and governmental/military structures have already been drawn,[60] but in any event most national jurisdictions, especially in the common law tradition, punish collective criminality through laws proscribing conspiracy.[61]

Overwhelmingly, however, when companies are involved in international crimes it is usually as indirect or accessory participants.[62] For the purposes of this analysis, secondary participation can be divided into two groups: corporate complicity and superior responsibility.

The most relevant[63] aspect of corporate complicity is direct complicity, more commonly known as aiding and abetting.[64] In order for

[57] A. Marston Danner and J. S. Martinez, 'Guilty Associations: Joint Criminal Enterprise, Command Responsibility and the Development of International Criminal Law', 93 *California Law Review* (2005) 75.

[58] See generally, J. D. Ohlin, 'Joint Intentions to Commit International Crimes', 11 *Chicago Journal of International Law* (2011) 721–5.

[59] ICJ Report, 29 citing *Prosecutor* v. *Tadic* (International Criminal Tribunal for the former Yugoslavia, case number IT-94-1), 15 July 1999, paras 188–92 and 226.

[60] See M. J. Kelly, 'Grafting the Command Responsibility Doctrine onto Corporate Criminal Liability for Atrocities', 24 *Emory International Law Review* (2010) 671–96.

[61] ICJ Report, 31–2; R. K. Punja, 'What is the Distinction between Joint Criminal Enterprise as Defined by the ICTY Case Law and Conspiracy in Common Law Jurisdictions?', Memorandum for the Office of the Prosecutor, International Criminal Tribunal for Rwanda, 2003: http://law.case.edu/war-crimes-research-portal/memoranda/JointCriminalEnterprise.pdf (accessed 16 January 2013).

[62] Fafo Assessing Liability, 29.

[63] Commentators also refer to 'beneficial' and 'silent' complicity: the former relating to circumstances when a company benefits from a human rights abuse committed by a third party, the latter where a corporation fails to raise concerns at systematic or continuous human rights abuses with the appropriate authorities, although, given the high standard of proof of criminal *mens rea*, such forms of complicity are more properly to be considered as questions of civil or administrative liability. See Engle, 'Extraterritorial Corporate Criminal Liability', 298; ICJ Report, 19–20.

[64] See also Fafo Survey 2006, 17–22.

an accused to be convicted of aiding and abetting a crime, two elements must be proven (to the requisite standard). First, that s/he has given practical assistance, encouragement or moral support that had a substantial effect on the perpetration of the crime,[65] and secondly, that such a contribution was intentional – although there is some debate as to the extent of this intent. From one perspective, the prosecution are simply required to prove that the accessory had knowledge of the principal's intention to commit the crime.[66] In contrast, Article 25(3)(c) of the Rome Statute requires proof that the accused aided or abetted for the *specific purpose* of facilitating the commission of the crime.[67]

How this apparent divergent standard might be resolved in relation to corporate defendants has been addressed by one commentator, who has suggested that:

> once a corporation is made aware of a likelihood of contributing to a crime committed by a group, then once it accepts that its actions may lead to elements of the crime occurring and it continues to act, it has the requisite mental involvement to give rise to a residual form of corporate complicity in international crimes.[68]

This appears to be a sensible conclusion as corporations are now being more frequently 'made aware' of their contributions to crimes than previously. Through instantaneous social media tools and the mobilisation of vocal online groups, companies that operate in areas where human rights violations are being committed are being subject not only to scrutiny but also to comment and criticism, making it much more difficult for a company plausibly to claim ignorance of a situation.

[65] The International Commission of Jurists argues that the jurisprudence of the ICTY on complicity can be equally applied in the corporate sphere, referring to: *Blagojevic and Jokic* Case no. IT-02-60 (Appeals Chamber), 9 May 2007, para. 127; *Simic* Case no. IT-95-09 (Appeals Chamber), 28 November 2006, para. 85; *Blaskic* Case no. IT-95-14 (Appeals Chamber), 29 July 2004, paras 45–6; *Vasiljevic* Case no. IT-98-32 (Appeals Chamber), 25 February 2004, para. 102; and the ICTR case of *Ntagerura* Case no. ICTR-99-46 (Appeals Chamber), 7 July 2006. See ICJ Report, 18 n. 55.

[66] For a discussion of this, see A. Clapham and S. Jerbi, 'Categories of Corporate Complicity in Human Rights Abuses', 24 *Hastings International and Comparative Law Journal* (2001) 342.

[67] However, the ICJ questions whether this 'notionally higher subjective standard will have a practical effect, given the way in which the state of mind of an aider and abettor is assessed by the courts': see ICJ Report, 22.

[68] A. Clapham 'Extending International Criminal Law beyond the Individual to Corporations and Armed Opposition Groups', 6 *JICJ* (2008) 911.

Superior or command responsibility is another potential tool that corporate actors should be aware of.[69] Characterised by a superior–subordinate hierarchy involving effective exercise of power or control, a superior is responsible for the acts of subordinates if s/he knew, or should have known, that the subordinate had committed, or was about to commit, the acts and that s/he did not take necessary and reasonable measures to prevent the acts or to punish the subordinate. The doctrine appears to be a good fit for holding senior executives responsible for the actions of their subordinates carried out in the name of the company, although the question of how a company could adequately 'punish' for retrospective abuses is yet to be resolved.[70]

The International Commission of Jurists has recommended that superior responsibility might be applicable to companies operating in conflict zones, particularly those hiring 'subordinate' private military or security companies (PMSCs) for whose actions the 'superior' employing company may be held criminally liable.[71] Additionally, the superior responsibility of corporate entities need not be limited to crimes physically committed by subordinate contractors or employees. As the ICJ suggests, complicity liability would also be a feasible mode of liability under which corporations or their executives might be held liable.[72]

As shall now be discussed, the business and human rights movement aims to transform the discussion on responsibility for violations into concrete action, which means encouraging states to enforce their existing domestic laws and to provide an adequate remedy when companies violate human rights.

[69] Kelly, 'Grafting the Command Responsibility Doctrine'.

[70] Note, however, that a higher threshold is required for civilian superior responsibility under the Rome Statute than for military command responsibility: Article 28(b)(i) 'The superior either knew or consciously disregarded information which clearly indicated that the subordinates were committing or about to commit such crimes', as opposed to Article 28(a)(i) '[The] military commander or person either knew or, owing to the circumstances at the time, should have known that the forces were committing or about to commit such crimes.' It is likely that applying superior responsibility to a corporation would require the stricter test under Article 28(b)(i).

[71] ICJ Report, 34. See the comments on PMSCs below.

[72] The International Commission of Jurists suggests the following example: 'if a local manager of private security forces is engaged in assisting in interrogations in a war zone which involve torture, by organising the guarding of interrogation rooms, he or she may be guilty of aiding and abetting torture and his or her superiors could be held responsible as superiors, if the other elements of this offence are made out': ICJ Report, 32.

Changing times and the influence of the business and human rights movement

All legal systems develop in response to changes in society and the priorities and values of those who live in them. Attitudes are influenced by significant events, natural or man-made catastrophe, chaos and disorder. Laws are passed and enforced to define or regulate standards of behaviour, but also to prohibit and punish harmful conduct.

Although aspects of what is today known and practised as corporate social responsibility have existed for many years,[73] a series of recent initiatives have developed into what can be distinctively styled the business and human rights movement. These developments will be briefly examined before considering their impact.

Creating a framework of human rights obligations and responsibilities for business enterprises has proved extremely challenging. The United Nations attempted to negotiate a Draft Code for Transnational Corporations as early as the 1970s and 1980s, but the efforts were deemed too contentious and the initiative was abandoned.[74] In 1999, former UN Secretary-General Kofi Annan launched the Global Compact with the goal of encouraging businesses to comply with ten fundamental principles on human rights, labour, environmental protection and corruption.[75] A large network of Global Compact groups operates in many countries in order to promote more sustainable, principled business. However, membership of the Global Compact is voluntary, and there has been criticism that monitoring and enforcement mechanisms are weak or non-existent,[76] or that the principles are somewhat basic and too generic.[77]

The next attempt to regulate the actions of business enterprises came in 2003 when experts in a United Nations human rights subcommittee drafted a set of guidelines for businesses on their human

[73] See generally, M. Blowfield and A. Murray, *Corporate Responsibility: A Critical Introduction* (Oxford: Oxford University Press, 2008).

[74] See American Society of International Law, *ASIL Insights* (1 August 2011), available at www.asil.org/insights/volume/15/issue/21/human-rights-council-endorses-%E2%80%9Cguiding-principles%E2%80%9D-corporations (hereinafter *ASIL Insights*, 2011), citing S. D. Murphy, 'Taking Multinational Codes of Conduct to the Next Level', 43 *Columbia Journal of Transnational Law* (2005) 403–5.

[75] See www.unglobalcompact.org/index.html.

[76] See, e.g., Global Compact Critics, a project of the Centre for Research on Multinational Corporations: www.globalcompactcritics.net (accessed 13 January 2013).

[77] See *ASIL Insights*, 2011.

rights responsibilities, otherwise known as the Draft Norms.[78] Although these again proved too controversial for agreement, the Human Rights Commission requested the UN Secretary-General in 2005 to appoint a Special Representative for Business and Human Rights to examine the issue of business and human rights more systematically. Harvard Professor John Ruggie was eventually selected for the role with a mandate to clarify the existing standards and elaborate on the role of states in regulating businesses.[79]

In 2008, Professor Ruggie submitted his 'Framework for Business and Human Rights' to the United Nations.[80] The Framework is based upon the 'Protect–Respect–Remedy' formula: the duty of every state to protect their citizens against human rights abuses, including those perpetrated by third parties, such as corporations; the responsibility of businesses to respect human rights; and the obligation to provide a more effective remedy for human rights abuses. This was later amplified by the publication and endorsement by the Human Rights Council of Ruggie's 31 detailed 'Guiding Principles' that, together with the accompanying commentary, explains how states and corporate entities should implement the Framework.[81]

There is little doubt that business enterprises have an obligation to respect IHL. The Guiding Principles specifically exhort business enterprises as well as states to respect the standards of IHL during armed conflict.[82] Similar comments were made during the Geneva Forum on Business and Human Rights in December 2012.[83] Earlier initiatives, such as the International Committee of the Red Cross's 2006 publication 'Business and International Humanitarian Law', state that business enterprises are indeed bound by IHL when their activities are 'closely

78 Sub-Commission on the Promotion and Protection of Human Rights (UN Doc. E/CN.4/Sub.2/2003/12/Rev.2) (2003).

79 'Secretary-General Appoints John Ruggie of United States Special Representative on Issue of Human Rights, Transnational Corporations, Other Business Enterprises', UN press release, 28 July 2005: www.un.org/News/Press/docs/2005/sga934.doc.htm (accessed 16 January 2013).

80 United Nations Human Rights Council, 7 April 2008, Doc. A/HRC/8/5.

81 For the full text of the Guiding Principles and accompanying commentary, see Guiding Principles on Business and Human Rights: Implementing the United Nations 'Protect, Respect, Remedy' Framework: www.ohchr.org/Documents/Publications/GuidingPrinciplesBusinessHR_EN.pdf (accessed 16 January 2013). Human Rights Council Resolution endorsing the Guiding Principles, 6 July 2011, Doc. A/HRC/RES/17/4.

82 See, e.g., the commentary to Guiding Principles 7 and 12: www.ohchr.org/Documents/Publications/GuidingPrinciplesBusinessHR_EN.pdf.

83 Author's own notes, Geneva Forum.

linked' to an armed conflict.[84] Moreover, as Professor Ruggie has himself identified, the worst business-related human rights abuses take place in conflict-affected areas and other situations of widespread violence,[85] hence the need not only for vigilance, but also for insistence on the application of the law.

In the first eighteen months since the Framework and Guiding Principles were unanimously endorsed by the United Nations in July 2011, the wider reaction to them has been extremely positive. Where previous efforts to regulate or codify business responsibility for human rights have foundered, Professor Ruggie's six years of exhaustive research and development appear to have created a lasting and tangible 'normative framework'.[86] Widely heralded as groundbreaking,[87] Ruggie's work is being endorsed by a fast-growing number of states, businesses and civil society groups.[88] The fact that such diverse stakeholders finally appear to be agreeing is a triumph, evincing, as one commentator has put it, an ethos 'to co-opt rather than to coerce' states and businesses into taking action.[89]

Although not without their critics,[90] the Framework and Guiding Principles are credible because of the growing appreciation of the impact of business enterprises on the communities with and through whom they trade, as well as of the need for increased corporate responsibility and accountability. They should also be seen as good for business too. Assuming that companies do not want to be complicit in serious human rights abuses, the Guiding Principles assist businesses to appreciate the

[84] *Business and International Humanitarian Law*, International Committee of the Red Cross, 30 November 2006, 13.

[85] 27 May 2011 (UN Doc. A/HRC/17/32).

[86] M. Martin, The Guiding Principles on Human Rights and Business – Implementation in Conflict-Affected Countries, Background Paper prepared for the Civil Society Dialogue Network, 29 October 2012.

[87] Interview with John Ruggie, *Business Ethics*, 30 October 2011: http://business-ethics.com/2011/10/30/8127-un-principles-on-business-and-human-rights-interview-with-john-ruggie/.

[88] See, e.g., the discussion by Sherman (n. 132, below) examining the broad adoption of the GPs 'by governments, companies, investors, international standard-setting organisations, and in the advocacy of civil society' (6).

[89] Martin, The Guiding Principles on Human Rights and Business', 6.

[90] See, e.g., P. Simons, 'International Law's Invisible Hand and the Future of Corporate Accountability for Violations of Human Rights', 3 *Journal of Human Rights and the Environment* (2012) 5–43 (arguing that the GPs and Ruggie's mission was misconceived, the root cause of the problem instead being the fundamentally flawed nature of the international legal system, which she argues 'protects and facilitates corporate activity' – instead, Ruggie's goal should have been to seek a binding international human rights mechanism for companies with regard to human rights standards).

boundaries of acceptable trade and the risks. Compliance will result in an enhanced reputation, shareholder confidence and commercial advantage over competitors.

The impact of the Guiding Principles has been magnified by several converging factors. First, the globalisation and liberalisation of trade and markets that have extended the reach of large corporations, which, combined with dramatic improvements in technology, have ensured that companies can operate in areas that have historically been off-limits but are still largely unregulated, unstable and unpoliced. Second, the communication revolution, which has enabled even the poorest, most isolated victims to publicise their plight globally. With the rise of the Internet and social media websites, victim groups can build powerful campaigns to expose corporate abuses. Third, a number of high-profile cases have been brought against business entities, both in civil and criminal jurisdictions, as shall be discussed later. Fourth, businesses – or at least some of them – are demonstrating a greater desire to trade more responsibly.[91]

There is a real possibility that, just as IHL developed exponentially in response to the conflicts of the 1990s, the development of corporate criminal responsibility will be shaped by changing attitudes towards greater accountability of people and institutions in civic and commercial life and by the increasing calls for an effective remedy where the obligations to protect and respect human rights are violated. As an illustration of the momentum being generated by the business and human rights movement, the Geneva Forum on Business and Human Rights in December 2012 attracted nearly a thousand delegates from eighty-five countries.[92] Every sector was represented, from senior politicians, through to indigenous groups, labour movements and large mining companies.

Professor Ruggie's Framework and Principles is one of the latest initiatives in a recent series of recommendations and guidelines for businesses.[93] Whilst not having the binding force of an international

[91] Whether this may be due to a moral imperative to trade responsibly or to a purely commercial appreciation is outside the scope of this chapter – but there is some evidence for the latter. See (on a related issue) A. Carroll and K. Shabana, 'The Business Case for Corporate Social Responsibility: A Review of Concepts, Research and Practice', *International Journal of Management Reviews* (2010) 85–105.

[92] Author's note of the Opening Session at the Geneva Forum.

[93] See also The Voluntary Principles on Security and Human Rights, 2000 www.voluntaryprinciples.org/files/voluntary_principles_english.pdf; Organisation for Economic Cooperation and Development (OECD), Guidelines for Multinational Enterprises,

convention, these efforts provide evidence of state practice that may evolve into customary international law,[94] as well as giving guidance to domestic courts attempting to interpret principles of both criminal and civil liability, as shall be examined below. It is still relatively early to predict, but the signs are that the debates emanating from the business and human rights movement will have a considerable impact on criminal prosecutions, particularly in light of a number of well-publicised recent cases.

Recent examples of corporate liability at the domestic level

On 23 December 2005, the District Court of The Hague in the Netherlands found Dutch businessman Frans van Anraat guilty of complicity in war crimes for providing Saddam Hussein's regime in Iraq with chemical components that were used in the gas attacks on the Kurds in 1988, in which tens of thousands of civilians were killed or maimed. The court held that van Anraat's chemical deliveries directly facilitated the attacks, although he was acquitted of a charge of complicity in genocide as the court was not satisfied that he knew the specific genocidal intent of the regime. He was eventually ordered to serve a sentence of sixteen and a half years for his crimes.[95]

Guus van Kouwenhoven was also tried by The Hague District Court on allegations of complicity in war crimes, sanctions violations and arms trafficking relating to his business dealings in timber and arms with the former Liberian President Charles Taylor. Specifically, it was alleged that he facilitated the importation of arms to Taylor in violation of UN sanctions and that the militias he hired for his timber companies massacred civilians. He was acquitted of war crimes but convicted of sanctions violation and sentenced to eight years. This conviction was reversed on

25 May 2011: www.oecd.org; International Organisation for Standardisation (ISO), Guidance on Social Responsibility, ISO 26000, September 2010: www.iso.org/iso/iso26000; the Revised International Finance Committee Sustainability Framework and Performance Standards, 1 January 2012: www1.ifc.org/wps/wcm/connect/topics_ext_content/ifc_external_corporate_site/ifc+sustainability+framework/2012+edition/2012-edition#PerformanceStandards (all accessed 16 January 2013).

94 See K. Magraw, 'Universally Liable? Corporate Complicity Liability under the Principle of Universal Jurisdiction', 18 *Minnesota Journal of International Law* (2009) 483–5.

95 For the original Dutch judgments and their English translations (District Court, Court of Appeal and Supreme Court), as well as the failed attempt to have the convictions quashed at the European Court of Human Rights, see the Asser Institute website: www.asser.nl/default.aspx?site_id=36&level1=15248&level2=&level3=&textid=40025 (accessed 13 January 2013).

appeal, but the Dutch Supreme Court quashed the acquittal in 2010. His retrial is ongoing.[96]

Both cases centred on theories of indirect perpetration as a mechanism to establish criminal responsibility. The Dutch Supreme Court upheld van Anraat's conviction for being an accessory to war crimes.[97] It found that the accused knew that the chemicals he was supplying to the Hussein regime were being used for the production of poisonous gas and, in the context of a longstanding war in which this gas was being used in the attacks, van Anraat's conduct constituted 'deliberate contribution' to the offences. In other words, he was found to have provided the opportunity and the means for the gas attacks.[98]

In 2011 and 2012, separate criminal complaints were filed before a Paris court alleging that French businesses were complicit in human rights violations committed in Libya and Syria. In the Libyan case, it was alleged, first, that the company provided communication surveillance equipment to the Gaddafi regime, which was then used to intercept private communications, and secondly, that the company assisted in developing and monitoring a surveillance network that the authorities used to identify opponents of the regime, whom the government then detained and tortured.[99] In the Syrian case, a second French enterprise was accused of supplying surveillance equipment to the Bashar El-Assad government, which allowed the government to monitor, target, arrest and torture dissidents and to suppress the opposition.[100] Both complaints have led to the opening of official criminal investigations against the two French companies.[101]

[96] For the original Dutch judgments and a selection of their English translations (District Court, Court of Appeal and Supreme Court), see the Asser Institute website: www.asser.nl/default.aspx?site_id=36&level1=15248&level2=&level3=&textid=39902 (accessed 13 January 2013). Van Kouwenhoven denies any wrongdoing.

[97] See the Asser Institute website.

[98] See para. 12.5, Judgment of the Court of Appeal, The Hague, 9 May 2007: www.asser.nl/default.aspx?site_id=36&level1=15248&level2=&level3=&textid=40025 (accessed 13 January 2013).

[99] For a summary of the criminal complaint against the operations of the Amesys corporation in Libya, see the Business and Human Rights Resource Centre website at http://business-humanrights.org/Categories/Lawlawsuits/Lawsuitsregulatoryaction/LawsuitsSelectedcases/AmesyslawsuitreLibya (accessed 16 January 2013).

[100] For a summary of the criminal complaint against the operations of the Qosmos corporation in Syria, see the Business and Human Rights Resource Centre website at http://business-humanrights.org/Categories/Lawlawsuits/Lawsuitsregulatoryaction/LawsuitsSelectedcases/QosmoslawsuitreSyria (accessed 16 January 2013).

[101] The Paris prosecutor opened investigations against Amesys on 21 May 2012 and against Qosmos on 26 June 2012. Both corporations have denied any wrongdoing,

The third group of cases concerns the investigation of corporate criminal acts in the civil courts through actions for damages for tortious liability. The most celebrated of these cases have been brought under the Alien Tort Statute (ATS) in the USA. The ATS gives US federal courts jurisdiction over 'any civil action by an alien for tort only, committed in violation of the law of nations or a treaty of the United States'.[102] Survivors of human rights abuses committed anywhere in the world have invoked the ATS to seek redress in the form of compensation from those responsible, whether the perpetrators are individuals or corporations, whenever the perpetrators are present in the USA.[103] Although the most recent Supreme Court opinion in the case of *Kiobel* v. *Royal Dutch Petroleum Company*[104] has considerably limited the application of the Statute, class action trial lawyers are continuing to push cases of alleged corporate complicity in human rights violations overseas. *Kiobel* has narrowed, but also focused, the requirements for any successful claim for extraterritorial torts and victims will no doubt redouble their efforts to hold companies accountable, whether in the USA or elsewhere.[105]

Some have suggested that these cases demonstrate how 'home' states are seeking to influence the overseas behaviour of companies domiciled within their borders.[106] A more accurate view is to see ATS litigation as a

and the cases are ongoing as at the date of writing. See the Business and Human Rights Resource Centre website (n. 100, above). As of January 2013, the Paris Cour d'Appel had ordered the investigation into Amesys to proceed, and five Libyan torture victims had been granted civil party status in the case.

102 28 United States Code of Federal Laws, para. 1350. See Magraw, 'Universally Liable?', 469–70.

103 See Clapham 'Extending International Criminal Law', 904–7; Business and Human Rights Resource Centre: www.business-humanrights.org/LegalPortal/Home/Countrywherelawsuitfiled/Americas (accessed 18 January 2013); and Fafo Assessing Liability, 24–8 and 30–2 for a discussion of cases brought under the ATS.

104 According to the United States Supreme Court in *Kiobel* v. *Royal Dutch Petroleum Company*, a claim will fail under the ATS unless it sufficiently 'touches and concerns' the territory of the US. However, the Court left open the possibility that where the allegations relate to 'serious violations of international law principles' or where the defendant's conduct 'substantially and adversely affects an important American national interest' there may be an actionable claim: 17 April 2013, No. 10-1491, available at www.supremecourt.gov/opinions/12pdf/10-1491_l6gn.pdf (accessed 10 July 2013).

105 See, e.g., Commentary: Door Still Open for Human Rights Claims after Kiobel, Supreme Court of the United States blog, 17 April 2013, K. Redford: www.scotusblog.com/2013/04/commentary-door-still-open-for-human-rights-claims-after-kiobel/ (accessed 10 July 2013).

106 See Ramasastry, 'Corporate Complicity: From Nuremberg to Rangoon', 92.

clear example of how properly mobilised victim groups can seek justice and compensation for extraterritorial acts. In certain respects, civil litigation holds a number of advantages for victims of international crimes seeking redress: establishing a tortious act requires a lower burden of proof; victims do not have to wait for the decision of a state prosecutor for the case to commence; and proving both liability and causation in a tortious suit may well be easier than attributing criminal liability and causation.[107]

All these cases are extremely significant, as they demonstrate a willingness to apply universal legal principles to investigate and punish egregious international crimes. As the Red Flags initiative puts it,

> As new international standards are incorporated into national laws, and as courts take a more expansive view of legal responsibility, the web of liability is expanding.[108]

The proliferation of such litigation and the development of the business and human rights movement have a symbiotic relationship: the growth of one stimulates the growth of the other and contributes to the prevailing climate that corporate impunity for involvement in serious human rights abuses can no longer be tolerated.

Towards greater accountability: new responsibilities for business enterprises

Professor Andrew Clapham, writing in 2008, said that it was imaginable that the jurisdiction of the international criminal tribunals could be expanded to include corporations, arguing that the exclusion of non-natural persons can be seen as 'the consequence of a rule of procedure rather than the inevitable result of application of international criminal law'.[109] Five years on, the only international tribunal with a worldwide mandate taking on new cases is the ICC and, whilst it does not appear likely that there will be an imminent expansion of its jurisdiction to include corporate entities, despite much vocal support in academic circles,[110] the concept of corporate criminal responsibility is becoming

107 For a discussion of these issues, see Fafo Assessing Liability, 24.
108 Red Flags website: www.redflags.info/.
109 Clapham, 'Extending International Criminal Law', 902.
110 Haigh, 'Extending the International Criminal Court's Jurisdiction to Corporations', 199–219; Kyriakakis, 'Corporate Criminal Liability and the ICC Statute'; Van den Herik, 'Subjecting Corporations to the ICC Regime', 155–74.

reality. Business enterprises and executives that become involved in human rights abuses or are complicit in international crimes are now being vigorously pursued in domestic jurisdictions.

As has been emphasised, the greatest risks of corporate criminal liability for international crimes occur in war zones and areas where violence is widespread.[111] In such unstable regions, companies are being warned to exercise particular vigilance. Even if 'host' states do not respect the rule of law within their borders, it is now entirely possible for the 'home' state to assert extraterritorial jurisdiction and, where the abuses are so egregious, universal jurisdiction may be asserted by any state willing to hear the case. Victims of human rights abuses now have more choice and greater chances of successfully pursuing their claims against companies.

Rather than *ex post facto* attempts to remedy abuses once they have occurred, the business and human rights movement has trained the focus on preventing the violations in the first place. This means ensuring that states should establish policies and pass legislation clearly to set out expectations on businesses operating or domiciled in their territory or jurisdiction with regard to respecting human rights.[112] The Guiding Principles also stress the importance of the state's early engagement with businesses operating in conflict-affected areas to provide guidance and support in identifying and mitigating potential human rights risks.[113] Finally, where abuses occur despite the efforts to educate, inform and regulate, it is incumbent upon states to ensure that victims have access to an appropriate and effective remedy.[114]

Equally, business enterprises themselves, 'regardless of their size, sector, operational context, ownership and structure',[115] are expected to conform, across their entire operations, to the new global standards of required conduct with regards to respecting human rights. More specifically, according to these expected standards companies have a responsibility not only to avoid causing or contributing to adverse human rights impacts themselves, and to address them when they

[111] See also S. Tripathi, 'Business in Armed Conflict Zones: How to Avoid Complicity and Comply with International Standards', 50 *Politorbis* (2010) 131.

[112] See the 'foundational principles' 1 and 2 of the Guiding Principles on Business and Human Rights (n. 81, above).

[113] Principle 7, Guiding Principles, *ibid.*

[114] See generally, Principle 25, Guiding Principles. An 'appropriate' remedy includes both judicial and non-judicial mechanisms – see Principles 26–31, *ibid.*

[115] Principle 14, Guiding Principles, *ibid.*

occur, but also to take steps to prevent or mitigate negative impacts that are 'directly linked' to their operations, products or services by their business relationships *even if they have not contributed to such impacts themselves.*[116] This would mean, in practice, that businesses would, to a certain extent, be responsible for the actions of their suppliers.

This has been of recent interest in relation to conflict minerals, especially from the DRC.[117] In 2010, the United States Congress passed the Dodd–Frank Act, which directed the US Securities and Exchange Commission to issue rules requiring certain companies to disclose their use of conflict minerals if those minerals are 'necessary to the functionality or production of a product' manufactured by those companies. Those rules were issued in August 2012 with the clear underlying purpose 'to further the humanitarian goal of ending the extremely violent conflict in the DRC, which has been partially financed by the exploitation and trade of conflict minerals originating in the DRC'.These rules require companies to file detailed reports disclosing the provenance and use of certain specified materials.[118] Although the application of the rules has been subject to some criticism and their future effectiveness remains to be seen,[119] they are indicative of the general trend for greater corporate accountability.

Another recent series of standard-setting initiatives, relative to the conduct of third-party suppliers, has been in the area of PMSCs, which are increasingly being employed to protect business assets in conflict-affected or other unstable regions. The status of PMSCs has been the subject of much debate and issues surrounding their control and accountability are still far from clear.[120] However, as the ICRC explained:

[116] Principle 13, Guiding Principles, *ibid.*

[117] Section 1502(e)(4) of the Dodd–Frank Act defines conflict minerals as '(A) columbite-tantalite, also known as coltan (the metal ore from which tantalum is extracted); cassiterite (the metal ore from which tin is extracted); gold; wolframite (the metal ore from which tungsten is extracted); or their derivatives; or (B) any other mineral or its derivatives determined by the Secretary of State to be financing conflict in the Democratic Republic of the Congo or an adjoining country'.

[118] Rules available online at www.sec.gov/rules/final/2012/34-67716.pdf (accessed 16 January 2013).

[119] See, e.g., Louise Bennetts, 'Dodd-Frank: Discretion in an Age of Uncertainty,' *Jurist* (2013): http://jurist.org/hotline/2013/01/louise-bennetts-dodd-frank.php (accessed 16 January 2013).

[120] For discussion, see O. Quirico, 'War Contexts: The Criminal Responsibility of Private Security Personnel', Academy of European Law, EUI Working Paper 2010; C. Lehnardt, 'Individual Liability of Private Military Personnel Under International Criminal Law', 19 *EJIL* (2008) 1015–34.

> Business enterprises that hire security or military forces who do not respect the rules of IHL while engaged in armed conflict may, under certain circumstances, be legally liable for assisting the commission of violations of IHL, even if they did not intend the violations to occur and if the offences were not perpetrated on their behalf.[121]

Wider issues of corporate accountability are neatly encapsulated in the debate on liability for the criminal or negligent acts of PMSC employees.[122] Initiatives, such as the 2008 Montreux Document on Pertinent International Legal Obligations and Good Practices for States Related to Operations of Private Military and Security Companies During Armed Conflict[123] and the 2010 International Code of Conduct for Private Security Service Providers,[124] set out voluntary best practices whilst reminding states and PMSCs that they should respect international law and human rights respectively.[125] Indeed, the 2010 Code specifically references Ruggie's Protect–Respect–Remedy Framework and the need for all companies to act with due diligence in relation to human rights. Although it is well argued that such voluntary self-regulation will primarily cover responsible PMSCs, rather than the worst offenders,[126] the ever-growing number of signatories to the scheme[127] is evidence that this is an industry standard in the making.

Ignorance and inaction will no longer be a defence for companies found to have been complicit in abuses, even those committed by third-party trading partners and suppliers. Although industry codes of conduct and other international commercial guidelines will be useful, as the Red Flags initiative pointedly explains, this may not be sufficient to ensure that companies avoid criminal liability.[128]

Corporations are now expected to ensure that they identify and mitigate, or eliminate, any risks that their commercial activities or

121 ICRC, Business and IHL, 19; see also IHL and Private Military/Security Companies, ICRC: www.icrc.org/eng/resources/documents/faq/pmsc-faq-150908.htm (accessed 15 January 2013).

122 See N. D. White, 'Due Diligence Obligations of Conduct: Developing a Responsibility Regime for PMSCs', 31 *Criminal Justice Ethics* (2012) 233–61.

123 The 2008 Montreux Document is available at www.icrc.org/eng/assets/files/other/icrc_002_0996.pdf (accessed 15 January 2013).

124 For the Code, see www.icoc-psp.org (accessed 10 July 2013).

125 See also the Voluntary Principles on Security and Human Rights (2000): www.voluntaryprinciples.org/files/voluntary_principles_english.pdf (accessed 10 July 2013).

126 White, 'Due Diligence Obligations of Conduct', 24.

127 As of 1 June 2013, 659 companies had signed up to the Code.

128 Red Flags website: www.redflags.info/.

business relationships will cause, or contribute towards, human rights abuses. The Guiding Principles require businesses to gauge these risks through a process that draws on both internal and independent external human rights expertise, as well as meaningful consultation with potentially affected stakeholder groups.[129] As the field of IHL and complicity in international crimes is almost certain to be outside the experience of a company's corporate social responsibility department, businesses would be well advised in future to ensure that they are properly advised and adequately prepared on all relevant issues of IHL and human rights.

Conclusion

As one of the diplomats at the Rome Statute has recently underlined:

> Rather than witnessing a retreat from corporate liability in international practice since 1998, there has been a marked progression towards adoption of corporate criminal liability among nations joining the International Criminal Court.[130]

As demonstrated above, there has been a notable increase in the number of domestic prosecutions and civil suits asserting extraterritorial jurisdiction over commercial activities actions that constitute or contribute towards human rights abuses. Although victims often face overwhelming practical and financial problems, as well as legal difficulties in proving their case in an unfamiliar overseas jurisdiction, the opportunities for companies to engage in abusive business practices with impunity are shrinking; gradually the obstacles to securing justice are being overcome.[131] It is no surprise, therefore, to see high-profile cases being brought in established jurisdictions against multinationals, many of them mining companies with operations in developing countries troubled by armed conflict and other serious violence.

The initiatives of the business and human rights movement, in particular the UN's Guiding Principles and the Protect–Respect–Remedy Framework, have created a paradigm shift in the field of corporate conduct. Previous difficulties in negotiating a specific treaty on business responsibility towards human rights are now virtually irrelevant. As Professor Ruggie has amply demonstrated, not only do mechanisms already exist to hold corporate entities accountable (particularly in the

129 Principle 18, Guiding Principles on Business and Human Rights (n. 81, above).

130 Scheffer, Kiobel amicus, 19.

131 Fafo Report 2010.

domestic sphere), it is becoming increasingly accepted, both by states and companies alike, that respecting human rights issues must be properly considered as part of standard business practice and everyday corporate compliance.

Such an emerging global consensus will inevitably find its way into judicial, legislative and administrative decisions, as well as into enforceable legal instruments.[132] More importantly, as one academic has recently argued, holding corporations criminally liable for involvement in genocide, crimes against humanity and war crimes is not only consistent with the broader goals of international criminal law, it is also reflective of transnational economics in the twenty-first century.[133]

Given the momentum currently being generated by the business and human rights movement, it is plausible that the ICC may soon revisit the question of corporate criminal complicity. In the meantime, businesses – particularly those operating in conflict zones – would do well to be vigilant. It is only a matter of time before victims bring a successful criminal case in a domestic jurisdiction against a high-profile company accused of complicity in international crimes.

[132] For more discussion on this, see J. F. Sherman III, Professional Responsibility of Lawyers under the Guiding Principles, Shift Project website available at www.shiftproject.org (accessed 16 January 2013).

[133] Stoitchkova, *Towards Corporate Liability in International Criminal Law*, 190.

14

The trial of prisoners of war by military courts in modern armed conflicts

PETER ROWE

Introduction

One important role for the Geneva Conventions 1949, and of subsequent relevant treaties, is to provide a framework of judicial (and disciplinary) procedures to be followed in the event of an international armed conflict in which prisoners of war (POWs) are detained. This chapter will consider one of these, namely, the trial by the detaining state of a POW. It will show that action may now be required by states to comply with their obligations under international humanitarian law (IHL), even if their actual participation in an international armed conflict is perceived to be highly unlikely and the possibility of acting as a detaining state of POWs even less likely. Such a bold claim is not made lightly.

The urgency of action on the part of states stems from the obligation, under Geneva Convention III 1949, to ensure that POWs are tried by 'the same courts according to the same procedure as in the case of members of the armed forces of the Detaining Power'.[1] The court envisaged is a military court and the Convention goes on to provide that such a court must 'offer the essential guarantees of independence and impartiality as generally recognised'.[2] If a state is unable to provide an independent and impartial military court to try members of its own armed forces, it will fail to comply with its obligations under Geneva Convention III 1949 should it be faced with the need to try a prisoner of war for a crime committed before, or after, capture.

On becoming parties to the Geneva Conventions 1949 it is unlikely that states considered the relevance of the form in which their own military courts operate in peacetime. However, this is the effect of their ratification or accession, apart from any obligations they will owe under

[1] Article 102 GC III 1949. [2] Article 84.

an applicable human rights treaty to ensure that their courts or tribunals are independent and impartial.[3] No state would wish to admit that, should the situation arise, it would be unable to comply with its obligations under Geneva Convention III. Nevertheless, it may have to do so unless it can provide an independent and impartial military court for members of its own armed forces, before any international armed conflict, in which it is involved, takes place.[4]

This chapter will consider how a military court could comply with the requirements of Geneva Convention III, should it be called upon to try a POW, and the consequences of failing to do so. It will also address the relationship between IHL and international human rights law in this context.

The context

The Hague Regulations 1907 established the principle that POWs were to be subject to the laws 'in force in the army' of the detaining state.[5] This was continued by the Geneva Convention 1929 with the addition that sentences for penal[6] offences were only to be imposed 'by the same tribunals and in accordance with the same procedures as in the case of persons belonging to the armed forces of the detaining power'.[7]

The 1929 Convention was interpreted as only applying penal procedures against POWs for an offence committed after capture. For war, or other, crimes committed prior to capture, the effect was that a POW could be tried by a court different in character from those provided for members of the armed forces of the detaining state.[8] By Geneva Convention III 1949 a POW could also be tried by the detaining state

[3] In addition, they will have an obligation under the International Covenant on Civil and Political Rights 1966 (ICCPR) to ensure that their courts or tribunals are 'competent'.

[4] The effect of Article 102 GC III is that it will be difficult for a state to make the required changes whilst it is engaged in an armed conflict.

[5] Article 8, Regulations Respecting the Laws and Customs of War on Land, Annexed to Hague Convention IV, 1907.

[6] The term 'penal' is to be compared with disciplinary offences.

[7] Article 63 Geneva Convention Relative to the Treatment of Prisoners of War 1929. See, e.g., the *Argus* (Melbourne), 14 September 1942, 2, which reported on the trial of a POW for the offence of causing actual bodily harm to a fellow POW following a 'quarrel in a mess hut'.

[8] See *Johnson* v. *Eisentrager* 339 US 763 (1950); N. Boister and R. Cryer, *The Tokyo International Military Tribunal: A Reappraisal* (Oxford: Oxford University Press, 2008), 45–6.

for crimes committed prior to capture.[9] Although this change in the law spawned a number of reservations,[10] it could have a significant effect on the use of trials of POWs by the detaining state as a means of holding an individual to account, against whom charges of a violation of IHL[11] could be brought. The option of transferring a POW to the International Criminal Court (ICC) for trial is closed as that Court is not a party to the Geneva Conventions.[12] Even if it were possible to do so, the Rome Statute 1998 contains a 'gravity threshold' so as to reserve only the most serious breaches for the attention of the Court.[13]

In considering whether a detaining state could place a POW on trial for a crime committed prior to capture, a preliminary issue will be whether it actually possesses jurisdiction, under its national law, to do so. This is less likely to be a problem if the alleged crime is committed on the territory of the detaining state than it would if that state is engaged in an armed conflict abroad, or where it accepts the transfer of a POW captured outside its territory. Even if this hurdle is successfully surmounted, it will face severe difficulties in attempting to prove genocide or crimes against humanity against the type of individuals normally taken as POWs, most of whom will be low- or middle-ranking members of the armed forces. The detaining state is unlikely to be in a position to investigate a series of alleged incidents against an individual. It has been shown that the detaining state cannot transfer him to the ICC. A POW can be confined awaiting trial for a maximum of three months, even if this occurs after all other POWs have been released and repatriated by the detaining state, providing that the criminal proceedings were pending at that time.[14] This is, in reality, too short a period in which to investigate allegations of genocide or crimes against humanity, although it might suffice for a war crimes charge. The most likely event is that the POW will be released and it will be then for another state (or the ICC) to try to assume jurisdiction over the alleged offences and secure his presence in the appropriate forum for trial.

9 Article 85.

10 On the basis that those convicted under the 'principles of the Nuremberg trials of war crimes [or] crimes against humanity' should not be treated as POWs. A number of states objected to these reservations.

11 Or, indeed, any criminal offence and not merely a grave breach of any of the Geneva Conventions 1949.

12 Article 12 GC III.

13 Article 17(1)(d) Rome Statute of the International Criminal Court (1998).

14 Articles 103 and 119 respectively GC III.

Although there is no limitation in Geneva Convention III that 'acts committed prior to capture'[15] must relate to the armed conflict itself, it is likely to be only in the very rare case that a detaining state will wish to put such an individual on trial as a POW for a crime unrelated to the conflict. In any event, to do so it will need sufficient evidence to begin judicial proceedings and to prove the case against him beyond reasonable doubt.[16] Since one or more states may possess jurisdiction to try an individual who has subsequently become a POW for a crime allegedly committed in his home state or, indeed, elsewhere, it may be more effective to transfer him to an appropriate state.[17] Compared with the case of a POW who is alleged to have committed a war crime on the territory of the detaining state prior to capture, there is likely to be little public interest in it taking on the responsibility of trying a POW for a crime, perhaps unrelated to the conflict, he has committed in another state.

The issues discussed in this chapter relate only to those who are entitled to POW status. Where this status is in doubt the detaining state is required to refer the matter to a 'competent tribunal' to make a determination.[18] Until this is done a person is entitled to POW status and will be able to take the benefit of Geneva Convention III, with all its trial provisions. To avoid the need to establish these tribunals retrospectively, all states will need to have such a procedure in place or, in a case where it seeks to prosecute someone whom it detains, refer this matter to the trial court as a preliminary issue.[19]

The obligation on a state requires these Article 5 tribunals to be 'competent'.[20] They will not involve the trial of a person claiming POW status, but the determination they make will be extremely important to him,

[15] Article 85. [16] See discussion below relating to fair trial rights.

[17] Examples include the case of Capt. Aztiz, an Argentine POW during the Falklands conflict 1982, requested by France, Sweden and General Noriega in 1983. For a detailed legal analysis of the Astiz case, see M. Meyer, 'Liability of Prisoners of War for Offences Committed Prior to Capture: The Astiz Affair', 32 *ICLQ* (1983) 948.

[18] Article 5 GC III. For the workings of such tribunals, see G. Risius, 'Prisoners of War in the United Kingdom', in P. Rowe (ed.), *The Gulf War 1990–91 in International and English Law* (London: Routledge, 1993), 295–7; Article 45 AP I 1977.

[19] For examples, see *The Public Prosecutor* v. *Oie Hee Koi* [1968] 2 WLR 715; *Osman bin Mohamed Ali* v. *The Public Prosecutor* [1969] 1 AC 430.

[20] A requirement that the tribunal be 'competent' suggests that it has been established by the law of the detaining state and that it has, at least, access to independent legal advice given that it may be composed solely of military personnel. The notion of a 'tribunal' also implies that it is independent and impartial, without this phrase being specifically mentioned in Article 5 GC III. It need not be a military tribunal; see J. S. Pictet (ed.), *Commentary on Geneva Convention III* (Geneva: ICRC, 1960) 77.

should he subsequently be placed on trial for acts committed prior to, or after, capture. In short, if it is determined that he is not entitled to POW status the trial procedures to be found in Geneva Convention III will not apply to him.[21] Even if it is determined that he is entitled to POW status it is possible, should he subsequently be placed on trial as a POW, that the trial court would decide that the earlier decision was wrong and that he cannot rely on Geneva Convention III.

An Article 5 tribunal could also decide that a particular civilian is entitled to POW status. Thus, authorised employees of defence contractors may be captured alongside the military personnel with whom they are working, for example, on weapons systems.[22] Should such an individual commit a crime after capture[23] he could face a trial before a military court since Articles 82–108 do not distinguish between different categories of POW. Any lack of concern in 1949 about civilians being tried by a military court does not reflect the current position held by some human rights bodies, although they have not been called upon to determine the issue involving POWs.[24]

There have recently been calls for a more flexible approach as to entitlement to POW status, so as to include non-state actors taking an active part in hostilities and who are subsequently captured.[25] Whilst the treatment of a POW in captivity is likely to be considerably better than that of a civilian detainee, the effect would be to make these civilians subject to a military court for offences committed prior to, or subsequent to, capture. Indeed, since they would not belong to the armed forces of a

[21] He will be able to take any trial benefits offered to him by GC IV 1949 if he is of a different nationality from, or owes no allegiance to, the detaining state and by Article 75 AP I (or customary international law).

[22] Article 4 GC III. See D. Turns, 'Cyber Warfare and the Notion of Participation in Hostilities', 17 *JCSL* (2012) 292.

[23] He could, in theory, also be a secondary party to a crime against humanity or a war crime committed before capture. An example would be if he agreed with senior military personnel to alter the program of an air-delivered bomb so as to prevent its guidance system from operating, with the effect that, on release, it indiscriminately killed a large number of civilians.

[24] See, e.g., the Inter-American Commission Report on Terrorism and Human Rights, OEA/Ser.1/V/II.116, 22 October 2002, para. 256, which accepts that POWs could be tried by military court. For concern expressed about civilians being tried by a military court, see n. 27, below.

[25] Although there is no suggestion in International Committee of the Red Cross (ICRC), 'Interpretive Guidance on the Notion of Direct Participation in Hostilities under International Humanitarian Law', 90 *IRRC* (2008) 991 that civilians taking a direct part in hostilities would be entitled to POW status if captured.

state party to the conflict they would not be entitled to the 'combatant's immunity'[26] for crimes committed prior to capture. These offences could, as a result, be tried by a military court of the detaining state[27] or, possibly, by a civilian court.

Trial by a military court

Geneva Convention III makes it clear that a POW is to be tried by a military court, unless the existing laws of the detaining state permit a civilian court to try a member of its armed forces for the same offence.[28] Individual states may give their military courts exclusive jurisdiction over all criminal offences committed by members of its armed forces, or concurrent jurisdiction with the civilian courts or give exclusive jurisdiction to the civilian courts. Whatever the arrangement between the military and the civilian courts of a state existing at the outbreak of any international armed conflict it will apply to POWs, who are subsequently detained by it, whether on capture or on subsequent transfer from another state.

It should not be thought that a military court comes in a standard shape or size. Its structure is likely to vary from one state to another.

[26] Had the accused in both *The Public Prosecutor* v. *Oie Hee Koi* [1968] 2 WLR 715 and *Osman bin Mohamed Ali* v. *The Public Prosecutor* [1969] 1 AC 430 been entitled to POW status they could not have been tried for a breach of the national law committed prior to capture.

[27] In *Martin* v. *United Kingdom*, Application No. 40426/98, Judgment, 24 October 2006, the European Court of Human Rights (ECtHR) stressed that 'the power of military criminal justice should not extend to civilians unless there are compelling reasons justifying such a situation, and if so only on a clear and foreseeable legal basis [. . .] the existence of such reasons must be substantiated in each specific case': para. 44. For suggestions that civilians should never be tried by a military court, see Report submitted by Emmanuel Decaux, *Administration of Justice through Military Tribunals*, E/CN.4/200658, 13 January 2006, Principle 5; UN Basic Principles on the Independence of the Judiciary, 1985, Principle 5; Report on Terrorism and Human Rights, Inter-American Commission on Human Rights, OEA/Ser.L/V/II.116, Doc.5 rev.1 corr., 22 October 2002, para. 232 (although it recognised that 'certain human rights bodies have found that in exceptional circumstances military tribunals or special courts might be used to try civilians, but only where the minimum protections of due process are granted); Human Rights Committee General Comment 32, Article 14, CCPR/C/GC/32 (2007); L. Doswald-Beck, *Human Rights in Times of Conflict and Terrorism* (Oxford: Oxford University Press, 2011), 340. See also Human Rights Watch, 'Righting Military Injustice: Addressing Uganda's Unlawful Prosecution of Civilians in Military Courts', available at: www.hrw.org/reports/2011/07/26/righting-military-injustice (accessed 2 January 2013).

[28] Article 84 GC III.

Some will be comprised of military officers only, whilst others will involve officers and non-commissioned officer(s) and one or more civilians. Some will have, as part of their membership, a civilian or military judge(s). Where a military court comprises of a judge and military members[29] it is more likely that the role of the latter will be restricted to the determination of guilt or innocence and the sentence, with the judge giving a binding direction on the applicable law.

In the same way that military courts vary amongst states, so will the composition of civilian courts. Some will provide one or more judges acting without any lay assistance, whilst others will be comprised of various combinations of judges and lay members. In this context, trial by civilian courts will not necessarily be preferable, in terms of providing a fair trial for a POW, since the involvement of lay members in deciding guilt or innocence may bring its own problems during the course of an armed conflict.[30]

Whether a POW is tried before a military or a civilian court, that court must 'offer the essential guarantees of independence and impartiality as generally recognised'.[31] In 1948, the Universal Declaration of Human Rights had used the term 'independent and impartial tribunal'[32] and so, perhaps, it was a precedent that the Geneva Conventions wished to set as a suitable benchmark for a military court to try POWs. Article 84 of Geneva Convention III referred to these terms being interpreted as 'generally recognised'. The parties to the Convention cannot have intended that they must be interpreted as they were understood in 1949. What constitutes an independent and impartial court must move with the times and be interpreted in the light of modern conditions, influenced through interpretation of the term by human rights bodies.

Attaining the standard of an independent and impartial court can be much more difficult for a military than for a civilian court, largely

[29] The term 'military member' is used in order to draw a distinction between a judge (either civilian or military) and non-legally qualified members. The ECtHR has indicated that 'the participation of lay judges [*sic*] on tribunals is not, as such, contrary to Article 6: the principles established in the case-law concerning independence and impartiality are to be applied to lay judges as to professional judges': *Cooper* v. *United Kingdom*, Application No. 48843/99, Judgment, 16 December 2003, para. 123. The terms 'lay' and 'professional' judges as used by the Court do not distinguish, as many common law countries do, between the separate roles in a trial performed by each.

[30] It was one of the main reasons for the establishment of trial by judge alone for crimes involving a terrorist element during the 'Troubles' in Northern Ireland from the 1970s (the so-called 'Diplock courts').

[31] Article 84 GC III. [32] Article 10.

because the accused and most (if not all) of the court will be members of the armed forces, with its unique hierarchical rank structure. A military (like a civilian) court must possess the required qualities of independence and impartiality, but the perception that it does so may be more difficult to establish. There can be no scope, therefore, for even the perception of command influence or interference, in its various forms, over a military court or over the investigation process. The ECtHR has been particularly active in considering the independence and impartiality of military courts. In a line of cases stretching from *Findlay* v. *United Kingdom* in 1997[33] the Court has stressed the need to ensure that the military members of a court martial are free from appraisal of their court decisions, for the purposes of pay levels or promotion, by someone higher in the chain of command than themselves. Their independence is relatively easy to establish where the military court is presided over by a civilian judge,[34] from whom the military members can be guided as to the appropriate law and sentence, where those members are required to take an oath to act independently and where there can be no review with a view to altering or varying the decision of the court by the military authorities.[35]

[33] Application No. 22107/93, Judgment, 25 February 1997. A significant number of 'look-alike' cases followed *Findlay*. See, in particular, *Cooper* v. *United Kingdom*, Application No. 48843/99, Judgment, 16 December 2003, para. 104 (stressing the manner of appointment of members of the court, their terms of office and the existence of guarantees against outside pressures); *Grieves* v. *United Kingdom*, Application No. 57067/00, Judgment, 16 December 2003. See also S. Joseph, J. Schultz and M. Castan, *The International Covenant on Civil and Political Rights, Cases, Materials and Commentary*, 2nd edn (Oxford: Oxford University Press, 2004), 406–8; L. Burgorgue-Larsen and A. De Torres, *The Inter-American Court of Human Rights, Case Law and Commentary* (Oxford: Oxford University Press, 2011), para. 25.17.

[34] Cf. two cases decided by the Grand Chamber in which judgment was given on the same day: *Cooper* v. *United Kingdom* (civilian Judge Advocate) with *Grieves* v. *United Kingdom* (naval legally qualified officer as Judge Advocate) paras 78, 89. It is suggested that *Grieves* does not decide that a legally qualified military officer could never be a judge (in the sense of giving binding legal directions to the other members of the military court). Rather, where such a person performed this role it would be much more difficult to establish the necessary guarantee of independence.

[35] In *Findlay* v. *United Kingdom*, the Court stressed that the ability of a non-judicial authority to alter the decision of a court went to the very notion of 'tribunal and can also be seen as a component of "independence" required by Article 6 para. 1': para. 77. However, in *Cooper* v. *United Kingdom* the Court was of the view that a non-judicial authority could review the finding of a military court, providing that the final decision was made by a court: paras 131, 133. Cf. the view of L. Doswald-Beck, *Human Rights in Times of Conflict and Terrorism* (Oxford: Oxford University Press, 2011), 339–40. The reviewing authority referred to in *Cooper* was abolished by the Armed Forces Act 2011.

Similar, but not identical, issues will arise where the military court is employed to try a POW for a crime committed prior to, or after, capture. There are, of course, marked differences between a soldier being tried by a military court established for his own armed forces and a POW being tried by that same court. The requirements of independence and impartiality of a military court relate to the relationship between its members and the military chain of command (or other organs of the executive of the state) to which they are subject and not towards the accused, who, by the very nature of being a POW, is not a member of the same armed forces. Relevant questions would include whether the members of the military court are independent of the chain of command in charge of the POW camp and whether those military commanders could alter, in any way, the judgment or sentence of the military court.

A summary trial of a POW will give rise to its own difficulties. This form of trial is quite common in the armed forces of many states and will vary, in format and jurisdiction, from state to state. Essentially, it is very unlikely that such a trial could be considered to be independent and impartial, although an appeal hearing from such a court may be. It is, however, the trial stage which must, according to Article 84, be held before an independent and impartial court. Although an accused may be able to waive this right under a particular international human rights treaty,[36] he will not be able to do so under Geneva Convention III.[37] The effect of this will be that the state may try its own soldiers by some form of summary trial involving a criminal offence, or which may impose a 'criminal-type' punishment,[38] but it will not be able to do so in respect of a POW.

Whether a trial of a POW is held before a military court or by way of a summary trial, difficulties for the detaining state will arise if either form of trial would not be considered to be 'independent and impartial'. An alternative forum for the trial will only be available in the detaining state if its national law permits members of its own armed forces to be tried by civilian courts in these circumstances. This is, however, unlikely always to be the case. In order to comply with Article 84 the detaining state may

36 The difficulties of doing so in practice are outlined in *Bell* v. *United Kingdom*, Application No. 41534/98, Judgment, 16 April 2007, paras 47, 48, 50.

37 Article 7 GC III.

38 *Engel and Others* v. *The Netherlands*, Application No. 5100/71, Judgment, 8 June 1976, para. 82.

have no option but to forego the opportunity of placing a POW on trial for a crime committed prior to, or after, capture.[39]

It is likely that the view taken by the ECtHR of military courts trying criminal offences would be accepted as the 'generally recognised' interpretation of the requirement that the military court must be independent and impartial.[40] It is not necessary to decide whether international human rights law becomes the *lex specialis*[41] as Article 84 Geneva Convention III contains within it all that is necessary to enable a proper understanding of its requirements.

Not only must the court be independent and impartial from the chain of command; so also must the investigation into an alleged offence committed by a POW. Many of the problems faced in this area, by bodies such as the police[42] and the armed forces,[43] will not arise where the accused is a POW as the investigation will not generally involve the armed forces members of the detaining state investigating the actions of their colleagues.

Geneva Convention III does not provide any mechanism whereby a state could determine whether, should it become a detaining state in the event of an international armed conflict, its military court is able to offer the 'essential guarantees of independence and impartiality', the necessary conditions precedent to an ability to place a POW on trial before this type of court. It is unlikely that a state would consider this issue in peacetime in the absence of a challenge brought by one or more members of its armed forces before a human rights court or body. To date, the number of instances where this has occurred is extremely small. The vast majority of states will assume (perhaps wrongly) that their military

[39] Even if the court trying a POW is the same as for a member of the armed forces of the detaining state, Article 102 GC III requires that 'the provisions of the present Chapter have been observed'. This would include the requirement that the court offers 'the essential guarantees of independence and impartiality' (Article 84).

[40] See n. 33, above. See also *Civil Liberties Organisation and Others* v. *Nigeria*, African Commission on Human and Peoples' Rights, Communication No. 218/98 (1998), which relied upon the ECtHR.

[41] *The Legality of the Threat or Use of Nuclear Weapons* (Advisory Opinion of 8 July 1996), ICJ Reports 1996, 226, para. 25. Both IHL and international human rights law could apply, *Case Concerning Armed Activities on the Territory of the Congo*, ICJ Reports 2005, 168, para. 216.

[42] See, e.g., *Ramsahai* v. *The Netherlands*, Application No. 52391/99, Judgment, 15 May 2007, paras 294–6.

[43] *Al-Skeini* v. *United Kingdom*, Application No. 55721/07, Judgment 7 July 2011, paras 167, 172–4; *R. (on the Application of Mousa)* v. *Secretary of State for Defence* [2011] EWCA Civ. 1334, para. 37.

courts will be adequate for the purpose laid down for them by Geneva Convention III.

In an attempt to provide some external surveillance of the trial process, Geneva Convention III imposes upon the protecting power[44] obligations where the detaining state intends to place a POW on trial. These involve the duty to notify the protecting power before the trial commences, failing which it must be adjourned,[45] and to permit that power to be present at the trial.[46] Following from this, it must be the case that the protecting power has an implied obligation to ensure that the military court, before which a POW is to be tried (along with the investigation preceding it), are conducted by independent and impartial bodies. Should it be believed that this is not the case, it will be for the protecting power to draw this to the attention of the detaining state.

Since a number of military courts may currently lack these required qualities of independence and impartiality, the protecting power has a significant responsibility to ensure the protection of a POW from an unfair and irregular trial.[47] It may have to undertake a considerable degree of research into the nature of the military court structure of the detaining state. Even if it does this, which is, perhaps, a counsel of perfection, there may be disagreement over whether a particular process involved in the trial is such as to deprive that court of the qualities required. Should a defect be found and accepted by the detaining state, it will be constrained in its ability to make an alteration to the procedure of its military court. Geneva Convention III requires a POW to be tried by the same procedure (as well as by the same court) as its own armed forces. Strictly, it cannot make a retrospective change unless that change is to apply concurrently to its own armed forces. Since the trial of a POW must be 'regular',[48] any change to the procedure of the military court should only be brought about through the constitutional processes of the detaining state.

The detaining state could take the view that communications from the protecting power of this type exceed its powers under Geneva

44 Or a substitute protecting power (such as the ICRC), Article 5(4), AP I, 1977.

45 Article 104 GC III 1949. This point arose in *The Public Prosecutor* v. *Oie Hee Koi* [1968] 2 WLR 715 and in *Osman bin Mohamed Ali* v. *The Public Prosecutor* [1969] 1 AC 430.

46 Article 105 GC III unless 'exceptionally, this is held *in camera* in the interests of State security'.

47 Through its ability to draw attention of the detaining state to the grave breach of wilfully depriving a prisoner of war of the rights of fair and regular trial in Article 130 GC III.

48 *Ibid.*

Convention III. The problem thrown up by the issues raised here is of considerable practical importance as the trial of a POW is not to proceed if the court does not offer the 'essential qualities of independence and impartiality'.[49] Should the trial proceed, notwithstanding this injunction, the personnel involved, who have full knowledge of these circumstances, will run the risk of committing a grave breach of Geneva Convention III or a war crime under the Rome Statute.[50] The consequences of proceeding with the trial are much more severe should the defendant be a POW, rather than a member of the armed forces of the detaining power, since, in this case, specific international crimes will have been committed. A state breaching its human rights obligations through trying a member of its armed forces before a military court that does not possess the qualities of independence and impartiality could only lead to a judgment by a human rights court or body of such a breach and a direction to change its national law to bring it into compliance.[51]

A detaining state faced with this difficulty may decide to forgo the trial of a POW and look to other states with the necessary jurisdiction to conduct a proper trial to which it could transfer the accused as a POW. Practical difficulties would, however, include the agreement of the necessary witnesses to give evidence at any trial to be held in the transferee state. In addition, the ability of that state to offer a trial by its military court may be no better than that of the potential transferor state. In reality, the transfer of a POW is unlikely to be an option available to the detaining state. The effect of that state not providing, under its own law, a military court able to offer guarantees of independence and impartiality would be that, should it subsequently detain POWs, it will not be able to place them on trial for crimes committed prior to, or after, capture. The consequences are serious since, for crimes committed after capture, this restriction of the detaining state will decrease its ability to maintain law and order within the confines of the POW camp, especially given the very limited penalties provided by Geneva Convention III to impose disciplinary punishments.[52] For allegations of the commission

[49] Article 84 GC III. [50] Article 130 GC III; Article 8(2)(a)(vi) Rome Statute.

[51] Even though the ECtHR has determined that a court martial lacks independence, it has not declared the finding of the court to be void: *Findlay* v. *United Kingdom*, and those decisions which followed it.

[52] Article 89 GC III. The maximum period of confinement is thirty days. This may be of shorter duration than commanding officers can impose by way of summary trial/hearing in the armed forces of some states but, unlike in some, it can apply to all POWs regardless of rank. By way of example, the maximum period of confinement can exceed

of an international crime committed prior to capture, the opportunity of placing that individual on trial, and thus being able to hold him accountable for his actions, will be blocked at the forum in which he is actually held in captivity. The most likely consequence is that he will never face trial, particularly if he is careful in not travelling, following his release and repatriation, to a state that might invoke universal jurisdiction in order to place him on trial before its own courts or extradite him to the ICC.

Problems of implementation of Geneva Convention III

States will vary in the way in which they see the relationship between their treaty obligations and national law. Some will draw a tight distinction between the two systems, requiring that obligations contained in a treaty must, if they are to apply in national law, be specifically implemented by some form of legislation. Others will accept that the ratification of, or accession to, a treaty will automatically have effect in their national law.[53] Where national law is to be relied upon it is, therefore, not sufficient to argue that Geneva Convention III sets out an obligation on a state without inquiring whether, in a due case, it has been implemented by legislation into a particular state's national law or that the constitutional arrangements of the state require nothing more.

Those Articles of Geneva Convention III relating to the trial of a POW are heavily dependent on the national law of a detaining state, simply because the trial is required to be before the same courts, using the same procedure as applicable to the armed forces of a detaining state. In addition, it is essential that judicial proceedings brought against a POW can be described as a 'fair and regular trial'.[54] A key issue will be

thirty days in the US armed forces, see Article 20 Uniform Code of Military Justice, 10 USC para. 820, and at a summary hearing in the UK armed forces, s. 133 Armed Forces Act 2006. In Canada, the maximum period is thirty days, s. 163(3)(a) National Defense Act (RSC 1985, c. N-5).

[53] For the position in the USA relating to GC III 1949, see M. Reichstein, *The Extradition of General Manuel Noriega: An Application of International Criminal Law and Humanitarian Law to Answer the Question, 'If So, Where Should He Go?'*, 22 *Emory International Law Review* (2008) 877–81.

[54] See n. 50, above. A 'fair and regular' trial is understood in the Elements of Crimes relating to Article 8(2)(a)(vi) Rome Statute as involving the denial of 'judicial guarantees as defined, in particular, in the third [Geneva Convention 1949]'. A reasonable interpretation of 'regular' in this context must be a trial procedure followed in a case against a POW which does not deviate from the procedure laid down by law. The terms 'fair' and 'regular' must be disjunctive.

whether the national law gives the military court of a detaining state jurisdiction over POWs, not only in relation to their status as POWs, but also in respect of an offence that may be tried by the court. An offence committed on the territory of the detaining state, such as one committed after capture, is likely to cause less of a difficulty than an offence committed extraterritorially, such as an international crime committed before capture.[55]

The discussion above refers to the implementation of international criminal law into national law, but an additional problem can occur where the national law of a state is at odds with international law. A simple example would be a provision of national law making it an offence against the law of a detaining state to attack, from the air, what could only be described as a military objective. Suppose a member of the aircrew of an attacking aircraft is captured following the loss of his aircraft, is taken as a POW[56] and is to be tried for this offence. Under international law this is, however, where the 'combatant's immunity' should come into play by preventing any national criminal law applying to someone who is entitled, by virtue of Geneva Convention III, to POW status.[57]

In general terms, there are two ways in which a POW could, under national law, be made subject to the same courts and procedures as a member of the armed forces of another state. First, a state could enact in its law that the relevant law governing the armed forces will apply also to POWs. Secondly, it could provide a separate legal regime for POWs modelled on its national military law, allowing for all necessary modifications. The first option could, clearly, be achieved with much less difficulty than the second. It will, ironically, ensure that members of the armed forces are treated, by way of judicial proceedings, in a way no less favourable than that owed by the state to POWs through the obligations contained in Geneva Convention III. A separate regime for POWs runs the risk of a divergence of the standards of Geneva Convention III from the treatment offered to members of a state's armed forces, more particularly where the law applying to its own

[55] An international crime related to the armed conflict could encompass genocide, crimes against humanity, war crimes, the crime of torture or the taking of hostages.

[56] Compare if he is wrongfully denied POW status: P. Rowe in P. Rowe (ed.), *The Gulf War 1990–91 in International and English Law* (London: Routledge, 1993), 189 nn. 4–6.

[57] See cases at n. 19, above, although note the (unusual) dissenting advice given in *The Public Prosecutor* v. *Oie Hee Koi* [1968] 2 WLR 715, 867. There would be no immunity if his acts amounted to a crime under international criminal law.

armed forces is subsequently altered without any corresponding alteration in the separate law applicable to POWs.

International humanitarian law or human rights law or both?

The trial of a POW by the detaining state will cause IHL and the human rights obligations of that particular state to clamour independently for attention. It has been shown that the phrase 'an independent and impartial' court can be interpreted without either branch of law assuming any ascendency over the other. However, this will not be the limit of their interplay. It will be assumed that the POW is to be within the jurisdiction of the detaining state for the purposes of a human rights treaty, even if the alleged crime was committed, or the POW is detained, outside its territory.

Taking the European Convention on Human Rights (ECHR) as an exemplar, two particular rights will be firmly placed in the foreground, namely, those of liberty and a fair trial. It seems reasonable to conclude that a POW is deprived of his liberty by virtue of Geneva Convention III and not by the ECHR and, in this sense, IHL is the *lex specialis*. But does this mean that Article 5 ECHR can have no significance at all? It could have if it is linked with Article 6, the right to a fair trial. Thus, if the detaining state wishes to conduct an investigation of a crime committed after capture, it may wish to ensure that the accused is unable to tamper with any of the witnesses and to keep him in more secure confinement. This is permitted by Geneva Convention III for up to three months.[58] Article 5(3) ECHR requires that the decision as to confinement, in relation to an investigation of a criminal offence, be made by 'a judge or other officer authorised by law to exercise judicial power'. There is no good reason why it should not apply. A decision made by the commanding officer of the POW camp to order confinement will fall short of this standard.[59] Whilst a POW could not use the ECHR to challenge the fact that he has

[58] Article 103 GC III.

[59] *Hood* v. *United Kingdom*, Application No. 27267/95, Judgment, 18 February 1999; *Boyle* v. *United Kingdom*, Application No. 55434/00, Judgment, 8 January 2008; *Bell* v. *United Kingdom*, Application No. 41534/98, Judgment, 16 April 2007. In the circumstances of a judicial investigation concerning a POW, that individual would be within the jurisdiction of a detaining state which is a party to the ECHR wherever the POW is detained. *Al-Jedda* v. *United Kingdom*, Application No. 27021/08, Judgment,

been detained as a POW,[60] there is no reason why he should not be able to challenge the lawfulness of his confinement under Article 5(3).

Specific rights involved with a fair trial are to be found under both IHL and human rights law. The right to appeal against a criminal conviction, although, not specifically, under IHL, is granted by human rights law. Both are discussed below.

Fair trial procedures

The international law obligations of the detaining state, in relation to the trial of a POW, are found primarily in IHL. In addition to independence and impartiality, a court assigned to try a POW must be able to offer him 'the rights and means of defence provided for in Article 105' Geneva Convention III.[61] These are stated to be the provision of a qualified advocate or counsel of his choice, the ability to call witnesses, the services of an interpreter (if necessary), to know of the charges against him in good time before the opening of the trial and the attendance of a representative of the protecting power at the trial. In addition, Article 75 Additional Protocol I[62] introduces further trial standards, which would be recognised by any human rights treaty, including the presumption of innocence and his attendance at the trial. All these would apply even where the accused is charged with war crimes or other breaches of IHL committed prior to capture.[63] In addition, the trial rights available under a human rights treaty to which the detaining state is a party will continue to apply as a POW will be within the jurisdiction of the detaining state for the purposes of that treaty.[64]

7 July 2011. The position is likely to be the same for states parties to the ICCPR, General Comment 31, para. 10.

[60] Although Article 5 ECHR applies during an armed conflict, except where a permitted derogation has been made, see *Al-Jedda* v. *United Kingdom*, Application No. 27021/08, Judgment, 7 July 2011, para. 99. The essence of Article 5 is 'arbitrariness': *Al Husin* v. *Bosnia and Herzegovina*, Application No. 3727/08, Judgment, 7 February 2012, para. 61. A person entitled to POW status is not, in these terms, detained arbitrarily.

[61] Article 84 GC III.

[62] It is recognised that this article reflects customary international law; see J.-M. Henckaerts and L. Doswald-Beck, *Customary International Humanitarian Law*, vol. 1, *Rules* (Cambridge: Cambridge University Press, 2005), Rule 100.

[63] Article 75(7) AP I. Although the crime of genocide is not specifically mentioned, it must be understood as being included.

[64] This will not be a contentious issue where the POW is held on the territory of the detaining state, but it will arise where the detaining state is conducting military operations outside its own territory and where it has established a POW camp or detaining

It has been demonstrated above that any trial of a POW will be based on the *national* law of the detaining state. It is this law that should be in conformity with international law. If it is not, the state will be in breach of its international obligations even though the trial is conducted in accordance with national law. However, there is little a POW could do if he finds that his trial rights and procedures do not match those to which he is entitled under IHL or international human rights law. In response to his concerns, it is likely that the detaining state will merely reply that members of its own armed forces are not entitled to more, by way of trial rights, and so he cannot expect any more than this.

Even if the national law of the detaining state is consistent with that state's international law obligations, it may be difficult to apply some of the trial rights to a POW who is to be tried by a military court for a crime committed prior to capture. Although he is entitled to call witnesses,[65] he will find it virtually impossible to secure the attendance of a member of his own armed forces, who has not become a POW, as a witness to guilt/innocence or to character. It is not beyond the bounds of possibility, however, that the national law[66] and the practicalities of the situation will enable evidence to be given by video or by written statement, but this is likely to occur only in a rare case.

Whenever the alleged crime was committed, a POW may find difficulty in securing an advocate of 'his own choice' if he is not provided with some form of legal aid. Since he is to be tried by a military court he may find that, in practice, he is offered a (or possibly a choice of) military lawyer of the detaining state to defend him. Whilst in a number of states he is likely to be very ably defended by such a lawyer, there are obvious risks in a military court if, for instance, defence lawyers are only permitted where they are of a subordinate military rank to that of the military members of the court.[67]

centre: *Al-Skeini* v. *United Kingdom*, Application No. 55721/07, Judgment, 7 July 2011, fifth applicant; *Al-Jedda* v. *United Kingdom*, both of whom were civilian detainees.

65 Article 105 GC III; Article 75(4)(g) AP I.

66 The main issue will be whether that law permits the admissibility of hearsay evidence where a video and a written statement are not made at the time of the trial itself and where the maker of any statement cannot be cross-examined. Whether hearsay should be admissible is a matter for national law: *Al Khawaya and Tahery* v. *United Kingdom*, Application No. 26766/05, Judgment, 15 December 2011, para. 118.

67 See, e.g., the allegations made in *Civil Liberties Organisation and Others* v. *Nigeria*, para. 28 (which related primarily to the dangers involved where an accused is unable to choose his counsel). It is, however, common in military courts for a defending officer to be junior in rank to the military members of the court. In this context, difficulty will arise

It seems reasonable to interpret the phrase 'the same courts according to the same procedure' in Article 102 Geneva Convention III as including pre-trial events that have an effect on the court procedures. This is so, even though there is no specific requirement in the Convention to provide pre-trial legal advice during the investigation stage to a POW.[68] The detaining state will also need to ensure that the pre-trial questioning and treatment of a POW is subject to the same limitations and safeguards provided to members of the armed forces of that state. In particular, the procedure by which a confession is made inadmissible in a subsequent trial, or the provision of pre-trial legal advice, must be applied to POWs as a legal requirement, not merely as *ex gratia* benevolence. The obligation in Article 75 Additional Protocol I, whereby a person must not be 'compelled to testify against himself or to confess guilt', whilst important, provides a lesser standard of safety against the possibility of an unfair trial than the law applicable in the military courts of many states.[69]

where a defence military lawyer is required to give priority, in relation to his military court duties, to his status as a military officer within a hierarchical structure and not to his professional responsibilities as a lawyer. If a POW rejects a defence lawyer he may find no option but to attempt to defend himself. Although Article 105 GC III provides that he could secure the 'assistance of one of his prisoner comrades' it would appear that a legally qualified prisoner comrade could not actually defend him as would a 'qualified advocate or counsel'. This conclusion is drawn from the use of the word 'assistance' in relation to the former and to 'defend' for the latter: Pictet, *Geneva Convention III*, 486. The International Criminal Tribunal for the former Yugoslavia has developed a practice for dealing with an accused who insists on representing himself; see C. Harvey, 'Self-Representation in International Criminal Procedure: Theoretical and Illusory or Practical and Effective?', PhD thesis, University of Lancaster (2012). Moreover, the national law of the detaining state may not give the right of audience (although it may enable assistance to be given) in a military court of the detaining state to a POW's 'prisoner comrade'. This is the case in the United Kingdom: Article 26(1), Prisoner of War (Discipline) Regulations 1958. See also the Armed Forces Act 2011, s.23.

68 Article 105 refers to a 'competent advocate or counsel to conduct the defence', whilst Article 75 AP I does not refer to legal advice or assistance. The defence advocate must have at least two weeks to prepare for the trial (Article 105), but legal advice is often needed before this stage, particularly where an accused is being questioned prior to any formal decision being made to place him on trial. Advice at this stage may prevent an improper 'confession' being made by an accused. A failure to permit access to a lawyer at this stage may have the effect of denying a detainee 'a fundamental safeguard against ill-treatment': *Othman (Abu Qatada)* v. *United Kingdom*, Application No. 8139/09, Judgment, 17 January 2012, para. 199.

69 There is, for instance, much more protection for an accused against the power of investigators if the prosecution has to prove that a confession has not been obtained as a result of anything said or done that would make it unreliable than where the only protection is that the accused should not be compelled to confess. In a number of states a statement made by one person implicating the accused, or where one accused

It will, therefore, be necessary to ensure that this adjectival law is actually made applicable to POWs should a state find itself as a detaining power in the future.

There can be little doubt that, under IHL and international human rights law,[70] it is for the prosecution to bear the burden of proving a POW guilty. This essential right will be of little significance if it is not mirrored in the national law of the detaining state and made applicable to the trial of POWs.[71] Similarly, the standard of proof as 'beyond reasonable doubt'[72] is a very important safeguard in preventing an unfair trial. Although no treaty establishes this principle, it has become the norm in international criminal tribunals and must be considered to reflect customary international law. For the same reasons as discussed in relation to the burden of proof above, it will be essential that this standard is applicable under the national law of the detaining state in a military court assigned to try a POW.

An appeal from a military court

In 1949, it was not uncommon for states to provide no appeal from the decision of a military court.[73] The principal reasons given for this policy were that military justice, in the form of judgment and sentence, must be

voluntarily confesses and implicates another, will not be admissible against an accused who has not, himself, confessed. This will be the case *a fortiori* if the evidence against an accused is obtained from the torture of another person: *Othman (Abu Qatada)* v. *United Kingdom*, para. 267.

70 Article 75(4)(d) AP I; Article 14(2) ICCPR; Article 6(2) ECHR; Article 8(2) American Convention on Human Rights; Article 7(1)(b) African Charter on Human and Peoples' Rights.

71 In considering any statutory reversal of the burden of proof the ECHR 'requires States to confine [presumptions of law or fact] within reasonable limits which take into account the importance of what is at stake and maintain the rights of the defence': *Salabiaku* v. *France*, Application No. 10519/83, Judgment, 7 October 1988, para. 28.

72 This is generally how the standard is stated in common law countries. In civil law countries the appropriate term is 'to the intimate conviction of the trier of fact': J.-M. Henckaerts and L. Doswald-Beck, *Customary International Humanitarian Law* (Cambridge: Cambridge University Press, 2005), 358. *Quaere* whether this standard follows inexorably from the placing of the burden of proof on the prosecution (*ibid.*).

73 In 1940, the *Report of the Army and Air Force Courts-Martial Committee*, Cmd 6200 rejected the option of establishing an appeal from a court martial on the grounds that 'the essence of the great majority of military offences is that they are offences against discipline. They must be punished from the point of view of discipline; and that they certainly would seem to be better handled at every stage by persons who are familiar with service discipline and the general situation and surroundings of officers

carried out promptly for the sake of preserving discipline and that the best judges of what that required were military officers and not civilian judges. Even when a right of appeal was granted it was limited, broadly for the same reasons, to the judgment of the court and not to the sentence imposed. It is not surprising, therefore, to see that a POW is accorded no right to appeal unless this procedure is available to members of the armed forces of the detaining state who have been convicted by the same military court.[74] As an alternative to appeal, Geneva Convention III recognises that a member of the armed forces, and therefore a POW, convicted by a military court may have the right to petition military authorities to quash his conviction or reduce his sentence.[75]

This is surprising as the power to institute an appeal from a conviction by a court is today considered to be a basic human right[76] and the right merely to petition military authorities would now be seen as a serious indicator that the military court was not independent of those authorities.[77] Should there be no right of appeal from a military court a POW could be convicted of a serious crime, ranging from genocide to war crimes committed before capture, or murder, or serious assault committed after capture, without any form of appeal. He could be retained by the detaining state after the conclusion of hostilities until he has served his sentence.[78] A crime committed before capture is likely to be a very serious one and would attract a long sentence of imprisonment so, unless he is repatriated under a 'prisoner transfer scheme' to serve his sentence in his home state, a convicted individual would remain a POW long after the cessation of hostilities.[79]

and men' (para. 22). The reason given for rejecting the idea of an appeal from a court martial was that a convicted soldier could petition the authorities, over which the Judge Advocate General (a lawyer) would have oversight. This practice is reflected in Article 106 GC III.

74 Article 106 GC III.

75 This was the only option available in a number of states to a person convicted by a court martial prior to the establishment of an appeal court. It would have been the practice in those states in 1949.

76 Article 14(5) ICCPR 1966. However, the Article 6 ECHR 'does not compel the contracting States to set up courts of appeal or of cassation': *Jovanovic* v. *Serbia*, Application No. 32299/08, Judgment, 2 October 2012, para. 46.

77 See n. 35, above, for discussion of the possibility that a non-judicial individual could alter the decisions of a court.

78 Article 119 GC III.

79 During this period he will remain entitled to the protection of GC III: see Article 5(1).

It might be thought that this is just the type of situation where, in the absence in IHL of an obligation on the part of a detaining state to provide an appeal against the verdict of a military court that has convicted a POW, the *lex specialis* should be international human rights law with its requirement that a conviction and sentence must be reviewable 'before a higher tribunal according to law'.[80] The difficulty, however, is that unless such an appeal court is in existence in the detaining state before the trial of a POW (and probably before the armed conflict), it might be difficult to establish it according to law during the course of it.[81] The effect will be that, although international human rights law requires an appeal from a military court in these circumstances, it has no means of compelling a detaining state to carry out its constitutional procedures to create one.

If the detaining state does provide an appeal from a military court that court must, itself, possess the essential guarantees of independence and impartiality, not as a direct result of Geneva Convention III, which is silent on the matter, but as a matter of logic and common sense. It would be absurd if the trial court (under Geneva Convention III) had to possess these qualities, but an appeal court could be exempted from them.

A further issue that arises is whether a state, which is detaining POWs, is under a legal obligation to provide an appeal from its military court, even where such an appeal is not permitted to members of its own armed forces and where Geneva Convention III does not place a specific obligation on a detaining state to do so. It could, of course, be said that the detaining state will be in breach of its obligation under the ICCPR in not providing such a court for its own armed forces. This may be the case where the protecting power would call upon the detaining state to institute an appeal process for all those convicted by its military courts so as to ensure an appeal is possible for a convicted POW. In making this call the protecting power would be acting outside its remit under Geneva Convention III and would, in effect, be requesting that the detaining state comply with its human

[80] See n. 76, above. This principle may not, however, be implemented into the law of the detaining state.

[81] Cf. where the impetus to create such a court is drawn from the detaining state wishing to provide an appeal for the members of its own armed forces with that where the pressure emanates from the protecting power (or ICRC) to establish an appeal for a POW convicted by a military court in that state.

rights obligations under the ICCPR, assuming that the detaining state had not entered a reservation to the ICCPR in respect of its armed forces[82] or had not derogated from Article 14(5).[83]

In the operation of judicial proceedings all POWs must be treated in the same way.[84] However, the discussion above shows that, within this particular group, there may be civilians entitled to POW status under Article 4 of Geneva Convention III. Some human rights courts and bodies have some difficulty accepting that a civilian could be tried by a military court.[85] The concern that they have expressed is only likely to be increased if no appeal from a military court is provided or even where an appeal court is comprised of military officers sitting alongside one or more civilian judges.[86]

[82] *Quaere* whether the UK reservation to the 1966 Covenant, relating to 'members of, and persons serving with, the armed forces of the Crown and to persons lawfully detained in penal establishments of whatever character such laws and procedures as they may from time to time deem to be necessary for the preservation of service and custodial discipline' would apply to POWs. The UK has no present intention of withdrawing this reservation: CCCPR/C/GBR/Q/6 Add.1, 18 June 2008. No such reservation had been made by the United Kingdom on its ratification of the ECHR. See also the reservation made by France relating to Articles 9 and 14 'to the effect that these articles cannot impede enforcement of the rules pertaining to the discipline regime in the armies [*sic*]'. A number of states, such as Azerbaijan, Czech Republic, Slovakia and Spain, have entered reservations concerning discipline in their armed forces to the ECHR, Article 6, but have not made any such reservation to the ICCPR.

[83] See Article 4. In theory, a state could derogate from the whole of Article 14 providing that, if it does so, it would not be inconsistent with its other obligations under international law. The obligations in Article 84 GC III would prevail over any purported derogation from Article 14 ICCPR, but this would not prevent a derogation from Article 14(5) of that Covenant since the 1949 Convention does not require an appeal court where one is not in existence.

[84] Article 16 GC III subject to permitted differences caused by their military rank, sex, age, health, professional qualifications.

[85] See n. 27, above.

[86] In *Incal* v. *Turkey*, Application No. 41/1997/825/1031, Judgment, 18 May 1998, a military judge, who underwent the same professional training as his civilian counterparts with whom he sat on the State Security Court, made the whole court lack independence. The reasons given for the lack of independence of military judges sitting in this Court were that 'they are servicemen who still belong to the army, which in turn takes its orders from the executive [. . .] they remain subject to military discipline and assessment reports are compiled on them by the army [. . .] their term of office is only four years and can be renewed [by the army]' (paras 67–8); *Gurkan* v. *Turkey*, Application No. 10987/10, Judgment, 3 July 2012, para. 19; *Constitutional Rights Project* v. *Nigeria*, African Commission on Human and Peoples' Rights, Comm. No. 60/91(1995), para. 14.

Conclusion

This chapter has attempted to establish that all states party to Geneva Convention III (effectively, all states in the world) are required by that Convention to provide a military court that possesses the 'essential guarantees of independence and impartiality' for the trial of POWs. The second prong to this obligation, that POWs are to be tried and sentenced by the same courts as members of the armed forces of the detaining state, has the effect of imposing on all states, in peacetime, a requirement that their military courts possess these 'essential guarantees' in anticipation of them, at some stage, becoming a detaining state. A number of states may well argue that it is unlikely they will ever be in this position and that they need not concern themselves with whether their military courts do actually offer these essential guarantees. This is a mistaken approach. It would prevent a state from complying with its obligations under Geneva Convention III, in peacetime,[87] in the event of it becoming a party to an international armed conflict or accepting the transfer of one or more POWs from states that are parties to the conflict. Moreover, any trial of a POW by a detaining state is likely to attract more publicity than would a trial of a member of its armed forces before one of its military courts. Any alleged failings under the Geneva Conventions 1949 would be very public indeed.

In peacetime states will also need to assess objectively whether their own military courts are able to offer the essential guarantees of independence and impartiality. The decisions of the ECtHR have shown that a detailed analysis is required to determine whether one or more significant features of a state's military court structure could lead an objective bystander to be concerned that the court is unable to offer these guarantees.[88]

For a number of states, some form of national legislation is required to give effect to their obligations under an international treaty, such as Geneva Convention III. This is to provide the legal foundation under the national law of the detaining state for the trial of a POW, including the procedural requirements applicable to the trial of a member of that

[87] Article 129, para. 3 GC III ('to take measures for the suppression of all acts contrary to the provisions of the present Convention other than grave breaches').

[88] See, e.g., *Findlay* v. *United Kingdom*; *Incal* v. *Turkey*, para. 71 where the Court stated that 'in deciding whether there is a legitimate reason to fear that a particular court lacks independence and impartiality, the standpoint of the accused is important without being decisive. What is decisive is whether his doubts can be objectively justified'.

state's own armed forces. States will need to consider whether such legislation is actually in place and whether it does provide the essential guarantees of independence and impartiality required by Article 84 Geneva Convention III, along with the rights and means of defence provided by Articles 105 and 75 Additional Protocol I. The effect of such an exercise could lead to the reform of a state's peacetime military courts to the advantage of members of its own armed forces and, if the need arises, those whom it detains as POWs.

Those states that have become a party to the Rome Statute 1998 and have, in some form, implemented the relevant crimes in their national law will have accepted that 'wilfully depriving a PoW of the rights of fair and regular trial prescribed in [Geneva Convention III]'[89] is a grave breach of that Convention or a war crime[90] under the Rome Statute. It is hardly a startling proposition to conclude that the trial of a POW before a military court (or indeed, any court) that is not independent and impartial would be to deprive him of a fair trial. Whether it would also deprive him of a 'regular' trial would depend on whether this word meant that the trial process was not established in accordance with the constitutional structure of the state and was, in consequence, 'an irregular' court and procedure, or whether it refers to a trial process that would be considered to be irregular when compared with those states that do comply with Article 84 of Geneva Convention III.

It might be argued that a POW is 'wilfully' deprived of a fair and regular trial where those who conduct the trial become aware, perhaps through the medium of the protecting power (or substitute), that the trial could not objectively be considered to meet the essential guarantees in Article 84 of Geneva Convention III. For them to carry on with the trial would be to commit a grave breach of the Convention or a war crime under the Rome Statute 1998.

[89] Article 130 GC III.

[90] Article 8(2)(a)(vi) Rome Statute of the International Criminal Court.

15

The 'right to conduct one's own defence in person' and a 'fair and expeditious trial' before the ICTY: an impossible balancing act?

CAROLINE HARVEY

Introduction

> [The ICTY] will not be judged by the number of convictions which it enters, or by the speed with which it concludes the Completion Strategy which the Security Council has endorsed, but by the fairness of its trials.[1]

The fairness of a trial is particularly important where a defendant chooses to represent himself and not to engage counsel, preferring instead to waive professional services in the presentation of his defence. This chapter examines the scope of the right to self-representation and the manner in which the exercise of this right has been controlled by reference to the practice of the United Nations (UN) International Criminal Tribunal for the former Yugoslavia (ICTY).[2] The ICTY, along with its fellow international criminal institutions, has been instrumental in the development of procedural law applicable in the holding to account of individuals for violations of the laws of war since the early 1990s. An interesting aspect is the interplay of the provision of the ICTY Statute granting a defendant before the ICTY the 'right to conduct his own defence' and the duty of ICTY Trial Chambers to conduct a 'fair and

Grateful thanks to Peter Rowe, Boris Kasolowsky and Dan Saxon for comments on earlier drafts. Also grateful thanks to Peter Rowe for his supervision of my PhD thesis in the field of international criminal procedure. This chapter is an offshoot of that thesis.

[1] *Prosecutor* v. *Slobodan Milošević*, IT-02-54-AR73.4, Dissenting Opinion of Judge David Hunt on Admissibility of Evidence in Chief in the Form of Written Statement (Majority Decision given 30 September 2003), 21 October 2003, para. 22.

[2] Although there is some case law from the ICTR and SCSL on the issue, the main decisions have been rendered by the ICTY. The scope of this contribution therefore does not include the ICTR and SCSL decisions.

expeditious trial'. The underlying question is whether this legal framework is workable and thus fit for purpose.

The body of ICTY jurisprudence on self-representation addressed in this contribution is of particular significance: the ICTY has dealt with the majority of self-representation cases in international criminal cases and has the richest international body of law on the topic. Although other international courts and tribunals are not bound by the decisions of the ICTY, they may wish to draw on the ICTY's experience. Furthermore, as the ICC Statute also contains a similar (as yet unused) provision on self-representation, the decisions of the ICTY on the issue may prove instructive, or perhaps even cautionary.

The scope of the right of a defendant to conduct his own defence before the ICTY

There is no overarching 'international' right to self-representation underlying the ICTY legal framework. Instead, in addition to different legal frameworks in national legal systems,[3] there are: (i) provisions of the statutes of various international criminal institutions, which each institution may independently interpret as it sees fit, and (ii) different interpretations of the applicable provisions of the different international human rights conventions.

In international law, prior to the 1990s, only the International Military Tribunal (IMT) at Nuremberg and the International Military Tribunal for the Far East (IMTFE) had tried and convicted individuals for violations of the laws of war, in both cases in the context of the Second World War. Established by the victorious powers, those tribunals aimed at the swift dispensation of punishment. The rights of the accused before the IMT were minimal, but included the right to self-representation.[4]

[3] In the Anglo-Saxon legal traditions it is generally possible. See, e.g., for England and Wales, Rules of the Supreme Court (Revision) 1965/1776, Schedule 1, Part 2 Commencement and Progress of Proceedings (5) Mode of Beginning Civil Proceedings in High Court, 6. Right to sue in person (containing the right to 'begin and carry on proceedings in the High Court by a solicitor or in person') and *R.* v. *Woodward* [1944] KB 118 and *R.* v. *Lyons* (1979) 68 Cr. App. R. 104; further, in the USA it has been found to be a constitutional right. See *Faretta* v. *California*, 422 US 806 (1975) 835–6. In contrast, in the Continental European tradition, the assistance of counsel is generally mandatory in the case of serious charges. See, e.g., for Germany, StPO (Code of Criminal Procedure), sect. 140. Note that in German criminal proceedings, however, the defendant generally has greater possibilities for participation, even when represented by counsel.

[4] Article 16, Nuremberg Charter provides for the accused the right to receive full particulars of the charges, the right to give an explanation relevant to the charges, the right to

However, none of the main Nuremberg defendants ultimately represented themself, although Alfred Jodl and Rudolf Hess appear to have considered doing so.[5]

Half a century later, the establishment of the ICTY in 1993 commenced a new era of individual criminal accountability for violations of the laws of war. Although the IMT laid important groundwork, it has been subjected to strong criticism, including charges of victor's justice, arbitrary selectivity in drawing up the list of defendants and deficits in due process. Whilst the ICTY has not escaped criticism, it was founded on the authority of the UN. Its establishment therefore represented a broader expression of the will of the international community than that of the Allied Powers in the aftermath of the Second World War.[6]

Incorporated into the constitutional documents of the ICTY is a much broader framework of human rights guarantees. Alongside the core principles of equality before the court, a fair and public hearing and the presumption of innocence, a defendant before the ICTY is entitled to the following 'minimum guarantees':

> (a) to be informed promptly and in detail in a language which he understands of the nature and cause of the charge against him;
> (b) to have adequate time and facilities for the preparation of his defence and to communicate with counsel of his own choosing;
> (c) to be tried without undue delay;

(i) receive particulars of charges and (ii) have the preliminary examination conducted in an accessible language, *the right to conduct their own defence* before the Tribunal or to have the assistance of counsel and the right to present evidence and cross-examine prosecution witnesses (emphasis added).

5 See report of the interview between British lawyer Airey Neave and Alfred Jodl, '[i]n answer to the question of what alternative [Jodl] had if he raised objections to counsel appointed by the court, I said that he would then have the right to conduct his own defence. I told him to get in touch with me if he had any further questions to ask on this': Memorandum for the General Secretary of the International Military Tribunal from Major Airey Neave, 24 October 1945, National Archives, ref. LCO2/2982 X/L06978, 10; and report of an interview with Rudolf Hess, '[Hess] asked whether he was allowed to be his own counsel and, on being assured that this was permissible, said "Then I wish to do so," ignoring Neave's advice to the contrary': Telford Taylor, *Anatomy of the Nuremberg Trials* (London: Bloomsbury, 1993), 133. Ultimately, however, both Hess and Jodl engaged counsel.

6 The ICTR in 1994, also established on the basis of a Security Council Resolution, followed soon after the establishment of the ICTY. Thereafter, the tribunal model began to diversify to incorporate participation of the hosting state in the form of so-called hybrid courts (including the Extraordinary Chambers in the Courts of Cambodia (ECCC) in 1997, the Special Court for Sierra Leone (SCSL) in 2002 and the Special Tribunal for Lebanon (STL) in 2009). A common feature of these institutions is their limited substantive and temporal jurisdiction.

(d) to be tried in his presence, and *to defend himself in person* or through legal assistance of his own choosing; to be informed, if he does not have legal assistance, of this right; and to have legal assistance assigned to him, in any case where the interests of justice so require, and without payment by him in any such case if he does not have sufficient means to pay for it;
(e) to examine, or have examined, the witnesses against him and to obtain the attendance and examination of witnesses on his behalf under the same conditions as witnesses against him;
(f) to have the free assistance of an interpreter if he cannot understand or speak the language used in the International Tribunal;
(g) not to be compelled to testify against himself or to confess guilt.[7]

As under the Nuremberg Charter, defendants are granted the possibility to defend themselves in person, without any criteria or requirements attached to the provision.

At the same time there is a polarisation of approaches in international human rights law, with the European Court of Human Rights (ECtHR) and the UN Human Rights Committee reaching opposite conclusions as to whether there is a presumptive right to self-representation in international human rights law. In fact, they have reached opposite conclusions in cases where the same individual, Carlos Matos, pursued exactly the same violation of rights on exactly the same set of facts before both institutions.[8]

The European Convention on Human Rights (ECHR) provides in Article 6(3)(c) for the right of a defendant: 'to defend himself in person or through legal assistance of his own choosing'.[9] In the *Matos* decision of the ECtHR, this was not interpreted as a presumptive right of the defendant to conduct his own defence, but rather a right to a defence, which may be guaranteed either through self-representation or representation by counsel at the discretion of the national courts.[10]

[7] Article 21, ICTY Statute (emphasis added).

[8] ECtHR: *Matos* v. *Portugal*, Application No. 48188/99, 15 November 2001 and UNHRC: *Matos* v. *Portugal*, Communication No. 1123/2002, UNDOC CCPR/C/86, 19 September 2006.

[9] Convention for the Protection of Human Rights and Fundamental Freedoms, 213 UNTS 222, entered into force 3 September 1953, as amended by Protocols 3, 5, 8 and 11, which entered into force on 21 September 1970, 20 December 1971, 1 January 1990 and 1 November 1998 respectively.

[10] *Matos* v. *Portugal*, Application No. 48188/99, 15 November 2001.

Article 14(3)(d) of the International Covenant on Civil and Political Rights (ICCPR) provides for the identical right of a defendant: 'to defend himself in person or through legal assistance of his own choosing'.[11] However, in contrast to the ECtHR, in the UN HRC *Matos* decision, the provision was interpreted to provide for the right of a defendant to conduct his own defence as under the Anglo-Saxon model, i.e., that where the assistance of counsel is mandatory, this breaches the defendant's rights.[12] This decision, however, post-dated the main ICTY decisions addressed in the analysis below.

When the ICTY was established, the UN Secretary-General expressly stated that its constitutional documents should, in matters of the rights of the accused, follow the ICCPR.[13] Thus, Article 21(4)(d) of the ICTY Statute ('Rights of the Accused') provides for the right of a defendant:

> to be tried in his presence, *and to defend himself in person or through legal assistance of his own choosing*; to be informed, if he does not have legal assistance, of this right; and to have legal assistance assigned to him, in any case where the interests of justice so require, and without payment by him in any such case if he does not have sufficient means to pay for it.
>
> (emphasis added)

Rule 45(F) ICTY Rules of Procedure and Evidence (RPE) clarifies the nature of that right:

> A suspect or an accused *electing to conduct his or her own defence* shall so notify the Registrar in writing at the first opportunity.
>
> (emphasis added)

So far, five defendants have conducted their own defences before the ICTY: Slobodan Milošević, intermittently until his death in 2006; Momčilo Krajišnik, on his appeal only; Vojislav Šešelj, also intermittently and currently in his ongoing trial; Radovan Karadžić, in his ongoing trial; and Zdravko Tolimir, on trial and now going into his

[11] International Covenant on Civil and Political Rights, opened for signature 16 December 1966, 999 UNTS 171, 6 ILM 368 (entered into force 23 March 1976).

[12] *Matos* v. *Portugal*, Communication No. 1123/2002, UNDOC CCPR/C/86, 19 September 2006.

[13] Report of the Secretary-General Pursuant to para. 2 of Security Council Resolution 808 (1993), 3 May 1993 (UN Doc. S/25704), para. 106 ('It is axiomatic that the International Tribunal must fully respect internationally recognised standards regarding the rights of the accused at all stages of its proceedings. In the view of the Secretary-General, such internationally recognised standards are, in particular, contained in article 14 of the International Covenant on Civil and Political Rights.').

appeal. Through these cases, the ICTY has developed a relatively detailed framework for the exercise of the right to self-representation. The following sections examine: (a) the integrity of a request to self-represent, (b) the relevance of the legal skills of the defendant and (c) fitness to exercise the right to self-representation before the ICTY.

(a) Integrity of a request to exercise the right to self-representation before the ICTY

Notification of the exercise of the right to self-representation must be given to the ICTY Registrar 'at the first opportunity'.[14] In practice, 'at the first opportunity' has been interpreted in line with the presumption in US law 'that, if the right is asserted prior to the beginning of trial, it will be given effect'.[15] Milošević exercised his right to self-representation on 3 July 2001, well before the trial commenced,[16] as did Šešelj,[17] Karadžić[18] and Tolimir.[19] All four defendants were permitted to represent themselves.

In cases where the defendant has sought to exercise the right to self-representation after commencement of the trial, Trial Chambers have been less willing to grant the request. Stanković filed a written statement that he wished to represent himself on 23 May 2005,[20] having been represented by counsel since 18 July 2002.[21] His request was denied, but primarily because it was found to be motivated by frustration that he was not permitted to be represented by his chosen counsel, who had been suspended for professional misconduct.[22] Krajišnik attempted to exercise his right to self-representation over a year into his trial and his request was denied because it was deemed to be motivated 'with what he saw as the poor performance of his defence' and 'insufficient resources'.

[14] ICTY RPE 45(F).

[15] *Prosecutor* v. *Momčilo Krajišnik*, IT-00-39-T, Reasons for Oral Decision Denying Mr Krajisnik's Request to Proceed Unrepresented by Counsel, 18 August 2005, para. 26.

[16] *Prosecutor* v. *Slobodan Milošević*, IT-02-54, Reasons for Decision on the Prosecution's Motion Concerning Assignment of Counsel, 4 April 2003, para. 2.

[17] *Prosecutor* v. *Vojislav Šešelj*, IT-03-67-I, Initial Appearance, 26 February 2003, T1 and *Prosecutor* v. *Šešelj*, IT-03-67-PT, Decision on Prosecution's Motion for Order Appointing Counsel to Assist Vojislav Seselj with his Defence, 9 May 2003, para. 2.

[18] See *Prosecutor* v. *Radovan Karadžić*, IT-95-5/18-T, Registry Decision, 19 November 2009.

[19] *Prosecutor* v. *Zdravko Tolimir*, IT-05-88/2-PT, Status Conference, 14 September 2007, T54.

[20] *Prosecutor* v. *Radovan Stanković*, IT-96-23/2-PT, Decision following Registrar's Notification of Radovan Stankovic's Request for Self Representation, 19 August 2005, para. 7.

[21] *Ibid.*, para. 3. [22] *Ibid.*, para. 18.

This, it appeared to the Trial Chamber, 'implied solutions less drastic than self-representation'.[23]

However, at the appeal stage Krajišnik was surprisingly permitted to represent himself.[24] Judge Schomburg of Germany, perhaps predictably coming from a jurisdiction where self-representation is not generally permitted, gave a powerful dissenting opinion.[25] The Appeals Chamber upheld the decision to grant self-representation, basing its conclusion on the absence of case-specific reasons for curtailing the right to self-representation on appeal[26] and the fact that the ICTY (unlike the USA)[27] does not draw a distinction between self-representation at the trial and appeal stages in its constitutional documents, with the result that there is 'no textual basis for concluding that the guarantee to self-representation [. . .] evaporates with the issuance of the trial judgement'.[28] Tolimir is also now representing himself on appeal, having already represented himself at trial.

Although the procedural rules of the ICTY do not set out any requirements for self-representation other than that written notice must be submitted to the Registrar at the first opportunity, an examination of the self-representation jurisprudence shows that Trial Chambers have sometimes utilised certain criteria to examine the integrity of requests. In *Milošević*, the Trial Chamber first noted that the declaration was made 'clearly and unequivocally'.[29] Secondly, the Trial Chamber noted that the defendant was 'literate, competent, and understanding, and voluntarily exercising his informed free will'.[30] These statements echo the tests in the leading US case on self-representation, *Faretta* v. *California*.[31] In contrast to this detailed examination in *Milošević*, in *Šešelj* the enquiry was, at least initially, much less extensive.[32]

23 *Prosecutor* v. *Momčilo Krajišnik* (n. 15, above), para. 9.

24 *Prosecutor* v. *Momčilo Krajišnik*, IT-00-39-A, Decision on *Momčilo Krajišnik*'s Request to Self-Represent, on Counsel's Motions in relation to Appointment of Amicus Curiae, and on the Prosecution Motion of 16 February 2007, 11 May 2007, para. 37.

25 See *ibid.*, Fundamentally Dissenting Opinion of Judge Schomburg on the Right to Self-Representation appended to *Prosecutor* v. *Momčilo Krajišnik*.

26 *Prosecutor* v. *Momčilo Krajišnik* (n. 24, above), para. 10.

27 *Ibid.*, para. 12 (in *Martinez* v. *Court of Appeal of California*, 528 US 152 (2000) it was found that there is no constitutional right to self-representation on direct appeal from a criminal conviction).

28 *Prosecutor* v. *Momčilo Krajišnik* (n. 24, above), para. 11.

29 *Prosecutor* v. *Slobodan Milošević* (n. 16, above), para. 39.

30 *Ibid.*, citing *Faretta* v. *California*, 422 US 806 (1975), 835.

31 *Faretta* v. *California* (n. 30, above), 835–6.

32 *Prosecutor* v. *Vojislav Šešelj*, IT-03-67-PT, Decision on Assignment of Counsel, 21 August 2006, para. 26 ('The Accused in this case has unequivocally expressed his

In *Krajišnik*, the defendant's request to exercise the right to self-representation was not fully examined because it was already found to be equivocal.[33] 'Equivocal' was interpreted to mean 'unclear in meaning or intention; ambiguous' and the accused must 'actually desire [. . .] the alternative of self-representation'.[34] The integrity of Krajišnik's successful request to represent himself on appeal does not appear to have been examined in any similar depth of detail, with the defendant describing himself as a 'literate and highly intelligent person who is certainly capable of defending himself in person' and who had made 'an informed waiver of professional legal representation'.[35]

In *Karadžić* and *Tolimir*, as in *Šešelj* the issue of the integrity of the requests received less attention. Interestingly, although Tolimir (perhaps equivocally) stated in open court 'I did not elect to defend myself because I wanted to do so but because the Registry wanted to impose counsel on me of his choice',[36] he was still permitted to represent himself.

(b) Relevance of the legal skills of the defendant before the ICTY

There is no express requirement that a defendant before the ICTY must have a particular level of legal expertise in order to be permitted to represent him/herself. If this is considered in light of the specified duties of ICTY defence counsel, it quickly becomes apparent that it is very difficult for a self-represented defendant to run his/her case effectively. After all, the duties of defence counsel include: filing 'a pre-trial brief addressing the factual and legal issues, and including a written statement setting out: (i) in general terms, the nature of the accused's defence; (ii) the matters with which the accused takes issue in the Prosecutor's pre-trial brief; and (iii) in the case of each such matter, the reason why the accused takes issue with it';[37] filing 'a list of witnesses the defence

intention to represent himself with the assistance of "legal advisors" [. . .] There appears not to have been an explicit preliminary enquiry to determine whether the request was unequivocal, informed and intelligent [. . .] The Prosecution has not contested that this expression of will was voluntary [. . .] There is no doubt that the Accused is literate [. . .] The parties have not raised any issue relating to the standards to be applied for the acceptance of this expression of will. The Chamber finds no reason to revisit this issue.').

33 *Prosecutor* v. *Momčilo Krajišnik* (n. 15, above), para. 7.

34 *Ibid.*, paras 5–21.

35 See *Prosecutor* v. *Momčilo Krajišnik* (n. 24, above), para. 8.

36 *Prosecutor* v. *Zdravko Tolimir*, IT-05-88/2-PT, Status Conference, 14 September 2007, T58.

37 ICTY RPE Rule 65 *ter* (F).

intends to call' with *inter alia* 'a summary of the facts on which each witness will testify', 'an indication of whether the witness will testify in person or [. . .] by way of written statement or use of a transcript of testimony from other proceedings before the Tribunal'; and filing 'a list of exhibits the defence intends to offer in its case, stating where possible whether the Prosecutor has any objection as to authenticity'.[38] Further, defence counsel must 'notify the Prosecutor of its intent to offer: (a) the defence of alibi [. . .] (b) any special defence, including that of diminished or lack of mental responsibility'.[39]

Although Milošević had received a legal education, the Appeals Chamber acknowledged that a defendant cannot conduct his defence to the same level as professional defence counsel but that defendants before the ICTY have 'a presumptive right to represent themselves notwithstanding a Trial Chamber's judgment that they would be better off if represented by counsel'.[40] Šešelj has a doctorate in law and in his trial it was similarly noted that '[t]he complex legal, evidential and procedural issues that arise in a case of this magnitude may fall outside the competence even of a legally qualified accused, especially where that accused is in detention without access to all the facilities he may need'.[41] In *Stanković*, although the defendant's request was denied for other reasons, the Trial Chamber also took the view that 'self-representation should not be disregarded solely on the basis of the negative effect on the Accused's position caused by inferior knowledge or skills compared to those of a professional legal counsel'.[42]

In *Krajišnik*, that Trial Chamber elaborated more extensively on the question of whether the defendant should be permitted effectively to sabotage his own defence by refusing the assistance of counsel and expressed serious concern that:

> a criminal case of the present magnitude, which has been experienced as a great strain even by learned defence counsel, would certainly collapse if put into the hands of Mr Krajišnik who in his limited cross-examination

[38] ICTY RPE Rule 65 *ter* (G). [39] ICTY RPE Rule 67(B).

[40] *Slobodan Milošević* v. *Prosecutor*, IT-02-54-AR73.7, Decision on Interlocutory Appeal of the Trial Chamber's Decision on the Assignment of Defense Counsel, 1 November 2004, para. 11.

[41] *Prosecutor* v. *Vojislav Šešelj*, IT-03-67-PT, Decision on Prosecution's Motion for Order Appointing Counsel to Assist Vojislav Šešelj with his Defence, 9 May 2003, para. 21.

[42] *Prosecutor* v. *Vojislav Šešelj*, IT-03-67-AR73.3, Decision on Appeal against the Trial Chamber's Decision on Assignment of Counsel, 20 October 2006, para. 43. *Prosecutor* v. *Radovan Stanković* (n. 20, above), para. 20.

> of witnesses [. . .] inadvertently revealed details of protected witnesses and was frequently cautioned by the bench for his improper questions and misunderstandings of procedure; and this is to say no more, and no less, than that the Accused does not know, and has no reason to know, how to run a criminal defence case.[43]

Although in this instance the request was refused, the Trial Chamber noted that 'an accused may to his detriment waive his right to be represented by counsel'.[44]

Unlike Milošević and Šešelj, Karadžić does not have any legal training. When at an early stage Karadžić was alone in court and was asked whether he wished to oppose a prosecution motion to amend his indictment and, if so, to state his reasons for opposing, Karadžić answered:

> THE ACCUSED: [Interpretation] This is too much of a major issue for me to state my views without consulting my legal advisors. [. . .]
>
> JUDGE BONOMY: [. . .] Now, what you're say [*sic*] is that you're trying to conduct this case but you're incapable of conducting, and that's an unsatisfactory situation for the Court to be in.[45]

Karadžić later acknowledged that his lack of legal training was an impediment to the conduct of his defence, stating: 'The fact that I'm representing myself and I'm not a lawyer is a handicap.'[46] He continues, however, to represent himself.

(c) Fitness to exercise the right to self-representation before the ICTY

There is no express standard in the ICTY Statute or ICTY Rules of Procedure and Evidence (RPE) for fitness of a defendant to conduct his own defence or, for that matter, for fitness to stand trial.[47] However, the issue of fitness to stand trial was examined by the ICTY in some depth in *Strugar*, which led to the elaboration of certain general principles.

[43] *Prosecutor* v. *Momcilo Krajišnik*, IT-00-39-T, Reasons for Oral Decision Denying Mr Krajisnik's Request to Proceed Unrepresented by Counsel, 18 August 2005, para. 34.

[44] *Ibid.*

[45] *Prosecutor* v. *Radovan Karadžić*, IT-95-5/18-PT, Status Conference, 20 February 2009, T109.

[46] *Ibid.*, Status Conference, 2 April 2009, T144.

[47] Rule 135, ICC RPE does not define a standard for fitness to stand trial, but provides that where a medical examination shows that a defendant is unfit to stand trial the trial should be adjourned and its status periodically reviewed.

In *Strugar*, the Trial Chamber based its analysis of the defendant's fitness to stand trial on the Report of the Secretary-General,[48] which states that the Tribunal must:

> decide on various personal defences which may relieve a person of individual criminal responsibility, such as minimum age or mental capacity, drawing upon general principles of law recognised by all nations.[49]

The Trial Chamber went on to note that the issue of fitness to stand trial appears to be 'on a similar footing' to such personal defences[50] and that the enjoyment of the procedural rights guaranteed to a defendant under Articles 20 and 21 ICTY Statute 'appear to presuppose that an accused has a level of mental and physical capacity'. In relation to Article 21(4)(d) ICTY Statute, it found that this specifically referred to the right to 'defend himself in person'.[51] The Trial Chamber did not include the exercise of the right to self-representation within the scope of the procedural defence rights the defendant must be able to exercise in order to be found fit to stand trial. It found that the 'rights to defend in person and examine witnesses appear to require for their exercise inter alia a capacity to: understand the purpose, including the consequences, of the proceedings, understand the course of the proceedings, including the nature and significance of pleading to the charges, understand the evidence, and testify (should the accused so choose)'.[52]

Without expressly considering a self-representing defendant, the Trial Chamber simply stated that:

> The availability of counsel to assist an accused in his defence is a feature of trials before the Tribunal. The availability of counsel may certainly enable an accused to more adequately deal with each of the above matters, and in a particular case may well adequately compensate for any deficiency of a relevant capacity.[53]

After defining the test for fitness to stand trial as 'whether [the defendant] is able to exercise effectively his rights in the proceedings against him', the Trial Chamber found that a non-exhaustive list of the capacities required for determining fitness to stand trial includes:

[48] UN Doc. S/25704, para. 58.
[49] *Prosecutor* v. *Pavle Strugar*, IT-01-42-T, Decision re the Defence Motion to Terminate Proceedings, 26 May 2004, para. 20.
[50] *Ibid.* [51] *Ibid.*, para. 21. [52] *Ibid.*, para. 22. [53] *Ibid.*

- to plead,
- to understand the nature of the charges,
- to understand the course of the proceedings,
- to understand the details of the evidence,
- to instruct counsel,
- to understand the consequences of the proceedings, and
- to testify.[54]

The dicta in *Strugar* suggests that a self-representing defendant may be found unfit to stand trial when conducting his own defence, yet still be found fit to stand trial if assisted by counsel. Further, it appears that in circumstances where unfitness to stand trial may only be temporary, the proceedings may simply be adjourned until the symptom has ameliorated or measures have been taken to compensate for the relevant deficiency, which the Trial Chamber specifically envisaged could consist of 'legal assistance to an accused'.[55]

Shortly after the *Strugar* decision, the *Milošević* Trial Chamber deliberated on the medical reports it had procured from experts on the state of health of the self-representing defendant.[56] The subjects covered by the medical reports did not address the question of the fitness of the defendant to stand trial, but rather his current health and his fitness to represent himself.[57] It is no surprise that the Trial Chamber claimed that it had no evidence before it as to whether the defendant was fit to stand trial[58] – the medical experts appear not to have been asked to consider the issue. When assigned counsel raised the issue of provisional release due to medical reasons,[59] the Appeals Chamber refused to equate fitness to stand trial whilst exercising the right to self-representation with fitness to stand trial whilst represented by counsel. The Appeals Chamber did not refer to *Strugar*, although it followed the approach in that case in finding that:

> We reject Assigned Counsel's contention that Milosevic's inability to represent himself necessarily rendered him unfit to stand trial at all. Trial litigation is an extraordinarily demanding profession. It cannot be

[54] *Ibid.*, para. 36. [55] *Ibid.*, para. 39.

[56] *Prosecutor* v. *Slobodan Milošević*, IT-02-54-T, Open Session, 2 September 2004, T32356 *et seq.*

[57] *Ibid.*, Reasons for Decision on Assignment of Defence Counsel, 22 September 2004, paras 1 and 60 and *Slobodan Milošević* v. *Prosecutor* (n. 42, above), para. 6.

[58] *Prosecutor* v. *Slobodan Milošević*, Reasons for Decision on Assignment of Defence Counsel, 22 September 2004, para. 12.

[59] *Ibid.*, para. 24.

that only those defendants capable of meeting its demands are formally fit to stand trial.[60]

When *Strugar* subsequently came to appeal, the Appeals Chamber upheld the Trial Chamber's determination of the defendant's fitness to stand trial and stated, by reference to a confidential order in *Milošević*, that it 'emphasizes that fitness to stand trial should be distinguished from fitness to represent oneself'.[61]

Judicial control of the right to self-representation by the ICTY

None of the five defendants who exercised the right to self-representation conducted their defence alone. They were supported 'backstage' by legal associates and support teams. In this regard, the right to self-representation is more of a 'right to a sole appearance'. Furthermore, the courtroom conduct of self-representing defendants before the ICTY has frequently caused disruption, offence, obstruction and delays. This has been sometimes due to circumstances beyond the control of the defendant, and sometimes due to intentional, disruptive conduct. The following sections examine judicial responses to: (a) intentional obstruction and (b) unintentional obstruction, as well as (c) the Trial Chambers' interpretation of their duty to ensure a fair and expeditious trial where defendants have exercised the right to self-representation.

(a) Intentional obstruction

The ICTY has struggled to control self-representing defendants who have insulted trial participants, made offensive and racist remarks and held irrelevant speeches. Whilst US law provides for specific ways of dealing with disruptive defendants, including binding and gagging the defendant[62] or using a 'stun belt' remotely to inflict a powerful electric shock effectively to silence him/her,[63] the ICTY only has the two options of: (i) removing the defendant from the courtroom, depriving the

60 *Slobodan Milošević* v. *Prosecutor* (n. 42, above), FN42.

61 *Prosecutor* v. *Pavle Strugar*, IT-01-42-A, Appeals Judgment, 17 July 2008, para. 60 and FN172.

62 *Illinois* v. *Allen*, 397 US 337, 344.

63 See P. Russev, 'Restraining US Violations of International Law: An Attempt to Curtail Stun Belt Use and Manufacture in the United States under the United Nations Convention against Torture', 19 *Georgia State University Law Review* (2002) 603, 604.

defendant of a defence, or (ii) appointing counsel to take over from the defendant.

Milošević often launched into long political speeches that were irrelevant to the issues being tried. Judge May controlled such speeches by simply switching off the defendant's microphone and interrupting him.[64] As Scharf has argued, there was simply no incentive for Milošević to heed admonitions from judges, being already in detention.[65] Šešelj has often made largely irrelevant submissions[66] and, upon filing motions running to tens of thousands of words beyond the word limit set by the Trial Chamber, was warned that if this continued counsel would be imposed.[67] Karadžić also made numerous irrelevant statements.[68]

Although Milošević's trial generally proceeded without obstruction during his periods of good health, there were some instances of contumacious, abusive conduct by the defendant. For example, the following statement to the court:

> [D]on't bother me and make me listen for hours on end to the reading of texts written at the intellectual level of a seven-year-old child – or rather – let me correct myself – a retarded seven-year-old.[69]

The Trial Chamber cut his subsequent speech short.[70] His conduct also included offensiveness to witnesses. For example, when cross-examining Nikola Samardžić, former Minister of Foreign Affairs of Montenegro – a man who had lost his legs through amputation as a result of diabetes complications – Milošević questioned him as follows:

MR. MILOSEVIC: [Interpretation] Q. Mr. Samardzic, do you know the Serbian saying that people who lie have short legs?

JUDGE MAY: You needn't bother to answer that.[71]

[64] *Prosecutor* v. *Slobodan Milošević*, IT-01-50-I, Initial Appearance, 3 July 2001, T5 and Initial Appearance, 29 October 2001, T41.

[65] M. P. Scharf, 'The Perils of Permitting Self-Representation in International War Crimes Trials', 4 *Journal of Human Rights* (2005) 513, 514.

[66] See, e.g., *Prosecutor* v. *Vojislav Šešelj* (n. 41, above), para. 7.

[67] *Prosecutor* v. *Vojislav Šešelj*, IT-03-67-PT, Status Conference, 22 November 2006, T804.

[68] See, e.g., *Prosecutor* v. *Radovan Karadžić*, IT-96-23/2-PT, Status Conference, 2 April 2009, T158, where Judge Bonomy commented 'You've obviously got something off your chest, and perhaps that's just as well [. . .] Let that be an end of the political grandstanding, and let us concentrate on the issues in the trial.'

[69] *Prosecutor* v. *Slobodan Milošević*, IT-01-50-PT, Status Conference, 30 October 2001, T64.

[70] *Ibid.*, T65.

[71] *Prosecutor* v. *Slobodan Milošević*, IT-01-50-T, Open Session, 10 October 2002, T11401.

The highly offensive nature of this remark was commented on by the Prosecution and noted by the Trial Chamber, but Milošević was not reprimanded.[72]

The other defendants brought greater challenges to their respective Trial Chambers. Stanković began a submission with the words 'To the Registry of the Monstrous Fascist Hague Tribunal', referred to his counsel in a submission as 'an immoral bastard who works for this grotesque Hague Tribunal' and 'a notorious scumbag' and to his counsel and the former ICTY Chief Prosecutor Carla Del Ponte as 'fascist spies and complete bastards'.[73]

Šešelj, who had previously published books which insulted some of the key participants of the ICTY,[74] severely disrupted his trial. One of the first statements made by Šešelj to the court when represented by assigned counsel was 'I will never speak to [assigned counsel], never in my life, or with any other spy of yours, whose goal it is to deny me my right to my defence'.[75] He also stated that he considered 'the attire of the Judges in Court inappropriate, since, in his view, it is reminiscent of the Catholic inquisition or of German SS or Gestapo uniforms'.[76]

Already at the pre-trial stage the Prosecution argued that counsel should be appointed in the interests of justice *inter alia* 'due to [...] the Accused's express intention to cause harm to the Tribunal [and the] possibility of a disorderly trial'[77] and the likelihood that Šešelj would behave in a 'disruptive, obstructionist or scandalous manner' based on remarks he had made.[78] In appointing standby counsel, the Trial Chamber noted a number of examples of the defendant's 'tendency to act in an obstructionist manner', including his refusal to accept the offer of a laptop or typewriter because he was 'afraid of receiving an electric shock'.[79] When the *Šešelj* Trial Chamber finally imposed defence counsel on the defendant in 2006, because of his 'obstructionist and disruptive behaviour; deliberate disrespect for the rules; intimidation of, and slanderous comments about, witnesses',[80] it further investigated the

72 *Ibid.*, T11425–6 ('the Trial Chamber takes no notice of that sort of question, and in its view, was no more than vulgar abuse, and the witness should hear that').

73 Referred to in *Prosecutor* v. *Radovan Stanković* (n. 20, above), para. 23. Stanković's case was transferred to the courts of Bosnia and Herzegovina.

74 Referred to in *Prosecutor* v. *Vojislav Šešelj* (n. 32, above), para. 30.

75 *Prosecutor* v. *Vojislav Šešelj*, Status Conference, 14 September 2006, T574.

76 Referred to in *Prosecutor* v. *Vojislav Šešelj* (n. 32, above), para. 34. Many far worse examples can be taken from the decision, which do not have to be repeated here.

77 *Prosecutor* v. *Vojislav Šešelj*, IT-03-67-PT (n. 17, above), para. 3.

78 *Ibid.*, para. 4.

79 *Ibid.*, para. 23.

80 *Prosecutor* v. *Vojislav Šešelj* (n. 32, above), para. 79.

threshold of obstructionism that precipitates forfeiture of the right to be present and/or to self-representation. Although a Trial Chamber may 'merely disallow [...] irrelevant remarks, it may also take stronger measures, even limiting the right of an accused to be tried in his presence ... [j]ust as the former right is not absolute, the latter may also be restricted in cases of substantial trial disruption'.[81]

The Trial Chamber found guidance in the US case *Illinois* v. *Allen*, in which it was held that:

> a defendant can lose his right to be present at trial if, after he has been warned by the judge that he will be removed if he continues his disruptive behaviour, he nevertheless insists on conducting himself in a manner so disorderly, disruptive and disrespectful of the court that his trial cannot be carried on with him in the courtroom.[82]

The Trial Chamber also cited the US case of *Brock* for the presumption that disruptive conduct at the pre-trial stage could be sufficiently indicative of likely conduct at trial so as to permit imposition of counsel.[83] It further found the case to be distinguishable from *Milošević* because the restriction of the right to self-representation was 'prompted by the persistent and wilful conduct of the Accused' rather than due to involuntary circumstances. Importantly, '[t]hat distinction [...] provides a proper foundation for a firmer and stricter approach in determining the role of the Accused in the proceedings'.[84]

The Appeals Chamber reversed the assignment of counsel as the Trial Chamber had failed to give Šešelj the requisite warning.[85] It confirmed that disruption may be intentional or unintentional (referring to Milošević's health problems)[86] and that a clear warning must be given to a defendant, in line with Rule 80(B), before counsel is imposed.[87] It also confirmed that pre-trial conduct, including behaviour outside the courtroom, could be taken into account in a decision to curtail the right to self-representation at trial.[88] Šešelj's self-representation was reinstated, but he vehemently protested against the simultaneous reassignment of standby counsel. Ten days later, on 1 November 2006, Šešelj disrupted a Status Conference so severely that, after being duly warned, he was removed from the courtroom pursuant to Rule 80(B).[89] On 11 November 2006, he commenced a hunger strike, which he ended on 8 December 2006 when

[81] *Ibid.*, para. 23. [82] *Ibid.* [83] *Ibid.*, para. 18, citing *US* v. *Brock* 159 F.3d 1077.
[84] *Ibid.*, para. 80. [85] *Prosecutor* v. *Vojislav Šešelj* (n. 42, above). [86] *Ibid.*, para. 8.
[87] *Ibid.*, paras 22–6. [88] *Ibid.*, para. 33.
[89] *Prosecutor* v. *Vojislav Šešelj*, IT-03-67-PT, Status Conference, 1 November 2006, T635–6.

his right to self-representation was restored, without assistance of standby counsel, and his trial was suspended until he regained health.[90]

It has been argued that 'the handling of self-representation in Šešelj's case reveals a system spinning out of control'[91] with the '[t]he Appeals Chamber's creation of a fundamental right out of self-representation, and its zealous enforcement of that right in the case of Šešelj, enabl[ing] Šešelj to dominate, manipulate, and retard the proceedings, with the ultimate aim, it seems, to force the Tribunal to set him free for having suffered excessively long preventive detention'.[92] Although this has not (yet) proven to be the case, it is difficult to argue that the judges have not been '[b]ending over backwards to maintain the appearance of fairness' and allowing conduct 'that would earn ordinary defence counsel expulsion from the courtroom'.[93] With the death of Milošević only six months previously, such leniency may be partly explained by the desire to avoid a second death in detention.

(b) Unintentional obstruction

In *Milošević*, the deterioration in the health of the defendant caused delays to the trial and ultimately led to the qualification of his right to self-representation. During the prosecution case, sixty-six trial days were lost through interruptions and adjournments.[94] With the stress of representing himself exacerbating his health problems, the Prosecution argued that counsel should be imposed because '[i]t cannot be right in principle for the scope of a criminal trial to be dictated by the fact that the accused elects to represent himself'.[95] Initially, the Trial Chamber did not agree, finding that 'there may be circumstances, as envisaged by Judge Gunawardana [in the *Barayagwiza* case before the ICTR], where it is in the interests of justice to appoint counsel. No such circumstances have, *as yet*, arisen in this trial. However, as the Trial Chamber has said, it will keep the position under review'.[96]

When the trial timetable continued to be delayed owing to the ill health of the defendant, the *Milošević* Trial Chamber decided that

[90] *Prosecutor* v. *Vojislav Šešelj*, IT-03-67-AR73.4, Decision on Appeal against the Trial Chamber's Decision (No. 2) on Assignment of Counsel, 8 December 2006.

[91] A. Zahar, 'Legal Aid, Self-Representation and the Crisis at the Hague Tribunal', 19 *Criminal Law Forum* (2008) 241, 255.

[92] *Ibid.*, 257. [93] M. P. Scharf, 'Is it International Enough?', 2 *JICJ* (2004) 330, 336.

[94] *Prosecutor* v. *Slobodan Milošević* (n. 57, above), para. 1, citing oral ruling of 2 September 2004.

[95] *Ibid.*, para. 19. [96] *Prosecutor* v. *Slobodan Milošević* (n. 16, above), para. 40.

counsel should be imposed because the delays and disruption caused by the exercise of the right to self-representation were jeopardising the fairness of the trial.[97] Commentators are divided as to whether this was justified. Should the exercise of the right to self-representation be permitted, with all of its consequences for the length of the trial, especially if the defendant is not well enough to conduct his defence on a full-time basis? Does delay entitle a Trial Chamber to curtail the right? It has been suggested that '[i]t is more appropriate to maintain that the Tribunal is presently facing only the unpleasant prospect of a very long trial, replete with interruptions'[98] and, further, that the length and unwieldy nature of the trial is of the Tribunal's own making, with the timing of the decision to impose counsel at the start of the defence case giving the impression of muzzling the defendant, risking the Tribunal's reputation for fairness.[99]

Controversially, the Trial Chamber found that '[t]here is no difference in principle between deliberate misconduct which disrupts the proceedings and any other circumstance which so disrupts the proceedings as to threaten the integrity of the trial'.[100] However, it has been argued that the health problems of the defendant may not have been entirely unintentional: the Trial Chamber did not discuss in any depth the Prosecution's allegations that Milošević was wilfully failing to take his medication in order further to disrupt the proceedings, but did note that there were 'irregularities in the medical findings relating to non-adherence to the prescribed medical regime'.[101]

The Trial Chamber acknowledged that there was no legal authority for the assignment of counsel to a self-representing defendant with ill health[102] and modified its earlier stance that the right of self-representation was a fundamental right (by reference to common law systems). The Trial Chamber now entered into an in-depth discussion of civil law practice on mandatory representation to bolster its conclusions in favour of the assignment of counsel[103] and found that, if the defendant failed to communicate with assigned counsel, any resulting deficit in the quality of defence was the defendant's own responsibility.[104]

[97] *Prosecutor* v. *Slobodan Milošević* (n. 57, above), para. 32.

[98] M. R. Damaška, 'Assignment of Counsel and Perceptions of Fairness', 3 *JICJ* (2005) 3, 7.

[99] *Ibid.* [100] *Prosecutor* v. *Slobodan Milošević* (n. 57, above), para. 33.

[101] *Ibid.*, para. 67 and G. Boas and T. McCormack 'Learning the Lessons of the Milosevic Trial', 9 *Yearbook of International Humanitarian Law* (2006) 65, 82.

[102] *Prosecutor* v. *Slobodan Milošević* (n. 57, above), para. 37. [103] *Ibid.*, para. 49.

[104] *Ibid.*, para. 70.

Once formally represented by counsel (against his will), Milošević refused to cooperate. Assigned counsel appealed against their assignment, alleging a 'complete and irrevocable breakdown in the relationship between them and the Accused'[105] and sought to withdraw.[106] The Trial Chamber refused, however, concluding that 'assigning counsel to an unwilling and uncooperative accused [. . .] cannot be said to impose pressure on counsel such that their integrity is compromised'.[107] The Appeals Chamber upheld the decision to assign counsel, but restored Milošević's role as leader of his defence.

(c) The duty to ensure a fair and expeditious trial as a means of judicial control

At the same time as respecting the rights of the accused, which, as set out above, have been interpreted to include the right to self-representation, ICTY trial chambers are also under a duty to ensure that a trial is fair and expeditious. Article 20(1) of the ICTY Statute (Commencement and Conduct of Trial Proceedings) provides:

> The Trial Chambers *shall ensure that a trial is fair and expeditious* and that proceedings are conducted in accordance with the rules of procedure and evidence, *with full respect for the rights of the accused* and due regard for the protection of victims and witnesses.
>
> (emphasis added)

As established above, a defendant has the option to conduct his own defence, which, if elected unequivocally at the commencement of the trial, will, in the absence of an indication of obstructive behaviour, generally be granted.

In those cases it has been demonstrated that although, on an objective analysis, it is inevitable that a self-representing defendant, generally without courtroom experience or international criminal legal experience, will take longer than professional counsel to conduct his defence, such defendants have generally behaved disruptively, thus causing

105 *Prosecutor* v. *Slobodan Milošević*, IT-02-54-T, Decision on Assigned Counsel's Motion for Withdrawal, 7 December 2004, para. 5.

106 *Ibid.*, para. 6, on the basis of 'good cause' pursuant to Article 9(B)(iv) of the Code of Professional Conduct for Counsel Appearing before the International Tribunal.

107 *Ibid.*, para. 23. This was affirmed by the ICTY President. See *Prosecutor* v. *Slobodan Milošević*, IT-02-54-T, President's Decision Affirming the Registrar's Denial of Assigned Counsel's Application to Withdraw, 7 February 2005.

additional delays and disruptions. Such delays and disruptions are sometimes considerable – for example, where the conduct of a defendant is disruptive to the point of having to be removed from the courtroom and/or replaced by standby counsel.

In seeking to ensure that a trial is fair and expeditious, Trial Chambers have therefore had to weigh: (i) the obligation to permit a defendant to bring his own, less-professional and more cumbersome defence, against (ii) the obligation to ensure that justice is dispensed in a fair and timely manner. The jurisprudence illustrates how the Trial Chambers have approached these competing priorities.

In *Milošević*, when the Prosecution sought to have counsel imposed, the Trial Chamber initially upheld the defendant's right to self-representation, finding that although '[a] Trial Chamber has indeed an obligation to ensure that a trial is fair and expeditious [. . .] where the health of the Accused is in issue, that obligation takes on special significance'. It went on, 'while ensuring that the trial is fair and expeditious, a Trial Chamber must also ensure that the rights of the accused, as set out in Article 21 of the Statute, are not infringed'.[108] This was the first time that the right to self-representation was weighed against the right to a fair and expeditious trial and, although the Trial Chamber expressed concern about the potential impact on a fair and expeditious trial, the disruption was not deemed severe enough for the right to self-representation to have to yield.

Shortly after this decision, the Trial Chamber in *Šešelj* invoked the fair and expeditious standard in order to appoint standby counsel. The basis for this was the express intention of the accused to use the ICTY as a vehicle to further his political aspirations, his tendency to act in an obstructionist fashion and his need for legal assistance. The Trial Chamber found that '[t]he need may arise for unforeseeable reasons to protect an accused's interests and ensure a fair and expeditious trial'[109] and '[i]n the context of the right to a fair trial, the length of the case, its size and complexity need to be taken into account [. . .] Moreover, the Tribunal has a legitimate interest in ensuring that the trial proceeds in a timely manner without interruptions, adjournments or disruptions'.[110] The Trial Chamber concluded that the wilful disruption of the proceedings by the defendant 'would not only result in an abuse of the valuable

[108] *Prosecutor* v. *Slobodan Milošević* (n. 16, above), para. 41.
[109] *Prosecutor* v. *Šešelj*, IT-03-67-PT (n. 17, above), para. 11. [110] *Ibid.*, para. 21.

judicial resources of the Tribunal but also hinder an expeditious trial'[111] and defined the role of standby counsel as 'safeguard[ing] a fair and expeditious trial'.[112]

When deciding to assign counsel in September 2004, due to the delays caused by the ongoing health problems of the defendant, the *Milošević* Trial Chamber identified as a risk to a fair and expeditious trial the 'real danger that this trial might either last for an unreasonably long time or, worse still, might not be concluded should the accused continue to represent himself without the assistance of counsel'. It viewed the assignment of counsel as the solution, alongside 'the duty of the Chamber to ensure that the role of assigned counsel is so fashioned that the trial process, while being expeditious, will protect the fundamental right of the accused to a fair trial'.[113] The Trial Chamber 'considered that there was evidence indicating that the health of the Accused was such that he might not be fit to continue to represent himself and that his continuing to represent himself could adversely affect the fair and expeditious conduct of the trial'.[114] Importantly, the Trial Chamber found:

> Whether by way of self-representation or legal assistance, the purpose of [Article 21(4)(d)] is to secure for an accused the right to a defence, which is a prerequisite for a fair trial. Defence 'in person' or 'through legal assistance of his own choosing' are simply means whereby the minimum guaranteed right to 'defend himself', i.e., to a defence, may be exercised.[115]

Envisaging disruption as a cause of the undermining of the integrity of a trial, and thus its fairness,[116] and referring to the 'overarching right to a fair trial' and an element of a fair trial being a trial without undue delay,[117] the Trial Chamber found that '[t]he right to represent oneself must therefore yield when it is necessary to ensure that the trial is fair' and '[t]he primary duty of the Trial Chamber, as reflected in Article 20 of the Statute, must always be to take such steps as are necessary and

[111] *Ibid.*, para. 22. [112] *Ibid.*, para. 28.

[113] *Prosecutor* v. *Slobodan Milošević* (n. 57, above), cited at para. 1. [114] *Ibid.*, para. 12.

[115] *Ibid.*, para. 32. This contrasts sharply with the statement of Judge Robinson at T18 that 'We have to act in accordance with the Statute and our Rules which, in any event, reflect the position under customary international law, which is that the accused has a right to counsel, but he also has a right not to have counsel. He has a right to defend himself, and it is quite clear that he has chosen to defend himself. He has made that abundantly clear. The strategy that the Chamber has employed of appointing an amicus curiae will take care of the problems that you have outlined, but I stress that it would be wrong for the Chamber to impose counsel on the accused, because that would be in breach of the position under customary international law.'

[116] *Ibid.*, para. 33. [117] *Ibid.*

available to ensure that the trial of the accused is completed fairly and expeditiously'.[118] The Trial Chamber found that its fundamental duty was to ensure a fair and expeditious trial and where a trial is severely disrupted, counsel may be assigned to a defendant and 'measures could be devised to ensure that the trial continues in a manner that is both fair and expeditious'.[119] The Trial Chamber found that '[i]t would be intolerable for any accused to have accusations as serious as those against this Accused left outstanding against him for an unreasonable time or, worse still, unresolved'.[120] Summing up, the Trial Chamber stated:

> In light of the history of the case and the conclusions that the Trial Chamber had reached, the Chamber was of the opinion that it was necessary to relieve the Accused of the burden of conducting his own case with a view to stabilising his health to ensure, so far as possible, that the trial proceeds with the minimum of interruption in a way that will permit the orderly presentation of the Accused's case and the completion of the trial within a reasonable time in his interests and the interests of justice: in other words, to secure for the Accused a fair and expeditious trial.[121]

The *Milošević* Appeals Chamber appeared to qualify the notion of expeditiousness, finding that 'any restrictions on Milosevic's right to represent himself must be limited to the minimum extent necessary to protect the Tribunal's interest in assuring a *reasonably* expeditious trial',[122] although it did not elaborate on the relevant criteria. When addressing the objection of assigned counsel that 'the appointment of counsel to an accused who is engaging in deliberate misconduct [. . .] is quite distinct from the situation where an accused would be allowed to continue [representing himself] but for a finding of medical unfitness', it found that it did not have to choose between releasing the defendant and allowing the trial to slow down unacceptably. The *Milošević* case therefore demonstrates the line between a (reasonably) expeditious trial with self-representation and a trial that is delayed to the point that it is no longer expeditious, at which point self-representation must yield.

The *Šešelj* Trial Chamber, in determining to impose counsel on the accused, noted that the conduct of the defendant in making frivolous and abusive submissions 'places a heavy burden on the resources of the Tribunal'.[123] After Šešelj appealed that decision, the Appeals Chamber

[118] *Ibid.*, para. 34. [119] *Ibid.*, para. 65. [120] *Ibid.*, para. 36. [121] *Ibid.*, para. 66.
[122] *Slobodan Milošević* v. *Prosecutor* (n. 42, above), para. 17 (emphasis added).
[123] *Prosecutor* v. *Vojislav Šešelj*, IT-03-67-PT, Decision on Assignment of the Counsel, 21 August 2006, para. 75.

affirmed that the decision to assign counsel is discretionary and stems from the obligation of a Trial Chamber to ensure a fair and expeditious trial.[124] However, the Appeals Chamber went on to utilise the standard of 'proper and expeditious', upholding the test used by the Trial Chamber with one change[125] (whether the pre-trial behaviour considered as a whole 'provides a strong indication that self-representation *would* [instead of *may*] substantially and persistently obstruct the proper and expeditious conduct of the proceedings').[126]

Conclusion

The language 'to defend himself in person or through legal assistance of his choosing' was adopted in the ICTY Statute, echoing the language of the ECHR and ICCPR. Rule 45(F) clarified the scope of the provision as permitting a defendant to conduct his own defence. Such an approach, whilst following the (tentative and unused) precedent of Nuremberg, is, however, only one of the two permissible approaches in modern international human rights law. Whilst the ECtHR has taken the approach that there is no presumptive right to self-representation and defence rights under international human rights law may be satisfied, either through self-representation or through representation by counsel, the UN HRC has, more recently, taken the alternative approach, i.e., that the right to self-representation may not be totally excluded.

The right to self-representation has now been exercised by several defendants before the ICTY. Their trials have been frequently disrupted through intentional obstruction, health problems and their lack of legal skills. Yet the ICTY has continued to find that defendants before it have a presumptive right to self-representation. This choice of philosophical approach to the right to a defence, as encompassing a presumptive right to self-representation, has forced judges to navigate between: (i) upholding the right to self-representation, potentially at the expense of the right to a fair and expeditious trial, and (ii) curtailing the right to self-representation, in order to be able to discharge the duty to ensure a fair and expeditious trial. In both cases, fairness is potentially compromised as both the right to self-representation and the duty to ensure a fair and expeditious trial are elements of the right to a fair trial before the

[124] *Prosecutor* v. *Vojislav Šešelj* (n. 42, above), para. 16. [125] *Ibid.*, para. 21.
[126] *Ibid.*, paras 27–8 (emphasis in the original).

ICTY and it has not proved possible to uphold both principles simultaneously.

Judges at the ICC may wish to consider taking the alternative approach, i.e., that there is no presumptive right to self-representation. They would be able to point to the more recent ECtHR *Matos* decision. Such a break with the practice of the ICTY would save the ICC time and resources and remove the need to balance the right to self-representation and the duty to ensure a fair and expeditious trial in an assessment that carries risks of unfairness, regardless of the outcome. The last consideration is of central importance, for only by ensuring fairness is it possible to ensure a legitimate and sustainable system of international criminal justice.

INDEX